THE LIBRARY OF HISTORY AND DOCTRINE

HEIRS OF THE REFORMATION

THE LIBRARY OF HISTORY AND DOCTRINE

The aim of this international Library is to enable scholars to answer questions about the development of the Christian tradition which are important for an understanding of Christianity today

HEIRS OF
THE REFORMATION

JACQUES DE SENARCLENS

*Professor of Dogmatics
in the University of Geneva*

Translated and edited by
G. W. BROMILEY

*Professor of Church History and Historical Theology
in Fuller Theological Seminary,
Pasadena, California*

with a Foreword by
T. F. TORRANCE

*Professor of Christian Dogmatics
in the University of Edinburgh*

Philadelphia
The Westminster Press

Translated by G. W. Bromiley from
Héritiers de la Reformation
(2 vols.), Labor et Fides, Geneva,
copyright © 1958 and 1959

PRINTED IN GREAT BRITAIN
Published by The Westminster Press_R, Philadelphia 7, Pennsylvania

CONTENTS

FOREWORD

by T. F. TORRANCE

Professor of Christian Dogmatics in the University of Edinburgh

THE reader of this book will soon find that it needs no commendation from me, for its brilliance and freshness and masterly handling of profound theological questions in lucid and transparent discussion leave little to be desired. Yet for this very reason it gives me great pleasure to introduce to English readers the work of a Genevan theologian which is bound to have the widest appeal to readers in the English-speaking world. Whether they are traditionally of 'Evangelical' or 'Catholic' persuasion they will be assailed with the conviction, long before they have finished reading the book, that true evangelical theology is deeply catholic, and true catholic theology is deeply evangelical. Moreover this is a work marked with prophetic insight and vigour, for in it the author penetrates to the basic questions that lie at the root of the modern development of theology, and shows how they cut across the divisions of our ecclesiastical allegiance, and points out the road ahead through a new and deeper unity in the primary beliefs of the whole historical Church.

Professor de Senarclens, who is himself an heir of the Swiss Reformation, writes for all of us in the modern world who are in different ways heirs of the great movements of the sixteenth century that have transformed the face of history. He does not write, however, with any polemical intention or with the spirit of a partisan; nor on the other hand is he concerned to offer a *via media* between Protestantism and Roman Catholicism. He is concerned rather to raise again the basic question which agitated the whole Church during the Reformation, the question as to the fidelity of the Church to its foundation in God's self-giving in Jesus Christ. That is both the supremely spiritual question and the fundamentally scientific question as to the Church's conformity to Jesus Christ, and as to the adequacy of its faith to the Word and Truth of God. But this is a question that the Church is bound to keep on asking from generation to generation, not only because it must ever remain vigilant over the truth of its preaching and teaching, but because it belongs to the very nature of the Church to be obedient to Christ and constantly to be renewed in his image through the Spirit. Far from being an abstract question of only academic interest, this is an essential part of the continuing life and mission of the Church, for it is concerned with the testing and clarifying of its faith, and the articulating and communicating of the Gospel to each generation in its involvement with the world and with history, and indeed with creation itself. Moreover the raising and answering of this question in its spiritual depth and scientific rigour is the very essence of evangelical and catholic theology, and hence its pursuit and development cannot but serve the unity of all the Churches in their common Lord, and so strengthen the whole Church in its mission as the Body of Christ to hold out his image for the contemplation of mankind.

Professor de Senarclens carries through his discussion by examining the main tendencies of modern theology, and by putting to them his basic question in two forms or stages, which divides his work into two main parts. In the first part he inquires into the starting-point of modern theology to see how far it is grounded in the divine self-revelation, and in the second he inquires into its fundamental frame of reference to see how far it is related to the central dogma of Christ. This does not mean that he brings forward uncritically ready-made formulations to serve as his criteria in posing and answering basic questions, but rather that his inquiry is so directed into modern theological tendencies that he lets the basic subject-matter of all theology disclose itself in its own nature, and so provide for him the proper norms and modes for the clarification of our understanding and the articulation of the truth.

In the course of this discussion three main tendencies in the modern development emerge, *Modern Protestantism* with roots in the rationalism of the Enlightenment and idealist philosophy, *Modern Catholicism* with its roots in mediaeval piety and rationalism, and a third which may be described as *Evangelical and Catholic* with its roots in Patristic and Reformation theology. In spite of their diverging characteristics and the apparent antithesis between them, Modern Protestantism and Modern Catholicism are shown to rest ultimately on a common basis, and to involve similar attempts to combine grace and nature more in ways that are determined by man himself in accordance with his own natural desires, than by consistent following of the action of God in Incarnation and Reconciliation. By pushing his inquiry in this way beyond the serious traditional divergences between Protestantism and Roman Catholicism into the really basic issues behind them, and then by disclosing and breaking through their common framework, de Senarclens reinterprets and points up the analogous insights and common basis of Patristic and Reformed theology, not least in regard to the central theme of the Nicene Creed in the *homoousion*. But the discussion does not stop short at that point, for de Senarclens goes on to think out the profound implications of this for the Church's mission and involvement in the world of today.

Thus *Heirs of the Reformation* turns out to be a positive and constructive interpretation of the fundamental convictions of the Christian faith that have always lain at the centre of Catholic and Evangelical tradition. Hence the discussion carries us into the basic ecumenical problem, for, as de Senarclens points out, the Christian Churches are not divided by their fidelity to the Gospel, but by their infidelities. It is only in a search for their common Lord and through faithful response to the Gospel in the centre of all their life and thought that the separated Churches will find one another, and learn to fulfil again their evangelical mission to hold out Christ and his Gospel to all men.

One of the most exciting and exhilarating characteristics of this fine book is the way in which its author moves forward through the gates that have been flung wide open by the critical and dogmatic labours of Karl Barth, open, that is, for the younger theologians of both professedly 'Evangelical' and 'Catholic' convictions to think out again the common basis of Christian doctrine in the prophetic and apostolic witness of the Early Church, and to interpret it afresh for the world mission of the Church. Here it becomes manifestly clear that the interpretation of the Gospel characterized by honesty and integrity has no need to lapse into shoddy expedients of reducing it to alien conceptual forms or denigrating its basic framework as obsolete and mythological in order to commend it to modern man or make it relevant to modern life. The mission of the Church, as the author rightly conceives it, is not to adapt the Christian message to suit the categories of secular man, but to expound the Christian

A*

message in such a way that modern man is brought to Christ and his Gospel, and is renewed through the transforming of his mind to be a faithful child of the heavenly Father.

From end to end of his book Professor de Senarclens appears as a thinker of outstanding freshness of mind and independence of judgment, who is imbued at the same time with a deep pastoral concern for human beings and the integrity of their faith in our distracted world.

PREFACE

HEIRS OF the Reformation! This title, borrowed from most of our Protestant ecclesiastical constitutions, is primarily a question. Are we still the heirs and continuers of the sixteenth-century Reformation? We voluntarily affirm this, and we are sincerely persuaded for the most part that we can do so with a good conscience. From the single standpoint of temporal continuity the description is undoubtedly correct, although, if we press this aspect, how does our conviction differ from the Roman dogma of apostolic succession? The Jews argued along these lines: 'We have Abraham to our father' (Matt. 3.9). The real point is whether there is such an evident and certain agreement between our faith and that of the Reformers that demonstration may be regarded as superfluous.

It is not that the faith of the Reformers can ever be for us a final norm of truth. The norm of our faith is to be found neither in Luther nor Calvin. But what was the starting-point of their action? Was it not the question which they put to the men of their age: In your faith, teaching and activity, are you really a witness and therefore an heir of the Gospel of the prophets and apostles? To mediaeval Catholicism this seemed to be an insolent and even an aggressive question, for it was quite convinced, as we are today in our own sphere, of its unshakable right to represent authentic Christian truth in spite of certain inherent weaknesses in the human condition of the Church. Nevertheless, the examination conducted by our fathers led them to a very different conviction, namely, that the form of Christianity then being taught could not be considered a faithful expression of the witness of Scripture. This inherently alarming discovery shaped their action.

Can we say that their analysis was perfectly accurate and that their conclusions were inerrant? This cannot be affirmed *a priori*. The question has always to be put again and again. It can hardly be contested, however, that their movement arose out of this question as it was put to the Church of their time, and out of the answer

which they thought they should give. If God is really self-revealed
in Jesus Christ, and if his Word is accessible to us by the Holy Spirit
in the testimony of Holy Scripture, how can we concede without
hesitation, as a self-evident truth, that any Church transmits the
message exactly? Is the Church infallible? Is it not composed of
sinners, i.e., of men who are distant from the truth, not only in time,
but in virtue of the abyss which their revolt has opened up between
them and their Lord? Who can prove to us that any Church truly
pronounces the Word of God?

The question posed by the Reformers expresses at once a dis-
quietude, a desire to obey, a demand for authenticity and the resolve
not to be held by traditions which, venerable though they are,
cannot offer any guarantee of agreement with the message of the
living God. Irrespective of the value of the decisions taken in the
sixteenth century, we are Protestants in virtue of the single fact that
we understand the permanent need for this kind of examination.
Furthermore, we are Protestants because this control of actual
preaching in the Church, achieved in terms of the norm of the first
instruction and deriving its life from the Lord, corresponds to the
most urgent imperative of a vigilant faith, to concern for a true submission to Jesus Christ and indeed to the true mission of a theology
conscious of its *raison d'être* in the Church. How can we really refuse
constantly to ask ourselves concerning our true fidelity and constantly to let ourselves be corrected by the Word of God, from which,
as we know, it is so easy to deviate?

Moreover, if this concern belongs to the essence of the Evangelical
Church both historically and doctrinally, it links up again quite
directly with the basic ecumenical problem. The Christian Churches
are not divided by their fidelity, but by their infidelities. Thus the
most urgent task, as recently proposed by J. Hromadka, is to lead
the separated confessions to put to themselves as stringently as possible the question of their relationship to the Gospel. It is in searching for their common Lord, not by habit or automatically but in
vital response to his living summons, that they will find one another.

In the pages which follow we have tried to put this question in
terms of the Protestant confession. Are we truly the Church of Jesus
Christ, the community willed by God? Yet we cannot question our
own Church as it now is four centuries after the Reformation without
also taking some small account of the Roman Catholicism which our
fathers challenged and without listening to the answer which it has

made, whether immediately after or in the course of its later develop-ment. We thus find ourselves in some sense on two fronts, that of modern Protestantism and that of Romanism, our relative norm being the teaching of the Reformation with which we compare them and our effective norm what we think we understand of the Gospel.

It will be seen that this attempt is not theoretical or abstract. The whole of the Church is called in question, in its faith no less than its witness, its structure no less than its theology. We are not impelled to make this attempt by motives of speculation. Pastoral concern lies at the heart of the work. What are we to preach to this distracted world? What image of the Body of Christ are we to hold out for its contemplation? Whence have we come, and where do we stand, in face of the great work which God has accomplished in our favour and which alone can relieve and console and strengthen and indeed save all men?

Our investigation will centre upon two points alone, but upon two which seem to us to determine the whole life of the Church, namely, revelation, the starting-point of faith, and Christology, its centre. In order to avoid unnecessary repetition on themes which are so closely related, since revelation is in effect identical with Jesus Christ, we have distributed the material over the two parts, which are thus complementary and only together can give any adequate answer to the question raised.

We thus hope to contribute to the clarification which many regard as more and more necessary to the effectiveness of our witness. For, although this depends always on the sole mercy of God, for this very reason it also depends on our own faithfulness to his message.

EDITOR'S NOTE

THE VOLUME now introduced to the English-speaking world is a translation of two studies which were originally published separately as the first and second parts of the author's *Héritiers de la Réformation*.

In the English version it has been thought preferable, for the sake of compactness and continuity, to combine the two smaller writings into a single larger production. The author has readily given his consent to this change.

A certain amount of abridgment has, however, been necessary. In the first place, there has been slight compression of some of the discussions of French Swiss theologians whose work is not quite so significant on the British and American scene. To give added point to the remaining expositions, Dr de Senarclens has provided brief notes of identification, and in this amended form the material used should prove of real interest and importance.

More seriously, the extended supplementary discussions in small print have been drastically reduced to references or much abbreviated footnotes. This is unfortunate, since one of the author's main qualities is his strength in historical and dogmatic analysis. Yet the substance of the book remains unaffected and there are compensations in the less broken pages and the livelier tempo of exposition. Specialists who wish to examine the supporting theological structure will probably in any case prefer to consult the original.

So far as possible, quotations from other writers are in familiar English renderings. Sometimes, however, these have not been available and original translations have had to be made. The author himself uses only a French *précis* of Schleiermacher's *Christian Faith*, so that there are no exact equivalents for the 'quotations' and these are no longer marked as such, though the relevant references are given. It is perhaps worth noting that the French edition of Barth's *Church Dogmatics* I, 2 follows a peculiar tripartite arrangement unlike either the German or the English.

G.W.B.

Pasadena

ABBREVIATIONS

CD   Karl Barth, *Church Dogmatics*, ET, Edinburgh, 1936ff.
DTC   *Dictionnaire de Théologie Catholique*, ed. A. Vacant and
        E. Mangenot, Paris, 1899ff.
ET   English translation.
ST   Thomas Aquinas, *Summa Theologica.*
TDNT *Theological Dictionary of the New Testament* (ET of
        TWNT), Eerdmans, Grand Rapids, Michigan, 1963ff.
TWNT *Theologisches Wörterbuch zum Neuen Testament*, ed. G.
        Kittel, Stuttgart, 1932ff.

PART ONE

Revelation
or
The Starting-point of Faith

INTRODUCTION

THE DECLARATIONS, confessions and catechisms of the Church seem for the most part to be suspended in the void. They usually begin with a peremptory affirmation which is neither explained nor justified: *Credo*, I believe. What is the source of this assurance? What is the foundation of the decision thus made? Are we not justified in asking the Church to explain the basis of its position before it states its faith? What is the impulsion to faith? By what route does one arrive at such a declaration, which in effect is more like a conclusion than a starting-point?

By way of example, we may refer to Luther's *Smaller Catechism*. Deciding to publish this because of the 'desolated state of the Church', he begins at once and without preamble to give a commentary on the Ten Commandments. But what is the authority of this Law? Luther simply puts himself in the established framework of the Mosaic Law, the Creed and the Lord's Prayer without apparently feeling any need to demonstrate the legitimacy of the choice. Again, Calvin affirms at once that the meaning of life is to know God. This is no doubt an interesting proposition, but it is not proved. Even more surprising is the first question of the Heidelberg Catechism: 'What is thy only comfort?' Do we need comfort, and if so can we be comforted in this way? Like the ancient creeds, the Reformation confessions begin with an abrupt declaration: 'We believe and confess.'

The Church advances and proclaims its faith without presenting any credentials. We do not have here argument or reasoning; we have a kind of axiom, a starting-point which is wholly gratuitous and for which there is no guarantee.

No one is concerned to establish the validity of this faith and its origin. It is simply there and it declares itself. There is something almost insolent and even a little irritating in the audacity of such a beginning.

It is true, of course, that the Scriptures are no less audacious. 'In

the beginning God . . .', says Genesis. And John opens his account
of the life of Jesus in much the same way. 'In the beginning was the
Word.' The Synoptists, whose outlook is more historical in the
current sense of the word, commence similarly with unexpected
events which can neither be demonstrated nor explained. Thus
Matthew, after a genealogy which is not very convincing from the
standpoint of purely historical succession, introduces the strange
episode of the Virgin Birth. Mark links his account to the Old
Testament and then moves on abruptly to the baptism of Jesus and
the voice from heaven. In Luke, after a few words of introduction,
the appearance of the angel to Zacharias is the true starting-point
of the Gospel. Acts begins with the ascension and Pentecost, and
Paul in his epistles begins by referring to the grace of God.

None of these 'beginnings' is rational. All of them introduce a
non-verifiable element which they cannot explain. Whether it is
illusion or reality, this new element stands at the entry to the
Christian sphere, protecting it like an intractable sentry. Whether
in the form of an intervention from above or of an act of faith, we
are dealing with an absolute and wholly gratuitous beginning which
is not linked to any known reality and beyond which it seems neither
legitimate nor possible to venture. The Church is thus set on a
territory apart, and to crown its misfortune it seems obstinately
unwilling to justify its attitude in a manner acceptable to those who
do not share its conviction.

This abrupt commencement has caused much unrest. Philosophers
and theologians have hurled themselves against this wall, seeking
some kind of liberation. Ought we not to establish this faith, to
explain its authorization, to attach it to known and universally
accepted realities? 'I should like to know,' asked Vinet, 'where they
derive their faith.' If it could be shown that this faith is simply a
particular, though remarkable, instance of our spontaneous feeling
for the infinite, of the natural religion which can hardly be contested,
of our innate sense of right and wrong and of our sense of possessing
an immortal soul, it would be more acceptable. For it would be seen
to rest finally on a sure and verifiable basis.

Perhaps the clearest expression of this impatience is to be found
in the dedicatory epistle of Descartes' *Méditations métaphysiques*
addressed to the deans and doctors of the sacred faculty of theology
at Paris. 'I have always thought,' he says, 'that the two questions of
God and the soul were the chief of those which should be demon-

strated by the reasons of philosophy rather than theology, for, although it is enough for us who are of the faithful to believe by faith that there is a God and that the human soul does not die with the body, it certainly does not seem possible to convince unbelievers of any religion, or even of any moral virtue, unless first we prove these things to them by natural reason.' Faith is thus adequate for believers; it has, as it were, an inward power. The Church may propose it to its members. But for unbelievers a preamble is indispensable. Faith cannot be affirmed in the first instance. Something must precede and justify it in order that unbelievers may finally accept it. A little lower down Descartes gives his reasons. 'Although it is absolutely true that we should believe that there is a God because this is what we are taught by Holy Scripture, and although we should also believe Holy Scripture because it comes from God . . . we cannot propose this to unbelievers, who might imagine that we have here the fault which logicians call a circle.'

The philosopher does not say precisely that this is a vicious circle. Nevertheless, he suggests it. If the Church refuses to give unbelievers a preliminary explanation justifying the audacity of its act of faith, it sets itself in grievous contradiction with the laws of logic. It may be noted in passing that for Descartes faith must rest either on the argument of authority (one should believe . . . because of Holy Scripture . . . which comes from God)—which is hardly faith—or on rational demonstration. No other possibility is envisaged. It is also specified that the question is that of believing that there is a God rather than believing in God, faith thus being assimilated to adherence to a truth.

The kind of demonstration which would force men to accept the existence of God and the immortality of the soul is thus a concern of philosophy. Theology works within the circle, whereas philosophy has the privilege of entering the more vast and exacting sphere which stands under the laws of logic. On its own grounds and with its own weapons philosophy offers to support the faith by a demonstration which will secure its foundation and an apology which will persuade those who are not yet under its yoke. Thus philosophy takes the Church and its faith under its own wing, justifying and presenting them. Nor should theology object to these pretensions of its eternal rival. On the contrary, it should rejoice to have found such a defender.

Innumerable questions call for investigation at this point. We may

content ourselves for the moment by observing that in this pro-
gramme philosophy is arrogating to itself the role which classical
theology has recognized to be that of the Holy Spirit. The assurance
of faith and the efficacy of witness have always been regarded as
fruits of the Spirit. But how are we to admit the existence of the
Spirit. Do we not have to prove this too? R. Otto explained this need
as follows: 'Every religion which is not mere faith in traditional
authority . . . must presuppose principles in the mind enabling it
to be independently recognized as true. . . . It has little meaning,
however edifying it may sound, to say that these are inscribed upon
the heart by the pencil of the Holy Spirit "in history".'[1] The circle
thus widens, but it does not open. Outside it, there is only natural
reason, and it is to this that we must refer for a demonstration which
will make faith acceptable. Witness gives place to apology.

These two attitudes—that of the Church which declares its faith
without preamble and that of the philosopher who seeks to prove
what he still believes—pose exactly the problem of this first part of
our investigation. Of what should we speak first in the sphere of
faith, the Church and theology? Of faith and its object, or of its
natural supports, if any? Where is the true commencement of the
whole Christian life? Our question is that of the starting-point from
which all the manifestations of faith proceed. It seems to us to be
the first and most important today, not merely because everything
in dogmatics depends on the reply given, but also because this reply
exerts an equally decisive influence on the structure of the Church
and its mission, as we hope to show in the pages which follow.

Now it is true that all Christian theologians claim to find their
starting-point in the unique Gospel of Jesus, in accordance with the
saying of Paul: 'Other foundation can no man lay than that is laid'
(I Cor. 3.11). Nevertheless, we have to recognize that the confessions
and schools differ widely both in their definition of this foundation
and in their way of building upon it. As a hypothesis which we have
yet to prove, we may suggest that three main replies have been given
to this question of a starting-point: that of Thomism, which has
become the classical position of official Roman Catholicism, that of
modern Protestantism and that of the Reformation. The importance
of the problem will emerge, and readers may make their own
responsible decisions, when each of these attitudes has been briefly
described in accordance with the purpose of the present study.

[1] *The Idea of the Holy*, ET, 2nd ed., 1950, p. 175.

I

The Starting-point of Roman Catholicism

THOMAS AQUINAS lays down in principle that the salvation of men
and therefore theology depend wholly on revelation. 'In order that
man may attain eternal salvation, it was necessary that in addition
to the philosophical sciences created by natural illumination there
should be another science resting on revelation and relating to the
things which surpass the range of our intelligence and many of the
matters which we can know of ourselves' (*ST* I, 1, 1). This opening
thesis of the *Summa* is explained as follows: 'If men had only reason
as their guide and light, a small number alone would finally attain,
after long efforts and through countless errors, to knowledge of the
supreme being.' Thus theology is a science which 'receives by faith
those things which are revealed from on high' (I, 1, 2) and which
'considers everything from the standpoint of the divine revelation'
(I, 1, 3). It is the 'reflection of divine science' (I, 1, 3), embracing
'the various aspects of philosophical sciences . . . as relative to
revelation' (I, 1, 4). Hence 'it does not borrow from the other
sciences; it makes use of them'. For 'it has not found its principles
on earth; it takes them from God himself by revelation' (I, 1, 5). If it
makes use of other sciences, this is because 'natural things help us
to understand supernatural' (*ibid.*).

It may be noted at once how Thomas approaches the problem.
His primary interest is to fix the position of theology in relation to
revelation, but also to natural philosophy. This second aspect of the
question had achieved a new significance in his day because of the
influence of Aristotle on all mediaeval thought. J. Congar believes
that this impact of Aristotle took place in three stages which he calls
the three incursions of Aristotle into Western thought. Up to the
time of Anselm only the 'grammatical elements', i.e., the 'rational

instruments of textual analysis', were introduced into the Middle Ages. The second stage leads in the twelfth century to a 'scientific study of the syllogism and of the various kinds of proofs'. Finally, the third 'introduces into sacred science a philosophical leaven which is no longer purely formal but which concerns the very order of objects and the content of thought'.[1]

There is a kind of historical necessity about this development, which places the theologian of the thirteenth century in a very different position from that of the eleventh. Thus, while Anselm remains in the Augustinian framework and develops theologically within the traditional evangelical *Credo*, Thomas is confronted at once by an external element, a given philosophy which provides him with knowledge of man and the world and which he feels obliged to take into account. A given sociological factor has also to be considered. The Church is now firmly established in the society which it aspires to direct. The *corpus christianum* has become a reality which impresses itself upon the minds of almost all men of the period. The role of the Church is no longer to remain apart preaching a Gospel which is quite new and which a hostile world rejects. It is rather to take over nature, not merely associating with it but subordinating it to Christian truth. These two elements lead Thomas to integrate Aristotelianism into a vast synthesis which subjects human reality to the truth of the faith and the Church.[2]

'God is the object of theology' (I, 1, 7), and it treats all subjects *sub ratione Dei* (*ibid.*), i.e., as they relate to him in some way. But at this point already there intervenes a precision which is pregnant with meaning and implication. 'As we do not know what God is, instead of proceeding according to the definition of his being, we begin with his effects, both natural and supernatural, in order to attain to his knowledge' (*ibid.*). The knowledge of God is primary, and in principle we receive it by revelation, because of the darkness which surrounds our natural capacities. At the same time, it must be admitted that God manifests himself in two ways, by effects which are both supernatural and natural. One may thus say that God is knowable not merely in his Word but equally by the way of nature.[3]

Thomas, then, will not say precisely that God may be known only

[1] *DTC*, art. 'Théologie'.
[2] This gives to the *Summa* its distinctive philosophical, systematic and static character.
[3] Cf. the comments of Karl Barth, *CD* I, 2, p. 866.

in Jesus Christ and by the Holy Spirit. He adds to the way of grace a way of nature. This means that he adopts a dualistic position which constitutes the main characteristic of his theology and which becomes the official position of Roman Catholicism. These two ways, if not of equal importance, are of equal validity. Though they must be placed in a certain order, and clearly delimited the one by the other, they both lead to the knowledge of God. In effect, 'we can know God in this life by the light of nature, not as he is in himself, but as the first and eminent cause of all things' (I, 12, 12). If reason cannot attain to the essence of God, it has a perception adequate for the knowledge of his existence (*ibid*.). 'We thus know by natural reason, first, that God has necessary relationships with creatures, i.e., that he is their first cause; then that he differs from them essentially, i.e., that he is not anything that he has made; and finally that he is separated from them, not by inferiority, but by pre-eminence' (*ibid*.).[1]

It is true that in this life 'man knows God more perfectly by grace than by natural reason' (I, 12, 13), and that revelation in the strict sense first enlightens reason to enable it to draw intelligible concepts from sensible images (*ibid*.). Yet within this framework reason has certain capacities and an important role. It will demonstrate the existence of God, not *a priori*, but *a posteriori*, moving back from effect to cause and thus establishing the preambles to faith which are indispensable to it and which constitute in Thomas not merely the first three books of the *Contra Gentiles*, which might be regarded as his philosophy of religion, but also the whole of the opening section of the *Summa*. 'The existence of God, and other truths which we can discover concerning His being by natural reason, according to the sayings of St Paul to the Romans, are not articles of faith, but the preambles of faith; for faith presupposes human knowledge, just as grace presupposes nature' (I, 2, 2). And later he adds: 'Is it not necessary to know that a thing is before one can say what it is?'

We should not underestimate the importance of these statements. If it is the duty of theology to discover the essence of God by revelation, natural reason is first called in to prove that the being in question exists. The movement in which God presents himself to us personally is not enough to demonstrate that he really exists. We must first make sure of this by a process of intellect which alone seems able to make it possible for us finally to accept revealed truths.

[1] Thomas here refers to Rom. 1.19, but does not mention Rom. 1.21–23 or I Cor. 2.14.

In this respect Thomas gives several examples which leave nothing to be desired by way of clarity. In relation to faith particularly he later asks whether demonstrative science can exist alongside faith in the true sense. Replying in the affirmative, he shows that we can demonstrate the unity of God, but not the trinity, which is a truth of revelation (I, 31, 1). 'We may thus have demonstrative knowledge of his unity and believe in his trinity' (II, 1, 5). This parallelism runs right through the *Summa*, which begins by establishing the five proofs of God's existence, then by the same light of natural reason defines the names of God, and finally investigates the Trinity as the object of revelation. This twofold way of knowledge is carefully followed in respect of all the themes which lend themselves to it.[1]

The preambles of faith are thus given a considerable role in the knowledge of God even though they cannot pretend to instruct us concerning his essence. They can demonstrate a number of truths on which theology builds in its own elaboration of revealed principles. In this respect the part of reason is primary. For not only does it establish preliminary truths; it also shows the self-consistency of a revealed truth. To be sure, it does not prove faith. But it helps faith 'to set in a clearer light the truths which it teaches' (I, I, 8). It is thus called in both to defend faith and to 'construct what is revealed', i.e., to co-ordinate the mysteries of faith.[2]

Strictly speaking, the preambles of faith are not truths of faith. Yet they are to be ranked with articles of faith which cannot be demonstrated. 'Among the articles of faith we rank truths which may be proved by demonstration, not that they are of faith purely and simply for the whole world, but because they are an indispensable preliminary to the things which belong to faith, and because those who cannot appreciate their demonstration should at least admit them by faith' (II, II, 1, 5). This is, no doubt, the reason why they are included not merely in the apologetics of Thomas but also in his dogmatics. They introduce and support faith, not by way of demonstration, but by way of authentication. There is indeed a danger that they will attenuate it by sparing it the risk which is inherent now that we walk by faith and not by sight: 'Rational proofs

---

[1] Thus God's goodness is a specific instance of the good in general, and the eternity of God may be known from time. Though many others before Thomas had used natural or philosophical knowledge, his systematization at this point is new.

[2] Cf. the duties of reason as defined in I, 1, 8 and I, 32, 1. Congar sees three main uses of reason: to establish the *praeambula fidei*; to defend Christian truths; and to construct a body of doctrine out of revealed mysteries.

destroy all the merit of faith, or at least diminish it, if they are applied to divine things with the object of making us adhere to them by faith; but if they tend only to make our faith more spontaneous and solid, they do not diminish its merit at all' (II, II, 2, 10). This conclusion is followed by the explanation: 'As concerns demonstrative reasons which establish the truths that serve as an introduction to faith, though without being themselves articles of faith, they may alter the nature of faith by making evident the things which they propose for belief, but they do not alter the nature of the charity which disposes the will to believe these things even if they are not evident; and for this reason they do not alter the nature of the merit' (*ibid.*).

The question which interests us specifically is to know the final basis of this dualistic or synthetic position of Thomas. What is its ultimate presupposition? This basis or presupposition is surely apparent in the two quotations already adduced: *Cum enim gratia non tollat naturam, sed perficiat,* reason ought to serve faith (I, 1, 8); and then: *Sic enim fides praesupponet cognitionem naturalem, sicut gratia naturam* (I, 2, 2). The role of reason, both as justification of the preambles and in association with supernatural revelation, thus rests on a relationship between grace and nature. The whole system has here its starting-point. If grace presupposes and perfects nature rather than destroying it, then it is not merely legitimate but imperative to take nature into account. Even if it does not present itself to us in a state of perfection, it waits for grace and appeals to it, and grace, when it comes, does not set it aside, but takes it up and adapts it to its proper end. Nature has only to be corrected to enter afresh into harmony with grace and to recover its place in creation as God willed it.

Thomas deals more precisely with these questions in I, 4, which treats of the divine perfections. Under 3, he here asks whether creatures can be like God. On the basis of Gen. 1.26 and John 3.2, he answers as follows: 'Since on the one hand God is the universal agent and principle of all beings, and since on the other he has neither genus nor species, creatures are like him, not in genus or species, but by a certain analogy' (I, 4, 3). Having then made some distinctions between form, genus and species, he concludes: 'Supposing, then, that the cause is not enclosed in any genus or species, its effects will have an even more remote relationship with it; they will be like it neither in species nor genus, but only by a certain analogy, inasmuch as all beings participate in being itself. We may thus see the relationship between creatures and God: they are like him because they are beings and he is the universal and primary principle of all being' (*ibid.*). The likeness between God and man thus rests on a simple line of reasoning. As we can show by reason, God is the essence and the principle of all being, and man is set in a certain relationship or analogy to him because God causes him to participate in being. Thus 'God is being by essence, and creatures by participation' (*ibid.*). This resemblance has been called the 'analogy of being' because it affirms a relationship of created being to the first being, i.e., a participation of the creature in the universal principle. The term 'proportion' is sometimes used in the same sense. The question is raised whether created intelligence can see God in his essence. The fourth objection is as follows: 'There must be proportion between the one who knows and the thing known. Now there is no proportion between the created intellect and God, since an infinite distance separates them. Hence the created intellect cannot see the essence of God' (I, 12, 1). To this Thomas replies: 'The word proportion has two meanings: first, it expresses the relationship between one quantity and another, as equal, double or triple; then it marks the relationship between one thing and another. In the latter sense there is a proportion between the creature and the Creator, for they are related as cause and effect or power and act. *Secundum hoc intellectus creatus proportionatus esse potest ad cognoscendum Deum* (*ibid.*).

If there is thus an analogy or proportion between the creature and God, this means that there is between them a certain continuity which authorizes the knowledge of God by created intelligence and therefore the association with supernature of a nature which is basically related to God in spite of its perversion. In this respect, it is important to note that Thomas never introduces the philosophy of Aristotle as such into theology. He corrects it, taking from it only what he believes to be authentic natural truth. The theologian adopts, as it were, a superior standpoint, surveying created and perverted reality, discerning in it the truth which it still seems to have maintained, linking this with his knowledge of grace and thus establishing the original harmony in a grandiose attempt to embrace all creation as reconciled to God. This ambition conforms to his definition of theology as a derivative of the divine knowledge (I, 1, 2). Like God, but in his own place, the theologian takes in at a sweep the whole of reality as already reconciled, thanks to the principles revealed to him from on high (*ibid.*).

This raises a decisive problem in the interpretation of Thomism. In thus seeing nature in its original perfection, and associating it with God, does the theologian find himself exclusively in the sphere of revelation, so that he cannot really do more than comment on it? It is evident that nature is assumed into the humanity of Jesus and therefore that it is already present before God. Thus, even if we can see redeemed creation only through a veil, certain natural implications of completed revelation can be known to us in him. Does this mean, then, that the synthesis of Thomas is simply an unfolding of the implications of Christ's redemption? Or does it rest on the very different presupposition of a relationship of being between the creature and the Creator which does not rest directly on the work of reconciliation, but on a prior definition of this common being, so that the theologian can speak of unity with God along two different lines? First, he can speak within the framework of the preambles of faith, by the reason which can apprehend one part of truth, in virtue of this relationship. Then, he can treat of revelation, which has been shown to be necessary because of the inadequacy of fallen reason. If this second alternative is correct, then we have a synthesis which is more original but also more dangerous and also very debatable from the biblical standpoint, since it assumes that nature is not entirely corrupt, and that it has its own power which grace is commissioned to release and direct by adding its own truth. In this case, the theologian has three tasks: first, with the help of the Holy Spirit, to establish the system of natural truths; then to gather the principles of revelation; and finally to bring the two systems together in a grandiose synthesis of truth.

There seems to be little doubt that this second interpretation of Thomas is the more correct.[1] If so, we may perhaps note already a basic resemblance between Thomism and the concerns of Neo-Protestantism. We may also point out that the reaction of the Reformers was in essence a vehement criticism of this synthesis.

The Thomistic synthesis serves to justify in Roman Catholicism several positions and enterprises which call for notice. First of all we

[1] In favour of this interpretation cf. Congar, Gilson and even more blatantly Pénido and Gardeil. Largely in reply to the criticisms of Barth, a different view has been advanced by G. Söhngen (*Catholica*, 1934, 3 and 4) and H. U. v. Balthasar (*K. Barth, Darstellung und Deutung seiner Theologie*, 1951), but this is hardly the official understanding.

have the so-called 'fundamental theology' which by and large corresponds to the philosophy of religion in Neo-Protestantism. This is an introduction to positive theology, its task being to elaborate the preambles of faith by rational demonstration. Congar finds for it temporary justification as follows: 'The humanist movement on the one hand and the exigencies of the Protestant controversy on the other raise many questions in the Church and thus stimulate the attempt to create a fundamental theology in which there is critical investigation of the sources, certainty and method of religious thought.'[1] Yet he also recognizes that in principle it derives from a deeper source and conforms to the very foundations of Roman Catholicism. There is little distinction from apologetics, as noted in the same dictionary by J. Michel: 'Rational apologetics, which tries to demonstrate scientifically the credibility of revelation, may be regarded as a fundamental theology. It is, in effect, fundamental in relation to special theology, for thanks to it the human mind is led to accept revealed truths.'[2] This discipline thus precedes, supports and establishes positive theology by demonstrating and even constituting the fundamentals of the faith by means of reason. It lays the foundations of the dualistic edifice of Roman Catholicism, starting with an element alien to revelation in the strict sense.

Apologetics for its part seeks 'to bring man to the act of faith', as plainly if somewhat imprudently stated by L. Maisonneuve in another article.[3] Quoting Racine: 'The reason in my verses leads man to faith,' the author bluntly claims that this is the principal end of apologetics. Of the numerous definitions which he cites we may refer to that of Weltzer and Welte: 'The science which deals systematically with the constitutive and guiding principles of the theological sciences,' and also to that of Ottigen: 'The scientific demonstration and defence of the Christian religion.' The author's own definition is as follows: 'Theology presupposes the faith whose teachings it expounds, connects, develops, confirms and enlarges; apologetics tries to make faith possible, to show that it is reasonable and necessary. . . . Yet the distinction is only in appearance; in effect, far from establishing opposition and separation between apologetics and dogmatics, reason is the faculty which unites them; for, if it is indispensable to the apologist in the construction of his

[1] *DTC*, art. 'Théologie'.   [2] *DTC*, art. 'Fondamentale'.
[3] *DTC*, art. 'Apologétique'.

arguments, it is no less essential to the theologian in drawing from revealed majors and minors the conclusions which enrich the treasury of faith.' Moreover: '. . . since revelation is certain and its transmission assured only after rational demonstration, apologetics is the absolutely necessary condition of theology.' In short, 'it is a science of the foundations of true religion, a theory of the principles which serve to establish the existence of a supernatural religion, the truth of the Christian revelation, the legitimacy and necessity of the social form which it takes in Catholicism and which maintains its unity and vitality in the Church of Jesus.' In terms of a temple, apologetics is like the solid foundations, the buttresses, and the porch by which one enters. In support of his thesis, the author quotes many authorities, especially Thomas: 'He would not believe if he did not see that it is necessary to believe,' and Cardinal Pius: 'That a thing must be believed is not seen by faith, but by reason.' It is most unlikely that Thomas would have expressed himself like Congar, but his dualism, however cautious, cannot defend itself successfully against such developments.[1]

These two procedures depend upon an essential ability to recognize 'the aptness of an assertion to be believed', or its credibility. Gardeil expresses himself quite unequivocally on this point. There are four degrees of credibility. The first is the simple credibility 'which makes faith possible for a human agent acting according to the requirements of reason', but not 'necessary'.[2] The other three degrees are supernatural: 'By the four qualities of natural knowability, rational credibility, supernatural credibility and visibility the divine intelligibility adapts itself to the continuous effort of the created intellect, supported by a progressive divine revelation, to enter into knowledge of the divine being, and in this way it assures the welding of the four orders of knowledge by which it attains this, namely, metaphysics, apologetics, theology and beatific knowledge.' This rational credibility justifies apologetics, the aim of which is to demonstrate 'the existence of God and of the attributes which establish his divine personality; the possibility of a revelation; its necessity; the possibility and cogency of the demonstrative signs of the credibility of revelation; the possibility of verification, etc.' Man thus has the power to accept the faith if it can be proved to him that

---

[1] On the distinction at this point between Thomas and Anselm, cf. K. Barth, *Anselm: Fides Quaerens Intellectum*, ET, 1960, *passim*.
[2] *DTC*, art. 'Crédibilité'.

it is reasonable. There is a smooth and progressive movement from nature to grace.

In all this Gardeil rests on four canonical decisions, the chief of which is that of the Vatican Council of 1870. Here there is an admirable balance between the part of God and that of man. The former is naturally predominant; they are not on the same level. Yet every statement concerning revelation or grace has a complementary indication of the part played by man. The Council was seeking to combat modernist rationalism and naturalism without falling into Reformed univocity, i.e., without abandoning the *via media* of a judicious synthesis. Its main concern was to defend a proper subordination of reason to faith which would allow it to avoid both a false contempt for nature and the abuse of nature by regarding it as autonomous.[1]

All that we have said shows us that from the moment when the theological supremacy of Thomas was practically imposed[2] the Roman Church has deliberately chosen this middle line of compromise, even though it runs contrary to Augustine, Anselm, Bernard, Bonaventura and in some respects Thomas himself. Thomas is undoubtedly the origin of the deviation effected in the Vatican Council, which is the true charter of modern Roman Catholicism. There may be variations from the main course, both to the right and to the left. But the teaching office keeps to it through every variation, authorizing the variations only to correct them, to play them off the one against the other, and finally to return to the course selected. This course discloses the basic structure of Roman Catholicism and explains its official acts, its teaching and its attitude in society.

The starting-point of the Roman Catholic position, especially since the time of Trent, is thus the knowledge of God received by the twofold way of grace and nature in virtue of revelation on the one side and of a 'profound structural similarity between nature and supernature' on the other, i.e. through the operation of a twofold alliance, the one set up by the participation of the creature in being and the other by the restitution effected in the reconciliation in Jesus Christ. This arrangement between two elements of unequal impor-

---

[1] Cf. the *Constitutio Dei Filius*.

[2] With regard to the authority of Thomas, he was hailed as the common doctor in 1317, canonized in 1327, and recognized as a doctor of the Church in 1567. His work is commended in Canon Law and has been eulogized in encyclicals by Leo XIII and Pius X.

tance ascribes to man and to the Church a certain power[1] which is expressed in the doctrines of free will, of tradition, of merits, of the authority of the teaching office and of Mariology, and which constitutes the chief characteristic of this whole attitude.

[1] This power is centred in reason, cf. *ST* I, 31; I, 12, 2; I, 16, 1; I, 83, 1; II, I, 73, 2; II, II, 4, 2.

B

2

The Starting-point of Modern Protestantism

As we now turn to more recent Protestantism in an attempt to pick out its basic features, we enter a very different world, even though the contrast in theological presuppositions is not perhaps at root so sharp as we are constantly told. According to a common view, the origin of this movement may be attributed to a need for liberation which became more and more urgent in face of scholastic intellectualism and authoritarianism. In part this is true enough. The first signs of the new spirit in theology are a reaction against the hardening of Reformed positions after the Synod of Dort, e.g., in the *Consensus Helveticus* of 1675. Yet this impatience is not the whole story. The development of Protestant theology during this period is part of a more general movement which fulfils the humanism of the sixteenth century and prepares the way for that of the eighteenth. The rise of the modern spirit carries theology along with it and affects it profoundly. Undoubtedly many of the features of the religious movement are as old as Christianity itself and have been with it throughout its history. Nevertheless, to understand the deep inspiration of this new thrust in Protestantism, the results of which are still vital, we need to trace it back to its origins in the age of the Enlightenment, in 'the most enlightened century of all', as Voltaire described it.

The characteristics of this century are well known and need not detain us long. We may simply recall that the eighteenth century was especially the century of the rise of human self-awareness and anthropocentricity. Previously in bondage to many different powers, man now undertook to loosen his bonds, to affirm his freedom and to impose his own standard on the things around him. Kant's definition of the *Aufklärung* might well be applied to the whole century: 'It is the movement by which man emerges from the state of inferiority which made it impossible for him to use his reason without submission to the direction of others. Previously man has been a minor, living in this dependence. He has not been without reason, but he has never had the boldness nor the resolution to break free from this supervision. Have the courage, therefore, to throw off these authorities and to take the direction of your life into your own hands according to your own spirit.' Voltaire for his part describes the rise of the new spirit as a veritable revolution. In his *Essai sur l'histoire générale* he mentions four centuries of particular glory: that of Philip and Alexander, that of Caesar and Augustus, that of the Medicis and finally that of Louis XIV, which 'of the four is perhaps the one that comes nearest to perfection'. 'Sound philosophy was not known until this age. In our arts, our minds, our manners, as also in our government, there has been a general revolution which should serve as an eternal monument to the true glory of our country.'[1]

It is with this rise of the modern spirit, which fulfils the movement of emancipation initiated by the Renaissance but restrained by the strongly theocentric influence of the Reformers, as also perhaps by a general lack of readiness, that we should link the development of modern Protestantism. It is carried on this wave in its journeying to new coasts. How indeed could it resist this glorious expansion without appearing to be reactionary and thus forfeiting all chance of a hearing?[2]

Initiated by Leibnitz, the century contributed such men as Rousseau and Voltaire, Lessing and Kant, who, in spite of every difference, were at one in proclaiming the priority of life over theory, of conscience over all external domination, of subject over object. They accepted the authority of their own minds and thus proclaimed their essential liberty, which was accompanied by a barely adequate scepticism and by a resultant toleration which was sincere but relativistic. For them, everything came into the sphere of natural morality, for once dead orthodoxy had been rejected with all its dogmas, what better basis could be found for man's pursuit of the ideal than his inner sense of right and wrong? Individualism was a consequence of these premises. If man is free, confident in his resources and rights, himself controlling truth, he naturally turns

[1] Ch. 165. Cf. also ch. 203.
[2] Cf. K. Barth, *From Rousseau to Ritschl*. ET, 1959, pp. 11, 15, 19, 36, 52.

inward and isolates himself. The only intolerable thing—and this is the limit of his liberalism—is the incursion of external forces into his personal experience. These aspects of mastery are far from excluding the exercise of the intellect which results in the strong intellectualism of the movement of the Enlightenment. Furthermore, in spite of its pretensions, the eighteenth century never claimed to reject Christianity. It sought rather to appropriate it, first making it acceptable to the reason and conscience of the new man in order that it, too, might contribute to the development of life. In short, confidence in man and his faculties is the main characteristic of the century.[1]

In other ages, theology could maintain, if not its control over thought, at least its own partial integrity in face of secular trends. In this age, however, we have to recognize that it could only follow the general movement. Resting on an orthodoxy which in spite of everything was fairly closed, it had to choose between fierce resistance to the new movement and a cautious, progressive and almost total acceptance. To be sure, it might also have rethought its message in the light of the new ideas. But it was slow to realize what was happening, and in spite of itself it was, as it were, dragged along by the powerful impetus of modernism.[2]

In general, the new arrangement between theology and humanism was achieved in four stages corresponding to the various trends in the Protestantism of the time. The first theologians affected by the new spirit belonged to the early days of the century. They had no intention of abandoning orthodox teaching, to which they sought to remain faithful at least in part. At this first stage, there was no question of a conscious transformation of the Gospel to adapt it to the new ideas. Sensitive to the needs of their time, these men, rather than shutting themselves in an ivory tower, entertained what seemed to be the legitimate ambition of making men see and accept the fact that authentic Christian faith is the only true divine and human truth. To their concern for fidelity there was added merely a pastoral or apologetic interest. When they appealed to reason, it was not consciously to raise it to the dignity of a second source of knowledge, but to show to those who claimed it that they had no serious grounds for rejecting the faith. This appeal to reason was simply the argument of the preacher and not a positive theological

[1] Cf. Rousseau's *Profession de foi du vicaire savoyard*, and similar passages in Voltaire, Lessing and Kant.
[2] Though the Church condemned Rousseau, Barth thinks that he was merely developing the presuppositions accepted by all eighteenth-century Protestants.

notion. By postulating the agreement between reason and faith, it was hoped above all to avoid the obstacles which the former might erect to prevent acceptance of the latter. The attempt was certainly not without its dangers, since the desire to make Christianity acceptable often grows in the theologian and leads him either seriously to pervert or at least to attenuate it. With the recoil, we may say that this mutilation took place, but it is only fair to recognize also that it was not the result of a deliberate intention on the part of these transitional theologians. In principle, their starting-point was still revelation, though in fact their apologetic desire introduced into theology the dualism which extended over the whole century.[1]

During the second stage reason or consciousness was deliberately placed on the same level as revelation, and an equilibrium was achieved which in theory surpassed even that of Thomas, though astonishingly resembling it in fact. As we have seen, the Thomistic synthesis tried to maintain a clear subordination of philosophy to theology, like the earlier eighteenth-century theologians, but it could not prevent this submission from frequently transforming itself into the equality and even the superiority of philosophy. Once the gate is opened to natural theology, even though it is given a strictly limited place, one cannot finally prevent it from sweeping the field. Reason was here deliberately set on an equal footing with revelation.[2]

There could be no halting at this point. The process moved forward irresistibly. In this respect we may note how differently such movements develop in Roman Catholicism and Protestantism. When the former had achieved the synthesis, and regarded it as balanced and judicious, it was able to impose it gradually by a series of decrees. The teaching office could not prevent certain individuals from going to extremes which were already contained in the premises themselves. But by maintaining the central line it was able to limit the mischief until the day came when the Vatican Council could openly confirm the best form of the alliance. Protestantism, however, had no authority but that of Scripture, which does not impose itself by papal, canonical or conciliar decisions. It had thus to pursue its own movement to the bitter end and to bear all the consequences of its folly. This is proved by the third and fourth stages of the process. In these reason took up a position of clear superiority to revelation, first in appropriation and then in

[1] Cf. Werenfels, Osterwald and J.-A. Turrettini, esp. the latter's *Treatise on the Truth of the Christian Religion.*   [2] Christian Wolff is a good example.

suppression. The group of theologians called the Neologists had no outstanding representative, so that interest centres less on the individuals concerned than on the highly significant phenomenon which they illustrate. They were not prepared to discard revelation altogether. Their method was more restrained, though it led to the same result. It consisted in a threefold process: revelation was reduced to a sum of notions or ideas concerning God, liberty, morality and immortality; it was accepted only to the extent that it conformed to natural religion; and this implied condemnation of the whole of the past with its unacceptable dogmas of hell, the devil, satisfaction by the death of Christ, etc. Quite naturally the authority of the ancient creeds, the inspiration of Scripture, original sin, justification by faith, the Virgin Birth, the descent to hell, the resurrection and ascension, the miracles and return of Christ, were rejected without the slightest regret. The fathers were no more than mischievous sophists, and all that was left was a vague natural religion analogous to that of Rousseau's *vicaire*. The final stage is hardly worth mentioning. It was an extreme expression of such brazen spirits as are often found on the periphery of the Church and whose delight is in the most outrageous utterances. For them Christianity was simply an opportunity to boast of a number of virtues with no great profundity.

In sum, Protestantism reflects in its own sphere the main characteristics of the century. Without wishing to abandon its own true object, it seeks to associate with it what it finds of value in the human world around. Without caricature, one may attribute to it the features outlined above: the predominance of inwardness over external authority; moralism; optimism; semi-Pelagianism and even Pelagianism, resulting from confidence in man; an intellectualism which became more and more pronounced, though it had been present from the very moment when orthodoxy was described as reasonable. After all the attacks on the predominance of the intellectual element in both Roman Catholic and Protestant orthodoxy, it is interesting to note that there arises a new rationalism which is even more implacable in its autonomy and self-sufficiency. All things considered, we are confronted during this period by a powerful resurgence of natural theology—sometimes disciplined, sometimes wildly unrestrained—which will remain an inalienable element in the whole theology of Neo-Protestantism.[1]

[1] The development of the authority of reason or consciousness is paralleled in

The early stages of this new alliance between nature and grace do not permit us to draw any conclusions concerning its starting-point. We shall have to see it in action during the nineteenth century and up to our own day. In so doing, we shall follow three parallel lines which shed a vivid light on its principles: first, the line of religious consciousness which inspired the whole movement originating in Schleiermacher; secondly, that of moral consciousness which, beginning in Kant, exercises a no less comprehensive influence; and thirdly, that which, initiated by Lessing but again affecting the whole period, lays primary emphasis on the importance of history.

1. *Religious Consciousness*

For Schleiermacher the starting-point is obviously consciousness. As he himself said again and again: 'The one point from which everything radiates, because it is there that everything concentrates, is, for me, consciousness.'[1] Christian consciousness is our starting-point; it develops in the community; it produces there many forms of expression; our task is to unite these into a single whole.[2] To put it simply, an individual religion such as we seek can arise only out of the fact that a specific intuition of the universe, whatever it may be, is made the central point of all religion, so that everything relates to this centre.[3] Thus the writer can also say again to Lücke: 'I have written scores of times that I hold aloof from philosophical systems and simply seek to analyse the Christian soul.'

Yet we do injustice to the theologian if we do not add that in spite of certain appearances his starting-point is not to be found in religious consciousness as such but in the object which it discovers and from which it receives an influence which gives it its whole value. Notwithstanding his own attenuations of this affirmation in his second *Discourse*, where he says that a religion without God might well be better than one with God,[4] Schleiermacher ascribes this importance to consciousness only because it is religious and therefore an intuition of God in his revelation. The apologetic procedures should not mislead us. The true starting-point of his thinking, as of his life, is the influence which he receives from the Gospel in his consciousness. The basic fact as he sees it is the appearance of an individual whose personality has exerted an influence on the

Roman Catholicism by a similar development of that of tradition from the days of Irenaeus, through Vincent of Lerins, to the Council of Trent.

[1] *Second Letter to Lücke.*   [2] *The Christian Faith*, §20.
[3] *Discourses.*   [4] *On Religion*, ET, 1958, p. 282.

consciousness of those who come after him.[1] His whole dogmatics revolves around this influence which determines him from without and which is none other than that of Jesus Christ. It is only in Jesus Christ, and in his religion, that redemption is the centre of piety. Any attempt to diminish this dignity of Jesus Christ, or to reduce his special work; any attempt to give to them, within the totality of the system, a different place from that here assigned to them, will deprive Christianity of its essential character (§11). Schleiermacher's dogmatics is undoubtedly subjective, as that of Kant is rationalistic. But this is because the Gospel is apprehended in and by consciousness. In truth Schleiermacher would have defended himself strongly against the charge of pantheism. For him, God and man are conjoined in religious consciousness, which is primary only to the degree that God influences it and is present in it. The object of faith is thus outside, and instead of speaking of integral subjectivism we should rather find Schleiermacher's starting-point in a kind of synthesis between God and man which is achieved in the domain of consciousness, where the encounter takes place. All the elements of religious life contain the sense of absolute dependence, or, in other words, all self-consciousness contains consciousness of God (§32). The totality of things and the world, or the world, does not place us in absolute dependence. God alone gives us this sense. In the bosom of consciousness, it is the only true encounter between God and myself (*loc. cit.*). Thus the subjectivism of Schleiermacher does not imply suppression of the divine object. It consists in the emphasizing of the subject which apprehends the truth rather than the work of the truth itself.[2]

The theology of Schleiermacher oscillates between the spontaneous intuition of consciousness and the revelation of God in Christ, which are intimately associated in a new kind of synthesis established in the domain of the inwardness of man and the Church. At each point the source of dogmatics is the inward state of the individual (§30). If we set this affirmation alongside the statement that Jesus Christ is the source of theology (§19), we can see the fusion plainly effected. The starting-point is to be found in the consciousness which adheres to the evangelical message, in Christ as he is absorbed in this consciousness, or in the consciousness as it is determined by him.

[1] *The Christian Faith*, §10.
[2] At root, this is simply a development of the *Discourses* (e.g., pp. 282ff.), though *The Christian Faith*, as an exposition rather than an apology, is far more precise (cf. §§ 10, 13, 19, 22, 29).

The characteristics of this consciousness have been so frequently delineated that we need not dwell on them. Yet two features are of sufficient importance to call for notice. It is both a sense of dependence and an intuition. Awareness of God is an immediate sense of absolute dependence and it can never be separated from sensual awareness (§5). This sense is identical with consciousness of God (§11). Thus there is at the outset no prior conception of God. There is rather an instinct, an expression of the state described. To feel absolutely dependent and to have a sense of fellowship with God are one and the same thing. In other words, God is first given to us in the feeling (§4). But this relationship with God carries with it an intuition which is not knowledge in the strict sense but a kind of internal vision. In effect, feeling, knowing and acting are united in piety. In it we have intuitive knowledge of the universe and God, and we feel that we are in relationship with him. By nature every intuition is linked with a feeling.[1] The second feature of this religious awareness is that it is inseparable from sensual awareness. The three states of self-consciousness are described in *The Christian Faith* (§5). The confused consciousness of infancy is followed by the sensual consciousness in which the soul affirms itself in face of nature and society and thus assures itself of both its liberty and its dependence. At the third stage the feeling of absolute dependence is predominant. The essence of religious consciousness lies in this feeling, which is always linked, of course, with sensual awareness. At every instant in the spiritual life, therefore, there are two elements, the one constant and essential, i.e., the feeling of absolute dependence; the other variable and formal, i.e., sensual awareness. Thus faith in classical theology was regarded as quite distinct from our feelings, intuitions and religious needs, being not merely the work of the Holy Spirit but his presence in us, so that the subjective element in revelation was neither more nor less than God in us taking over our human faculties, though without confusion with them. But religious consciousness is finally only a higher degree of human consciousness, an achievement, but hardly another reality. Awareness of God is enclosed in self-awareness. They are inseparable (§4). This is why the opening sections of *The Christian Faith* deal primarily with psychological considerations. If we begin with the human soul, we must first define Christian consciousness. The confidence placed in human nature results in a humanizing of

---

[1] *On Religion*, p. 280.

B*

religion which will finally lead to an exaggerated psychology which does not merely study the religious phenomenon but apprehends even the miracle of faith. Thus the religious consciousness, though set under the influence of Christ and the Church, is ultimately only a specific instance of general human consciousness.[1]

This profound integration of faith into human experience has incalculable results for the whole of Protestantism. For if faith is both a supreme expression of nature and an influence of the divine, we must investigate it both from the human standpoint and from the standpoint of revelation. Furthermore, even though the human standpoint is subordinated to the study of revelation, it precedes, introduces and finally judges it. This explains why the dogmatics of Schleiermacher opens with some deductions from ethics, i.e., some sociological considerations on the Church, and then continues with some deductions from the philosophy of religion, which contain an examination of the development from religious feeling in the first religious societies to the Christian revelation. The field is the same, and the evolution takes place without a break. Finally, Schleiermacher sets before his dogmatic teaching some deductions from apologetics, the role of which is to establish the essence of religion, Christianity being only a particular, though distinct, instance of the religious phenomenon in general.

Ethics comprehends the study of laws manifested in the sum of facts. It is to history what philosophy is to natural science. The philosophy of religion expounds and criticizes the different forms of religious societies as expressions of piety. Apologetics isolates the essence of Christianity and demonstrates its truth in relation to other beliefs (§2). Schleiermacher makes his concern quite clear in his *First Letter to Lücke*: 'If I had begun with the Redeemer, his person and work, I should have plunged at once into full Christianity and my general conception would have remained obscure.' The preambles of faith and fundamental theology are no less necessary here than in the Roman system. Christianity is not self-vindicated. In both cases a need is felt to begin with some general conception of religion, God, the world and man. The content of the preambles differs at certain points (the proofs of God, etc.) in virtue of the differing interests of the age. But the principle accepted in both systems is the same.

This alliance between the Christian, the religious and the human

[1] Cf. also §§ 6, 13, 33.

incontestably rests on a presumed relationship between God and man which is the Protestant counterpart of the analogy of being. The only difference is that another faculty of nature is found to be spontaneously associated with grace, namely, feeling, consciousness, or the knowledge of good and evil. These are preferred to reason, although this often appears too at a later stage. If Neo-Protestantism seldom expressed this relationship so precisely and systematically as Thomism, the reason is that it regarded it as so self-evident that no theory of it needed to be worked out. To be sure, this pre-established alliance is more refined and sometimes more extreme than that of Roman Catholicism. Nevertheless, it is plainly analogous in principle.[1]

The system does not rest on an impossible association between revelation and reason, but on a prior association between revelation and consciousness or experience, which is quite acceptable if it is solidly established that this consciousness derives from the Holy Spirit who leads us into all truth (John 16.13). Unfortunately it is rather this mixture of sensuous, religious and Christian consciousness which must be our guide in the world of revealed truth and even in respect of norms. Schleiermacher's whole dogmatics is simply an expression of this religious consciousness, or of what it apprehends of revelation. The task is no longer to bear witness to the Word of God as it is incarnate in Jesus Christ and as the Scriptures enable us to receive it by the illumination of the Holy Spirit. It is simply to co-ordinate the religious impressions of the consciousness enlightened by the Gospel. Some claim that the two formulations overlap, since revelation must become experience to be a living and expressible reality. But a question of proportion arises. Revelation is certainly to be received. But if it is revelation which produces experience, more importance is to be attached to it than to its effects. Once we admit that the results are more important than the cause, and that they intermingle from the very outset with spontaneous intuitions, revelation will inevitably be subordinated to our impression of it.

Neo-Protestant theology illustrates this absorption of revelation into experience, whether in its Pietist, mediating or Liberal forms. Once it is admitted that man can choose the truth which fits his own intuition, some, who are orthodox by temperament, tradition or the

---

[1] Although Schleiermacher believes that Christianity is rational, he is in reaction against intellectualism (cf. §§ 10, 13, 14, 16, 33). There is a certain parallel in Kant.

demands of deeper piety, will accept Scripture in its totality even to
the point of literalism, whereas others, who are more concerned to
keep abreast of a scientific and rational century, will take from the
Bible just enough to preserve the distinctive value of Christianity
without isolation from the world around. Thus modern man, culture
and the Church become the masters of theology. 'Exile in the
fortress, remote from contemporary culture, is what I fear for our
theology.'[1]

A final point calling for notice in this investigation of the theological presuppositions of Neo-Protestantism is the conception of the
Church. When we first scan *The Christian Faith*, we are quite surprised to find that its effective starting-point is the reality of the
Church. Dogmatics is a theological discipline which has its origin
in the Church and is related to it (§2). This is a common opening in
Roman Catholic dogmatics, as may be seen particularly from the
statement of Bartmann: 'A dogma is any religious truth super-
naturally revealed by God and proposed as such for belief by the
Church.'[2] This is followed by a classical declaration of the Vatican
Council. The same trend may be seen in Barth's adoption of the
title *Church Dogmatics* in place of the original *Christian Dogmatics*.
The essential point, however, is to discover the meaning and role of
the word Church. For Schleiermacher, the Church is a society born
of piety and formed to maintain and develop it (§3). It is thus a
product of piety and its role is to conserve and stimulate it. And
piety is a state of feeling or immediate consciousness (§3). Thus to
begin with the Church is again to begin with feeling. The domain of
piety is not that of knowledge or action; it is that of feeling. Piety
has its origin neither in thought nor volition, but in certain states
of the soul. Now, since the feeling of absolute dependence is the
climax of all affection, it is here that true piety will have its source.
Piety is the source of the Church and the immediate sense of God
is the source of piety.

But how is the transition made? Schleiermacher understands it in
terms of ethics. Man tends to form a society, for we remember that
each of us has a sense of species which leads us to exert our influence
on others and to receive their influence on us. We also remember
that, when it has reached a certain power and maturity, what is

---

[1] *Second Letter to Lücke.* Cf. *The Christian Faith*, §28, which finds the basic matter
of dogmatics in the inward fact of religious consciousness. There is a close parallel
between the consciousness of Schleiermacher and the tradition of Roman Catholicism.
[2] *Précis de théologie dogmatique*, 1944, I, p. 22.

inward has to express itself. This is the law of all feeling. The feeling of absolute dependence is thus stirred by this force to communicate and to reproduce itself, like everything truly human (§6). The process is thus a natural one. Piety, the expression of a feeling under constraint to communicate itself, produces a society of men who are equally desirous of imparting the riches of their inner life. This gives us the Church, which gradually takes on a stable character to permit and to promote these exchanges. Thus the family, partly because it enjoys a relationship of faith and partly because it shares common circumstances, gradually forms a particular spiritual atmosphere. Enlarging the circle, we find an analogous phenomenon between men of a common language and customs. In this way there arises a society which is sufficiently distinct to stand out from others and within which piety lives and renews and propagates itself in a special way, so that we can distinguish between those who belong and those who do not. This is the Church (§6). What we have here is a kind of hierarchy in feeling and consciousness. The Church is the climax of such natural societies as the family and nation. Like them, it develops out of a certain relationship, not merely at the stage of lower feelings, but at the stage of the consciousness of God which is the highest of all. Such societies are found in all religions, for where religious feeling is manifested we see the Church, understanding by this term the character and the states of soul which piety produces and the reflection of which forms a body of ideas (*loc. cit.*).

The Church, therefore, is no longer a product primarily of the grace of God, nor is its centre a miraculous and constantly renewed attachment to the Word of Christ. It is a natural consequence of the pious feeling which remains its *raison d'être*, and the supreme manifestation of all the religious societies which have existed since men aspired to the infinite. In the *Discourses* Schleiermacher describes as follows the feeling which produces the Church and which it ought to cultivate: 'This sacred melancholy—for this is the only term which language offers—accompanies all joy and sorrow, all love and fear; no less in pride than in humility it is the fundamental note to which all else is related.' This, then, is the nature of the Church. If it is true that feelings are more lasting than ideas, then one must recognize that this heritage of ecclesiastical sentimentality is still very much with us. The task of the preacher in such a community corresponds to the basic definition. His role is not to teach, for piety does not have its origin in thought. Intellectualism in the broadest sense of the term is out of place in the Christian pulpit. The task of the preacher is to stir up religious feelings, i.e., piety, by the communication of his own feelings and experiences. As a religious virtuoso, he must communicate his impressions and intuitions to help those whose piety is still feeble to rise up above themselves.[1]

The theology of Schleiermacher is thus entrenched in a sphere which Neo-Protestantism never leaves in spite of several other influences and numerous oscillations. The framework is sketched in a most precise and yet also a very subtle way in a little work entitled *Christmas Eve*[2] which is well worth studying both as a whole and in detail. The features which clearly emerge are the predominance of feeling, the imperceptible transition from spontaneous emotion to a deeper intuition which grasps its object directly, and the presence of this intuition in the background. The explanations which may be given, and therefore theology, are of secondary value, so that theories may vary without hurt to faith. Allusion is made to the Moravians, who are attacked by one speaker and defended by another on the ground that doctrines are unimportant, since language is in any case inadequate to convey the warmth of feeling. We can never be sure that what the speakers say represents exactly the view of the author, since there are many different possibilities within the same framework and the variations and even the excesses are of little importance so long as they remain within the piety awakened supremely by primary and childish intuition. What counts is the balance of the whole. Doctrines matter little so long as the common feeling is present. Such a position rests on a clear presupposition, namely, the pre-established harmony between man and God in an immediate and spontaneous adherence to the divine influence. Strictly speaking, reconciliation is not effected in Christ. It is produced in Christ, and therefore it becomes a possibility of our nature as this lays hold of grace and associates with it in a communion of which Christ is the occasion but not the unique cause. This natural mysticism, which leads to a spontaneous synthesis in a progressive knowledge of the divine, corresponds fully to the Thomistic synthesis established prior in being to revelation. The only difference is that the organ of encounter is no longer reason

---

[1] This is how Schleiermacher defends great religious leaders in the *Discourses* (pp. 151, 156).
[2] ET by W. Hastie, 1890.

or the moral consciousness, but religious feeling. In the last analysis this view rests on an optimistic view of man's ability to attain to God, undoubtedly with the help of God, yet also in his own strength, so that the work of God is necessarily weakened and revelation mutilated.

Neo-Protestantism as a whole belongs to this field. In spite of every variation, there is the common feature of spontaneous adherence to the Christian religious reality. Sometimes there is closer approximation to revelation, sometimes to conscience, and sometimes to reason. But these variations make no decisive difference so long as the basis is the same. Through the various currents, it thus steers a course very similar to the main drift of Roman Catholicism, maintaining the line which corresponds to the unity of the Church and excluding only that which endangers the consciousness of the Church as determined not merely by the teaching office but by the majority tendencies within the Church at large. In Roman Catholicism the reality of the Church dominates and envelops revelation, whereas here revelation is absorbed into the religious consciousness. But the difference is small, for we have seen that this consciousness immediately gives rise to a community whose aspirations, though less well directed and therefore subject to greater variations, still become the ultimate norm of truth. According to this novel conception, it is inevitable that tradition should take on an authority at least equal and more likely superior to that of Scripture. This tradition is no more than the expression of the permanence of an attitude which is maintained not merely by fidelity to revelation but by a kind of sentimental and even passionate attachment. Natural feeling linked with religious feeling constitutes a far more binding imperative than that of doctrines, because it is rooted in the very depths of being. Ultimately, this reality of feeling is indeed the final reason on which Roman Catholicism itself rests.[1]

As we have seen, this position justifies the philosophy of religion since Christian feeling is simply a special instance of religious feeling in general. It also justifies apologetics, which grasps the essence of religion within a wider whole which is the sense of human life and culture. Finally, it justifies ethics, which discusses the religious society in its relationship with human life as a totality. If human nature is directly associated with grace, and if the transition from the

---

[1] Cf. the emotional attachment of the priest to his church, the place of the aesthetic in the cultus, etc.

one to the other takes place in a progressive upward movement, Christianity must be introduced by way of the most immediate human realities, and as in Roman Catholicism, though with a different content, we then have preambles of faith based upon the history of religion, philosophy and contemporary culture. This gives us the characteristic dualism of the two positions which reveals itself in a twofold source of knowledge and which influences both the definition of faith and the practice of the Church. This dualism corresponds to a more or less pronounced secularization of Christian truth, which is incarnate in the human context and often more or less identical with it. It has been justly observed that in Protestantism this secularization goes hand in hand with its adaptation to the middle classes whose growth accompanied its rise and whose reactions it very largely adopted. Once again this enterprise represents the victory of natural theology, which carries with it all the human substance that it is thought should be associated with grace.

It is neither possible nor necessary to follow the line of religious consciousness through all its variations in modern Protestantism. We shall simply give some examples of oscillations within the common framework, remembering that most of the positions defended cannot be attributed to Schleiermacher alone, but give evidence of the intermingling of his influence with that of moral consciousness and historicism. This process of borrowing, which was often indirect and which owed much to the climate of the time, produced in French-speaking Switzerland what has been called the theology of experience, which unites these different elements and links them with revelation in an alliance sometimes dominated by the one pole and sometimes by the other.

Our first example is Vinet.[1] There can be little doubt that his emphasis is primarily on revelation and only secondarily on the associated consciousness. Yet the latter has its own value, for there is an assumption of nature into grace, not merely in the incarnation of the Son of God, in which we are all implicated, but in each Christian. We thus have a kind of second incarnation in each consciousness. This presupposes the spontaneous association of our

[1] Alexandre Vinet, b. 1797. In 1817 he was appointed teacher of French language and literature at Basel High School. Ordained in 1819, he became Professor of Practical Theology at the Lausanne Academy in 1837, and of French Literature in 1845. He played an important part in the creation of the Free Church. Apart from literary criticism, his main works are *Théologie pastorale*, *Essai sur la manifestation des convictions religieuses et sur la séparation de l'église et de l'état* (1848), *Discours* and *Nouveaux Discours* and *Méditations évangéliques*.

nature with grace and justifies a certain humanism. As a result, a legitimate place is found for apologetics and the philosophy of religion. In Vinet, however, the human response to grace is located more in the moral consciousness than in pure feeling, important though the latter is. Schleiermacher is thus admixed with Kant.[1] Vinet has exerted an immense influence on all subsequent Swiss theology. His delicate dualism means that almost all the various trends in the general movement can appeal to him, either expounding his basic affirmations or taking advantage of his voluntary or involuntary concessions to religious or moral consciousness, to reason, or in a word to the humanism of the period, surreptitiously associated with the Gospel.[2]

Our next two examples are J. Bovon[3] and A. Bouvier[4] in Lausanne and Geneva. Both champion Christian experience as the norm of revealed truth. Their formal starting-point is reaction to orthodox intellectualism. This rather exaggerated reaction allows them to introduce by contrast their conception of inward Christianity. We should identify the Word of God, not with doctrine, but with experience, which Bovet believes to be the original intention of Protestantism. Profession of faith is legitimate only to the degree that each article corresponds to a real need of life. Experience is thus the true criterion. Yet this is not just individual. There is the collective norm of response to the actual needs of the age, the Church being a spiritual democracy subject, like all democracies, to the law of the majority. Piety, then, is the judge of revelation. To the extent that it is profound or superficial, traditionally attached to the Bible or influenced by the problems of the hour, it will preserve a greater or smaller measure of evangelical truth, and dogmatics will be no more than a wise mixture of what is or is not acceptable in revelation, and therefore an adaptation of revelation to contemporary spiritual

---

[1] Cf. J.-F. Astié, *Esprit d'Alexandre Vinet*, 1861, I, pp. 41, 122; P. Bridel, *La Pensée de Vinet*, pp. 9, 12, 67ff., 105, 124, 156, 192ff., 340, 410; Frommel, *Etudes littéraires et morales*, 1908, pp. 264ff., 279f.

[2] For the inner conflicts of Vinet, cf. his famous 1838 letter (C. Secrétan, *La civilisation et la croyance*, 1893, p. 377).

[3] Jules Bovon, b. 1852. He studied at Lausanne and Berlin, and after a pastorate served from 1880 to his death in 1904 as Professor of Systematic Theology in the Free Church College at Lausanne. His main works are *Etude sur l'oeuvre de la rédemption* (6 vols.) and *Dogmatique chrétienne* (2 vols.).

[4] Auguste Bouvier, b. 1826. He was Professor of Systematic Theology at the University of Geneva from 1862 to his death in 1893. His *Dogmatique chrétienne* was compiled posthumously from his lecture material and published in 1903.

needs.[1] This principle explains all the variations from Grétillat[2] to Chapuis,[3] from Godet[4] to Fulliquet, etc. In Bouvier we see the same concerns in a wider setting. The main thing is to communicate the divine life manifested in Jesus. The object of religion is revelation, but in a broad sense. Our criterion is consciousness as Christian knowledge of oneself and particularly as the sense of the restoration and possession of the divine life. But again there is the further criterion of collective Christian consciousness, and it is important not to become isolated from the contemporary climate of culture. These premises explain the various dogmatic conclusions, e.g., that 'the divine is the perfection of the human, i.e., of the spiritual and moral element in man', so that the divine life in man is simply 'the human ideal in a state of reality'.[5]

A further example is G. Frommel,[6] who exercised a decisive influence on a whole generation of conscientious pastors. Yet several questions arise in relation to his system with its careful balance between historic revelation and the experience of grace and nature. Frommel is in many ways the systematizer of the implications of Vinet's thought, though he comes closer to the second pole. His two main works are his dogmatics entitled *L'expérience chrétienne* and his apologetics *La vérité humaine*. The heart of the former is christonomic experience. Frommel aimed to put the person of Christ in the centre, though strictly the centre is experience of Christ rather than Christ himself. The starting-point is intuition of the subject, which may take various forms. The criterion is the obligation of consciousness. We thus have a new interfusion of Kant and Schleiermacher in which dogmatics rests on internal evidence, i.e., an experience of

[1] Cf. Bovon's *Dogmatique chrétienne*, 1895, I, pp. 5, 11f., 26, 29, 39f., 46.

[2] A. Grétillat, b. 1837. After a pastorate he served as Professor of Theology at Neuchâtel from 1870 to his death in 1894. His chief work is *Exposé de théologie systématique* (6 vols.). He espoused the so-called Kenotic theory.

[3] Paul Chapuis, b. 1851. After pastoral work, he was Professor of New Testament Exegesis at Lausanne Academy from 1876 to 1886. In 1886 he was dismissed on account of a conflict with the state, but he was reinstated in 1901 and remained until his death in 1904. A radical Liberal.

[4] Frédéric Godet, 1812–1900. He served as pastor and Professor at Neuchâtel. His reverent work of exegesis is still used. 'Let us concede to the Papist Church', he said, 'the honour of maintaining, in the face of unbelieving Protestantism, the two pillars of the Gospel of salvation—the Incarnation and expiation' (quoted by P. Godet in a work on his father, 1913).

[5] *Dogmatique chrétienne*, 1903, I, pp. 5, 8, 17, 20f.; II, p. 157.

[6] Gaston Frommel, b. 1862. After studying at Neuchâtel, Erlangen and Berlin, he served as a pastor and then became Professor of Systematic Theology at the University of Geneva in 1894, dying in 1906. A man of profound piety, he developed a theology of experience along the lines of Vinet and Secrétan.

the authority of Jesus Christ over our religious consciousness.[1] Apologetics naturally precedes dogmatics, and Frommel devotes three volumes to proving that Christian truth is the best, the most human and indeed the only human truth which stands up to examination.[2] This clears the ground for dogmatic study, which consists primarily in investigation of the impression made on us by the divine action. While the continuing work of God by the Holy Spirit is not to be underestimated, one cannot but deplore at this point the attenuation of Christology in the strict sense and the exaltation of 'actual' inspiration in a Hegelian separation which finally leads to the humanization of faith. The final result is a mystical naturalism parallel to that of Schleiermacher. Jesus Christ is the object, but the starting-point is a human consciousness attaining to perception of God. Psychological considerations thus take precedence of the exposition of the faith, so that Gétaz can write concerning Frommel: 'Leaving on one side the historical aspect of Christianity, he gives to an introspective psychology the final word in theological explanation of Christianity. The work of Frommel thus seems to be . . . the systematized expression of a personal religious experience, of a certain manner of laying hold of God in prayer.'[3] If this is too severe a judgment, it is basically sound. An inward fact rather than the incarnation is the starting-point. Christ in experience is the norm. Religious man stands in the forefront. Belief in Christianity rests on belief in consciousness. The analogy of being finally holds sway in the sense that if we were not by nature of divine origin we should be incapable of experiencing and realizing the implied moral and religious relationship.[4] On the other hand, the piety of Frommel includes a sufficiently strong biblical impress to make it bear witness in a very positive form to the grace of God.

Our final example of this general movement is Lemaître,[5] who in his dogmatics expounds Christianity in a similar synthesis of revelation, moral consciousness, religious intuition and history. He starts out from revelation together with the states of consciousness of the believer and the belief of the Church. Scripture and Christian experience are his two sources of reference. His norm is the Gospel

---

[1] Cf. *L'expérience chrétienne*, I, pp. 9, 11, 17, 194.   [2] *La vérité humaine*, I, pp. 6f.
[3] *Les variations de la doctrine christologique chez les théologiens protestants de la Suisse romande au XIXe siècle*, pp. 186-7.
[4] *L'expérience chrétienne*, II, pp. 38ff., 59, 151, 178, 227.
[5] Auguste Lemaître, b. 1887. He was Professor of Systematic Theology at the University of Geneva from 1928 to 1960. In addition to *Foi et vérité*, he has published sermons and meditations.

of salvation, not the Bible regarded as an 'intangible block'. We should not be enslaved to philosophy, but it can help us to understand the religious phenomenon of which Christianity is a particular example. On the basis of an original relationship between our finite spirits and the Creator Spirit, philosophy can recognize the eminent value of the Christian revelation. Nature is thus associated with grace to such a degree that its role is almost equal in importance. The biblical revelation is not alone. The Bible itself is perhaps the primary source, but it is not a unique source. Church history as well as the Bible affords several normative experiences. Tradition thus stages a reappearance in a new guise. Religious knowledge is possible only if we concede to man an ability to recognize revelation and to confer upon it its true value. Christian experience, while it is the product of the work of God, is thus the basis and norm of the authority of the supreme Revealer.[1] Christ is indeed 'the centre of all evangelical doctrine'.[2] But we are forced to ask: What Christ? And the centre of what? The Christ of experience or of Scripture, of general revelation or special? Who is to say what he is or what he teaches? Religious philosophy, religious consciousness, the normative experience of the first Christians, or that of great religious personalities in Christian history? Is the personal religion of salvation really our final authority? And if so, who is to define it, Jesus himself, critical scholarship, the intuition of the believer or the piety of a given church? Do the religious impressions of believers finally decide whether truths attributed to Christ are acceptable or not? And what is the centre of evangelical doctrine? Is not this doctrine introduced by the philosophy of religion and followed by apologetics? Does it not assume all kinds of moral, philosophical and human manifestations regarded as compatible with the Gospel? Is it not a vast divine-human organism, supporting a Church which is itself mounted on the Gospel and on the world and embracing all the values of a humanity which is fallen no doubt but still close to God? Too much importance is not to be attached to such questions. For what finally counts, as Schleiermacher taught, is piety, the religion of the heart. Intellectual formulations are secondary and ineffectual. 'Only the adoration and utterances of poetry and music can serve to evoke this triumph of the total presence of God in the irradiating of eternal love.'[3]

[1] *Foi et vérité, dogmatique protestante*, 1954, pp. 10, 15f., 21ff., 28, 52f.
[2] *Ibid.*, p. 63.   [3] *Ibid.*, p. 537.

THE STARTING-POINT OF MODERN PROTESTANTISM 53

2. *Moral Consciousness*

A child of the Enlightenment, Kant also goes beyond it. For he is not content merely to affirm the power of reason; he justifies this power and subjects all spheres of life and thought to it. The term 'critique' which he uses in his two principal works—*Critique of Pure Reason* and *Critique of Practical Reason*—does not imply depreciation. In this context it denotes analysis. Kant measures the power of reason and directs its use. The two works are thus an exercise in self-consciousness on the part of reason. Having come of age, self-reliant man establishes his rule. The criticism, as a theory of knowledge, is of great interest to theology, for, as we have noted, the choice of method is essential. Thus, while Kant does not aspire to do theological work, he certainly wishes to influence this whole discipline.[1]

His method brings about a real revolution and consists in a movement which is both negative and positive. Reacting against the Wolffian system and all metaphysics, whether Scholastic, Cartesian or modern, especially the attempt to give rational proofs of God, Kant maintains the powerlessness of pure reason. Theology can only accept this first part of his demonstration on the grounds of the famous adage: *finitum non capax infiniti*, and rejoice to see reason brought back to a more correct estimation of its true powers. If God may be known only in the revelation of his Son by the Holy Spirit, he is not accessible by the natural way of speculation, which does not lead to knowledge of God the Creator and of the Father of our Lord Jesus Christ. The whole enterprise of natural theology is here called in question in its scholastic form.[2]

Practical reason is not a second faculty, as though we had two instruments of knowledge. It is a second way in which one and the same reason operates. Having described the impossibility of direct, theoretical apprehension uniting experience and metaphysics, Kant discovers that reason can follow the different direction of action. Though inaccessible to pure reason, the reality beyond time and space acts upon us and accuses us by the moral law in our conscience. In this respect, theology has less reason for satisfaction. In place of purely rational investigation the philosopher substitutes, not the knowledge of grace by revelation, but that which proceeds from

[1] Cf. *Religion within the Limits of Reason Alone*, ET by Greene and Hudson, 1934, p. 9.
[2] Pure reason cannot lead us to the *Ding an sich* and it is therefore unable to prove or disprove such ideas as God, freedom, immortality, etc.

moral obligation. The inaccessible God reveals himself, not in the event of Christmas, but in the moral consciousness.[1]

Thus reason leaves the sphere of speculation to appear again in that of morality, where it can know being as such, not by demonstration, but by a kind of act of faith answering a primary and incontestable obligation. On this new field reason reassumes its full power. The transition from pure to practical reason has two features which are in full keeping with the spirit of the eighteenth century and which are still accepted as essential truths. The first is the return to inwardness. The criterion of truth is decisively located in us. While the moral law is the voice of God to us, it is also part of our own being. Man finds the principle of truth in himself. The second is that truth is moral. As such, it is both divine and human, both rational and practical.[2]

The philosopher seeks to apply this discovery in every sphere of life and especially in theology. In the first instance he does not claim to substitute his religious philosophy for theology. With some condescension, he admits the existence of an ecclesiastical branch of study called biblical theology, and, as we shall see, he thinks this to be justifiable in some respects. His intention is rather to give to religion a place in the system of life based on moral reason. For religion as he sees it is one element in a much larger, and indeed the only universal, domain where practical reason rules. While giving to religion a certain autonomy in its own sector, he subjects it to the empire of philosophy.

How does this annexation take place in the philosopher of the categorical imperative? The first sentence in the preface to his *Religion within the Limits of Reason Alone* states the foundation of his conception quite unambiguously: 'So far as morality is based upon the conception of man as a free agent who, just because he is free, binds himself through his reason to unconditioned laws, it stands in need neither of the idea of another Being over him, for him to apprehend his duty, nor of an incentive other than the law itself, for him to do his duty.' The basis of morality is thus man himself. Biblical religion and the resultant morality cannot be universal, since they are only for the elect. A wider basis of morality has thus to be found. This lies in the absolute nature of the moral law in all

[1] We thus encounter true being in the existence of the inner law rather than in abstract thought.
[2] The replacement of metaphysics, first by philosophy and psychology (e.g., Renan), then by economics (Marx), looks to Kant for rational justification.

men. Moreover, man as the basis of morality is free, since freedom is the absolute condition of authentic moral effort. If man were not free to choose and practise the good, what would be the use of knowing it? The moralist is forced to be a Pelagian. There has to be in our nature 'a predisposition on which it is absolutely impossible to graft anything evil' (*op. cit.*, p. 23). This particle of good is indispensable to any conception which bases right conduct on man's own power. Man endowed with this capacity rationally binds himself to obedience to the unconditioned laws which he discovers in himself. He has no need of a supreme Being to know his duty, nor of any motive apart from the law to do it. In this sense, morality does not really need religion. It is autonomous and self-sufficient, thanks to practical reason.

To seek another motive of right conduct would be to pervert and depreciate morality, introducing self-interest and robbing morality of its gratuitous character. On the other hand, while no final end is needed, 'it is quite possible that morality is necessarily related to such an end, taken not as the ground but as the sum of inevitable consequences of maxims adopted as conformable to that end' (p. 4). In other words, morality is grounded in itself and yet it leads to an end, i.e., happiness, and therefore to 'the idea of a highest good in the world for whose possibility we must postulate a higher, moral, most holy, and omnipotent Being which alone can unite the two elements of this highest good', i.e., duty and happiness (pp. 4f.). 'Man gives evidence of the need, morally effected in him, of also conceiving a final end for his duties, as their consequence' (p. 5). 'Morality thus leads ineluctably to religion, through which it extends itself to the idea of a powerful moral Lawgiver, outside of mankind, for whose will that is the final end (of creation) which at the same time can and ought to be man's final end' (pp. 5f.).

We thus have a systematic moralizing of the Christian faith, not by immediate absorption, but by a juxtaposition of moral religion and biblical religion, the latter being hardly more than an instrument to serve the former. We may best examine this novel scheme in terms of some of the classical Christian doctrines.

(i) Revelation plays a distinctly secondary role in Kant. It is thought of in purely historical terms, being limited to the epoch which produced the Bible. Subordinated to practical reason, it serves pure moral religion. There is here a certain disjunction between past revelation considered as a compendium of principles and living rational and moral knowledge. 'Recognition and respect must be accorded, in Christian dogmatic, to universal human reason as the supremely commanding principle in a natural religion, and the revealed doctrine, upon which a church is founded and which stands in need of the learned as interpreters and conservers, must be cherished and cultivated as merely a means, but a most precious means, of making this doctrine comprehensible, even to the ignorant, as well as widely diffused and permanent' (pp. 152f.).

Exposition of this revelation is necessary, but it must conform to moral religion. Revelation cannot contradict natural intuition, otherwise 'it would be a dangerous religious illusion' (p. 159). 'If such an empirical faith . . . is to be united with the basis of a moral faith . . . an exposition of the revelation which has come into our possession is required, that is, a thorough-going interpretation of it in a sense agreeing with the universal practical rules of a religion of pure reason. For the theoretical part of ecclesiastical faith cannot interest us morally if it does not conduce to the performance of all human duties as divine commands' (p. 100).[1]

(ii) What, then, is this pure moral religion? Supremely, it is man's striving after the good. 'All religions, however, can be divided into those which are endeavours to win favour (mere worship) and moral religions, i.e., religions of good life-conduct' (p. 47). Kant refers scornfully to religions in which 'man flatters himself by believing . . . that God can make him eternally happy . . . without his having to become a better man' (loc. cit.). Moreover, religions which teach us to rely more on God than on man are an enticement to sloth and also do injury to man by condemning him to passivity, with an implied depreciation of morality, whose role is to summon man to action. 'It is not essential, and hence not necessary, for every one to know what God does or has done for his salvation; but it is essential to know what man himself must do in order to become worthy of this assistance' (p. 47). This is the real point at issue. Moral religion is that whereby man saves himself. It is practical in this sense. Other religion is theoretical because it relies on the work of God rather than the striving of man.

It is important to grasp the meaning of these two words which are so much used today and which are made in some respects the test of Christian truth. The practical is that which demands human

---

[1] Revelation is thus adapted to, as well as associated with, the knowledge of practical reason (cf. pp. 103f., 144, 170).

effort, whether in action, self-giving or self-fulfilment; and we are constantly told that this is supremely required of the laity. The theoretical is the mystical element which stresses the work of God and insists that we must receive before we can act. In sum, it is God's work rather than man's. 'The acceptance of the first requisite for salvation, namely, faith in a vicarious atonement, is in any case necessary only for the theoretical concept. . . . In contrast, the necessity for the second principle is practical and, indeed, purely moral. We can certainly hope to partake of another's atoning merit, and so of salvation, only by qualifying for it through our own efforts to fulfil every human duty—and this obedience must be the effect of our own action and not, once again, of a foreign influence in the presence of which we are passive' (pp. 108f.). This statement throws a vivid light on Kant's whole enterprise. Pure, theoretical reason is not just metaphysics. It also comprises all theology based supremely on the work of God accomplishing our salvation in Jesus Christ. Loyal to the spirit of his age, Kant decides to put salvation in the hands of man himself, who now that he is of age will not merely dominate nature and science but also forge his own destiny as the principal architect of salvation. Pure moral religion is simply an expression of this pretension.

Here is undoubtedly the basic thesis of the work. It marks a true revolution in theology at the hands of philosophy. It is seldom adopted in full by later theologians, who prefer to this Pelagianism a semi-Pelagianism in which man's work is associated with that of God. But we need to understand it clearly since it is the real starting-point of Kant. As he himself puts it: 'Yet he (man) must be able to hope through his own efforts to reach the road which leads thither, and which is pointed out to him by a fundamentally improved disposition, because he ought to become a good man and is to be adjudged morally good only by virtue of that which can be imputed to him as performed by himself' (p. 46). Or again: 'Now it is our common duty as men to elevate ourselves to this ideal of moral perfection, that is, to this archetype of the moral disposition in all its purity—and for this the idea itself, which reason presents to us for our zealous emulation, can give us power' (p. 54). The refrain refers constantly and is sometimes given a biblical form: 'Thus, "Not they who say Lord! Lord! but they who do the will of God", they who seek to become well-pleasing to him not by praising him (or his envoy, as a being of divine origin) according to revealed concepts which not every man can have, but by a good course of life, regarding which everyone knows his will—these are they who offer him the true veneration which he desires' (pp. 95f.). 'It is tedious to be a good servant . . . man would therefore rather be a favourite, where much is overlooked' (p. 188). This linking of the Christian who relies on the grace of God with a favourite secured by privileges reveals the profound contempt of Kant for traditional religion. 'True religion is to consist not in the knowing or considering of what God does or has done for our salvation but in what we must do to become worthy of it . . . and of its necessity every man can become wholly certain without any Scriptural learning whatever' (p. 123).

(iii) We must now turn to an idea which has sometimes been regarded as a foreign body in Kant's thinking, namely, that of radical evil. Goethe in particular thought this too close to the doctrine of original sin and quite contrary to the optimism of the century. To the extent that it might hinder man's effort to improve himself, it ought to be rejected. Kant distinguishes in man two inclinations, the one to good, the other to evil. He defines the second as follows: 'There is in man a natural propensity to evil; and since this very propensity must in the end be sought in a will which is free, and can therefore be imputed, it is morally evil. This evil is radical, because it corrupts the ground of all maxims; it is, moreover, as a natural propensity, inextirpable by human powers, since extirpation could occur only through good maxims, and cannot take place when the ultimate subjective ground of all maxims is postulated as corrupt; yet at the same time it must be possible to overcome it, since it is found in man, a being whose actions are free' (p. 32). The following points are to be noted. First, evil is moral and not spiritual. It is not revolt against God, but the reverse of virtue and of human integrity. Secondly, even though radical, it does not suppress freedom, and therefore radical does not mean total. It takes from man the will or desire to accept the absolute sway of the moral law. It thus suppresses the motive of self-amelioration. It is a neutralization or short-circuiting of good conduct, preventing man from following the maxims of the categorical imperative. It is an obstacle to the realization of the moral ideal, but not strictly to faith. Thirdly, it is imputable and must be overcome since it is a purely subjective reality. It will not be overcome by pardon but by the omnipotence of the moral law, which cannot be stopped by an obstacle of this nature. Evil 'lies in the disposition and the maxims in general', and is a violation of the law (p. 66). Finally, the idea of original sin cannot be accepted, since it humiliates man and is also an excuse for not attempting improvement. The origin of evil is not to be sought in the fault of a first ancestor but in the actual propensity of the free will. The discord in our will can be overcome because man 'is not basically corrupt . . . but still capable of an improvement. . . . For man, therefore, who despite a corrupted heart yet possesses a good will, there remains hope of a return to the good from which he has strayed' (p. 39).

Thus, although Kant takes evil much more seriously than his contemporaries, the threat is not so great as to force him to adopt a true doctrine of redemption.[1]

(iv) Regeneration and conversion are dealt with under the title 'Concerning the Restoration to its Power of the Original Predisposition to Good'. The victory over evil is described as follows: 'Man himself must make or have made himself into whatever, in a moral sense, whether good or evil, he is or is to become' (p. 40). It is thus his own work.[2]

(v) In relation to Christology a new and decisive element seems to be introduced. If regeneration is progress to an ideal, and if this ideal is personified in the Son of God, how is moral religion to view the role of the divine Son? Jesus is in fact 'the personified idea of the good principle' (p. 54). He is the incarnation of moral good, or of humanity in its moral perfection. He is thus the only man pleasing to God. 'It is our common duty as men to elevate ourselves to this idea of moral perfection, that is, to this archetype of the moral disposition in all its purity' (p. 54). Now this archetype 'has come down to us from heaven' (p. 54) and represents 'the ideal of a humanity pleasing to God' (p. 55) in the form of a person 'who would be willing not merely to discharge all human duties himself and to spread about him goodness as widely as possible by precept and example, but even, though tempted by the greatest allurements, to take upon himself every affliction, up to the most ignominious death, for the good of the world and even for his enemies' (p. 55). This idea is set before us in order that we may fulfil our duty by conforming to it. It thus follows that we can. 'Man may then hope to become acceptable to God . . . through a practical faith in this

---

[1] In spite of resemblances to Paul, evil for Kant is not so serious as to prevent man from regenerating himself.   [2] Cf. pp. 42f.

Son of God' and as, 'by faithful imitation, he remains true to his exemplar' (p. 55).

The end pursued is thus the return to a morally perfect humanity corresponding to the goal of creation and bringing with it happiness. Jesus Christ is the model, and by his example he is also the power to help us to attain the goal. Belief in him is confidence that in spite of the temptations and sufferings which he also endured we can cleave to this archetype of humanity and not be an 'object unworthy of divine approval' (p. 55). Kant adds that the idea of this moral perfection is present already in our reason, so that the exemplary life of Christ simply confirms the idea of holiness which we find in ourselves and which we have to realize.[1]

(vi) The doctrine of expiation follows. Kant does not evade it, and his argument is typical. He distinguishes two kinds of faith. Pure religious faith is moral; that is to say, it is confidence in the process of improvement by the triumph of the idea of good, personified in Jesus and now to be incarnated in us. Historic faith is the faith of the Church. He does not deny that the doctrine of expiation is essential to the second kind of faith, but he cannot allow it in the first. At this central point there is thus contradiction between the two faiths. Kant asks whether accommodation is really possible or whether we should desire the victory of the first over the second (pp. 106f.).

The first point in his discussion is that expiation is unacceptable to any thinking person. 'It is quite impossible to see how a reasonable man, who knows himself to merit punishment, can in all seriousness believe that he needs only to credit the news of an atonement rendered for him, and to accept this atonement *utiliter* (as the lawyers say), in order to regard his guilt as annihilated—indeed, so completely annihilated . . . that good life-conduct, for which he has hitherto not taken the least pains, will in the future be the inevitable consequence of this faith, and this acceptance of the proffered favour. No thoughtful person can bring himself to believe this' (p. 107). Even if the doctrine were logically necessary, it would have to succeed effort rather than precede it. In fact, however, expiation is a theoretical doctrine on which one cannot pronounce, so that it is better to leave it on one side and to concentrate on the practical doctrine which consists in the exercise of free will (pp. 107f.). The

---

[1] Cf. p. 56. Faith here is strictly faith in oneself, and it may thus be asked whether Kant's morality is not in fact a supreme form of sin.

solution is thus offered: 'The acceptance of the first requisite for
salvation, namely, faith in a vicarious atonement, is in any case
necessary only for the theoretical concept.... In contrast, the necessity for the second principle is practical and, indeed, purely moral'
(p. 108). In other words, doing, which is the distinctive feature of
practical moral religion, should take precedence of knowing, which
is the mark of the theoretical and historical faith of the Church.[1]

The two positions are finely stated by the author in a passage
which throws light on the effective point of departure of the whole
of modernism: 'The proposition: We must believe that there was
once a man ... who through his holiness and merit rendered satisfaction both for himself (with reference to his duty) and for all
others (with their shortcomings, in the light of their duty), if we are
to hope that we ourselves, though in a good course of life, will be
saved by virtue of that faith alone—this proposition says something
very different from the following: With all our strength we must
strive after the holy disposition of a course of life well-pleasing to
God, to be able to believe that the love (already assured us through
reason) of God toward man, so far as man does endeavour with all
his strength to do the will of God, will make good, in consideration
of an upright disposition, the deficiency of the deed, whatever this
deficiency may be' (p. 110). The first conception must be rejected
because it leads to the negation of reason, and one can only wish
that a 'new order of affairs' will be established by the 'gradual transition of ecclesiastical faith to the universal religion of reason, and
so to a (divine) ethical state on earth' (p. 113).

(vii) The interpretation of Scripture authorizes a systematic
adaptation of Christian dogmas to the new religion. The Bible as a
document of historical revelation contains two elements of unequal
worth. It is both the canon of moral religion and the basis of
ecclesiastical faith. Its utility does not lie in its teaching concerning
God but in its influence on the people in promoting and facilitating
the coming of pure moral religion. In this respect, it may be taken
as the starting-point of true faith. To be sure, authentic religion may
dispense with it. But it is wiser to uphold it in view of its genuine,
if limited, influence.

Exegesis should be utilized slowly to transform a narrow and
sombre religion into one which is wise and open. 'An attempt such

[1] Theologians who reject the doctrine of expiation as unbiblical might well ask
whether their true motive is not openly stated by Kant.

as the present . . . to discover in Scripture that sense which har-
monizes with the most holy teachings of reason is not only allowable
but must be deemed a duty' (p. 78). The avowed principle of all
biblical exposition is as follows: 'If such an empirical faith . . . is to
be united with the basis of a moral faith (be the first an end or
merely a means), an exposition of the revelation which has come
into our possession is required, that is, a thorough-going interpretation of it in a sense agreeing with the universal practical rules
of a religion of pure reason' (p. 100). This rule has in fact been largely
followed in the history of the Church, not only in relation to ethics,
but also in respect of philosophy, sentiment, politics, etc. It is
indeed an expression of the most natural tendency of the human
heart, which always seeks to adapt the Bible to its own impulses.
Kant makes it a definite law: 'For the final purpose even of reading
these holy scriptures, or of investigating their content, is to make
men better; the historical element, which contributes nothing to
this end, is something which is in itself quite indifferent, and we
can do with it what we like' (p. 102). The two interpreters of
Scripture are thus the religion of rational religion and learning
(p. 104). Kant asks whether we should also add inner feeling, but
'a knowledge of laws, and of their morality, can scarcely be derived
from any sort of feeling; still less can there be inferred or discovered
from a feeling certain evidence of a direct divine influence' (p. 104).
The Bible, therefore, has a symbolical signification which reason can
utilize to establish pure moral faith.[1]

(viii) Of other dogmas mentioned, the Trinity is explained as
follows: The Father is God in his love for the man animated by a
good moral will; the Son is the expression of the idea of humanity;
the Spirit is wisdom manifesting its goodness to those who recognize
it. There is no real place for incarnation, since the Son represents the
world of morality which is only within and not outside us. This ideal
is to be realized in a man who is perfectly obedient to the absolute
demand of moral reason. Passing allusion is made to the resurrection
and ascension, which, 'merely as ideas of reason, would signify the
commencement of another life and entrance into the seat of salvation, i.e., into the society of all the good' (p. 119, n.). The kingdom
of God is simply moral rule recognizable by reason alone. Prayer is
'a superstitious illusion . . . for it is no more than a stated wish

---

[1] Many followers of Kant dissent from this attack on feeling and prefer a synthesis
with Schleiermacher.

directed to a Being who needs no such information regarding the inner dispositions of the wisher' (p. 183). For it there should be substituted the 'spirit of prayer' which should accompany 'all our actions, to perform these as though they were being executed in the service of God' (*loc. cit.*).

(ix) To these dual conceptions of revelation, religion, the Bible, faith and even the person and work of Christ, there corresponds a dual conception of the Church. Kant affirms the existence of a traditional Church, which is not to be rejected. But in place of this he desires the gradual substitution of a community of good men. The former is historical; its main aim is cultic; it rests on a rationally incomprehensible revelation and submits to all kinds of ordinances and statutes; it seeks to serve God 'through ceremonies, confessions of faith in revealed laws, and observances of the ordinances requisite to the form of the church. . . . All these observances are at bottom morally indifferent actions; yet, just because they are to be performed merely for his sake, they are held to be all the more pleasing to him' (p. 97). Such a Church is based on Scripture as expounded and commentated by 'like unto consecrated persons' (p. 98). Here 'reason avails nothing in face of the decisive assertion, which beats down every objection: Thus it is written' (*loc. cit.*). Kant likes to recount the misdeeds of such a Church. Nevertheless, he recognizes its durability. While it must yield to the true Church, it may be used as a means to prepare for its coming.

The true Church, by contrast, is 'an ethical commonwealth under divine legislation' (p. 92). It consists of the invisible Church: 'a mere idea of the union of all the righteous under direct and moral divine world-government, an idea serving all as the archetype of what is to be established by men' (p. 92). Of its chief marks, the first is universality: 'Pure religious faith alone can found a universal church; for only rational faith can be believed in and shared by everyone, whereas an historical faith, grounded solely on facts, can extend its influence no further than tidings of it can reach, subject to circumstances of time and place and dependent upon the capacity to judge the credibility of such tidings' (p. 94). Religious faith is accessible to all. It is quite natural and can be shared by any honest man. An area of agreement with unbelievers is thus found in the moral sentiment common to all.[1]

---

[1] On the twofold basis of revelation and moral or religious consciousness, many churches now accept members without confession of faith. Only on the basis of the

Purity is a second mark. This is 'union under no motivating forces other than moral ones (purified of the stupidity of superstition and the madness of fanaticism)' (p. 93). Then follows liberty in the sense of full toleration. This Church can give the widest possible scope, for in principle no authentic human value is irreconcilable with faith. Yet this is a liberty within morality, and it excludes metaphysics, dogmatism, theory, morally indifferent ordinances, etc. It can quickly become intolerant in the face of threats to the new religion. It is the liberty of autocratic morality resisting as authoritarian any competing forces.[1] Finally, this community will have a moral constitution with established principles within the framework as thus defined.

(x) In relation to the task of theology, Kant's dualism enables him to admit the existence of a biblical theology side by side with the philosophy of religion. Linked with the Bible, the Church, and the catechisms and confessions of the Church, this is an associated rather than a rival discipline. All that is needed is demarcation and the recommendation that each should keep to his special field. Kant's advice to theologians is that they should not interfere in philosophy nor try to give philosophical proofs of the articles of faith. Engaged in exegesis, theology does not rest on moral reason, but on the teaching of men inspired by the Bible. Its role is not to interpolate biblical declarations nor to attach to them moral signification. It has the more modest task of explaining the teaching of the Bible; to elaborate its content within the limits of reason is the work of philosophy. The theologian cannot prove that God speaks effectively in the Bible. He must accept this as an *a priori*. On this ground he will confine himself to the diligent exposition of Scripture. He is thus a scholar and exegete. Other matters are in the province of the philosopher.[2]

This moralism has affected the whole of so-called Christian culture, including Protestant theology, spiritual philosophy and the world of the middle-class. In a variable alliance with religious feeling, rationalism, the mythology of progression or mere aspiration towards a better world, it has become the most common explanation

_____

sole grace of God can there be a true confessing Church and not a mere religious, political and apologetic institution.
[1] Cf. p. 153.
[2] It is ironical that in the little work *The Conflict of Faculties* the philosopher roams over all fields but tells theologians to keep to their own. Yet Kant's advice is basically sound.

of the Gospel as primarily a compendium of moral precepts. Two points stand out, the predominance of practice over theory and the reduction of all truth to moral requirements. As Lagneau puts it, 'God is the immanent principle of the good.' Or Loisy: 'Faith has always been, and is, the great moral resource of humanity. From the very first it sustains humanity in its hard and dangerous Odyssey.' Or Saint-Simon: The aim of the new Christianity is 'to organize the whole human race according to the basic principle of divine morality'. Everywhere the refrain is the same. When God is pushed into the background, the only power which can conduct humanity to the ideal and to happiness is its inner sense of right and wrong. The sense of duty and the hope of progress are the basis of every hope, of every noble and useful action. Only recently have the attacks of Marxism and Existentialism, and above all the events of the twentieth century, succeeded in discrediting the cult of humanity on the basis of morality.

Again, we can only illustrate this movement in terms of one or two typical theologians and philosophers. We have already noted the fusion of pietism and moralism in Vinet.[1] In order to prevent the complete moralization of Christianity, Vinet brings faith and morality into closer association, as excellently stated by Frommel: 'By an intuition no less true than profound, he summed up the Gospel in the person of Christ and human nature in the moral consciousness, which he made the supreme organ of knowledge and of the spiritual life.'[2] This definition might well be applied to all Protestant moralism, which did not go so far as Kant in substituting morality for faith, but was content to associate the two in a synthesis which might favour either revelation on the one side or morality on the other. In this respect, the assessment of Vinet by E. Scherer is worth quoting: 'Vinet . . . unwittingly became the author of a revolution in Protestantism. . . . The moment religious truth was justified by its accord with the religious needs of the soul, it was naturally concluded that only what is religious in religion is true, and that what is religious is what responds to holy desires which produce pious emotions. This was already a striking reduction and transformation of belief. Yet it was difficult to stop here. For if moral or religious feeling is the only *raison d'être* of religion, the supernatural origin of religion is no longer of any great importance. Whether a truth is natural or revealed, whether it comes from the

---

[1] Cf. *Mélanges*, 1865, pp. 44–46.   [2] *Etudes littéraires et morales*, 1908, p. 267.

C

depths of human consciousness or descends from the open heavens, it is true because it is salutary, and it is salutary because it is true in itself, intrinsically, independently of the source from which it is drawn. Thus Vinet's method led at once, on a fatal slope, to rationalism. No one would have been more alarmed than he by the consequences; no one would have insisted more firmly than he on the necessity of a revelation from above; but no one worked more effectively in a direction contrary to his own intentions.'[1]

The supreme Christian moralist along these lines was Charles Secrétan,[2] whose conception is clearly attested in the little work *Théologie et Religion* and in *La civilisation et la croyance*. His method is quite plain. He examines the various doctrines according to the norm of moral consciousness and finds them quite satisfactory.[3] We are all sons of God and there is no essential difference between Jesus Christ and us. The ancient formulations are at this point a hindrance (p. 30) because the two natures are one (p. 43). The holiness of Jesus is his divinity, and it is divine because human (pp. 40f.). Sterile speculation is thus avoided. The miracle of incarnation is the moral fact of conversion (pp. 36f.). Salvation is simply our moral transformation (p. 42). Expiation is the sanctification which we can acquire by imitating Jesus (p. 62). Each believer can expiate part of the sins of all by the sorrows of his conversion (p. 67). The preservation of true and effective religion as distinct from verbal metaphysics depends on our maintaining Jesus Christ as our model, his imitation as our hope, and holiness as our supreme goal (pp. 39f.).

This is obvious Pelagianism. Man is to save himself by imitating Jesus Christ. Humanity is to convert itself by an act which will consist in a series of individual acts (p. 65). If this is possible, however, it is because the corruption of humanity is only slight. It still participates in deity. God is sanctified humanity (pp. 68f.). Feuerbach could hardly be more radical. If Secrétan was a pantheist, it was for religious rather than philosophical reasons. He had no sense of bondage to sin. Full of confidence in himself and the race, he thought himself capable of developing to the point of a superior

---

[1] *Etudes critiques sur la littérature contemporaine*, 1863, pp. 291f.
[2] Charles Sécretan, 1815–95. After commencing theology, he came under the influence of Schelling at Munich. On his return he studied law and for a time practised at the bar. He became Professor of Philosophy at Lausanne Academy in 1838. Recalled during the 1848 revolution, he went to Neuchâtel in 1850. In 1866 he resumed his chair at Lausanne, where he remained until his death. Although a philosopher, he was primarily concerned with theology according to the criterion of the moral consciousness.
[3] *Théologie et Religion*, 1883, p. 60.

humanity full of nobility and dignity. He tried to integrate Christianity into his general search of the good. His starting-point was the liberty of man, his intrinsic worth, his sense of duty and his capacity for salvation.

To supporters of Moral Rearmament I would recommend *La civilisation et la croyance*, for Secrétan might well be regarded as in many respects the prophet of Caux according to this work. The theme is simple. The times are out of joint; the political situation is unstable; the economic position is little better; egotism creates all kinds of conflicts of interests. Moral collapse, or the lack of love, is responsible for these evils. If there is to be improvement, it must come from moral reconstruction under the leadership of the rich.[1] For man is above all a moral being. 'The only *a priori* of the human spirit is duty' (p. 10). But duty presupposes liberty. Nothing is more false or disastrous than to regard man as impotent and enslaved. Man is free and able. God stands behind duty; he is the inner voice of justice. Thus the foundations of human life are God, right and liberty (p. vii). 'The supremacy of the moral idea is the vital element in modern thought; it is the seed of truth which we must conserve and cultivate at all costs' (p. 10).

If, then, man is a moral being, he must be urged to seek perfection. This is the aim of morality and religion. Morality may be reduced to the two principles of justice and love, or even to the single principle: 'Act in accordance with nature' (p. 113). In philosophy Secrétan opposes both empiricism and materialism in favour of a doctrine of duty, which consists in the fulfilment of humanity (p. 195). God is the ideal, the perfect being, and therefore the sum of moral attributes. Faith in such a God is a logical rather than a supernatural act (p. 257). He calls this attitude 'philosophical faith' (p. 294). It is the only valid one. Thus religion must enter this framework, for moral and spiritual life are ultimately one (p. 314). 'The religion of moral consciousness is the only true religion' (p. 360). 'Society cannot continue without a common mind; this is necessarily a religion, and modern society can accept only a religion which is reconcilable with the facts gained from science, an intelligible religion which answers without clash or hiatus to the needs of moral consciousness, a religion which is the expression of conscience itself, a religion of liberty' (p. 380). This is the 'rational religion' (p. 380) prepared by the 'inconsistencies of the Reformation'

---

[1] *Op. cit.*, 3rd ed., 1893, p. 89.

(pp. 393f.) and pointing to the glorious future of a 'new evolution'. Of the many other theologians we might cite, C. Malan[1] deserves brief mention. Although not so prominent as he merited, he was a specialist in the field of moral consciousness and had much influence on Frommel and Fulliquet.[2] His great point is the accord between the three revelations in conscience, nature and Scripture.[3] Fulliquet, too, bases everything on moral obligation. F. Klein, in a work dedicated to his master, recalls that the *Précis de dogmatique* begins by describing the person and work of Jesus, then has a chapter on Christian experience, moves on to the kingdom of God and finally deals with the relation between science and faith. He adds, 'If we have not followed this plan literally, it is first because it does not give sufficient prominence to moral obligation, the key-stone of the whole edifice.'[4] This is true. To understand Fulliquet we should begin, not with his view of Christ, but with his work on moral consciousness, which is the basis and criterion of all his theology. Anthropology again takes precedence of Christology. It is unnecessary to adduce further quotations; this is the starting-point of all his works. In a manuscript on *La Doctrine de Dieu*, quoted by Klein, we read: 'Modern thought depends directly on Kant, who gives us, not a conception of God, nor a chain of affirmations and reasonings to establish the reality of God, but an exact appreciation of moral phenomena whereby our reason may rise to God by analysis and induction.'[5]

Similarly, W. Monod writes: 'Superior piety is based precisely on a pre-existent morality. Religion prolongs, intensifies and crowns morality.'[6] 'As a recent moralist has written, there is every advantage in pursuing the path from morality to religion. More exactly, as we have tried to see, there is no access to true religion apart from morality, or moral faith. It seems to us to be quite impossible to go directly to God except by way of at least a rudiment of moral experience.'[7]

---

[1] César Malan. The father was one of the founders of the movement of awakening who defended orthodoxy against J. J. C. Chenevière, the very liberal Professor of Theology at Geneva (1831). Our present concern is with the son, who bore the same name and who had a great influence on Frommel.

[2] Georges Fulliquet (1863–1924). After a pastorate he succeeded Frommel as Professor of Theology at the University of Geneva, in 1906. He wrote several works of apologetics, moral theology, doctrinal history and dogmatics.

[3] *La conscience morale*, Geneva, 1886, p. 167.

[4] *La Pensée religieuse de G. Fulliquet*, 1942, p. 18.

[5] *Op. cit.*, p. 134.   [6] *Vers Dieu ou l'ascension de l'homme*, 1922, p. 35.

[7] J. Bois, *Le Problème de la morale chrétienne*, 1948, p. 117.

3. *Historical Method*

Once Protestantism came to be linked with human values, such as the inner sense of good and evil, there was nothing to prevent it finding other supports for its knowledge of revelation either in nature or humanity. The principle, once admitted, necessarily came to be applied to other realities according to the new trends of culture, e.g., to history, science and psychology. We thus have new syntheses which, like those already mentioned, sometimes maintained a judicious balance, but still combined nature and supernature and even absorbed the latter in the former. The most characteristic of these movements is historicism, which has its source at the end of the age of the Enlightenment and with which are associated some of the greatest names in philosophy and theology. Together with the rise of a sense of history and the great development of philosophies of history which sought to assimilate truth to the movement of the spirit manifested in historical evolution, this new synthesis dragged theology along with it with a force almost as irresistible as that of feeling or practical reason.

Behind the larger attempts we can see, if not pantheism, which the various writers all tried to avoid, at least a conformity of the deeper nature of man with God which allowed the almost complete identification of the spirit of humanity with deity. The proponent of this differentiated identity was undoubtedly Hegel, for whom there is, not an immediate, but a mediated relation between man and God: 'I and God are different from one another; if both were One, there would then be immediate relation, free from any mediation. . . . Because they are different . . . mediation takes place more strictly in a Third.'[1] 'Spirit bears witness to Spirit; this witness is the peculiar inner nature of Spirit. In this the weighty idea is involved that religion is not brought into man from outside, but lies hidden in himself, in his reason, in freedom. If we abstract from this relation, and consider what this knowledge is, how this religious feeling, this revelation in the Spirit is constituted, it is seen to be immediacy indeed, like all knowledge, but immediacy which likewise contains mediation in itself. For if I form an idea of God, this directly involves mediation, although the reference to God is quite direct and immediate. I exist as knowledge, and then there is an object, namely, God, and therefore a relation, and knowledge

[1] *The Philosophy of Religion*, ET, Speirs, Vol. I, pp. 166f.

representing this relation is mediation' (p. 165). In other words, the spirit, which is from God, is found in reality, and especially in the evolution of humanity which it impels, so that man here participates directly by elevating himself to the infinitude of the idea which is God, both in himself and in all things. Religion is simply this elevation: 'The elevation and the movement of the objective content, however, actually come to form one process, namely, in Thought. I, in so far as I think, am myself this passing over, or transition, this spiritual movement' (p. 172).

Another theoretician of historicism, namely, R. Eucken, unambiguously defines this assimilation of the divine and the human which in a more or less emphatic form constitutes the most typical feature of modernism, as of Neo-Protestantism. Christianity for him represents a union of essence. 'It brings the divine in all its magnificence into human nature. It thus raises the latter to divinity. Hence the divine life becomes that of man. Man shares in the perfection, eternity and infinity of the divine life. He is thus lifted above the limitations and errors of the world, above suffering, misery and guilt.'[1]

The spontaneous association of God and man thus takes the third form of an assimilation of revelation to the movements of history. We must now study this new aspect of modern Protestantism, for, if it is less prominent than the other two, it has played a considerable role and produced results which are still present in religious consciousness today.

The trend begins with Lessing, and especially with his *Education of the Human Race*, 1795. Here revelation is compared to education and identified with the education of the race throughout history. 'What education is to the individual man, revelation is to the whole human race' (§1). The only difference is that 'education is revelation coming to the individual man; and revelation is education which has come, and is still coming, to the human race' (§2). This 'education gives man nothing which he could not also get from within himself; it gives him that . . . only quicker and more easily. In the same way too, revelation gives nothing to the human race which human reason could not arrive at on its own; only it has given, and still gives to it, the most important of these things sooner' (§4). There follows an

[1] *Problèmes capitaux de la philosophie de la religion au temps présent*, 1910, pp. 109f. This point of view helps us to understand the rejection of Chalcedon and the general depreciation of the supernatural.

account of this education through the three great stages of humanity: Judaism, primitive Christianity and the age of maturity: 'It will assuredly come! the time of a new eternal gospel, which is promised us in the primers of the New Covenant itself' (§86). 'Perhaps even some enthusiasts of the thirteenth and fourteenth century had caught a glimmer of this new eternal gospel' (§87), but 'they were premature. They believed that they could make their contemporaries, who had scarcely outgrown their childhood, without enlightenment, without preparation, at one stroke men worthy of their third age' (§89). Here, then, revelation consists in the actual movement of history, which leads from obscure beginnings to the reign of reason, i.e., to light. This scheme underlies all the great philosophies of history, e.g., of Condorcet, Hegel, Comte and even Marx.

Herder adds a significant emphasis by making humanity the centre of attention on the historical field. But it is Hegel who develops most grandly the idea of the development of humanity. In the present context we can only refer to some of his main points.

God is reason, spirit, idea, the general or the universal self-realized in triumph over subjectivity. He is reason in itself, reason in all things, and thought disengaging itself from matter to reconcile itself with itself by a long process. One can consider thought in itself, in its abstraction—this is logic. But one can also grasp it in its externality, in nature, by the philosophy of nature; it will then disengage itself from its opposite through the slow evolution of history, and return to self-consciousness as spirit—this is the philosophy of history; and the triumph of spirit, which has returned to itself after this long detour in nature and history, is the subject of the philosophy of spirit. Thus Hegel's system describes the activity of the spirit going out from itself to find itself in its opposite and then disengaging itself in self-reconciliation. The movement by which the spirit triumphs after its descent and progressively disengages itself is the signification of history, which is simply the return of spirit to itself, its progress from the primitive ages of obscurity to its triumph in the modern epoch. The meaning of history is to allow the progressive liberation of thought. Hence truth is not outside history. It is within it, in an ineluctable movement of disengagement and manifestation through the three ages of the Father, the Son and the Holy Spirit. 'We may distinguish these periods as Kingdoms of the Father, the Son, and the Spirit. The Kingdom of the Father is the consolidated, undistinguished mass, presenting a self-repeating cycle. . . . The Kingdom of the Son is the manifestation of God merely in a relation to secular existence—shining upon it as upon an alien object. The Kingdom of the Spirit is the harmonizing of the antithesis.'[1] Thus truth is in history, not only in the incarnation of the Son in Jesus Christ, but in the movement of history itself. From the dawn of Chinese civilization to our own day it is identical with the spirit in its gradual self-disengagement from its opposite. And this truth is God, universal reason, or human thought, enclosed in the opposition but slowly coming to itself and finding itself in the plenitude which is the idea re-established in full self-possession. History is thus the chief place where one can see truth at work, for 'reason is the sovereign of the world . . . that by which and in which all reality has its being and subsistence . . . the energizing power realizing its aim' (p. 9). Revelation in the classical sense is not suppressed; it is completed by what history contributes in its invincible progress to light.[2]

Universal history replaces biblical history, which is integrated into it as a single stage, in the revelation of the work of the spirit. Redemption takes place, not at one point, but over the whole course. Here is a movement which God effects, not by a direction intervention which, even though it is prepared in advance and has resultant consequences, is concentrated on the time between Christmas and Easter, but in a vaster movement which begins with the dawn of history and goes right up to the age of the philosopher. Truth is identified with the dialectical progression of both divine and human thought in history, which is 'the rational necessary course of the World-Spirit' (p. 10). Thus we have historicization and humanization. Both are partial, since reason first dwells in God and returns to him. But both are real, since history is the chief place where it manifests itself and where we may thus discern it. This perspective has had a profound influence on Protestant theology, which also concentrates on history and adopts this evolutionary view that truth makes itself rather than gives itself, and in its evolution embraces all the values of human culture, as noted by Bréhier: 'The high point of the spirit in Hegelian doctrine is human culture; even religion is regarded as an aspect of culture . . . if we take away the

[1] *The Philosophy of History*, ET, Sibree, 1956, p. 345.
[2] Hegel's thinking is panentheistic rather than pantheistic. History is the main source of revelation, since in it we trace the emergence of the spirit or reason which is both God and ourselves, and therefore the reconciliation of self-estranged thought, and therein of God and man.

mysticism, Hegel gives us little more than Comte's cult of humanity.'[1] Religion is an element in the self-recovery of the ideal; it is an aspect of thought.

To delineate the theological form taken by this movement in Neo-Protestantism, we may refer to its main proponent, Ernst Troeltsch, who has given us a full and typical analysis in *Das Historismus und seine Probleme*.[2] But before studying this work, with which we might also consider the essay *Historical and Dogmatic Method in Theology*,[3] we may first mention a work of R. Eucken entitled *Religion et Histoire* (*Problèmes capitaux de la philosophie de la religion au temps présent*), which clearly outlines the whole problem.

Eucken first notes that the most singular feature of the nineteenth century is the progress in seeing things from the historical standpoint. If the eighteenth century was the philosophical century, the nineteenth is the historical. We have been brought into closer touch with reality 'by considering the actual state of existence as the result of a long movement and by learning to view the present as a link in a long chain' (p. 49). This new outlook is not merely scientific. Indeed, it first appeared in the sphere of the spiritual life and only then spread to science. It has necessarily affected religion. Here, however, a difficulty arises, since the ancient view regarded religion as descending from a high point where it originated in a superior, miraculous act, in the personal revelation of God imposed on human existence from above. This led to veneration of the past and involved religion primarily in the task of conservation. The historical method necessarily challenges this whole approach. It is prepared to scrutinize the point of origin and the surrounding circumstances, and finally, for all its dominance, to integrate it into a vaster movement and totality. The result is a progressive dispersal of the abrupt antithesis between the human and the divine. The human, too, is invited to co-operate in the great work, and, since it recognizes in this work an eternal truth, it is inwardly ennobled; while the divine approaches the soul more intimately, and therefore life gains in inner unity and religion acquires a broader foundation (pp. 50–52).

In other words, the first result of the historical method as regards religion is to make its starting-point—the personal revelation of God—less extraordinary and unique and more relative. By bringing this event into line with analogous phenomena, it reduces it from

---

[1] *Histoire de la Philosophie*, 1938–41, II, 2, pp. 783f.
[2] *Gesammelte Schriften*, III, 1922.   [3] *Gesammelte Schriften*, II, 1913.

C*

a kind of miracle to something more common. It is still a culminating point, but it is also the result of an unbroken evolution. The antithesis between the divine and the human is replaced by a progressive ascent of the human to the divine. This is to the benefit of religion, which now embraces all human values and can raise them to the supreme height. The chief effect of this method, which is philosophical rather than scientific, is thus to abase the divine by making it more human and to elevate the human by making it more divine. 'The rigour of an absolute conception must yield to the attenuations of a relative' (p. 52). This statement is fully in the spirit of the age, which centres on man and which is eager to use even religion in the cause of humanity perpetually progressing towards the truth. It justifies the history of religions leading up to their supreme expression in Christianity, the philosophy of the religious phenomenon considered as a simple affirmation of life, and apologetics as the attempt to show that this vital expression is the loftiest of human values. All religions, as ramifications of a general tendency, have value, even though they are not equal (p. 52). This discovery rests on certain other intuitions. Thus history becomes the locus of truth, yet not merely in the brief biblical period, which is traditionally regarded as witness to revelation, but over the wider sweep of all ages and all peoples, so that one can follow truth in its development not only from the first beginnings to its full manifestation in Christ, but also in the spirit which goes beyond the biblical revelation and works itself out in modernism. For the evolution cannot stop with Jesus Christ. It goes on in the history of the Church, which, as Lemaître said, cannot be subordinated to the canonical documents but must be considered as a prolongation of revelation, as Roman Catholic theology also maintains. It goes on, too, in universal history, and especially in the history of philosophy which shows us the spirit moving to its fulfilment. Again, this truth which is suprahistorical in origin is now identified with the essence of history. It is the underlying divine meaning of history, obscured by many false and unworthy phenomena which have to be set aside in order that we may discern it. Hence historical criticism has to engage in a task of discriminating the secondary from the essential. Man is under many influences, especially subjective, which lead him to distort facts. Historical criticism seeks to recover the truth hidden behind subjective phenomena which are of no value. This task is particularly em anding in relation to the underlying facts of religion. 'In a sphere

where passionate desire and hope stir up the most violent feelings
in the soul, where the wishes of the heart take poetic form in plastic
images, and where the force of the total impression prevents the
sober assessment of detail, one must pay attention to the many contributions and corrections to be made by historical criticism (p. 53).'[1]

Like Frommel after him, Eucken asks whether there is not a clash
of interests between science and religion. Science seeks uniformity
whereas religion demands contrast (p. 54). Science cannot tolerate
miracle in any sense (p. 55). It is thus impossible to separate sacred
and secular history. They must be treated on the same level and as
a totality (p. 56). Taking them in this way, historical criticism must
say 'how badly attested are some objects on which we build with
confidence, how many accounts and conceptions differ from and
even contradict one another, not merely in secondary matters, but
in essentials' (p. 56).[2]

Like Frommel again, Eucken sees some of the limits of historicism.
He cannot allow the eternal to be completely subjected to and
absorbed in the temporal, so that religion becomes a mere appearance or shadow (pp. 58f.). While evolutionism may be fully accepted
in the realm of nature, it cannot encompass all the heights of the
spiritual life (p. 64). The movement of history does not affect all
reality. A fixed factor is found in the 'inner unity' which unites men.
Behind the flux of appearance is a stable reality: 'What gives history
its value is simply that something eternal is revealed in it, that it is a
struggle for the eternal. . . . In such a view, all true historical work
is an attempt to rise above mere history . . . and to penetrate to the
sphere . . . where there can be an intimate living fellowship. We
shall be careful not to follow the ancient method by linking the
spiritual movement to a sole point in history and thus immobilizing
it; but we shall also avoid the error of the moderns in making successive variations the main thing . . . ; we shall view the totality as the
deployment of an eternal order, and throughout its course it is at the
eternal that we shall grasp' (p. 69).

We perceive that, although Eucken reacts against extreme historicism, he follows the general tendency of the movement which
seeks historical truth, not in the external phenomena, but in the
deeper realities of history. In this way historical truth—intimate

---

[1] Though the champions of biblical criticism often claim objectivity, Eucken shows
that their work will always rest on a view of life which to some degree restricts its value.
[2] Cf. the impressive analysis of this problem in Frommel's 'Franche Explication'.
Etudes morales et religieuses, 1913, pp. 3f., 5, 7, 9, 11, 14, 16.

living fellowship—links up with psychological truth. Religion thus rests on the twin foundations of history and psychology, which are one in essence. 'Only in this way', Eucken writes, 'can religion be given an internal foundation, for such experiences are well adapted to certify the presence of a superior order' (p. 17). Contrary to what one might suppose, the internal foundation links up with the external, since the ultimate point of both is man in encounter with the divine.

These two foundations are characteristically linked in a writer like A. Sabatier.[1] In his *Esquisse d'une philosophie de la religion, d'après la psychologie et l'histoire* (1901), Sabatier defines religion as the expression both of human consciousness and of the development of humanity. His method is very typical, for he first begins with the religious phenomenon in general, then turns to the essence of Christianity and finally considers Christian dogma. He tells us that he is trying 'to develop a series of related and progressive views in which I hope there will be seen, not a system, but the firm applications and the first results of the method of strict psychological and historical observation' (p. i). In this attempt he seeks to unite 'the twofold cult of scientific method and the moral ideal' which are the great concerns of the century (p. ii), and he hopes to help the young people who are walking 'between the two high walls of modern science . . . and the dogmas and habits of the religious institution' (p. v). For we do not have to choose between pious ignorance and brutal knowledge. Conciliation is possible. We have only to show that religion is both the product of historical evolution—'on our planet the moral life is born slowly and painfully from the womb of organic life' (p. vii)—and 'the true and mysterious co-existence of a particular cause which is myself with a universal cause which is God' (p. viii). Thus history and experience conjoin in a single reality, namely, individual and collective, internal and progressive humanity. In the seventeenth century Protestant orthodoxy maintained that revelation was complete and guaranteed in an authentic form—a view shared by Leo XIII (p. xiv). In reality, humanity has always been religious and therefore it 'has never been without reve-

---

[1] Auguste Sabatier (1839–1901). After serving as pastor, he became Professor of Reformed Dogmatics at Strasbourg in 1867. Expelled in 1873, he helped to establish a Faculty of Reformed Theology at Paris and was Professor from its inception in 1877. His main works are *L'apôtre Paul* (1870), *Essai d'une théorie de la connaissance religieuse* (1893), *Esquisse d'une philosophie de la religion* (1901) and *Les religions d'autorité et la religion de l'esprit* (1903).

lation, i.e., without more or less obscure and more or less well interpreted testimonies to the presence and action of God within it' (p. 35). It is internal, evident and progresive (p. 52), so that psychology and history are automatically identified, for humanity, i.e., a common moral life, is realized in each individual. Moral goods are universal. If they do not exist outside the consciousness of the individual, no consciousness acquires them for itself alone and not in principle for all (p. 55). Whether the religious phenomenon is studied in the evolution of humanity or the individual consciousness, it is the same. Psychology certainly precedes history. But the study of the progress of the race confirms what is discovered within. Now religion has its origin in a contradiction found in man's inner life (p. 19) between 'the action of external things on the self by sensation (passivity)' and 'the reaction of the self on things by the will (activity)' (p. 15). How is this to be resolved? By religion, which is 'the inward and happy crisis whereby human life is transformed and a new prospect is opened on the ideal life' (p. 23). Thus 'it reconciles the two antithetical elements which constitute religious feeling: the passive element and the active, the sense of dependence and the movement of freedom' (p. 25). In this sense religion is 'inherent in man . . . he could not tear it from his heart without being condemned to self-alienation and without destroying that which strictly constitutes humanity in him' (p. 27).

It makes no odds whether this humanity is found in the individual or history, since these are both spheres in the development of consciousness. The opening psychological chapters are thus followed by 'an account of the religious progress of the race' which confirms the first intuitions. The advance of religion leads to a first stage which proves to be the soul and work of Christ, in which 'the early evolution has found its *raison d'être* and its final goal' (p. 125), and is now pursued 'in my own consciousness' where 'this practical demonstration takes place' (p. 133). The value of Christianity lies in the fact that 'it offers the term and consummation of the religious evolution of humanity' (p. 175). The consciousness of Jesus thus becomes 'the principle of Christianity' and the model of our own, though, seeing the author always defines the latter first, it may be asked whether he does not expound Jesus in the light of his own conception of religion: 'What we call the religious consciousness of man is the sense of relationship in which he stands, and wishes to stand, with the universal principle on which he knows he depends, and with the universe of which he sees himself to be a part. If, then, we would know the content and essential basis of the consciousness of Jesus, we must ask in what relationship he feels himself to be with God and the universe' (pp. 183f.). The filial relationship of Jesus with God thus becomes the essence of an inward, invisible, ideal Christianity which is best formulated in Protestantism: 'In our faith in Christ, what have we found to be the essence of perfect and eternal piety? No other than moral repentance, trust in the love of the Father and the sense of his immediate and active presence in the heart—the indestructible basis of our liberty, of our moral dignity, and of our assurance in face of the enigmas of the universe and the mysteries of death' (p. 254).

He applies the same method to dogma. Religion does not depend on formulae, for 'our ideas are psychical phenomena which are to be explained by prior phenomena of the same kind. In other words, the historical method has brought with it the triumph of the standpoint of evolution' (p. 324). Thus the task of dogmatics is the criticism of dogmas with a view to progress towards increasing light and liberty and according to the norm of religious experience. What is not in religious experience 'can find no place in religious scholarship and should be banished from it' (p. 349). By psychology and history —or 'the sense of history'—the theologian can distinguish between 'substance and accident' in dogmas (p. 403), remembering that 'the essential basis of dogmas and symbols is religious reality itself, the vital process created by the infinite and eternal Spirit as he reveals himself in the spirit of man and the experiences of piety. The twofold task of critical dogmatics is to seize and describe exactly the inward religious fact and to take account of the psychological conditions which precede the constantly renewed forms of religious thought; it thus legitimates the distinction which we have just made and which underlies this theory of symbolism' (p. 404).

Sabatier's reference to 'the sense of history' is most significant. For it is obvious that historicism, based on a philosophy of life or religion, finally dissolves its object. The controlling factor is no longer history but the consciousness of truth seeking justification of its intuition in history. History is called in to verify and confirm the idea to which it is thought to have led. In both philosophers and theologians the historical method is made to serve the philosophical or religious consciousness. It does so by two methods which are only apparently contradictory, i.e., by rejecting a religious intuition on the ground that its historical basis is inauthentic and yet also by claiming that truth does not lie in appearance but in the depths of history, so that one has to pierce the shell to reach the essence which corresponds to the intuition in question. These two procedures have both contributed to the dissolution of history by a movement which sought to exalt it.[1]

We now turn to Troeltsch. In reply to a semi-orthodox criticism, he summed up his position by comparing it with the dogmatic method which he condemns. He himself seeks to apply the pure historical method to the Bible and the Church, and he thinks that this will transform all our insights and bring out forms which have hitherto been obscured by the theological method.[2] But what is implied by the historical method, historical thinking and the sense of history? First, there will be a relativization of truth in this sphere, only judgments of probability being accepted as valid and no absolute value being attached to traditions or documents. Secondly, the key to understanding will be sought in analogy, which links past events with later or present events in terms of a likeness of principle which unites historical phenomena in spite of their diversity. 'The analogy between what takes place before our eyes and what results in us is the key to criticism' (p. 732). This analogy between similar historical processes permits us to ascribe probable authenticity to them and to understand what is unknown in some of them in terms of what is known in others. Thus Judaeo-Christian history must be taken out of its isolation and set in the context of universal history. This necessary levelling leads to a third principle, namely, that of the reciprocal action of the various expressions of historical life on one another, so that modification at any one point has repercussions at others. Each event is thus seen in relation to the whole, which is presented as a great stream. The Bible, for example, is integrated into the political, social and spiritual history of antiquity, and Christianity is evaluated in the framework of the history of religion and culture (p. 733).

By criticism, analogy and correlation, the historical method is impelled by irresistible internal necessity to erect a grand totality

[1] Cf. the historical dissolution brought about by the attempt to write a life of Jesus. Lemaître's handling of the Virgin Birth (*Dogmatique protestante*, p. 299) is a typical example. Indeed, the whole pursuit of the so-called 'historical Jesus' carries with it the loss of the true Jesus of history as he is brought before us in the apostolic and early Christian witness.

[2] 'Über historische und dogmatische Methode in der Theologie', *Gesammelte Schriften*, II, 1913, p. 730.

which embraces all the various manifestations of the human spirit, none of which can be isolated or regarded as absolute (p. 734). Like all methods, the historical does not arise independently of general theory. Its importance, however, lies in its application, the results of which are undeniably startling. It produces a revolution in our whole manner of thought similar to that brought about by natural science in relation to ancient and mediaeval conceptions (p. 735). The widespread talk of revolutions is worth noting. The moral revolution is now succeeded by the historical.

The main point here is not the mere use of a simple technique, but the transformation in thought which this produces. A new conception of things results from the systematic 'historicization' of all human truth. The ancient conception attributed absolute value to some realities and made history submit to them. There now succeeds a more pliable method which gives precedence to history. History itself, by observation and interpretation of facts, will decide what is true and what is false. This attitude has brought about a particularly radical transformation in theology (p. 735). If it has introduced insecurity, it has also brought to light immanent necessities. Theory and system have had to bow to the historical object.[1]

Historical method has produced two main modifications in theology. Specific, individual events become uncertain, and therefore a system of faith cannot be constructed on any one of them. The only certain facts are those which, by integration into the whole, exert an influence today. The link between religious belief and isolated facts is weakened in favour of the great complexes of life. Secondly, the total situations which underlie religious conceptions must be set in larger historical contexts and finally in universal history, not to the suppression of their originality, but for the sake of their interpretation in terms of similar phenomena. Thus the personalities we meet with in the Judaeo-Christian world are seen to be neither more nor less irrational than those in Greece or Persia. The historical method, then, has succeeded in 'relativizing all things, not with the idea of suppressing value judgments and confusing the whole in nihilist scepticism, but because each historical moment or representation can be considered only in relation to others and ultimately in the totality of universal history' (p. 737). This applies equally to Christianity (p. 738). Theology is to be built on the field of universal history. It will thus be a product of the history of

---

[1] Everything depends on our definition of this 'historical object'.

religion, a *religionsgeschichtliche Theologie* (p. 738), of which there are hints prior to the age of Deism and which was practised by Lessing, Kant, Herder, Schleiermacher, de Wette, Hegel, and finally Baur and Lagarde (p. 738). More extensive analyses of these systems may be found in *Das Historismus und seine Probleme*. What matters is the method practised by these men rather than their rationalistic systems or, in the case of Hegel, the dialectic of the absolute. Since those early days there has been much progress, and the author refers to men like Simmel, Rickert and Max Weber, who have replaced the great syntheses by a more sober technique.

While this method pretends to be objective, there can be no doubt that it implies a whole new *Weltanschauung* (cf. p. 745), and especially a conception of religion which is in accord with the current of modernism: 'All human religion has its root in a religious intuition or in a divine revelation which takes shape in individual religious personalities who founded communities, and which later believers revive with lesser originality. The faith in God contained in this intuition is at first concealed in the religion of nature; it bursts this framework in several parallel movements and leads to the religion of Yahweh and the teaching of Jesus, to continue in an evolution of infinite richness . . .' (p. 739). This is the phenomenon which the historical method calls religion. And here we have also the theological method of Troeltsch. It does not rest on the idea that this development might be reduced to chaos, but on 'faith in reason acting on history and progressively revealing itself in it' (p. 746). 'In my view this faith, which is also ethico-religious in origin, is confirmed by the deepening of personal life produced in history' (*loc. cit.*). From this standpoint, Christianity may be regarded as 'the loftiest religious force in history' (p. 747). On this whole point Troeltsch agrees with Hegel, who conceived of history as the development of divine reason (*loc. cit.*).[1]

Conclusion

The starting-point of modern Protestantism is an immediate association between God and man, based on the hypothesis of a

[1] To understand the historical studies of the nineteenth century, we must recognize the underlying philosophical and theological presuppositions. In effect Troeltsch presented a complete dogmatic system irreconcilably opposed to classical orthodoxy. For him Christianity was little more than faith in humanity, a perception of the goal of life through history, and European civilization in its nineteenth-century form. We can appreciate the violent reactions of isolated figures like Overbeck, Nietzsche, Kierkegaard, Bloy and Chestov.

direct relation, and first established in the alliance miraculously achieved, according to the Gospel, in the person of Jesus Christ, true God and true man. In Christology, this may also be presented in terms of the fatherhood of God, which corresponds to the most legitimate aspirations of the creature. In this whole alliance the accent may sometimes fall on the divine side and sometimes on the human, such human values as nature, feeling, moral consciousness, reason, history, culture, or the ecclesiastical institution either succeeding or intermingling with one another. Within this framework any position is justifiable so long as it can be comprehended in the synthesis. It is unfortunate that the whole scheme gradually reduces revelation, and the work of reconciliation in the strict sense, to secondary rank.

The result is a Christianity deeply embedded in the culture of the age and bearing its main features. Man and his transports become the centre rather than God or Jesus Christ. The general trend is to minimize the miracle of reconciliation by the self-abasement of God in the crucifixion of the Son. The seriousness of sin is similarly depreciated, and confidence is placed in man and his powers rather than in God and his mercy.

This Protestant scheme differs in many respects from the Roman Catholic system. Apart from philosophical differences attributable to the difference in culture, and also divergences in theological and ecclesiastical expression, the predominance of the human element sometimes seems to be more pronounced in the Protestant scheme, which is also less disciplined and more inclined to extremes. Nevertheless, the essentials are the same—the principle of a spontaneous relationship between God and man, the incorporation of faith into culture and history, the movement from nature to grace, a mitigated immanentism, an inevitable semi-Pelagianism and a more or less pronounced secularization, whether in a religious context or against a wider background.

While the Thomist synthesis is marked by stability and homogeneity in spite of temporary variations, Neo-Protestantism is characterized more by a climate within which theology oscillates from one side to the other, from the first rational orthodoxy to Strauss and Feuerbach, the pendulum preferably coming to rest in the middle, i.e., in an enlightened piety, at once sentimental, moral and historical, composed of religious zeal and good will.

It has often been claimed that Liberalism is only a method. But, apart from variations, it unquestionably rests on a view of life and leads to dogmatic results far beyond the mere enunciation of a working rule. In effect, Neo-Protestantism as a whole is a particular interpretation of the Christian faith which is sharply divided from its Reformation origins and which links up in essentials with the basic intuition of the Roman Catholic heresy.

A melancholy misunderstanding dominated the period. Accepting with enthusiasm the view of Kant that reality is to be found in man rather than God, i.e., in the practical rather than the metaphysical, it deliberately identified all classical theology with intellectual speculation. The most eminent fathers were discounted as more concerned to elaborate theories than to love and serve Jesus Christ and their neighbours. Athanasius, Augustine, Anselm, the Reformers and the seventeenth-century orthodox were systematically presented as dogmatists who tried to assimilate faith to dogma, who preached rational truths, who enclosed the hope of salvation, the whole Gospel, in formulae, and who loved disputation. Once their witness had been distorted, it was easy to dismiss them and to replace their arid and authoritarian intellectualism by feeling, morality and experience. There was thus joined a relentless battle, now latent and now more acute, between a supposed speculative orthodoxy, narrow and lifeless, and a kindly liberalism attentive to human needs and truly charitable.

Now there can be no denying that orthodoxy has always been tempted to exaggerate the importance of doctrine. But there can also be no denying that its champions, in formulating it to the best of their ability, were responding to a far more urgent need to bear witness to the living person of Jesus Christ their Lord and Saviour, to confess his love and to edify the Church, in faith, obedience and knowledge. The image given of these men under the sign of tolerance and charity contradicts quite clearly the historical reality. Furthermore, in the attempt to approach more closely to real man, has there not been a systematic yielding to the rather demagogic temptation to talk to him in a language which he can understand directly, i.e., without the victorious overpowering of his unbelief by God? To meet him in his sin, as though God had not already done so, the foolishness of the Gospel has been tempered and witness in the true sense has been replaced by presumptuous apologetics.

By thus substituting a rationalism of the left for that of the right, one could hardly hope to make headway. The two extremes display the same error. This is why the well-known conflicts between tendencies different in expression but similar in basis, and easily excused by the image of the pendulum, can never end. The only remedy to this situation which is no less anti-evangelical than sterile is the personal intervention of the Saviour himself imposing his truly emancipating Word. The theology which counts on him more than the watchman on the dawn builds on very different ground, which is neither that of a lofty dogmatism nor of a hesitant naturalism, but the rock of the personal and miraculous revelation of God in Jesus Christ, who lays hold of us by the Holy Spirit in the witness of Scripture to deliver us from the idols which constantly turn us aside from him and subject us to foolish pretensions.

Is there such a theology? This is the question which we must now try to answer in the next chapter.

3

The Evangelical Starting-point

WE HAVE been seeking the basis of the Roman Catholic and the modern Protestant attitudes in face of revelation. We must now turn to the Evangelical or Reformation form of the Christian faith. As before, we shall study the main representatives, though without burying ourselves in the remote past. Like the others, this position cannot be simply identified with an episode in Church history. It illustrates a constant factor more or less faithfully attested throughout this history and thus constituting a possible confession of faith in every age. Starting with its classical formulation by the Reformers, we shall try to grasp its permanent and therefore its living characteristics, comparing it with the positions analysed in the preceding chapters.

1. *The Classical Protestant Position*

The origin and main objectives of this movement may be seen already in the early catechisms and even in the prefaces to them. The most significant text in this regard is probably the first *French Catechism* of Calvin (1537).[1]

Before expounding the 'law of the Saviour' the Reformer here introduces a preamble—almost prolegomena—on three decisive points: revelation, man and salvation. In regard to the first, Calvin says that there is in all men an effective embryo of religion, but that this leads neither to the knowledge nor to the service of the true God, since 'they worship, not the eternal God, but the dreams and imaginings of their own hearts in place of God' (p. 5). In fact, they boldly make a god to suit themselves instead of seeking the knowledge which the true God grants them. They thus fall into a false religion. If we are to know the true God, we have to seek him, therefore, 'in his works'. But here, too, 'our perversity is such that

[1] Cited from the Geneva edition of 1878.

there is nothing which it does not corrupt and pervert in considering the works of God, and it completely subverts all the celestial wisdom which for its part clearly shines out in them' (p. 8). The possibility of a knowledge of God from nature is thus admitted, since the Creator God is plainly reflected in it, but the blindness of men prevents them from profiting by it. They distort and subvert it. 'We must turn, then, to the Word of God where God describes his works in order that we may estimate them, not according to the perversity of our own judgment, but by the rule of eternal truth' (p. 8). In view of the failure of other ways, this is the only possibility. Short though this exposition is, it contains the essence of the Reformation reaction. While the *praeambula fidei* postulate a twofold knowledge of God beginning with spontaneous and natural religious manifestations, moving on to an apprehension of God in creation and only then coming to revelation in the strict sense in Jesus Christ, Calvin plainly rejects the first two ways and confines himself to the third. This attitude belongs to the very inward core of the Reformation.

Secondly, Calvin describes man. Here again there are three main points: the actual state of the creature, free will and sin. The thrust of the argument is plain. In this man who is totally corrupt there is no basis for truth. Man's likeness to God has been effaced (p. 10) so that he is no more than 'flesh of flesh': 'No matter to which part of man we turn, it is not possible to see anything but what is impure, profane and abominable to God' (p. 10). A total sinner, man is not 'constrained by any violent necessity, but sins by most apt and ready consent of the will' (p. 11). Since he 'greatly abhors the righteousness of God, and is fervent in every kind of evil, he is said to have no free power to choose between good and evil, i.e., free will' (p. 11). This is why he is subject to God's wrath and retribution (p. 12). 'This reflection, although it strikes man with terror and brings him to despair, is necessary in order that, stripped of our own righteousness, deprived of confidence in our own virtue, robbed of all expectation of life, we may learn from our poverty, misery and shame to prostrate ourselves before the Lord' (p. 12).

This account raises many questions. Should we start with sin to establish the necessity of salvation? Can we deal with man's condition before we preach Jesus Christ? Is sin to be known apart from the revelation of the love of God in the death and resurrection of Christ? Calvin's schema could be used later by a questionable apologetics which thought it should inspire men with terror in order to force them to seek refuge in Christ. Again, is it true that the divine image in man is completely effaced? While the definition of flesh is Pauline, man being seen in a state of revolt against God and therefore as completely carnal, i.e., fallen in both soul and body, does not Calvin's conception of total corruption rest on a definition of the divine image which is not perhaps the last word in biblical interpretation? Yet, though we may question the order of treatment and the details of understanding, there can be no doubt that the intention of the reformer is sound and that it corresponds to an obvious concern to eliminate from the very outset any optimistic view of human capabilities. Calvin has evidently perceived that underlying the origins of 'papist' dualism is little more than an unjustifiable and completely erroneous assumption concerning man, that this rests on the hypothesis of man's likeness to the Creator (the analogy of being) and on the freedom of the will which attributes to him a certain natural capacity and which underlies the attempt to prove God by reason and the whole Aristotelianism of Thomism, and that the result is an attenuation of sin, nature being regarded as only sick and not in fact dead.

Now, as Calvin sees it, we must realize our true situation if we are to be prevented from trusting in ourselves and to be compelled to trust in God alone. This is the third point in his preface. Here he shows plainly that knowledge of sin can only be a result of grace: 'For he has, as it were, already opened a first door into his kingdom when he has destroyed these two most evil pests, namely, assurance in face of his judgment and false confidence in ourselves. For then we begin to lift to heaven the eyes which previously were fixed on earth, and we who trusted in ourselves sigh for the Lord' (p. 13). There follows a fine description of the restoration effected in us by the 'ineffable benignity' of God.

These three points are of decisive import from the standpoint of the Reformation. In face of the Christianity of his day Calvin thought it necessary to emphasize the basic truths of the sole validity of God's revelation in Jesus Christ, of man's radical inability to know God of himself, and of his hopeless plight apart from the intervention of Christ. This new type of preamble presupposes that the author has recognized the corresponding defects in the theology of his time, the association of natural theology with revealed, a relative but real confidence in man, and man's co-operation in redemption by works, indulgences, etc. These are the three basic and essential charges which Calvin brings against Romanism from the very outset and which inspire his reaction. The rest is simply illustration of this diagnosis of the root of the evil.

Before asking whether Calvin is justified in his position by the teaching of the Bible, we must first recognize the justice of his analysis of Roman Catholic theology and the relevance of his attack. But we must also admit that the three points of Roman Catholicism are the principles underlying modern Protestantism, namely, dualism in revelation almost to the point of the total absorption of the biblical revelation in a natural revelation linked with religious feeling, moral consciousness or history; the exaltation of man as able to come of himself to at least a partial, if not a complete, knowledge of God; and the combining of man's part with God's in the work of redemption. One might almost suppose that Calvin had foreseen the final evolution of Protestantism. The truth is, of course, that he found in medieval Catholicism the heresy *par excellence* which will always reproduce itself in different forms so long as there are men, simply because it corresponds to the most natural inclination of the human heart. For nothing is more alien than to trust in God alone. The essence of sin is to trust in oneself. How are we to break free from this propensity? Nothing is indeed more common than to seek self-elevation to the infinite in one's own strength. Systematic atheism was rare in Calvin's day. It is probably not as natural to man as some make out. Basically, man is a religious being. Hence his most common fault is not to deny God, but to imprison God and Christianity in a natural religion in order to keep control while not losing any of the benefits of established religion. This is at least the constant reaction of a certain class which is alive to the value of a secular culture in which human ambitions merge admirably with the religious consolations which the difficulties of life and the prospect of death make highly desirable. The linking of human and divine riches thus seems to be the most satisfactory solution for the average man who wants to have it both ways. Calvin learned this, not merely from his own age, but from his study of the Bible, which instructed him both in the work of God and also in the secret resources of the human heart with its incessant inclination to revolt, especially in the form of an appropriation of God. At these three points, then, Calvin's primary concern is with sin. Attacking it, he condemns the forms which in its tenacity it has taken, and will take, even in Christianity itself.

The rest of the catechism, like the work of Calvin as a whole, draws constant attention to these three insights, which finally come together in a single insight that constitutes the starting-point of the Reformation, namely, that our only hope is in the Word of God which alone can convict of sin and to which we must listen with all our power if we are not to go astray. The section devoted to pastors is particularly relevant. Everything finally depends on their ministry, since the Church cannot live or act without this Word. Hence those who intermingle human traditions with their teaching must be expelled.

In more familiar style Luther expresses the same insight in his *Greater Catechism*. He was moved to write this work by the terrible ignorance and sloth of ministers. If the Gospel is not correctly preached, the faithful will inevitably fall back upon themselves and seek their support elsewhere. They will leave the faith, or more likely add to it all kinds of human ideas and demands, so that the Church will again fall into the association of the human and the divine from which the Word comes to save it. In this way it will settle into a false security, not listening properly to the Gospel. Rather than pretending to grow up, man should really be prepared to remain a child, a life-long scholar. The best way to resist the devil, the world and the flesh, and all evil thoughts, is to study the Word of God, to speak of it and to meditate upon it. This is the real holy water. We must love reading the catechism in order to chase the devil, who cannot hear or endure the Word of God. For our part we need this Word every day, and it is deplorable that ministers and preachers despise it when it is so full of virtue. This is the basic reason for the sorry state of Christianity.

This supremely active attitude, with its bold impatience, its tension in relation to the truth, its humility and self-renunciation, its attentiveness only to God's Word, is the essential characteristic of Reformation piety. The proud think they know everything and can learn nothing. But the more Christians study the catechism, the more they see their ignorance and the need to learn more. Once the appetite is roused, they will acquire a taste for the study which now fills them with aversion. The subjective starting-point comes to view here. We must lose our natural repugnance for the Word of God, to which we prefer all sorts of doctrines already latent in us and therefore apparently closer to us. Instead, we must acquire the taste for this teaching, so that we receive it with pleasure and even with passion. Only the Holy Spirit can create this appetite. Luther thus shows that everything depends on the attitude which we adopt to revelation. His teaching on the Lord's Day drives home the same lesson. The point of this day is that in loving and fearing God we should not despise preaching or the Word, but treat the Word with respect and delight to hear and study it. Keeping Sunday implies a ceasing from our own works, ambitions and efforts in order that we may hear God and let him work in us. The two movements outlined in the previous chapters might perhaps be summed up in the brief judgment that they have little appetite for, or delight in, the study of the Word of God. Human values have suddenly become so interesting that simple Christian instruction is finally neglected.

Zwingli in his *Short Christian Instruction* adopts the same starting-point as Calvin and Luther. The source of the conflicts of the time is found in ignorance. And since all human teaching is vain unless God inwardly enlightens and draws us, both individually and corporately we must pray fervently that God may cause the light of his Word to shine and that he may draw us by his grace, poor and ignorant that we are. Beza says much the same in the preface to his *Confession of the Christian Faith.* He singles out two errors as the source of all others. One is the error of thinking that good intentions are enough to make an act good. The other is that of persuading the poor that they need not read Scripture nor be instructed in individual doctrines, but that implicit faith is sufficient. As Beza puts it, 'the kingdom of God is not a kingdom of ignorance, but of faith and therefore of knowledge; for none can believe what he does not know'. It is interesting that his confession starts abruptly with the doctrine of the Trinity, i.e., with a witness to revelation, the effective starting-point of faith, of the existence of the Church and of all theology.

Everywhere we meet with the same charge that lack of attention to God's Word in Scripture has meant seduction by other doctrines which have taken control because there is no appetite for the Gospel. The major defect in dualistic systems is not their over-estimation of man—in this respect the negative reaction of the Reformation is only secondary—but their neglect of scriptural instruction and their lack of interest in revelation, which necessarily lead to the establishment of human values regarded as no less essential than the Gospel, and therefore to the doctrines of free will and synergism, and their inevitable consequences. From this angle the starting-point of the

Reformation is positive. An attempt is made once again to centre the interest of theologians and believers solely on the God of revelation and not on an alliance of nature and supernature. All the resultant breaks, e.g., with natural theology, tradition, the teaching office, the preambles of faith, etc., are only signs of this primary attitude, which at root is not a dogmatic proposition but an act of faith.

There is, of course, another aspect. The Church is undeniably influenced by prevailing sociological, cultural and psychological conditions. While we do not diminish in the very slightest the authority of the Lord over the Church, nor seek to explain its movements in terms of a philosophy of history or social phenomena, we may rightly take these conditions into account as signs of the providence of God sovereignly at work in history. Now the reaction of the Reformation was undoubtedly prepared by two converging phenomena of the period, namely, the decadence of mediaeval society and the rise of the new Renaissance humanism. From the standpoint of social structure, economic development and culture as well as theology, the sixteenth century was one of transition. Universally recognized values were slowly decaying and therefore losing their interest. Established conventions and constantly analysed ideas still dominated life, but they had lost their vitality. In the meantime a movement which had been growing over a long period, but which had hitherto been held in check by the solid forces of the social order, gradually gained the mastery with the strength proper to what is new. The conflict between the *status quo* and the new forces was mortal, and was bound to issue in favour of the latter, even though the revolution was not basic, since it consisted merely in the replacement of one set of relative human values by another. It did, however, create a general state of unrest irrespective of the question of truth or error. From the theological standpoint, one of the main contributions of the sixteenth-century humanists was simply to call in question the supports on which faith, the Church and theology thought they could rest. Perhaps without them the Reformers would not have succeeded in shaking the imposing edifice of the mediaeval order and in rousing the sense of the plight of man and the almost desperate longing for grace. While these attitudes may be ascribed to the intervention of God, the uncertainty of the age was certainly of assistance. Poverty of spirit may not depend on external circumstances but it flourishes less easily in opulence than in insecurity. Thus, without advancing any binding rule, we may suggest that ages of crisis have been more favourable to theology than periods of spiritual and moral wealth.

The same phenomenon was repeated three centuries later when the middle-class order, which resulted from the Reformation and reached its climax in the century of the Enlightenment, Idealism and the general veneration of man, was brutally called in question, first by Marxism, then by Existentialism. Attacking established culture and the whole social structure, these two movements also challenged systematically the supports of a theology which, in the words of Schleiermacher, had been careful not to lose contact with the spirit of the age. Hard blows were directed against the spiritual conscious-ness, the moralism and the whole theologico-cultural edifice in which the Church seemed secure. What most scholars thought had been finally established was suddenly threatened by a pitiless criticism. Such pillars as religious feeling, the moral consciousness, history and the whole humanism of the epoch suddenly seemed to an important part of the race—the youngest and most active—to be mere illusions, the dreams of well-fed *bourgeois*. The offensive shook the Church to its foundations and forced it to self-isolation in its piety, which many now regarded as a venerable survival. It is thus that the younger generation, stirred by eloquent attacks and in-flamed by international conflicts, has in turn challenged the values sanctified by its elders but evoking in it only feeble echoes. It is thus that it has questioned the resources of the past, which it finds so feeble that, even if they exist at all, they have no constraining power and certainly cannot form the foundation of life or of faith.

From the Christian angle, Marxism and Existentialism are neither more nor less respectable and significant than sixteenth-century humanism. They have performed the same service for the Church, attacking at root the values customarily associated with grace and thus destroying their security. In face of this attack the Church, if it is not too pharisaical and self-sufficient, must engage in the hard and unwelcome self-examination which will reveal its progressive secularization. It is seldom that the official Church does this except when compelled by circumstances. The best of reasons are usually found for soothing its conscience and closing it to external influences. But if the Word of God chooses these times of shaking to intervene, it can happen that Christians, deprived of all other props and realizing the absolute need of grace, will turn to it alone. Thus in a new age of transition there is resurgent witness to the grace of God which is passionately received as the only help in a turbulent situation.

These initial observations are not enough to point us to the true starting-point of the Reformation. The ultimate basis of the movement must be more profound, or it would lose most of its interest. Our problem is to know why the Reformers thought they should challenge the theological foundations of their time. We may answer that they felt constrained to do this by their discovery of Scripture. But how are we to explain this sudden return to Scripture and the new interpretation of it? Others in their day studied the Bible without coming to the same conclusions. Are we to regard the series of causes which brought about this revelation as a purely fortuitous chain, and the authority of the movement, accepted by reason of the circumstances outlined, merely as the result of the initiative of individuals? Where is the true source of this offensive? How are we to explain its secret power? Is it enough to say with Frommel that man fashions the destiny of the Bible, in different ages bringing it out of the obscurity in which history has buried it, so that, 'if we see the work of God, we see supremely the work of man in the perpetual salvaging and constant resurrection of the Bible'?[1] If this is so, then the Reformation is primarily the result of a human choice and work encouraged by a remote divine inspiration. In strict conjunction with the Renaissance, it has brought certain ancient documents out of partial oblivion and found in them truths which it thinks superior to others. The influence and authority of the Bible are subordinate to the needs and decisions of man. In their adherence to the past the Reformers have simply followed a religious but essentially human impulse.[2]

If Scripture is simply a collection of human experiences, evoked from above but directly accessible like other elements of culture which may be buried for a time and then suddenly brought to the surface, then it is no more or less interesting than any conception of the world which may be forgotten yesterday and today exhumed from the ashes of an indifferent past. At most it can only take the first place in our scale of values, as Neo-Protestantism constantly proclaimed. But it has no decisive authority over us, and the

[1] *L'Expérience chrétienne*, I, p. 178.
[2] Cf. the pertinent criticism of this view by Kierkegaard in his *Training in Christianity*, ET, 1941, pp. 39, 134f.

Reformers were simply doing for it what others in their day did for Greek and Roman antiquity. Such an interpretation reduces the sixteenth-century movement to a religious episode which justifies all the later relativisms in which the Bible is mostly used as an effective support, if possible, for intuitions born of current needs. There is always the possibility, however, that Scripture is something quite different, so that the whole outlook changes. The truth may be that it is the witness to God's personal work, and itself the product of a divine intervention, so that none can bring it to life save God alone, and the Reformation, in accepting it, was not following its own decision but acting under constraint.

The real question which faces us is whether we have here choice or obedience. Are the Reformers responding to inner impulse or constraint from above? Is the Reformation man's work or God's? There is no proof that the second view is the correct one. Indeed, everything inclines us to reject it either by flat denial or by combining it with a simple awakening of certain enlightened men of the period. How can we recognize and admit that a historical and religious movement is the direct effect of divine intervention? The fact that the Reformers regarded themselves as God's spokesmen is no proof. Perhaps, like many others, they were the victims of an illusion. Have not all prophets claimed to be pure servants of the deity? The decisive question is whether God really spoke through these men or whether they themselves made him speak thus. The first view, if admitted too easily, leads us into the most dangerous fanaticism in which we make faith an evidence, an immediate certainty, a dogma, a human assurance. In fact, this possibility will always be a mystery to us, and to the degree that it does not enter into our normal categories, we are inclined to dismiss it as highly improbable.[1]

Thus one of the first features of the Reformation attitude is a radical disengagement from all forms of pantheism, even the most attenuated. God is enclosed neither in the Church, the religious consciousness, nor morality. He is free in relation to nature, religion and even the Bible. If he exists, he can only affirm himself against us, for what do we know of him, and what do we really want of him? Even if a demonstration of his existence and work were possible, it would be improper and even injurious, for though we

[1] Cf. Kierkegaard's important concepts of the divine incognito and of the scandal of the Gospel and faith.

might decide that he exists and is interested in us, what is the good of this discovery if it is only the fruit of our own intuition and reasoning? Who can convince us of the relevance of our hypotheses? Even if we are completely certain of his existence, who is to guarantee that God is as we have found, and that he acts according to our conclusions? Once he is exposed to even the slightest risk of confusion with an invention of our own mind, he ceases to be the one in whom we hope and whom we really need. Two conditions are decisive: if he exists, he must be himself, autonomous and sovereign; and our knowledge of him must be, not a dream, hypothesis or invention, but a true encounter. The real problem is not to know whether man has a natural capacity to know God, but to know whether God is indeed the living God, whether he has intervened, whether there are signs of his presence and activity. For, if God exists and wills to come to us, his will necessarily produces such encounters. Thus the crux of the matter is with him rather than us. For only his initiative can truly assure us of his existence and will. In other words, the only proof of God's existence is the event in which he shows himself to be living and acting. God alone, as he acts, can demonstrate his existence and action.

This applies in respect of the Bible and all the ways used by God to make himself present. If the Bible is only a document of religious history, it falls in human categories, comes under our evaluations, and loses its decisive significance. On the other hand, if even in its historicity it is the imperious and constraining echo of the sovereign intervention of God, we can be persuaded of this only by God himself. Thus none can presume to choose or adopt it, for such presumption would prove only that the Bible, subjected to our control, is not the effective sign of a divine action, but the expression of our own aspirations. Either its authority depends on our acceptance, and it tells us nothing but what we know or will know (as Kant stated with obvious satisfaction), or it is witness to the full 'newness' of God, so that he rules over it and can either give or withdraw it. We cannot make God be and do what we want him to be and do.

The Reformation falls under these conditions. It is essential only if it derives from a personal intervention of God in the form of the victory of his Word over our imaginings, of the Bible over the Church. But who can convince us that this is really so? No one, not even the Reformers! The only way to clear conviction on this point,

which will always be an act of faith, and therefore to discernment of
the true starting-point of the movement, is that God, if he exists
and wills to make himself known, should confirm this for us. The
basically paradoxical character of this position is that it is totally
non-demonstrable, and therefore unacceptable, to supporters as well
as adversaries, so that it has to depend absolutely on the miracle of
divine intervention.

We are thus led to three decisive propositions.

(i) God, his Word, the Bible, the Holy Spirit and all associated
realities, if they exist, can be proved only by their own activity
independently of all our own prior hypotheses concerning them. In
face of them we have no power of our own; we are bereft of supports and arguments. Even if we had them, it would be necessary
to abandon them and to be open only to the influence of the realities
themselves. We cannot force these to be or to act. To establish their
authenticity and to assure our own salvation, we can only seek,
listen, hope and receive.

(ii) For the same reasons, if these realities enter into account they
will necessarily be against us. What do we really know of them?
How can we adopt them? They provoke our astonishment and
hostility, just because we are blind and powerless before them. Far
from choosing them, we can only choose to reject them. For they
do not belong to our world. If we were to accept them from the
outset, it could only be because we found in them something familiar
or recognized the God of our own conceiving. But who can prove
that God is thus? Who authorizes us to make prior judgment concerning him? The very presumption throws doubt on the whole
procedure. We are simply looking for a God who will suit us.

(iii) The Reformers themselves did not expatiate on such possibilities. Their action did not derive from speculative reflections on
what might exist or not exist, nor from negations or criticisms of
various theological or religious interpretations of this possible or
probable reality. They were confronted, not by a choice, but by a
completed, sovereign and compelling event which mastered them.
This was their objective starting-point, which found its subjective
counterpart in a wholly positive act of faith. Having been led to see
the full sufficiency of this event, they could only believe in it to the
exclusion of all other claims, whose validity paled before this
decisive act. Apprehended by this decree, they could not think, will
or act except in the light of it. God has decided, fulfilled and

achieved everything in Jesus Christ. This is the fact. What more do we need? Why do we need to ask further what he might do or not do, or what we should add or retract? The achievement is given. Where else should we begin? Listening showed them that God is not as we imagine, and that all wisdom and truth are found in his work, i.e., in Jesus Christ alone. All that we have said thus far on the Reformation starting-point—the disengagement and demonstration by God alone—would be useless speculation were it not a simple commentary on this event. Since grace is effectively granted, since God has truly acted, since everything is accomplished in the story of his love, only unbelief and fantasy can build on anything other than this event which truly comprises all things and which rules with sovereign power all thoughts and actions claiming to be Christian.

The starting-point of the Reformation is that God has demonstrated himself in Christ. That he should take the initiative in this intervention and conflict is indispensable to the authenticity of faith, knowledge and salvation. He has done so. Hence what we say and do can depend on no other source. The very discovery of this starting-point is itself a miracle produced by him.[1]

To describe this new starting-point, Barth uses a fine expression which is not too dogmatic in the current sense but which meets all the demands of Reformation faith and theology. He refers to the 'good pleasure' of God, i.e., to the absolutely unforeseeable and gratuitous movement in which his love and freedom, his mercy and faithfulness, his whole being, come into action. Our only anchor is this act in which God gives himself according to the requirements of his own being, and triumphs over all the obstacles in his path, to restore a situation which he alone can meet and of which we are unable either to recognize the gravity or to avoid the peril. This divine initiative forces us to seek the solution in itself alone. To the good pleasure of God we thus reply with gratitude, acceptance and praise.

The main formulations of this theology are thus commentaries on this central intuition expressed in the famous *Soli Deo gloria* and bearing witness, in face of every dualism, to the full sufficiency of the divine love. We shall now consider the chief points, not treating

---

[1] We recall that in substituting the inner evidence of experience, feeling, etc. for the older proofs, modern theology can give no better demonstration of God. The only possible demonstration is that of God himself in his work.

D

them merely as historical truths, but rather as the constant elements in a position which is always possible, and which, in contrast to Roman Catholic and Neo-Protestant dualism, we may describe as Protestant, Evangelical, or in the wider sense Reformed.

(i) The source of this faith is necessarily found in divine revelation alone, independent of any prior judgment or any factual situation represented by the Church or its traditions. It clings to this unique demonstration from above, for the only thing which counts for it, if God exists, is that he manifests himself, coming to us to open us to him. The Reformed position is not ashamed to be involved in a *petitio principii*. For this circle, which is closed from our point of view, is in fact the only means to breach the vicious circle in which we are enclosed by sin.

This starting-point corresponds neither to religious or moral intuition, to the Jesus of history of modern theology, nor to the speculative or mythical conception of a semi-celestial, semi-terrestrial revelation. On the other hand, it is fully in line with the confessions of the early Christians, for whom faith could be summed up in the primitive formula: 'Jesus is Lord.' Now what does this mean but that they see in Jesus the Messiah, the Christ, the Lord? This confession is for them a simple commentary on the name of Jesus Christ, Son of Man and Son of God, very man and very God. Proclaiming his sovereignty, they attest his deity and yet also his humanity. The Jesus of history in whom they believed and whom they proclaimed was the crucified and risen Lord. His historicity was not simply his more or less inspired humanity; it was his lordship. It was as Lord that he was born, lived, died, rose again and ascended. A description of the Jesus of history is necessarily a description of the incarnate Word, of the real presence and therefore the revelation of the living God in this man (Matt. 16.16). God became a figure of history, and in this figure of history they perceived the concrete presence of God.[1]

If this is so, then to begin with revelation is to begin with the historical person of Jesus Christ, the man and Lord. But this starting-point forces us to open our eyes to the mystery of God himself present in history and yet also in person. This mystery arises the moment we confess faith in Jesus the Son of God. It finds

---

[1] The Jesus of history is not found by isolating his supposedly less mysterious humanity. In truth, the humanity of Jesus is no less mysterious than his deity, and the two go together. 'Jesus is Lord' aptly describes this historical figure.

expression in the doctrine of the Trinity. This doctrine does not try to explain or to dissipate the mystery. It simply bears witness. It has its source in the primary obligation to confess that God is this man without ceasing to be himself, and that we can know him only by his own intervention in us by the Holy Spirit. Trinitarian faith is a commentary on the original act of faith expressed by Peter at Caesarea Philippi: 'Thou art . . . the Son.' What art thou then in relation to the Father? And what enables me to know that thou and the Father are one?

Thus to begin with revelation is to begin with the Jesus of history in the sense of the first Christian confession, and this is to begin with the doctrine of the Trinity which explicates this act of initial faith. So long as we really accept faith's description of the true Jesus, there is no contradiction in these three beginnings.[1]

(ii) The doctrine of grace, with the bondage of the will as corollary, reflects adherence to God's own self-demonstration by the Word. It does not merely say that if God exists he can establish this on his own initiative. It says that he has given this demonstration by presenting himself to us in the person of Jesus. The fact replaces the hypothesis. God has done it. Nor is the act in which he has done it to be interpreted merely as a communication of truths hitherto unknown but now placed within our grasp. Grace is more than a message. It is a victory over all obstacles, the achievement of restoration, the accomplishment of revelation. In it, everything is effected: sin is conquered, the new man created, life re-established, God and man reconciled. Grace is the consummation in man of everything which needed to be done. Thus the starting-point, content and perfection of all Christian truths are to be found in this wholly gratuitous act to which we must look to the exclusion of every other reality. Captive to this event, theology states with complete satisfaction that it brings all that man really needs. It thus keeps to this incomparable plenitude with full thanksgiving. Any attempt to add to it would not merely weaken but destroy it, since its whole value rests in the totality of its accomplishment.

The doctrine of election, or predestination, simply confirms and protects the sovereignty of grace. Salvation depends on God and not on us. Certainly, the decision or election of God is strictly

[1] Historically the doctrine of the Trinity rests on the ancient confession: 'Jesus is Lord.' This is why it stands implicitly at the beginning of Reformation theology, though seldom treated first in the confessions, etc.

identical with the person of Jesus Christ, as stated in the Scots Confession. Perhaps the main fault of the Calvinist doctrine, as we see from most of the other confessions, is to envisage a predestination more or less independent of its realization in Christ. Yet the intention of the Reformers in elaborating this doctrine, to which we shall return in connection with Christology, was to put the origin of our salvation, to the exclusion of any possible deviation, in the sole mercy of God. Sin at this point is failure to be quite content with this work of God accomplished in Jesus.

(iii) The discovery of the perfection of this divine gift naturally imposes a third dogmatic demand which in its own way expresses the same astonished gratitude and claims the whole faith and thinking of the Reformers, namely, that Christology, as used to describe the person and work of Jesus, should dominate and penetrate all aspects of theology. The name of Jesus itself carries with it all the fulness of God and man. The Reformers did not recognize this explicitly. They violated the principle at many points. Nevertheless, we cannot seriously deny that their intention was to relate everything to Jesus Christ without any kind of preamble or complement. Their Christian thinking was reflection on Christ. It was witness to the only Saviour who has done everything for us.[1]

But what is meant by this Protestant Christocentricity? It is not merely a question of method. It expresses an act of faith. Here is true faith as distinct from other forms. At this point we come to the heart of the controversy with Roman Catholicism and Neo-Protestantism. The key-point of the whole ecumenical problem is also to be found here. If all is grace, and our salvation is fully effected by God, then it is wholly and completely in Jesus Christ. Whether we treat of God or man, judgment or pardon, election, justification or sanctification, the new man or eternal life, we have to avoid two constant temptations to faith and theology. On the one hand, the truth of these declarations is not to be traced back to a distant divinity seated beyond history in an inaccessible infinite. God is no longer the hidden and terrifying figure of our imagination. He is among us. On the other hand, we are not to identify him with ourselves, with our moral consciousness, or spiritual life, or religious experiences. He is in Jesus. This is his location. At this concrete point God and man are together. Hence anything authentic concerning them must be in the form of a commentary on the name of

[1] Cf. on this point Barth, CD I, 2, pp. 297, 350.

Jesus. His birth, life, death, resurrection and ascension contain the sum of our knowledge and worship.

Christology is both the truth of God and our truth, since the Son recapitulates in himself all that concerns God and affects us. Our theology, worship and service automatically disqualify themselves if they are guilty of even the slightest deviation from this one point of reference in favour of another object which is thought to be more accessible, e.g., the Church, the sacraments, religious feeling, pure or practical reason.[1]

(iv) Perhaps it has not been sufficiently noted that the three preceding criteria of an Evangelical theology can have their full significance only if we emphasize the doctrine of the Holy Spirit. There are three reasons why this point is so important. If we must look to God, and if he has already given us all things in Jesus Christ, how are we to receive these riches placed at our disposal? Grace might simply deposit the gifts in Christ and leave it for us to take them to our profit. In this case salvation would be God's work but its appropriation ours. And such a view assumes that we have the power to recognize the truth wherever it may be, and then to assimilate it. Thus a balanced system is again achieved in which man's work is of value even though the work of Jesus is not disparaged.

Now it will be seen that, if we set aside the Holy Spirit in this way, or identify him with a vague inspiration, leaving it to man to claim his salvation even though he cannot merit it, then we again place all faith and theology in jeopardy. Thus, if man had this power to see God in Jesus and to respond to him, it would have been unnecessary for Jesus to die under the burden of the divine malediction, for by his saintly life and devotion he could have summoned us to perceive the love of God and not to doubt the pardon which God of his fatherly goodness would give us. Stirred by this appeal, our latent capacities would throw off egotism and pride and rise to the divine. On this view, the death of Jesus is simply the sad end of a disinterested, dedicated life.

Neo-Protestantism is pleased to find in man powers which render the work of the Holy Spirit almost completely superfluous. Roman Catholicism attributes similar capacities to the Church. In these

---

[1] All heresy finally implies this basic heresy. We need not be surprised to see some failure at this point in all theologians, including the Reformers. The important thing is that their main intention was clear and sound.

systems the Holy Spirit is little more than a mysterious influence. But the Reformation, standing on biblical ground, has to confess man's total blindness to God and opposition to his work. If he is to find God in Jesus Christ, a new miracle is needed, not in Christ now, but in man himself. His closed eyes must be opened, his revolt overcome, and the death and resurrection of Christ must become his death and resurrection. This discovery of Jesus and his history is the work of God by the Holy Spirit. Without this, revelation would be incomplete and grace insufficient, and to Christology there would have to be added man's own effort to appropriate the merits of Christ.

But there is more to it than that. God is hidden from us in the apparently incompatible guise of an infant and a condemned male-factor. If we had the power to see him in this contradictory form, it would really prove that he is within our grasp. We should recognize him because we resemble him. There would be no need of triumph over our incredulity. He would only have to give himself and we should accept him in virtue of what we have in common with him. In both Roman Catholicism and Neo-Protestantism the analogy of being, the natural proportion between the fallen creature and a holy God, is an attack on the doctrine of the Holy Spirit and even a sin against the Holy Spirit himself. For it enables us to ignore him. Sin is not so serious as to prevent us accepting our Creator. He must come to us, but once he is incarnate everything impels us to accept him. Flesh and blood, far from crucifying him, receive him gladly.

In this way it is possible to keep to the main lines of Christology and yet, by slightly attenuating the work of the Spirit, to reintroduce the co-operation of man, his freedom of will, his participation in salvation. Roman Catholicism does this with great skill in its Mariology. Mariology is not so much an attack on Christology; it is rather a powerful threat to the work of the Holy Spirit.[1]

The Reformation doctrine of the Holy Spirit is basic, since it attributes to God under the form of the third person of the Trinity all that Neo-Protestantism ascribes to the moral consciousness, religious feeling and history. The Holy Spirit is our power to respond to Jesus Christ, to live in him and to witness to him. Similarly, he contains all the powers which Roman Catholicism

[1] In the infancy stories it is offset by the conception by the Holy Ghost, which also excludes the Neo-Protestant view of co-operation in the figure of Joseph.

allots to nature and the Church and which find their classic expression in Mariology. Thus the doctrine of the Holy Spirit is typically Protestant. Here we see most clearly, perhaps, the deep gulf between the three forms of faith. The Reformation doctrine implies that God alone responds to his own address to us, so that faith is not an achievement of our own nature but a miracle of the living God.

(v) At this point we should mention the doctrine of Scripture. God's action can come to us only by the means which he has chosen, i.e., his incarnation and earthly work, to which Scripture alone bears witness. Hence the unique and decisive authority of this book. The Church does not select the Bible and make it canonical. The divine mercy alone has chosen to give us this means of hearing. Scripture has been given to the Church as the incomparable means of coming to meet the Lord. What a privilege to have received it! Its authority is not a dogma; it is a grace whose vast implications are to be discovered afresh by each generation.

By referring to the sole authority of Scripture, the Reformers did not wish to exalt a religious document. They were simply expressing their astonished gratitude that they could find Jesus Christ by means of this witness which was so obviously human and yet which was destined miraculously to bring us the Word of God. In itself the Bible has no more power than the Church or experience. But if God chooses to speak through it, in his hands and according to his promise it becomes the occasion of hearing him and the only norm of the Church. It can be abused in many ways. It can be rejected or appropriated, deformed or added to. Only those whom God enables can begin to listen to it and discover its wealth and authority.

Again, everything depends on the decision of God. Neither history nor psychology, reason nor the Church, nor our pious experiences, can bring us through the letter to the Spirit. Only the Spirit himself can lead us along this path. The analogy between Christ's humanity and ours, between his consciousness of God, that of the apostles and our own, is of no help at this point. It can only have the deplorable result of reducing Jesus to our stature and explaining him in terms of our own doubts and hesitations, instead of allowing ourselves to be taught by his fulness. Only the Holy Spirit can illumine us to the point where we accept the realities which are fortunately alien to our sin, and where we are thus released from sin.

(vi) By these different means, God assures us that our whole

salvation is in Christ and not in ourselves. Our justification, sanctification and religious life do not first take place within us, but in
his person and through the successive stages of his history. It is to
him that we should look to know the meaning of such words as
conversion, the new birth, truth, life, love and hope. The Roman
Catholic and Neo-Protestant attacks on what they call purely
external, forensic grace are a typical illustration of their lack of
understanding. The Reformers never thought salvation to be
unattainable. They simply insisted that this transformation, even
when accomplished in us, is always the work and presence of God
alone. It thus takes place in Christ, with whom we are linked,
though his deity is not confounded with our feelings or the imperatives of our conscience, any more than it is admixed with his own
true humanity. God is God, and if he takes us to be with himself he
begins by uniting us and all our aspirations with the death of his
Son, to raise us from the dead and thus to make us, not more
spiritual, but new creatures.

Thus justification is a decree of God, not in the sense of a bare
declaration, but as a total transformation—an act and a mystery
which includes everything else. Even though we do not yet realize it,
Christ has incorporated us into his death, so that his end is ours.
He has also brought us before the Father in his resurrection, so that
his life is ours. The Holy Spirit enables us to see that his history is
ours and that what he has accepted and overcome, he has done to
give to us. Our sanctification, too, is achieved in him, and we receive
it to the degree of our identification with him.

There is something profoundly annoying about the objection that
the Reformation doctrine is merely external. It accuses the Reformers
of neglecting any essential coming of grace to man, whereas there is
in fact a strong emphasis on the presence of Christ in us. The real
point at issue is quite different. What the Reformers wished to avoid
was a confusion in us between what is of God and what is of man,
i.e., between faith as a miracle of God and natural capacities. On
the other hand, Roman Catholics and Neo-Protestants affirm the
union between human religion and Christian faith, between religious
feeling and grace. This is the source of conflict. For the latter view
gives us a real transubstantiation of nature, which can be not merely
conjoined with the work of God, but actually divinized, as if the
cross were not the end of what we have become through sin. Hence
faith is a mixture of the human and the divine, of human aspirations

and divine influence. In opposition to Chalcedon, the two natures are here very largely confounded. Fundamentalists are guilty of this confusion in regard to the Bible, the letter of which they identify with the Word of God. In Neo-Protestantism, the two natures are confounded in religious intuition, of which faith is only a superior manifestation. In Roman Catholicism, they are confounded in the Church, which is elevated to infallibility even in its humanity.

Faithful both to the Gospel and to Chalcedon, the Reformers rejected all these confusions. Yet they did not fall into the opposite extreme of a radical separation between man and God. Man is assumed into Christ, receiving all his perfections, so that he is truly exalted, through death, to become a new creature, though not himself God. The Lord takes him as he is, judges him, and begins to destroy him in order to restore him to life, delivered from sin, yet not ceasing to be himself. He finds himself in possession of his true human nature—and not the divine—at the very moment when, delivered from his false pretensions, he sees them replaced by the mind of Christ, by his work, in short, by the presence in him of the divine and human fulness of Jesus. This is the teaching of the Reformers.

(vii) On this view the Church is neither a society called to cultivate its religious feelings nor an institution traversing the centuries in its own power and to the exclusion of all other truth. It is always a miracle of grace, a creation *ex nihilo*, the Body of Christ, i.e., a magnitude which Jesus carries in himself and manifests solely by the power of his Word. It lives to the degree that Christ is its life, being and substance. In itself, it is nothing, and its pretensions derive from an imperialism far more serious than any forms of human domination. Since all things come to it from God, and truth is comprised for it in Christ, its only desire is to be able to state faithfully what it believes, namely, that everything is accomplished in him. It does not exist to find self-satisfaction in religion, as though superior to those deprived of intercourse with the Master of the universe. Its sole task is to witness. The true Church is necessarily the confessing Church. It proclaims what has been revealed to it in spite of its constant opposition to grace. Far from distributing its own largesse in an attempt to dominate society, it simply testifies that Christ is risen, triumphing over its own unbelief. It is not as it were a holy place in a secular world. Christ alone is holy, and it is conscious of its own fallibility. It can bear witness to holiness only as he enables

D*

it. It never looks to itself, but always to him. It is strong as it forgets and even loses itself. Otherwise, it substitutes itself for grace, for the Holy Spirit, for revelation, and, as often happens, it becomes the most serious obstacle to the fulfilment of the divine work.

This is why the Reformers never try to define the Church except in relation to Jesus Christ and his work. Once it becomes a tangible and definable entity in itself, it is nothing. If it sees that Christ is everything, it becomes his life, his truth, the efficacy of his message. This disengagement is the condition of its authenticity, and ecclesiological deviations and intra-confessional struggles may all be traced back to the self-concern of the Church. Bound by traditions and customs, it prefers itself to the truth, and identifies itself with the truth. This is the chief sin of the Church, and once again it means self-love in place of love for God.

(viii) The discipline of this theology is rigorous, at least in intention. It is expressed in words like 'alone' which constantly qualify the main affirmations of the Gospel: revelation alone, grace alone, Scripture alone, faith alone. The point here is to direct us to trust only in God's work to the exclusion of any prior participation of man. For if man's participation is not itself the gift of grace, it entails deformation, dissimulation, and the final destruction of hope.

More or less obscurely, the Church has always known that all its wealth is in Christ. Yet, even if unconsciously, it has always attempted surreptitiously to add natural and religious elements. It is fatally impelled in this direction by sin. Nothing is more contrary to man, especially religious man, than to be content with Jesus Christ alone. He must always play his own role and add some natural supports.

To avoid these catastrophic deviations, which result in the actual destruction as well as the mutilation of Christian witness, theology, like the Church, must accept a discipline which is expressed positively in contemplation of Christ alone, i.e., in a vigilant Christology applied to the whole of the Christian sphere, and negatively in the rejection of natural theology.[1] We must distinguish at this point between the intention of the Reformers and its expression in the circumstances of the time. Luther's violent attacks on Aristotle and reason are surely designed to confirm his adherence to revelation alone to the exclusion of all natural authorities. Of his many sayings on this point, the following will suffice: 'In faith, one must see

[1] Cf. Barth, *CD* II, 1, pp. 129ff.

nothing but the Word of God. The man who lets himself imagine anything but the Word is already lost. Faith cleaves to the one Word alone, keeps its gaze on it, and sees naught else, whether work or merit. If the heart does not have this singleness, all is lost.'[1]

If Melanchthon yielded too much ground in this respect, the central intention is clear. Grace alone can deliver us from the natural temptation to turn back to ourselves. This return to realities condemned in the death of Jesus Christ attests our strong unbelief, ignorance and ingratitude. Any addition to grace, however insignificant at a first glance, is a revolt against it and is sin *par excellence*. Instead of leaving to God the sole initiative, and receiving from him the only assurance, natural theology seeks more tangible supports which seem better adapted to our weakness. In so doing, it plunges us into uncertainty, substituting for God's faithfulness the relative and deceptive assurances of reason and experience. The hesitations at this point, even within the new sixteenth-century theology, show how hard it is for grace to triumph over our pretensions and how urgent it is to insist upon grace alone. Recent research has shown that even Zwingli, hitherto considered the most humanistic of the Reformers, was open to this basic intuition, as may be seen at various points in his works. As for Calvin, opinions vary. On the whole, however, one must allow that his intention was to place all his trust in revelation, even though he made moderate use of natural ideas in certain matters.[2]

We may deplore the inconsistencies in Reformation theology. Yet they need not surprise us, since the Reformers themselves taught that the truth of God affirms itself in the confusion of man. And in any case the movement as a whole occupies solid ground. Its common rule, in spite of every deviation, is that attention is fixed on revelation in Christ, that no trust is put in other things, and that it seeks always to follow the teaching of Scripture alone.[3]

This attitude cannot be regarded as only a question of theological method. It is an act of faith, gratitude, humility and confidence. It is obedience. If all the treasures of wisdom and knowledge are hidden in Christ (Col. 2.3), and the fulness of the Godhead dwells bodily in him (Col. 2.9), we can receive this fulness only from him, and we

[1] *Sermon* on John 4.4.
[2] This is the conclusion of P. Barth, P. Maury, Niesel and more recently Wendel, as opposed to Doumergue, E. Brunner and U. von Balthasar. Cf. esp. P. Barth, *Theologische Existenz heute*, No. 18, p. 18.
[3] Cf. Calvin, *Inst.* II, 16, 10; II, 16, 19.

can never boast of having received it. Rather than wasting time and energy in seeking truth outside him, or in completing his truth by supposed human truths, we do better to keep to his benefits alone. Like faith, theology is an act of gratitude. It is pressed to receive the precious gift offered and promised by the mercy of God; it is always ready to turn from its own intuitions; and it receives from Christ alone wisdom, truth and life.

One may thus say quite truly that the main feature of the Evangelical attitude is the singleness of heart to which Luther refers, or the strait way of Calvin, i.e., the hunger and thirst for righteousness, or humility, not in the sense of modesty, but of exclusive dependence on God and his grace in face of every cleavage, dualism or vacillation.[1]

Protestant faith and theology rest on the basis of revelation alone, i.e., of the incarnation and reconciliation, of the covenant which God has concluded with men in Jesus Christ. In this sense, they are everywhere dependent on Christ and therefore strictly christological. This attitude is not merely verbal. It is the actual point of departure. They thus differ sharply from all movements operating on the basis of a prior union between God and man in terms either of the analogy of being or of man's likeness to God in feeling, duty or historical development. We do not have to conclude that three such different principles necessarily produce three conflicting faiths, for in his faithfulness God never leaves the Church wholly destitute of his help. For all the human hesitation and confusion, the Lord himself has always been at work. Nevertheless, it is difficult to contest the fact that the only truly solid ground for an instructed and obedient faith is where grace alone rules. This is why the Evangelical Church can and should proclaim, even against itself and its own failings, that its own basis alone is the authentically Christian basis.[2]

---

[1] One can hardly think that U. von Balthasar is right when he argues that the main difference between Protestantism and Roman Catholicism is in respect of the sacraments and the Church rather than natural theology. Bouyer, too, obscures the main problem in his argument that the Reformation truths are authentically Roman Catholic, so that the only dispute is in relation to peripheral errors.

[2] In this respect we may note three different conceptions of theology: first, the Roman Catholic which would have theology express and analyse dogmas; secondly, the Neo-Protestant, which expects it to systematize the truths of the religious consciousness, feeling, experience, etc.; and thirdly, that of the Reformation, which gives it the role of testing the faithfulness of the Church's ongoing proclamation.

2. *A Contemporary Reformed Position*

The Reformation is deeply rooted in the most primitive Christian tradition. In part or in whole, it is illustrated in various confessions, conciliar decisions and theological works. It has constituted the true response of communities and individuals to the revelation of God in Jesus Christ, and it is fortunately a present and future possibility. One may say that it corresponds to the main stream of Christian history as the Church has been constantly led back, like Israel, to more complete submission to its only Lord. The best moments have always been when God has attacked the Church to take away its idols, to bring it to repentance, and to cause it to confess more clearly the work of its crucified Head as the only ground of salvation.[1]

If, then, the Reformation is more than a mere historical and passing movement, we are forced to ask whether this attitude is represented today. Are the criteria which define it respected in any quarter, and applied with a vigilance worthy of the Reformers? No honest and informed person could deny that the theology of Karl Barth more than any other gives us the answer to this question. It is here that Christianity is most powerfully and persistently called to examine itself with a view to greater obedience and gratitude. Before investigating this claim in detail, we may remark that, if the true intention of Barth was to take up this attitude and to return to the Gospel under the guidance of seventeenth-century orthodoxy and the Reformation, then he had no option but to make the corrections which mark his work and at the same time to break with the theology of the day. The prolegomena to the *Church Dogmatics* attest both the return and the break, emphasizing the essential points at which they must be effected. We shall now discuss these briefly.

(i) The attitude did not emerge at once; it matured slowly and painfully. The first stage is marked by the famous *Commentary on Romans* (1918), which breached the dominant Neo-Protestantism of the age. The various addresses which followed give evidence of a process of disengagement, in which a theology centred on the Word of God is substituted for thinking riveted on man. Important in this

---

[1] Along these lines the Reformers could make a true appeal to the past as the guardians of the genuine apostolic tradition. They are representatives of both real Catholicism and real Protestantism against Roman Catholic and Neo-Protestant deviations. The problem of modern ecumenism is to work through the deviations to the place where Catholicism and Protestantism coincide.

respect is the address entitled 'The Doctrinal Task of the Reformed Churches', where we read: 'The question of right doctrine introduces us to the vacuum inside our churches and inside Christianity.'[1] These churches are no longer occupied with the true content of preaching. They prefer to seek practical solutions, moral and material assistance, and an organization which will unite spiritual forces against Rome and modern unbelief. Convinced that doctrine is secondary to life, and that theology means sterility, they have given themselves to direct action, forgetting that a church does not 'live upon truths, however many and vital and profound those truths may be; a church lives upon truth, which men do not take up selectively . . . but which they take up of necessity because it has first taken them, and thus of itself has established the church' (p. 233). The characteristic of the Reformation confessions is that 'to them truth is God—not their thought about God but God himself and God alone, as he speaks through his own word in Scripture and in Spirit' (p. 235). The problem raised is that of the unique source of all truth, which is not man or religion, but 'the revelation witnessed to and perceived in the Scriptures [which] is itself no idea, no principle, no doctrine, but the origin of all doctrine and the standard by which all doctrine is and forever must be measured' (p. 235). The only thing which can make us Reformed is 'the recognition of the one truth, the recognition of that word of God which must prevail, if the worst comes to the worst, even against our own ideals' (p. 235). The content of God's self-witness is 'immeasurable and inimitable, unalterable and inexhaustible; and as such too great to be identical with the content of this or that particular viewpoint or experience—even with the experience of the forgiveness of sins. No such particular viewpoint or experience could contain the concept: "God is speaking", when the fact is that all particular viewpoints and experiences are themselves contained by that concept. God is speaking—he!—and not even the highest and most specifically religious element in the experiences of grace through which he speaks may itself take the place of God . . . [For the fathers] it was a basic thing that needed no basing: spirit is recognized only by spirit, God only by God. The appeal to this principle was meant in a sense neither mechanical and rational nor experimental and irrational . . . but as a simple submission to God's manifestation of himself . . . God does not ask "Why?" What he wills and speaks and does depends both for its

[1] *The Word of God and the Word of Man*, 1928, p. 221.

reality and its human realization only upon himself . . . God not only is the truth . . . but he is also the revelation that he is the truth' (pp. 243f.).

These quotations, which could easily be multiplied, show us that the young theologian has now recognized: firstly, that the starting-point of the theology in which he was nurtured is to be found in the choice, feelings, experiences or morality of the religious man; secondly, that the Reformers were constrained to return to another source, this being the chief mark of the movement; and, thirdly, that he himself in this century must choose a similar attitude in which 'the truth . . . stands or falls with the reality of this sovereign act proceeding from God and authenticated by him' (p. 244). Barth is startled by the plight of modern Protestantism: 'Doctrine, parted from its life-giving origin, hardened into Orthodoxy; Christian experience . . . taking refuge in Pietism; truth . . . shrivelled into the moral and sentimental maxims of the Enlightenment; and finally even Christian experience reduced in Schleiermacher and his followers, both of the left wing and the right, to the highest expression of a religious instinct common to all men' (p. 246). What he proposes is to try to break away from this assimilation of revelation to human realities, as did the Reformers, by whom he is now instructed. It is useless to discuss detailed problems of theology before clarifying this basic attitude: 'It has seemed to me that the first question before us today is concerned with the genesis of doctrine' (p. 247). What is the value of tackling details 'if we are not agreed as to the reason for that attitude . . . ? Only upon the basis of such an agreement can we speak of these or any kindred themes with the old authority' (p. 248). Everything depends on the primary attitude. Today we see two main attitudes in the Christian world, that of Roman Catholicism, which starts with the Church, and that of Neo-Protestantism, which starts with experience. Barth opposes to both the Reformed attitude, which starts with revelation. His whole work is to be explained in terms of this insight and its application to theology as a whole. Attempts have been made to assimilate it to Existentialism, Hegelianism and dogmatism, but in vain. These are only matters of form. Behind them lies the true protestation which is typically Reformed.

The addresses collected under the title *Die Theologie und die Kirche* (1928; ET, 1962), which belong to the same period, work out this theme in relation to Schleiermacher, Feuerbach, Hermann,

Roman Catholicism and culture. The most important are 'Kirche und Theologie' (1925), where Barth insists that the role of theology is to serve revelation and preaching, and 'Der römische Katholizismus als Frage an die protestantische Kirche' (1928), where he points out the profound identity between the new Protestantism and Roman Catholicism, and calls for a second reformation within Protestantism itself. Barth himself was learning at this period that Christian doctrine must be wholly and utterly the teaching of Jesus Christ, God's living Word to us. Its task is to serve his name and to edify the Church. Looking back, he can only wonder that he was so slow to see it and that he did not express himself far more clearly and vigorously.

Worth noting is the part played by the study of Anselm in his final development. As he examined the text, he was led to a novel interpretation of the author of the ontological proof, very different from that given by Thomas Aquinas and almost all subsequent philosophy. As Barth saw it, Anselm was not a rationalist using his intellect side by side with revelation. He was not laying a twofold foundation of reason on the one side and faith on the other.[1] His *sola ratione* did not mean *solitaria ratione*. This reason was no less subject to revelation than Luther's works to faith. In fact, he begins strictly with the Word of God and faith (pp. 100f.). Only a strange lack of logic could confuse the ground taken by Anselm with that of the 'fool'. This truly non-historical interpretation has been invented to justify the Thomistic dualism which has prevailed in Roman Catholicism and in philosophy. Anselm was in fact combating the alliance of theology and philosophy. Hence Barth can find in him a secure and joyous theology firmly attached to revelation, and he can reject the foolish enterprise of those who try to harmonize nature and supernature in some form. The folly of the fool is precisely to put himself in the place where God might not exist—and this is the place of natural thought even in Christian guise (p. 165). Faith cannot think thus. Starting with revelation, it rests on the finished work, though this does not prevent it from reflecting on itself in the light of its true reality. Unlike Thomas, Descartes, Leibnitz and Kant, Anselm is thus a prisoner of grace, and he can teach us what theology truly is. The ground occupied by the fool is that of the Roman Catholic and Neo-Protestant alliance of nature and grace. On this ground one can only think awry. Everything becomes dis-

---

[1] *Anselm: Fides quaerens intellectum*, ET, 1960, pp. 40f.

torted even though it is orthodox, and it is essential to let the Word of God direct us away from this position. The true distinction between Roman Catholicism and Neo-Protestantism on the one side, and Evangelicalism on the other, is not to be found in individual doctrines or secondary differences, but in the whole framework within which theology is pursued.

Now the modern framework common to the first two groups leads into the void, since it rests, not on the irresistible power of God's personal revelation, but in the illusion of self-confident man. This is the point expounded by Barth in the *Prolegomena*. These are necessary because one cannot engage in theology until one has clarified the starting-point, and yet one cannot establish a true and solid starting-point apart from theology. Hence this introduction to dogmatics is not a preamble to faith on the basis of philosophy, history and psychology. What is needed is to receive the starting-point from the Word of God itself. In other words, only strict theological reflection can tell us on what ground it is possible to practise an Evangelical or Church dogmatics (*CD* I, 1, pp. 26ff.). Dogmatics itself is an act of faith which nothing external can support or justify, so that the preambles to dogmatics themselves proceed from an act of faith and from no other source. What is to be shown in them is that all utterance concerning God comes from God's Word. 'Prolegomena to dogmatics is our name for the introductory part of dogmatics in which our concern is to understand its particular way of knowledge' (p. 26). This way is to be found neither in feeling, experience, duty, nor history, but in the act by which God makes himself known. Barth rejects even the suggestion of Brunner that there is an additional task of theology, called eristics, which will prepare the ground for theology by criticizing the ideas of the period and especially the axiom which makes reason the final reality (p. 28). This is still a form of apologetics, and all planned apologetics must necessarily be irresponsible, irrelevant and therefore ineffective (pp. 31f.). For in it unbelief is taken too seriously. An attempt is made to overcome it by discussion and argument, when in fact only grace faithfully preached can gain the victory. The theologian is diverted to another sphere instead of seeing to it that the preaching of the Church is really faithful to the decisive message of God. For this preaching is constantly menaced by theological presuppositions which can only turn it aside from its true task by detaching it from its authentic source. These presuppositions are heresies, i.e., faith which has the externalities of truth but a contradictory content. There thus arises an inner conflict of faith. It is unitary only in appearance. Different truths are really facing one another under the guise of unity.

The role of prolegomena is to unmask the contradictory origins of faith in the light of the Gospel so as to bring the Church back to faithfulness and true unity. Today there are two heresies or manifestations of faith which are certainly Christian in form, but which it is hard to acknowledge as Christian, since their content is a negation of faith (pp. 33f.). The first is modern Protestantism, for which 'the Church and faith are to be understood as part of a larger essential context, and dogmatics as part of a larger scientific problem-context, from the general structural laws of which we are to read off its special epistemological conditions, and to recognize its special scientific claims. This problem-context is, however, that of an ontology, and ever since Descartes that must mean a comprehensively explicated self-interpretation of man's existence, such as will, among other things, also help at the right point, to the preliminary understanding of an existence in the Church, i.e., in faith, and so to a preliminary understanding and criterion of theological knowledge' (p. 39). Such an attitude has forsaken the *Soli Deo gloria* in favour of a system of human glory associated with divine grace. Its prolegomena will consist in a slow ascent of man to the divine, in a philosophy which sets revelation within the larger phenomenon of religion. In this case faith is only 'a determination of man's reality' (p. 41). How can we accept this kind of interpretation of the Gospel unless we are prepared to fall into a relativism quite contrary to the Reformation? There could have been no Reformation on this view.

The second heresy is Roman Catholicism, which the Reformers were contesting and which is still with us. This takes it for granted 'that the essence of the Church, Jesus Christ, no longer the free Lord of their existence, but bound up with the existence of the Church, is finally limited and conditioned by definite concrete formulations of man's understanding of his revelation and of the faith that grasps it' (p. 43). Hence we again have an appearance of faith, but 'once more our community with this faith breaks off, in view of the way in which grace here becomes nature, in which here God's action disappears at once and dissolves into the action of man visited by grace, in which what is outside all human possibility is here at once transformed into a something enclosed within the

Church's reality, and the personal act of a divine approach into a continuously present and objective relation. Roman Catholic faith believes in this transformation' (p. 44).

On both sides faith is corrupted by its conjunction with man, by its absorption into the human, so that a position which seeks to be Evangelical today is limited both on the left hand, where it must renounce 'the presupposition of an existing ontological possibility for the essence of the Church', and on the right, where it must renounce 'the presupposition of a continuously present inherence of the essence of the Church in a creaturely form' (p. 44). The recent debate between Barth and a new orthodox and liturgical institutionalism reveals a no less serious difference. Institutionalism, too, is a kind of alliance with nature, as orthodoxy has often been when, detached from its living origin, it has conserved dogmas which are rationally preferable but already ossified. Institutionalism and liturgism hide a carnal attachment, a humanist participation in grace which will not let itself be called in question by grace for fear of being left without support. Confidence in the Gospel is here not strong enough to accept it as the only security.

The task of prolegomena is to establish in face of these deviations that our security lies only in the event through which God speaks to us and brings us out of our illusions at essential points where everything is at stake. If it is true that the divergence takes place in respect of the very foundation of knowledge, i.e., the starting-point, then it is here that the decision is made, for the threats already active at this point will overhang all the theological propositions developed later.

(ii) The prolegomena are grouped under the title 'The Word of God', the true and only starting-point. It was essential to show clearly that this is at issue rather than the human starting-points mentioned earlier. To be Reformed, Barth had to take this view. But he states it very forcefully. What is his philosophy, is Existentialism or any other 'ism', compared with the clarity and power of this witness? 'In practice it is not in our power to prevent this inroad of philosophy into dogmatics. Neither is it in our power to give to critically reflective human thought . . . such a relation to the divine object or such a determination in terms of it. But it is, of course, in our power to keep before us the need for such a right relation and definition, and therefore to refuse any philosophy this right of irruption, to give the last word not to any immanent regulations of critically reflective thought, not to any longing on the part of man's need for thought, but solely to the needs of the object here in question' (p. 94). Dogmatics uses these instruments simply to direct us to revelation. It is thus marked by openness to the active grace of God coming to us in the Christ of Scripture, and by a distrust in principle of any other source of knowledge.[1]

The starting-point is the event which is to be designated by the phrase: *Deus dixit*. This means that 'God was with us, with us his enemies, with us who were struck and shattered by his wrath. God was with us, with the reality and completeness with which God does what he does; he was with us as one of us. His Word became flesh of our flesh, blood of our blood. His glory was seen here in the depth of our plight, and what was the deepest depth of our plight was first revealed when it was there and then illumined by the glory of the Lord; when, that is, in his Word he descended into the lowest parts of the earth (Eph. 4.9), so that there and thus he might take the power from death and bring life and imperishable being to light (II Tim. 1.10)' (pp. 129f.). This event can be known only from Scripture, which has the power to instruct us in it because it is itself a product of this event: 'Revelation engenders the Bible that attests it' (p. 129). Always God himself speaks, both in Christ and Scripture. He also speaks in us through the Holy Spirit to permit us to hear. 'God speaks' thus sums up all the work of God by which we may know, love and serve him. Without it we should be alone and the victim of our own illusions. The most urgent message which the Church has to preach is that 'this "God with us" has happened' (p. 130). The movement has taken place; it does not have to be repeated; it has simply to be proclaimed as the only liberating message (cf. p. 133).

The description of this Word as the Word preached, written and revealed, and then as the speech, act and mystery of God, constitutes the basic category of this theology, the corner-stone, the starting-point, the centre and the end. It is a human and therefore a fallible attempt to give an account of this act of God, the one necessary and vital thing without which nothing makes sense.

If it is of God, this intervention can be received only in his power: 'The Word of God becomes knowable by making itself knowable.

[1] It is surprising how many friends of Barth as well as opponents have failed to see the real significance of this clear and erudite attempt to establish a theology of the Word of God.

The application of what has just been said to the epistemological problem consists in the fact that we hold fast to this statement and not one step beyond do we take. The possibility of knowing the Word of God is God's miracle on and in us . . . as the creator of the possibility of knowing the Word of God man must be set aside and God himself introduced' (pp. 282f.). Here we can see clearly the distinction from the other two attitudes, which both find in man a spontaneous capacity for knowledge. The question is crucial: 'Is there a general truth with regard to man which can be made generally realizable, which would also include in itself his capacity for knowing the Word of God? We must put this question because an almost overpowering development in the history of Protestant theology since the Reformation has led to an impressive affirmative to this question throughout the entire movement in the Church which we have described as modernist' (p. 218). Schleiermacher was the first basically to connect the 'newly discovered and independent reality of religion with a corresponding possibility generally demonstrable on anthropological grounds' and to undertake 'to interpret Christianity itself in the form of a concretely historical analysis of human existence along the lines of a general doctrine of man: 1. Man's meeting with God to be regarded as a human religious experience historically and psychologically fixable; 2. This experience to be regarded as the realization of a religious potentiality in man generally demonstrable' (pp. 218f.).

All Neo-Protestantism has followed this path. Barth is forced to oppose it because God alone can rescue us from ourselves, from sin and death, as the Bible constantly tells us. The encounter between God and man takes place in the incarnation, the only point of contact between the two worlds, and in the miracle of the Holy Spirit. It is true that man is to participate in God's work. But this is the result of God's intervention and not a prior truth which makes the cross of Christ unnecessary. In Kant as in Schleiermacher, in Secrétan as in Fulliquet, Christ is not strictly a Saviour, but an Inspirer, a Pattern, who saves us only by summoning and helping us to follow him. If expiation is here rejected, it is because it is unnecessary. Man can meet his own needs. To preach this is to corrupt the Gospel. That is why Barth, who thinks it the task of theology to help preaching to bring man an effective remedy to his true situation rather than to nourish his illusions, is so firm on this point: 'God's Word ceases to be grace or grace itself ceases to be grace when we ascribe to man . . . a possibility of knowledge independent of it and peculiar in itself' (p. 221).

Paul taught this, as did also Luther and Calvin. But Neo-Protestantism has seen fit to reverse the Evangelical teaching. Nor is it a mere matter of divergent opinion. The whole basis is here at issue: man's salvation, the reality of the Church, its preaching to men who are crushed yet still capable of illusions. God alone gives power to man, or the Gospel is neither taught nor practised. Experience is the determination of man's existence by the Word of God (p. 227). It is not a spontaneous sense of the infinite, a vague intuition of the force which rules the universe, an inner sense of right and wrong, nor a remote impression of the superiority of the Christian message of the God of love. It is the action within us of the Christ of Scripture, received by us in spite of ourselves through the intervention of the Holy Spirit. The Christian is no spectator. He does not simply select a convenient truth. Apprehended by grace, he has to witness. Experience implies true knowledge of the Word of God, the love and gratitude induced by this Word, and the responsibilities which it lays upon us. Although authentically human, since it involves the whole man, experience in this sense is more than human, since it is God in us. To refuse to see this is inevitably to make the believer 'the criterion of pronouncements upon the Word of God' (p. 243). The Word no longer rules, for man can now approve or reject what it says. The believer retains of the Gospel only what corresponds to his inward experience. His religion controls revelation by passing it through the crucible of his religious appreciation. The result is uncertainty and even a detached scepticism which cannot be too serious about any of the different alternatives, since good and saintly men have held divergent and even contradictory views without detriment to their usefulness or success. It has thus to be admitted that experience is our teacher, that piety and good will are more important than doctrine, and that we are to study humanity and piety rather than truth. Protestantism has undoubtedly embraced this relativism and made it a dogma and even its sole principle. This is a mark of age and fatigue, the relic of a period which since Descartes has devoted most of its energy to the exaltation of man. 'In theology at least thought cannot proceed along Cartesian lines' (p. 223).

The same criticisms apply equally to Roman Catholicism, which buries the truth, not in consciousness, but in the Church, the power of which rests on a capacity of nature as well as a promise of God. The result is an identification of the Word of God with the Church, which is at least partially sound in nature. As an intermediary between God and man, however, the Church does not really alter the problem. For in spite of its pretension, it is still a human reality which appropriates grace no less decisively than the religious consciousness. The analogy of being is the real root of the evil both in its more refined classical form and in its naiver and less prudent Neo-Protestant form. In the identification of the Word of God and Church dogma we can see the grandiose solitude of a Church which has so appropriated the Word that it can no longer hear any voice from without (p. 306). This loss of openness to the Gospel is perhaps the best proof that even religious man has no capacity for knowledge of God. The more he affirms it, the more he shows his impotence and hostility to the Word which alone can deliver him from bondage.[1]

(iii) When God speaks, the theologian must give his whole attention, not to supposed human capacities or opinions, but to this Word. The more he listens, the more the power of the Lord can illumine and conquer and therefore act through him. Untroubled by inevitable misunderstandings, he can find power and joy in humble reflection which owes its profundity to the Word. It is to study of the Word that Barth gives himself with remarkable strength and tenacity.[2]

The Word of God is identical with revelation. But the Bible tells us that revelation has three aspects or moments. God decides to come to our rescue; he comes to us at a point in history; and he comes to enable us to receive with new depth what this history teaches.

The aim of the dogma of the Trinity is to indicate this decisive event of revelation which includes all divine and human truth. The doctrine is not the truth, nor does it even contain it. Like all dogmas, it can only indicate it, since the truth lies in God and is Christ himself. The Trinity describes the fulness of God in action as the origin and end of all things. For this imperative reason, and not out of mere respect for tradition, Barth puts it first. This is good Reformation procedure, for essential problems are resolved and serious errors avoided by this commencement.

[1] Cf. *CD* I, 1, pp. 395ff.
[2] Note the way in which he engaged in study of the doctrine of predestination during the very period of the great Church conflict against the Third Reich.

As Athanasius emphasized, this doctrine protects the most simple faith. In his three modes of action, God is always himself, so that each time we meet him to our salvation. If the Son were not God, how could we be sure of meeting God in him and therefore of salvation? If the Holy Spirit were not equal to the Father, how could we know that through him we have dealings with the Son and the Father? If God alone can give us grace by assuring us of his existence, forgiveness and love, then it is absolutely necessary that he should be present, and self-identical, in each moment of revelation, always the living and personal God. If any moment were lacking, or there were no unity, God would be inaccessible and salvation a myth.

The dogma also defends three crucial truths of faith and theology. If the Creator is also the Reconciler and Redeemer in the differentiated unity of God, we cannot treat of the Father apart from the Son and the Spirit. This cuts off natural theology with its attempt to reach the Creator directly by way of proofs of existence and external evidence, i.e., apart from Christ, as in the Vatican Council and all Neo-Protestant theology. Access to the Creator is possible only through the incarnate Son by the Holy Spirit. This knowledge is simply an act of faith in the incarnate Word. Any disjunction between the orders of creation and redemption, any dualism in the sources of revelation, is thus excluded from the very outset, whether in the pronounced form assumed in Thomas, Schleiermacher, Kant and Troeltsch, or in the modified form championed by Brunner, who refers to orders of creation left intact by the fall. A precise definition and conscientious application of this dogma rules out these deviations. The fathers of Nicaea saw this, and it is strange that later defenders of the Nicene statement do not always perceive it. The moderns, of course, reject the dogma altogether if they follow their insights consistently. Barth's doctrine of creation naturally conforms to his primary tenet, the work of the Creator being firmly linked with the covenant concluded by the Father in the Son.

The dogma also emphasizes the full identification of revelation and reconciliation, thus placing Christ's person at the centre of all theology. In spite of what some people think, Christology as a theological method does not do despite to the Father and the Spirit, but is rooted in the formulation of the Trinity. 'So far as God's revelation as such achieves what only God can achieve, namely, the restoration of man's communion with God, destroyed, nay annihilated by us, so far as, in the fact of revelation, God's enemies are already his friends, revelation itself is reconciliation' (p. 468). It is necessary that Christ should be God the Son to overcome sin. It is equally necessary that he should be man to take away our sin. This central event in which God's work is done cannot be replaced by an evolution as in Hegelian and Roman modernism. It cannot be assigned to past history. If it is history, it has also a living relevance in every age. It includes all men and is thus the centre of history, of all our lives. It is God's verdict on the whole human drama. Nothing can be added or substituted. Doctrines of progress, evolution and experience, all forms of subjectivism, pantheism and institutionalism, break on this enduring rock of our eternal salvation. Identifying the Father and the Son even in their differentiation, the dogma of the Trinity establishes the only framework within which truly Christian thinking can move, and this framework is typically Reformed.

Finally, the climax is reached in the doctrine of the Holy Spirit. As God, he can lead us to God. Only if one insists on the power of man can we ignore this truth; the choice is once more between grace and works (Rom. 11.6). Again we are shown plainly that salvation, i.e., our adherence to Christ, is God's work and not ours. It is the Holy Spirit who 'guarantees man . . . his personal participation in revelation' (p. 518). This position dominates all dogmatics, including not only the doctrines of Holy Scripture and the Church but also ethics and eschatology.

One can hardly deny that here we have the most important points in Barth's whole work. He fixes the ground on which he will build, makes the principal articulations and defines the limits, especially in relation to the main heresies. All that follows is already implied and virtually present in this first volume, which even alone might well serve to chart the course of modern Reformed theology.

(iv) The work of the total revelation in which Father, Son and Spirit are co-equally God is enacted at the heart of history, on Christmas Day, Good Friday and Easter Day. It is identical with the incarnation of the Son of God in Jesus. Although apparently innocent, Subordinationism is probably the most dangerous of Christological deviations. Docetism and Ebionitism are less dangerous because they are so crude. But Subordinationism, which can appeal to many Pauline texts, makes possible an exaltation of the Father in creation and reduces the importance of reconciliation, so that Christ is demoted and the work of man is exalted. This threat must be averted at the very outset if we are to prevent the incursion of Roman Catholicism and Neo-Protestantism, with their confidence in man himself. This is why the doctrine of the incarnation follows that of the Trinity. It deals with the person of Jesus Christ, the mystery which contains all truth in his humanity and deity. The Chalcedonian dogma, Christ as very God and very man, is naturally adopted and approved. We need not dwell on this, since the second half of this volume is to be devoted to it. It is enough that we should note the extraordinary perspicacity of those fifth-century fathers, or rather the wonderful providence of God in the confusion of man, which in that supposedly primitive time gave us a formula which, in spite of all its faults, is after the Nicene definition the best adapted to ward off fatal deviations in the Church.[1]

It is not a question of according a place to Jesus Christ, but of recognizing that God has set him in the centre of all that is. 'The majesty of God in his condescension to the creature—that is the most general truth always told us by the reality of Jesus Christ . . . if God wished to reveal himself, if he wished to be free for us, this very miracle had to take place, namely, that without ceasing to be himself he entered our sphere, assumed our nature. He had to if he wished to impart himself to us, to become the Mediator of himself to us. That is what we mean when we say that he is God, not only in himself but also in us and among us. In that case we are saying that he becomes a Mediator, God in himself, but also a reality in our cosmos. That he can be both and that this possibility of his as such is the possibility of his revelation, is the most general meaning of the incarnation of the Word of God, of the name of Jesus Christ, of his God-ness and his man-ness.'[2]

God reveals himself by becoming visible. He saves us by assuming our condition, although without confusion with us. This is a miracle of far greater import than the Virgin birth. The point of the latter is to indicate this, like a sentinel on the threshold of the Gospel.[3]

We can now see what is the central insight of Barth's theology, as it ought to be of all Christian theology. It might be described as christological concentration. What does this mean? The term

---

[1] Cf. *CD* I, 2, pp. 350ff.

[2] *CD* I, 2, pp. 31f. Christology is the only relevant answer to natural theology. It excludes all extensions of incarnation and prevents all prior unions of God and man.

[3] The Virgin Birth shows Mariology to be an expression of the analogy of being and discloses the latent pantheism in Neo-Protestantism (cf. I, 2, pp. 132ff.).

Christology can be used in two distinct but related senses. More narrowly, it applies to the person and work of Christ, and more broadly, it signifies the discussion of every problem—God, creation, man, reconciliation, the Church, ethics, redemption and eschatology —only in the light of this one place where all wisdom and truth are recapitulated and proffered. From this angle, all theology in all its details is knowledge of Jesus Christ and therefore Christology.[1]

This attitude is an act of faith in the work of God which comprises our justification and sanctification, life and obedience, love and hope. This is what brings us under submission to Scripture, by which we receive liberty, fulness and autonomy, since God enlarges rather than crushes us by attaching us to himself. At the same time, this attitude is a discipline which rigidly excludes anything that might veil this fulness by adding other sources, norms or criteria. It is obedience to the first commandment, which ordains love for God alone and therefore the rejection of all self-fabricated idols. It is a vigilant application of the *Soli Deo gloria* to every sector of Christian faith, theology and action. One can hardly deny that Barth is one of the select company in Church history to have given concrete testimony to this total trust in Christ and to have practised this discipline with resolution and tenacity. This is the main reason why U. von Balthasar regards him as the most typical representative of the Reformed faith.

(v) The third section of Chapter II of the *Church Dogmatics* deals with the work of the Holy Spirit. The Holy Spirit expresses both the liberty of God and the liberty of man who is made capable of receiving him. He is thus our only possibility of becoming and remaining Christians and of confessing our faith. All human action is praise of God by the Spirit, whether in witness, obedience, or hope of a future consummation. Hence 'we have no right . . . to import into the reality of God's process of revelation to and among men any contribution learned from a source of knowledge different from Holy Scripture' (I, 2, pp. 207f.).

Having already emphasized this point in relation to Neo-Protestantism and Roman Catholicism, we can only confirm our earlier statements by quotations. 'If we are to call the special dogmas of the Reformation subjective dogmas, we can do so only in the sense . . . that they treat particularly, not so much of God's freedom for man become an event in Christ, as man's freedom for God actualized in

[1] Cf. *CD* I, 2, pp. 123, 872.

the Holy Spirit. And it was at this point that Neo-Protestantism failed. It claimed to be fostering the particular interest of the Reformers, indeed, it appeared to do so. But it was so interested in man's freedom that it forgot the divinity of the Holy Spirit. . . . And the final result was that God's freedom became simply a more precise establishing of the all-dominating "freedom from man's side". . . . It was concerned with man in himself, the man who understands himself because he controls himself' (p. 209). In contrast, our liberty is to be found in the deliverance brought by the Holy Spirit when he brings us to see and accept the resurrection of Christ as our own liberation. Thus, Neo-Protestantism has substituted for the liberating power of the Holy Spirit the power of supposedly free man to attach himself to the Lord.

This deviation did not appear at once in its full seriousness. The first step was to detach the Holy Spirit from Jesus Christ. The result was to attribute to the Spirit all kinds of non-biblical and therefore human and religious inspirations, for who can control the Spirit? Little by little the presumed impulses of the Spirit came to be confused with our own spirituality, which finally dominated the field: 'Neo-Protestantism did not at first install the human factor in its many forms as a second divine revelation side by side with the revelation of Christ. It did not at first allow this second revelation to evolve into the real revelation. But long before, and even where it still did not appear to do this, or concealed the fact that it did, it separated itself from the New Testament Church by setting over against the knowledge and life of faith in Christ an autonomous knowledge and faith deriving from the Holy Ghost . . . Neo-Protestantism in its noblest and earliest form was in every sense a godly and serious piety. It was godly and serious in all the important forms of its second or Enlightenment stage. Even today we shall miss the mark if we accuse it of a lack of seriousness or godliness. On the contrary, it must be soberly admitted that as far as seriousness and godliness go it has often had the advantage over the representatives of the official teaching. The one reproach we can and must bring against it is that it abandoned an insight which was unambiguously indicated in the New Testament, not so unambiguously asserted in the Middle Ages, and unforgettably renewed in the Reformation theology of justification and sanctification. This was the insight that the Holy Spirit is none other than the Spirit of Jesus Christ. By abandoning it, it opened the doors with only too much seriousness and godliness *quibuslibet deliriis et imposturis*, i.e., to a recognition of all possible idols, including those with which we have to do today' (p. 252). Mysticism and moralism replaced the Holy Spirit who proceeds from the Father and the Son. An autonomous piety emerged, attested by our hymns and religious ideas. Where piety is the fruit of the Spirit, it cannot be confused with our religious aspirations. But from the eighteenth century there has been a replacement of revelation by the general phenomenon of religion, which retains the title of revelation but regards it as the most exalted expression of man's natural religious feelings. The root of this perversion is the misconception of the Christian doctrine of the third person of the Trinity, or rather the blind pretensions which impel man to reject this dogma. The clearest result of the process is the secularization into which Protestantism is forced by its abandonment of the authentic Gospel (p. 257). 'It was and is a characteristic of its theological thinking . . . that in its great representatives and outstanding tendencies what it has discerned and declared is not the religion of revelation but the revelation of religion' (p. 284).

At the same time the doctrine of the Holy Spirit challenges the Church and its authority. For the Church has its origin in Jesus Christ, yet not merely in the sense that he gave it a first push which enables it to live in its own strength, though no doubt with his aid. No, he always creates, impels and directs the Church, or else it would have no continuing vitality. In itself the Church is no more lasting than manna. But we can count on the faithfulness of the Lord who is constantly at work to renew it. This is why it may be said that the Church is 'the sphere in which God's revelation is subjectively real' (p. 228). It is not the sphere of mere recollection, or of a continuing life owed to organization. It is the effect of a living, actual, personal revelation of God by the Holy Spirit. If Easter cannot be reproduced, Pentecost must be.

Once this truth is blurred, institutionalism develops. Whether in its Roman, Neo-Protestant or Orthodox form, institutionalism sins at this point. It finds truth in duration or tradition, not in the direct action of grace. It ascribes grace to an influence rather than a direct communication. Whether sacramental or pietistic, this influence stimulates religion rather than the creation of faith by living preaching of the Word in the Spirit. For the lasting faithfulness of God is substituted the persistence of religion as an ecclesiastical or human phenomenon. This view can be justified only if we assume the

infallibility of the Church or implicitly of the religious consciousness. But how can we accept this transfer of the infallibility of the
Holy Spirit to human magnitudes? The Church is here usurping an
unlawful privilege, as we can see from the history of rebellious Israel
and the early Church. This pretension always arises when the
efficacy of the Holy Spirit is even slightly forgotten. The more the
Church is deceived, the more it must proclaim itself infallible. How
else can it justify its existence and decisions in which its own
insights take precedence of the imperatives of Scripture? We can
see this happening at Trent, at the Vatican Council and in the
definition of the assumption of the Virgin Mary. When the Bible,
tradition and the consensus of the Church as a whole are so obviously
set aside, to what other court can there be appeal? Yet Neo-
Protestantism, with its appeal to the universal, national or pietist
Church, is in no position to throw stones. Thus on the subject of
baptism Lemaître can write: 'The baptism of infants is observed by
the majority of churches. There is no reason to abandon it.'[1] This is
exactly the spirit of Trent. It will defend an established position
even against the Bible, let alone the Reformation. Dissociating the
Spirit from the Christ of Scripture, it thinks it has the Spirit itself.
Apostolic succession and tradition guarantee this conception of the
Church where the event of grace coincides with the persistence of
the institution. There is, of course, an institution in Evangelical
theology. Yet it is not the Church. Strictly, it is Christ himself,
Scripture and the apostolate, implying the constant and constantly
renewed action of the Spirit of God. 'We stand here at the point at
which the Evangelical conception of the Church diverges abruptly
from the Roman Catholic and also the Modernist Protestant. . . .
But the act of the objective revelation of God is an act in the
existence of Jesus Christ as very God who is also very man. So, too,
the act of sign-giving by which the objective revelation comes to us
is an act in the existence of these signs as they were given us once
and for all at the inauguration of the apostolate. And since it is a
sign-giving which awaits the seeing eyes and hearing ears of ever
new men, this sign-giving must receive an ever new recognition and
understanding in the Church with each new generation. And it must
do so in such a way that never even in part can the Church believe
that it has mastered it, that it has learned what Christ really wants of
us in the message of the apostles, what preaching and sacrament

[1] *Foi et vérité*, p. 467.

ought really to be in our midst. It must do so in such a way that at any time in the Church, naturally with respectful consideration for what the fathers apprehended and taught, there exists a challenge to render an account *ab ovo* . . . whether it stands with this sign-giving as it was originally intended to stand' (pp. 227f.). The main fault of the ecclesiastical institution is its strong sense of being the daughter of Abraham and its failure to repent of what it has become. It is self-confident and deaf to the call of the Spirit. The recent Protestant attempt in this direction, far from being of decisive value, e.g., to the ecumenical movement, is simply the prolongation of an orthodoxy established on the prior existence of nature and grace, the Church and the Holy Spirit—an ontology which is neither that of Chalcedon nor of the Reformation. Alien elements are inter-fused with the Gospel, e.g., the need for security, mystical and rationalist demands, and even attachment to social and cultural values.

In face of the many dangers involved, e.g., moral or emotional secularization, illuminism or institutionalism, there is great need of the restoration of the doctrine of the Holy Spirit. While this will not be developed until Barth comes to the theme of redemption in the narrower sense, the foundations are already laid in a form appro-priate to the goal of the prolegomena, and the importance of the matter in the present situation of theology and the Church is plainly revealed.

(vi) The definition of the place and role of Scripture depends on the starting-point adopted. Where the Church is predominant, Scripture will be subjected to it on such grounds as the biblical origin of tradition, the incompetence of the believer, the anarchy caused by free investigation, etc. Similarly, when emphasis is placed on the religious consciousness, the Bible is treated along the same lines in a different context, and historical criticism can neutralize demands which are thought to be incompatible with present insights. On the other hand, when the Word of God is the sole source of faith, the Bible is placed on a different level, as finely stated in the *Second Helvetic Confession*: 'For God himself spake to the fathers, prophets, apostles, and still speaks to us through the Holy Scripture. And in this Holy Scripture, the universal Church of Christ has all things fully expounded which belong to a saving faith, and also to the framing of a life acceptable to God; and in this respect it is expressly commanded of God that nothing be either put to or taken from the same.'[1] In Chapter III Barth confirms, develops and explains this supreme Reformation principle, contrasting it with various deviations both to the right and the left.

'The Bible is the witness of divine revelation'.[2] This controlling thesis has the following implications.

(1) God has chosen the Bible and given it to us in order that its witness may come to us and lead us to its subject, i.e., Christ. A marvellous gift of grace, it is the vehicle of revelation and may become revelation as God decides.

(2) Yet it is plainly human and thus a legitimate object of historical criticism. The demand that it should be studied historically 'can never be taken too seriously. The Bible itself posits this demand: even where it appeals expressly to divine commissionings and promptings, in its actual composition it is everywhere a human word, and this human word is obviously intended to be taken seriously and read and understood and expounded as such. To do anything else would be to miss the reality of the Bible' (p. 464).

(3) Even in its humanity, however, it is witness to an object which surpasses it. Now the first duty of historical criticism is to respect the object. But here the object is not simply a human fact. It is witness to the personal revelation of God in Christ. Thus hermeneutics, to be truly adapted to the object and therefore genuinely objective, must apprehend this reality both in its historicity and in its movement elsewhere. Failure at this point made nineteenth-century historicism extremely unhistorical.

(4) The canon is not a choice of the Church but an act of faith by which the Church recognizes that God has given it these books to reveal himself to it and to reign over it. The Bible has imposed itself, and in virtue of its power as God's Word it can impose itself afresh on us.

(5) The dogma of biblical authority is not a demonstration or principle but the confession of the Church as convinced by God himself that his Word is found in these testimonies alone.

(6) It is thus an illusion to think we can subject the Bible either to our own judgment or to ecclesiastical decisions. In spite of all our attempts to tame it, the Bible is always free to arise again, strong enough to make itself understood and dangerous to those who think they are at peace because they have imprisoned it in their systems.[3]

---

[1] Ch. 1, Schaff, *Creeds of Christendom*, III, p. 833.
[2] *CD* I, 2, p. 462.   [3] Cf. *CD* I, 2, p. 470.

(vii) This attitude implies a conception of the Church which, for the sake of consistency with what precedes, must respect the sovereignty of grace alone to the exclusion of every other authority. As it emerges in the last part of the prolegomena, this ecclesiology is marked by a constant concern not to concede anything that might obscure the lordship of the Head of the Church who not only founds but also maintains and renews it. Such a Church is not to be defined from below, but only in terms of the power which creates and sustains it, namely, the Word of God, or Jesus Christ himself. We have here the same reversal as in the case of experience. Since the Church, like faith, is the creation of God, it is better to concentrate on its origin, which contains its fulfilment, than to enlarge on the results, at the risk of separating the effects from the cause. In other words, the Church is to be defined solely in terms of Jesus Christ. It exists only in its Head. It is borne by him. If we take our eyes from him it is only a human institution which is of no particular interest and may even be a hindrance to faith. Here more than ever the theologian must be vigilant, looking not to what is seen but to what is not seen (II Cor. 4.18). For the risk of being seduced by appearance is greater here than in any other sector.

The development of this doctrine is wholly in line with the first inspiration of the Reformers, though their views are sometimes criticized, e.g., on the relation of Church and State. Luther's teaching on the hidden Church will be recalled: *abscondita est ecclesia, latent sancti*. Like our life, it is hidden with Christ in God (Col. 3.3). Calvin, too, defines the Church in terms of the Word: 'Therefore, although they exhibit a temple, a priesthood, and other similar masks, the empty glare by which they dazzle the eyes of the simple should not move us in the least to admit that there is a Church where the word of God appears not'; and a little lower down: 'In short, since the Church is the kingdom of Christ, and he reigns only by his word, can there be any doubt as to the falsehood of those statements by which the kingdom of Christ is represented without his sceptre, in other words, without his sacred word?' (*Inst.* IV, 2, 4). Elsewhere Calvin says that 'the doctrine of Christ is the life of the Church' (IV, 12, 1). He means that Christ's teaching or Word is the very essence of the Church, as Barth is constantly saying. Thus, we may reach the point when 'the position which Jesus Christ occupies in its midst becomes only honorary. He ceases to be the actual ruler of the Church. It bears his name, but in practice it is the Church that

E

governs itself by its own will and action. But where this is the case every word of the Church's proclamation is a deviation, even if anything seriously deserving the name of heresy is still in the remote distance' (*CD* I, 2, p. 808). The Church, then, exists only where the Word is faithfully preached and the sacraments are duly administered. It is the place where the efficacy of God's work is seen. Though we may anticipate what the Word will do, we must rely on its power alone and not on ideas suggested by observation of the great religious societies. 'The sphere of Christian faith is the sphere in which God's Word exercises its power' (p. 687). Thus the best way to grasp the authentic reality of the Church is to turn from the visible reality and to let oneself be grasped by this Word which alone can create and renew, for 'the critical and reviving power of the Word of God in the Church is the power of the Word of God itself and its power alone' (p. 854), and one of the main tasks posed by obedience to it is to prevent the Church from becoming an autonomous institution. Once the Church comes to rely upon itself, it is lost.

These principles, which constitute a definite discipline, take on concrete significance in the description of the Church. Since it is created only by the living Word of God, its first mark will be its constant striving to hear this Word: 'The Church is constituted as the Church by a common hearing and receiving of the Word of God' (p. 588). Listening is its first activity. Its whole organization must be fashioned to aid, encourage and stimulate this study of the Word in Holy Scripture. This is the supreme concern. All other tasks depend on this primary task of interpreting Scripture. This is the chief end of its organization: 'We can declare positively that the Church as a whole is an organization which exists for this mediatorial work (i.e., interpretation). For this reason no member can remain unconcerned, idle and inactive in face of this duty' (p. 714). In this respect there are not two categories, the active and the passive. All must study the Word and all must proclaim it. This is 'the only kind of activity by which it can really be justified before God and man' (pp. 760f.).

This sole activity, which is its only *raison d'être*, consists in its commission to preach the Gospel. But it cannot preach unless it first receives. Nor can it separate the two elements of listening and acting. Its preaching derives from hearing. Its duty of speaking, living, acting and confessing is given when it listens and receives. Its work, like its very existence, is an effect of the activity of its

Lord, of his miracles, of his promise to serve his Church in order to attest his own work and to confirm that of the Church. This is why, in face of its humanly impossible task, the Church can only believe, hope and pray that God may accomplish it.

This does not mean that the Church is a passive instrument in the hands of its Lord. On the contrary, it is responsible for its acts, or more properly for its obedience. God takes it up and frees it by giving himself to it. He makes it autonomous by subjecting it to his Word. It is perhaps surprising how much space Barth gives to the freedom and autonomy of the Church. It has a great part to play, not in independence and revolt, but in gratitude and praise. Our freedom, 'as freedom under the Word, is not a secure possession, or a merit, but a gift . . . and in that it implies at the same time a task, an obligation of care and concern laid upon man, we must accept it as a vocation in the fulfilment of which we are not our own masters, but servants' (pp. 697f.). The liberty of the Church is a fruit of the liberty of the Word of God in it, i.e., of its authority over it. We have thus to begin by defining this authority. What is it? It consists neither in tradition, hierarchy nor government, but in Scripture, the fathers and confession. 'To say that Jesus Christ rules the Church is equivalent to saying that Scripture rules the Church' (p. 693). This is the primary dogma of the Reformation. God rules by his Word, and therefore by Scripture. Church authorities are its servants. It alone gives authority. The fathers and confessions have their authority from fidelity to Scripture. Thus the Church today is dependent for its authority on the fidelity of its confession. It derives authority neither from the power nor prestige of its deliberative assemblies, but only from the conformity of its witness to the biblical revelation, and therefore only from its obedience. This is the centre of debate.

The Church has probably never been defined so fully in terms of its origin and vocation. Every related problem comes back to the one preoccupation whether it is faithful to the impelling of the living God. Its authority and liberty, its organization and efficacy, its very being, all depend solely on its openness to grace and the authenticity of its praise and obedience. Its work is vain if not prescribed by Scripture. Once it ceases to question and to let itself be questioned by it, turning instead to traditions and customs, it loses its savour and becomes useless and even harmful. Thus we must devote our supreme energies to recapturing this fidelity, pursuing it relentlessly and at all costs. This is no mere question of academic or aesthetic consistency, or even of doctrinal purity. It is a matter of efficacy. The Church is truly strong only when it is biblical.[1]

(viii) To avoid the numerous pitfalls which endanger it and oppose God's plan, the Church has the means of constant self-examination in the light of its controlling authority. By submitting its preaching, acts and conduct to this authority, it can measure its obedience. This examination does not give absolute security, for God alone can make it truly faithful to his Word. But since the Word is incarnate in Jesus Christ, and since it has produced a human witness to which it binds us, the Church must constantly scrutinize its relationship to Scripture. This scrutiny poses the task of theology, whether exegetical, dogmatic or practical. The final pages of the prolegomena are devoted to this theme, and thus take up again the opening discussion.

It is clear that this definition of theology and its ministry in the Church exactly describes the work of the Reformers and indicates the starting-point of the whole sixteenth-century movement. The aim of the Reformers was to test the preaching, work and life of the Church of their day by the Gospels, and their protest was based on the results of this examination. If the investigation had not had these negative results, there would have been no Reformation. Similarly, Barth's dogmatics would have remained Neo-Protestant if he had found that current preaching corresponded with the teaching of Scripture. This kind of control involves more than simple comparison or criticism. The theologian can see the distinctions only as he is prepared himself to rethink the total message of Scripture in the light of historical theology and the concrete circumstances of the age. The deviations of the Church can be seen only in the mirror of the fulness of scriptural revelation.

In this regard we should note the following essential points. (1) Theology, and especially dogmatics as its main branch, answers to a vital need in the Church, namely, that of its fidelity and therefore its existence. It is not an academic exercise for specialists with intellectual gifts. It is not a game or a luxury. It arises from the most profound and legitimate need of faith, i.e., for authenticity. 'Dogmatics springs from the salutary unrest which must not and cannot

---

[1] The simple test of the Church's authenticity is whether it is open to the Gospel or preoccupied with questions of success, prestige, etc. (cf. R. de Pury, *Job*, 1955). The inner danger to the Church is probably more acute than outward attack (cf. *CD* I, 2, pp. 503, 643f.).

leave the Church. It is the unrest of knowing that its work is not done simply by speaking about God somehow or other . . .' (p. 780). When the Church speaks badly or haphazardly about God, it forfeits its right to exist. It deceives those whom it addresses by giving them false ideas and imaginations instead of the Gospel of salvation. Its position becomes untenable, for it is both illogical and dishonest from the standpoint both of faith and of simple human correction. Its situation is undoubtedly delicate. It is called to preach the Gospel of God. But this involves the human 'impossibility of the attempt to speak about God' (p. 750). Yet it has the promise that this miracle will take place, even though it lives under the threat of every possible corruption due to external pressure or its own blindness. Hence it must exert all its power to control its message, constantly seeking more exact fidelity and fighting against dangerous alterations. Theological concern is simply that of obedience, of the inward consistency of the Church with its message, and of love for men, to whom no conscientious Christian can give a haphazard message. At stake here is our own salvation and that of those to whom we speak. The Gospel alone can remedy their evils and reconcile them to God. How can we fail to address ourselves to the question whether we are really giving them this powerful message of liberation? Only complacency, pharisaism or sloth can be indifferent to this summons, which comes to us no less from the concern of love than that of faith.

(2) This is a concern, not merely of theologians, but of all Church members. Once they realize that their gatherings and activities, their outreach and service, depend on the truth of their faith, witness and conduct, how can they evade this problem? Who can refuse this responsibility without plunging both himself and his brethren into the night of a diffuse and deceptive religiosity? The theological problem thus affects the most concrete elements in the common life of the Church. 'It is in the thick of the Church's life, i.e., as the hearing Church has to be a teaching Church, that the decision about the purity or impurity of its doctrine is made: in its preaching and instruction, in its pastoral work, in its administration of the sacraments, in its worship, in the discipline which it exercises towards its members, in its message to the world, and last and not least in its concrete attitude over against state and society' (p. 770). By his mere participation in this activity the Christian is forced to examine its basis if he is not to act irresponsibly. The Church which refuses to

be questioned on the authenticity of its customs and practices shows more confidence in itself than in the Lord. It regards itself as sufficiently enlightened, though not perhaps infallible. It really lives on the assumption of infallibility. This attitude is profoundly un-christian, for the truth is in Christ and not in us. It explains all the schisms and the difficulty in healing them. Theological concern is the very reverse of ecclesiastical complacency. It derives from an act of repentance at the goodness of God and our corruptions of his message. It has its source in the humility of the Christian who is open to grace and sadly aware of his own infidelities. It is born of a total insecurity and yet also an unlimited confidence in the power of God's faithfulness. 'The autonomy in which dogmatics has to choose its method must consist solely in the recognition of its theonomy, i.e., in its free submission to the sovereignty of the Word of God alone' (p. 866). Can there be any other attitude to grace? Yes, there can be that of the owner, the interested spectator, the assured beneficiary. Here faith becomes human security. But the Holy Spirit sets us in a very different situation where we can count only on the mercy of God. Dogmatics is impossible in a Church which is sure of itself and closed to the judgments and promises of its Lord.

(3) In this situation, the role of theology is quite clear. It has first to bring preachers and hearers to 'accept as the exclusive possibility and the exclusive norm of their reflection and action the fact that, in what Church preaching says of God, God himself speaks for himself' (p. 800). It must then demand unceasing attention to this Word in order that the Church may overcome its weakness and do its work. This gives it its main task, i.e., to help the Church the better to listen to its Lord by itself listening in prayer and hope, and then teaching what it hears. In this process it perceives that 'even the slightest menace to pure doctrine is a serious and fatal menace to Christian preaching and the Christian Church as such' (p. 777). If dogmatic control had always been properly maintained, what deviations, betrayals, conflicts and schisms might have been avoided! It is not enough to intervene when heresy is rampant. In the name of the Church, with its support and in expression of its consecration, dogmatics is a watchman scanning the horizon and warning against possible dangers even before they appear. Its task is not to condemn heresy; it is to warn against incipient danger. It is 'a call to unity and order in the Church' (p. 802). It is constantly summoning the Church back to its true being. 'Its concern can only be to make

clear what its position involves in face of the possible deviations of today' (p. 811). 'In face of possible aberrations it must show the threatened consequences' (p. 812).

(4) In this sense, dogmatics expresses the Church's vigilance as it is convinced by the Holy Spirit that its life and mission and influence depend exclusively on Christ's presence in it. Only the Word of God can make it a valid magnitude, not a conception of this Word, or an idea, but the personal message of the living God. 'It is the task of dogmatics to remind it that the Word of God is not the Word of God if it is not *viva vox*, a message that goes forth as directed by the Church. . . . The whole desire of the Word of God is for man. . . . The same Word of God is also the Reconciler of man, through whose decision his existence, plunged into sin and guilt, is either preserved by justification and sanctification, or not preserved. The same Word is also the Redeemer of men, through whose work the ruined existence of man is either restored to its former splendour. . . . The attitude of man required by this Word of God is faith. . . . But that he may believe the Word of God it must have come to him, he must have heard it, and therefore it must have been spoken to him. By himself he neither knows it . . . nor can say to himself what it has to say to him. . . . The Word is therefore precipitated into this human vacuum with all the weight of the divine will and power of fulfilment' (pp. 848f.). The most important thing for the Church is to proclaim this Word on which everything depends. The role of theology is to enable it to know the message which it must deliver and to prepare it for the task. Theology must not take the place of preaching, let alone of God. Its work is auxiliary. It looks, not to itself, but to revelation. This is why it must not enclose the truth in a system. Truth resides in Christ and not in dogmatic formulations. These can only point to Christ as reflection on his message. But how can they do this unless centred on him in the form of Christology? Theology must resist any attempt to deflect it from revelation. In this way it expresses the first and final concern of the Church, i.e., to listen to its Lord and to declare him. 'The best and most significant thing that is done in this matter is that again and again we are directed to look back to the centre and foundation of it all' (p. 868). Its starting-point is the revelation of the triune God received through the Holy Spirit in the Scriptures which lead us to the Son and the Father. 'It is quite evident that there can be no dogmatic system. . . . In dogmatics, laying the foundation means recollection

that the foundation is already laid and expectation that it will continually be laid' (p. 868).

Dogmatics is thus the centre of the battle for the fidelity and therefore the life of the Church. It expresses the Church's passionate attempt under the Spirit to receive the one thing necessary. It can start only with the event where this most precious thing is given. Of what avail are history, experience, science and moral consciousness compared with this extraordinary gift of God's love? These realities are of value only on the basis of this event. A conscientious Church can only lift up its hands to the Word to the exclusion of all else. Dogmatics does this for and with the community. It is of value only as it does. Otherwise it is superfluous and even harmful. Diverting the Church from essentials, it threatens its very life.[1]

(ix) The propositions just stated all derive from a common inspiration expressed in a new criterion which is probably the most characteristic of a consistent Evangelicalism. In its negative and positive form this fundamental insight is the main point of demarcation from other interpretations, revealing the essential divergencies. Even more than the preceding formulas, it is primarily an elementary and spontaneous act of faith and a discipline which must be elaborated in conformity with the spirit of the Reformation.

To bring out its decisive significance we must first formulate it as simply as possible. It is contentment with the grace of God alone. To lack this is to show that one has not really grasped the richness of revelation and what it has accomplished. As we may go on to say, faith is not truly evangelical unless it is constrained to put all its trust in the unique and perfect work which God has done for us in Jesus Christ, not looking for anything more or for any other prop, but looking to this alone in joyous thanksgiving, full liberty and total consecration. This raises the problem of natural theology.

Before discussing the above formulation, we may recall the main objectives of what is called natural theology. Barth has given a definition which brings us to the heart of the problem: 'Natural theology is the doctrine of a union of man with God existing outside God's revelation in Jesus Christ. It works out the knowledge of God that is possible and real on the basis of this independent union with

---

[1] We owe a supreme debt to men like the Reformers and Barth who have seen this and who have pursued their theological work accordingly. It is a mark of the blindness and prejudice of the Church that Barth can still be discussed in terms of Neo-Hegelianism, Existentialism, Existential Fundamentalism, etc.

God, and its consequences for the whole relationship of God, world and man' (*CD* II, 1, p. 168). This description prevents us from assimilating natural theology, as Schleiermacher did, to the wholly secular attempt of man to discover God and to reconstruct his person and work from the natural and general sources of knowledge at his disposal. This is too simple. In fact, natural theology can recognize and respect revelation in principle, merely seeking to complete it. On the basis of the idea that even in his present condition, and especially if he is religious, man has certain real, though inadequate capacities and resources, it combines what is revealed with ideas discovered along these other lines. It is not really interesting unless it is religious, i.e., unless it becomes Christian natural theology. But in this form it is also far more dangerous.

It is not surprising that outside the sphere of the Church unbelief, philosophy and mysticism should try to replace revelation by developing their own intuitions. The really acute problem in theology and Church life is that Christians themselves, who are summoned by God and brought face to face with the miraculous fulfilment of his love, should still feel the need of appealing to other courts. This is the final pretension summed up under the term natural theology. Natural theology deserves serious consideration only in its Christian form.

But what does it represent as such? It meets a number of concerns, all of which are highly suspect.

(1) First, it admits the possibility of an effective encounter with God apart from the incarnation. While God is supremely present in Christ, he is also present in religious and moral consciousness, in the evolution of humanity and in Church tradition represented by the teaching office. God was in Christ, but he is also in us in virtue of our divine likeness. Hence the incarnation is no longer a unique fact on which everything depends. It is extended in the Church and Christian experience, and is only a supreme form of man's general relationship to God.

(2) These human and religious values represent positive values in us. This is true in the sense that they are a kind of religious capital embracing man's aspirations and available to sustain and renew faith. It is also true in the sense that they enable us to find in ourselves certain truths concerning God and salvation which may have their source in revelation but which are now our property and the criterion of participation in grace.

E*

(3) These inner riches ensure the continuity of faith, enabling believers and the Church to live, not merely by new acts of grace or the Word of God, but by an inner state of grace which is an essential aspect of the religious deposit committed to us. On this view, the Christian is not constantly dependent on grace. He desires it ardently, and knows that he needs it, but, if he has to wait, he has accumulated treasures of faith by which to live.

(4) This conception radically changes the view of the Christian and his attitude. If there is this deposit, he can approach the Gospel confidently. He is no longer a suppliant, a needy sinner, a penitent publican. His faith and his knowledge of God are lasting values which are not to be compared with transitory manna. His religion has solidity. What he has already received is even a criterion by which to assess the credibility and efficacy of new interventions.

(5) In this case, the main objective of the Church and its cultus is to maintain its inward fulness by suitable nourishment. Various means will be used at various times and places, e.g., religious discourse, which passes on the profound insights of the specialist in mediation; the sacraments, which act directly on the emotions and produce inward elevation by bathing the believer in a sacred and kindly mystery; prayer as the exultant rapture of a community wholly dedicated to the contemplation of spiritual things; devotion; friendship; above all mutual love, which can strengthen these riches that are hard to express externally but can still convey enthusiasm and peace.

(6) The sacred is to be found in us as well as Jesus. There are two classes of men, those who cultivate religious sentiments and those who, in violent or calm aberration, deprive themselves of these inner riches. The latter see in them only the survival of primitive superstitions or the development of a psychism in which the affective element is dangerously predominant over the rational and volitional. Scientific progress has helped to discredit this sentimental and emotional mythology. Such attacks have been regarded by believers as blasphemies which do violence not merely to God but above all to man. Attempts have been made to show that religion belongs to a perfect humanity, together with the arts and moral sciences.

These are some of the implications of natural theology. It does not seek merely to postulate a knowledge of God apart from revelation, though in accordance with it. It presupposes all kinds of truths concerning God, man, the world and the Church. Its main result is to change the centre of gravity of the Christian message. This no longer lies exclusively in Christ, in his living, written and preached Word, so that we have to turn away from ourselves to him. It lies both in him and in us. The believer's attention is claimed by Jesus, but also by the Church and by inner experiences, which constitute a sacred sphere within the secular world. Religion is a virtue. To develop it, we must not merely look to Jesus, which would be too intellectualistic. We must also look in upon ourselves, combining all the sources of authentic spirituality. To be Christian and religious means to concentrate on oneself in order to make contact with one's better self and to come under the benign influence of the spirituality of Jesus shining out in Scripture, in the works of the great mystics, and in great personalities through whom God imparts to us his divine influence.[1]

Rejecting natural theology, Evangelical theology attacks this great edifice. It sees its religious and mystical grandeur. It appreciates its deep piety. It finds no pleasure in destroying it. But it must raze it to the foundations to safeguard the full sufficiency of the work of Christ, the Way, the Truth and the Life, wherein our own faith and worship and obedience are already contained and achieved.[2]

But on what grounds can Evangelical theology justify its rejection of natural theology? In reply to the six characteristics of the latter, the following points may be made.

(1) Faith is not a free choice. It is always a victory of grace over our opposition. This is good, for where would be our assurance if faith depended on us? It is sure only as it is grounded solely in the goodness and triumphant faithfulness of God.

(2) Christian knowledge, far from being a discovery of our own, is obedience to the divine summons. It is recognition of the sufficiency of God's work—the love which is aroused in us by the fact that God gives us all things. It is the faith which receives this finished work. It is preceded only by its accomplishment in Christ, in which the Holy Spirit enables us to participate.

(3) There is no analogy allowing us to rise up from man to God. Our likeness is attested and revealed only in the God-man. To try to find any other link is a sign of ingratitude and egocentricity, i.e., of

---

[1] For why should the divine influence be restricted to Scripture? (Cf. Lemaître, *Foi et vérité*, p. 45.)

[2] At root, Liberal Protestantism is simply natural theology. It involves not merely deviation from Scripture, the fathers and the Reformation, but resistance to grace. At this ultimate level, it joins forces with Roman Catholicism.

the supreme sin which imprisons us in ourselves instead of bringing us to God to find our fulness in him as he has ordained for our good. The tenacity of natural theology is simply that of our sin. This is why we do not exaggerate in blaming it for all the evils in the Church during the course of its long history.

(4) Faith demands that we turn from ourselves to live only in Christ. It takes seriously his resurrection in spite of all our doubts, aspirations and experiences. It is life in him. Why should theology deflect us even slightly from this one point of reference to peripheral concerns? Is not the temptation to turn from him strong enough already without theology confirming and amplifying it?

(5) In view of the many combinations of natural theology, Christian preaching should not try to fight it. It can assume its defeat already in Christ's death, and proclaim the victory of God. Only the Gospel can effectively overcome it, and it has already done so in its promises and achievements. Only a rigorously christological theology can reveal its failings and render it innocuous. Against it, the only remedy is declaration of the Gospel, of Christ's person, of life in him, in a word, of the good news.

(x) A final observation may be added to this review of the constant elements in an Evangelical theology. It is often said that the main difference between a supposedly modern theology and traditional perspectives is in respect of the doctrine of man. Those who champion the former take a more comprehensive view of man. They are more aware of his weaknesses, closer to him, and more optimistic and charitable. Those who cling to classical orthodoxy are dangerously pessimistic and seem to take pleasure in depreciating man and crushing him. What truth is there in this?

(1) Appearances seem to confirm it. Reformation doctrine usually begins with a severe analysis of man's impotence. Barth has established with pitiless lucidity man's incapacity to know God and to co-operate in the achievement of his own salvation.

(2) Yet is this the whole truth? Have we not to show that in the Reformers the doctrine of sin is only a corollary of that of grace, a commentary on the work of grace and therefore on the love of God manifested in Jesus Christ? If God had to accomplish man's salvation, then man could not do so. It is the miracle of divine intervention that reveals man's impotence to solve his own problem. But if so, then we surely err if we emphasize the negative implication at the expense of the positive witness to God's all-sufficient mercy. In

context, the judgment on man is only a deduction from the fulness of the divine work.

(3) This throws a new light on the derogatory judgments. For if God has done everything, why continue to make further demands on man? He has only to receive as God enables him. Why require of him what God has chosen to give freely? Is the victory of Easter incomplete or insufficient? What God has done for us and in our place, can we do in his?

(4) Man's impotence is simply an implicate of God's triumphant omnipotence. To confess it is part of the knowledge of faith. It derives from an act of faith in the full sufficiency of the divine decision. Since God has judged it necessary to intervene, submitting himself in his Son to the curse which overwhelms us, even to the death of the cross, do we not deceive man if we let him think he can escape his situation by some other means? Do we not turn him from the one remedy chosen and administered by God, and thus leave him to his plight? Pretending to spare him by hiding the gravity of his position, do we not rob him of the only possible solution, and leave him to his illusions?

(5) In any case, what do we mean by optimism and pessimism? If we look on the bright side, are we not concealing the remedy so as not to hurt the patient, and thus abandoning him to his malady? Are we truly optimistic if we look to man instead of looking to God? On the other hand, are we looking on the dark side if we take God's love so seriously and welcome it with such gratitude that we expect no more from man but everything from God and his grace? The terms surely stand in need of radical reinterpretation. True optimism is to take God at his word and joyfully to declare his benefits. True pessimism is to doubt this miraculous achievement and to leave man to his illusory capacities, his attempts and his failures.

(6) When he gave himself to us, entering our situation and giving us life by the death of his Son, did not God know how to meet our needs? Is it possible to come closer to man than Christ did in his incarnation and crucifixion? Do we really show compassion on man by respecting him in his faults instead of fighting them to restore him to his right mind? If charity demands that we spare him by excusing his defects, how can it help him? Do we serve man by plunging him into self-deception, and demanding that in spite of repeated failures he should strive towards a goal which he can never reach? Is not this to take him more seriously in his sin than in his

resurrection, the supreme form of unbelief? Does not true charity require that we show him at once the only solution? The common use of terms like charity reveals a facile but dangerous demagogy.

(7) If man is impotent and basically corrupt, does this mean that he can never regain his true condition as a free and good creature? Is not the very question foolish? Is God no less impotent than his rebellious creature? Is his work ineffective? If he intervened, was it not to win back his children? Did he pursue a purely individual and egotistic goal? Was it not to save man from his crushing enemies that Jesus died and rose again? This history of God's love has a double aspect, being far more than a mere spiritual conception. It is the shining forth of the divine perfection and it is also man's greatest possible benefit. An accomplishment of deity, it also achieves the elevation of the creature. It brings back to man his lost freedom, his violated righteousness, his forfeited holiness. It restores to him his humanity. There is no more effective means to raise man to perfection than this death in which all that ruins him is destroyed and this resurrection in which life triumphs over nothingness. What more is to be desired than reconciliation to God? Does not this restoration re-establish man in all his privileges? The very idea that a faith which contemplates only the work of Christ should neglect the effect of this victory in man is absurd, for the whole point of the work is the rehabilitation of man.[1]

(8) Nothing is more false, therefore, than to deny man's co-operation, his liberty, his full humanity, not as his own conquest, but as a reality contained in the resurrection of Jesus Christ and offered to us by the Holy Spirit. Man cannot protect himself, but God defends him with sovereign power. He gives him life, and makes him capable and responsible. He does not crush him; he sets him free, so that in submission to his Lord he is truly responsible and active, not merely in soul, but in body. Grace humanizes him. To begin with God's work is to ascribe to him the new things which God gives, to see him passing from death to life, from sin to freedom, from revolt to righteousness. A doctrine of man based on Christ's resurrection can only exalt man in a dependence which makes him truly autonomous and under a direction which gives him mastery. He becomes a 'fellow-labourer with God' by the Holy Spirit, and is engaged in

---

[1] It is true that orthodoxy has sometimes missed the full implication of the resurrection, and thus opened the way for the dangerous reactions of a false humanism. Yet the true Gospel message includes man's exaltation, as finely brought out by Barth in *CD* IV, 2.

glorious enterprises. Far from being negative and gloomy, a true theology of grace is a theology, if not of the glory which we have not yet attained, at least of liberty, joy and hope, which looks forward to the time when at his return Jesus Christ will reveal and confirm the definitive restoration of man already secured in his incarnation. A true commentary on revelation will be wholly positive even in its assessment of man, which is only a necessary protection of his true rehabilitation, effectively attained in God's intervention and in his victory over all destructive forces.

We have now established clearly the starting-point of such a theology. It is to be found in the 'divine object' which is 'the foundation of the human subject' (CD I, 2, p. 849), i.e., in the movement in which God reveals himself, gives himself and triumphs in Jesus Christ, who alone has sovereign authority. No other court can be associated with him or substituted for him. If this authority does not reign alone, grace is not grace. 'The Word of God may not be replaced even vicariously by any basic interpretation of the "essence of Christianity", however pregnant, deep and well founded. The simple reason for this is that while its content is indeed the truth, it is the truth of the reality of the work of God taking place within it. As such it is not to be condensed and summarized in any view, or idea, or principle. It can only be reported concretely, i.e., in relation to what is at any given time the most recent stage of the process or action or sovereign act of which it is the occurrence' (p. 862). This theology of free grace sets aside from the very outset any human support apart from the humanity of the Son of God, the only encounter between heaven and earth, which contains all others within itself. On man's side there can be only concentration upon this event, the only possible assurance. This is why 'in dogmatics . . . traditional notions as to what is fundamental or not, central or peripheral, more or less important, have to be suspended, so that they can become a matter for vital new decision by the Word of God itself' (p. 865). In other words, the starting-point is not to have one, so that God himself may fill this role. For 'the position usually occupied by an arbitrarily chosen basic view belongs by right to the Word of God, and to the Word of God alone' (p. 866). This declaration is the golden rule, the disciplinary principle and the leading and decisive feature of any theology which claims to be Evangelical and therefore ecumenical.[1]

---

[1] Cf. also CD I, 2, pp. 824ff.

Conclusion

This attempt to note the main trends in the current theological situation has shown us three positions which may all be understood in the light of their starting-points. In spite of serious differences, the first two are based on an analogous insight. This is the strange result, paradoxical more in appearance than in reality, which we have reached. The real points of divergence in the three positions are not to be found where they have usually been sought.

Roman Catholicism is unacceptable to modern Protestantism because of the primacy of the pope, the authority of the hierarchy, the mass, tradition, the sacraments, Mariology, and dogmatism. Protestantism is rejected by modern Roman Catholicism because the latter is convinced of the sole legitimacy of Rome on the grounds of its age, power and miracles, and because it deplores the disorders of Protestantism, its doctrinal inconsistencies, sects, right of free investigation, aridity, etc.

Neither can contest the fact, however, that their religious conceptions finally rest on the common ground of a prior alliance between God and man and a twofold starting-point which can allow emphasis either on the humanistic or the ecclesiastical side without any modification of fundamental principle. Once God's authority is not given sole place, deviations are inevitable and yet they may all be reduced to a single common denominator.

This is why an eminent theologian like J. A. Moehler, the father of modern Roman Catholicism in Germany, can easily achieve a synthesis between Idealism and Pietism on the one side and official Roman Catholic doctrine on the other, thus preparing the ground for the conclusions of the Vatican Council. Similarly, Neo-Protestantism, which must respond to human aspiration, finds no difficulty in combining with Roman ecclesiology and sacerdotalism when the need in a troubled age is more mystical and traditionalist. Neo-Protestantism can never be too imperious, since it does not seek unity in the truth which it confesses but in the feelings which it experiences.

Only a true submission to Scripture can bring a new element into this confused situation in which brothers confront one another as enemies on secondary points without examining the deeper issues and therefore breaking the common framework of their distinctive definitions.

The common context is given by the fact that both Neo-Protestantism and Roman Catholicism accept a natural authority alongside revelation. The acceptance itself is more significant than the actual choice of the associated element or the form of its co-operation with grace. The identity between the two systems is to be found in the pre-existent association. God and man are already supposed to be united alongside or even apart from Jesus Christ. There is an obvious dualism, and the resultant theology is at every point one of 'both . . . and', as it has been called. In reality, the only point where this is legitimate, because there is genuine encounter between God and man, is in Jesus Christ, who is *both* very God *and* very man.

The Evangelical reaction is clear-cut. It rejects all additions and confesses the sole lordship of Jesus. In opposition to its own failings, it thus brings the new factor of the Gospel itself into debates previously dominated either by man's own concerns and aspirations or the preoccupation and pretension of the Church.

In this respect, then, Neo-Protestantism is a new form of mediaeval Catholicism. In less orderly fashion, but with greater spontaneity and in a different context—Hegel taking the place of Aristotle—it takes up again the essential principles against which the Reformation protested in the name of the Gospel. Our eighteenth- and nineteenth-century predecessors were quite right to claim that they were effecting a new reformation. Our present task is to choose which of the two reformations we are to follow as loyal successors and heirs.

The divisions of the Church are real even where they seem to be chastely covered by an appearance of tranquillity. They should move us primarily to repentance and humility. Then we can take up the more tenaciously the search for truth. For the different conceptions expounded in the foregoing chapters concern all of us. They are so many voices speaking loudly and clearly, not outside us in movements which we may easily condemn, but in our own hearts. Heresy is first found within ourselves. For this reason the main goal of the present examination is not to cite certain classical doctrines before some tribunal but to attempt a clarification of our own witness. The concern impelling us to the task corresponds to a precise need to know the influences which have made us what we are in the hope of grasping more clearly the requirements of fidelity. In this vital work theological relativism, which is the fashion in many quarters, can give us little help. In face of each difficulty it seeks escape in sentimentality and can never provide any solution. But God seems to be tackling with new vigour his divided Church, challenging its traditional preferences, customs and dispositions. This is our hope.

For why should we be surprised if the Church succumbs to the many temptations which threaten it? Even as a believer, can man do other than resist or pervert the Word of God? Does not history give us a sorry picture of this perpetual alienation? Nevertheless, the faithfulness of the Lord is stronger than our opposition. For this reason, taking his grace more seriously than our defection, Calvin describes the history of the Church, not as a series of failures, but as a 'story of many resurrections'.[1] And having quoted Calvin, Visser't Hooft adds a little later: 'We need not become obsessed with the human, all too human, side of the story. For the Holy Spirit works mightily to save the churches from this self-inflicted imprisonment, and breaks through the hardened institutionalized forms' (p. 111). The Lord himself comes, and therefore we should look to him and not to ourselves. The truth is not the preserve of any one party. It is Christ living and already triumphant, making all things new. By what other assurance can we live?

[1] W. A. Visser't Hooft, *The Renewal of the Church*, 1956, pp. 68f.

PART TWO

Christology
or
The Centre of Faith

INTRODUCTION

SHALL WE find again at the heart of Christian witness the differences which we have observed in respect of the starting-point? Thus far we have analysed a number of attitudes taken in face of the event of revelation. When we turn to Christology, shall we find similar divergences, or shall we discover that the attraction of the person and work of Jesus Christ, which is in principle the final criterion of faith for all Christians, is adequate to reduce every difference? This is our theme in this second part.

It may be noted that in approaching this new topic, the most classical theme of all, we are in the same area as before, since the act of revelation is identical with the person and work of Christ. We are thus considering another aspect of the same truth, not this time its origin, but its fulfilment and true content.

To bring out the essential points, we shall present the subject, in constant confrontation, in three chapters dealing successively with the postulates which underlie the various christological systems, with the person and work of Christ in his humiliation and exaltation, and with the implications of his life and action for us.

Slight misunderstandings which seem to have been occasioned by the tone of the first part make it necessary for us to repeat that this enquiry is not undertaken with any polemical intention. Our concern is to try to see where we stand. Can the Protestantism practised among us today claim to be in the true Reformation succession? Do we not have to put the same question which our fathers put to the mediaeval church: 'In your teaching and practices, are you truly faithful to your origins?' As regards Roman Catholicism, more and more voices are heard contesting its current interpretation. The situation is fluid, and the various movements hold out great promise for the future. We are faced by many forms of both Protestantism and Roman Catholicism, and the various truths and errors seem to converge in spite of confessional barriers. Our study should help us to discern a possible meeting-place and stir us to make the necessary renunciations and to stride in this direction with renewed energy.

4

Christological Presuppositions

In CHRISTOLOGY as elsewhere the disagreements go much deeper than the dogmatic formulations. The ultimate decisions are explicable in terms of a series of prior conditions and attitudes which are often hidden, either because the author is not concerned to disclose them or because he is not himself fully aware of them. It is in these depths that we are to seek the real causes of divergence. These underlying factors may be described as the presuppositions or impulses, and we shall now try to bring them to light before turning to the doctrines themselves.

1. *The Impulses of Neo-Protestant Christology*

Modern Protestantism, as we have seen, has deliberately established itself in the domain of religious or moral consciousness, of experience and history. We must now try to see the bearing of these postulates on the essential realities of reconciliation, expiation and justification, i.e., on the person and work of Jesus Christ.

Although vast and variegated, Neo-Protestantism may be reduced, the more deeply one studies it, to certain constant principles on which each theologian has constructed his edifice, emphasizing certain features but not modifying the commonly accepted foundation. To know the orientation of the movement as a whole it is thus necessary merely to concentrate on its most prominent insights. Schleiermacher supplied the main inspiration and he is still the master, so it is to him that we must turn in the first instance. The thought of Kant is already known to us; we shall consult him only in passing. More recently, Ritschl devoted three whole volumes to the subject.[1] His theology, however, is simply an illustration of the main perspectives of his great predecessors, and these are equally

---

[1] *Die christliche Lehre von der Rechtfertigung und Versöhnung*, 1870–4.

represented by a great French theologian of the period, Auguste Sabatier, who will introduce us into this whole sphere. Finally, among the French Swiss, we need not go into details, since our concern is to fix an attitude rather than to sketch a history of Christology. Frommel is certainly very explicit on these various points with his personalist theories of Jesus and his solidarity theories of expiation. For preference, however, we go to the most recent of the Swiss writers to express himself on this theme, namely, A. Lemaître, and we shall try to analyse the conditions which have given rise to his Christology.

(i) Faithful to the subjective spirit of his dogmatics (*The Christian Faith*, §83), Schleiermacher gave to his Christology the significant title 'Development of the Religious Consciousness as determined by Redemption', and he devoted the second part of his *Glaubenslehre* to it. The subjective sphere in which he sets himself is constantly redefined. He sets aside everything objective to enclose himself in the subjective sphere (§75). What does he mean by the terms objective and subjective? The former denotes the domain of metaphysics and speculation, the latter that of consciousness, experience and the soul. We are to take as a foundation the impression which we receive of Christ (§98). Hence we are not to begin with hypotheses on the decrees made by God, nor with the teachings which the Bible is supposed to give us on these initiatory divine acts. What matters is the impression made on us by these external realities. We begin with the effect and work back to the cause. We begin with the incontestable fact of the impression produced by holiness, and then go on to seek its origin (§88). Now the effect which is the starting-point and norm of religious thought is experience. We rest primarily on the territory of experience and it is to this that we must confine ourselves (§94). The *a priori* is not our domain. Consulting the Christian consciousness, we have shown that its needs are met when it knows that it is united with Jesus Christ as previously described (§100).

This criterion is certainly new. Truth is not as God reveals it in the witness of the prophets and apostles made alive by the Holy Spirit, but as we ourselves experience it. At a first glance, one might think that these two perspectives are complementary and that they finally merge, since the divine action must be known to attain its end. The difference, however, is in the choice of ultimate norm. Where does the decision come from?—from an authority which is external and which instructs us, or from our own feelings and needs? Schleiermacher contends for the second alternative, not because he underestimates the divine influence—he constantly accepts it—but because its authority depends on our awareness of it and therefore on the approval that we can give it. At the heart of every association lies a moral force which imposes its precepts, namely, the consciousness (§83). This is not autonomous; it lives in the association with God. Nevertheless, it is this consciousness which imposes its laws. Produced by an external influence, it thus becomes the criterion of authenticity. If it were simply a direct product of the revelation in Christ, the work of the Holy Spirit, the danger in these proposals would be less. But while it is this, it is also a human reality which remains valid in man after the fall, which is regarded as an effect of the general revelation of God and which is concretely independent of God's full self-communication in Christ. The consciousness is God's voice to all men. It persists in the depths of our being. It is a primitive revelation attested by experience (§83). It is a part of our being, a spontaneous intuition which without proof is attributed to God and associated with his special revelation. This allows the author to build on it no less and perhaps more than on Scripture in determining the role of Christ in the faith. It might be asked whether it is not necessary for a full conception of God to investigate the divine decrees. Since these are never immediate expressions of the consciousness, this question does not even arise for us. Moreover, if we do not enter the domain of speculation but intentionally describe redemption as it takes place in our soul, we shall come across the content of the divine decrees by another route (§90). In this section we can see the process fully developed. The work of redemption is not defined in terms of what God decides and ordains. To do this would plunge us into metaphysics and speculation.

From heaven we come back to earth. Making this movement in the sphere of religion, Schleiermacher is a man of his age. He nowhere disguises the fact that the secret of his whole theological enterprise is to be found in this change in starting-point. Nevertheless, he tries to follow a middle path. If he rejects speculation, he does not intend to build on a secular humanism which substitutes for the Word of God pure reason, current moralism or natural theology. He is still religious, and he must therefore rest on an element which is certainly subjective but not secular. It is for this reason that in preference to

Kant's categorical imperative he turns to the sense of dependence on God and to the consciousness which is religious and even Christian in so far as it is linked with Christ. He repeatedly emphasizes that everything comes from Christ, from his influence, though this does not alter the fact that the source on which he really draws is rather the effect or impression which this work produces in us, namely, the direct expressions of consciousness, religion as it flourishes spontaneously in us. His originality resides precisely in the adoption of this starting-point which is subjective and yet religious. Scholasticism, as he saw it, complicated the problem by not separating faith from speculation but intermingling the two in a singularly adventurous manner. The result was that in his day some rejected the heritage of tradition to adopt a starting-point prior to the actual rise of the questions, while others accepted everything hallowed by tradition. This led to inevitable oscillation between the two extremes. Instead, Schleiermacher sought his criterion in the Christian consciousness (§95).[1]

Furthermore, there supervenes at this point a third element which is equally subjective, namely, the collective element, or the Church. The consciousness does not judge in isolation. It is integrated into a religious society, so that the individual, far from resting on purely personal intuitions, takes into account the impressions of the religious community to which he belongs. We, too, can have the experience of the first Christians. We, too, can be brought to salvation. The only difference is that the influence of the person of the Saviour is now replaced by that of the religious society, and this influence is hardly equal to that of the perfection of Christ (§88). Thus Christ acts through the Church to influence individuals. At this point, Schleiermacher has been accused of approximating to Roman Catholicism. He himself resisted the accusation, but it is difficult to ignore the rapprochement.

This, then, is the subjective mode of reflection adopted by the father of Neo-Protestantism. Dogmas are simply the expression of the Christian consciousness or of the inner experience of Christians (§64). The term 'Christian consciousness' accurately describes the principle of this theology. Dogmas and precepts have value only in so far as they are related to Jesus Christ (§93). Knowledge is the product of this association in which it is difficult to distinguish what

---

[1] Cf. §83, where the holiness of God is discussed in terms of this consciousness rather than the Word of God.

comes from the primitive revelation in the consciousness, i.e., from the inner depths of our own being, and what comes from Jesus Christ, the more so as the influence of the latter is not very clearly defined. What is at issue is not so much a doctrine, word or message which God himself quickens by his Spirit, but a vague inspiration, a diffuse persuasion, which certainly comes through the Bible, but also through the religious society, through its spiritual atmosphere and through the emotions of its members. There is confusion between the two influences, between that from above and that from below. Everywhere there is posited on the one hand the activity of God which commences in a supernatural manner and on the other the receptivity of man which continues in a natural manner (§88).

The dogmatics of Schleiermacher focuses and displays that which man in community may experience when placed in the sphere of full accord between his innermost being and God. If anyone refuses to recognize *a priori* the essential difference between the scriptural method which places authority in the witness of the Bible and the method of experience as thus defined, we invite him to compare the results of the two processes. Does the consciousness really speak in the same way as Scripture? On this point the following brief observations may be made.

1. What primarily interests the Berlin theologian is not the fact that God has overcome the distance separating us from him in order to be with us, to triumph over our revolt and to reconcile us to himself; it is that in Jesus Christ we have the image of perfect man. The accent is not on the intervention of God, on his Word; it is on the natural achievement produced in this ideal person. Jesus is the perfect realization of the perfect ideal (§94). In him our nature has reached perfection, as Schleiermacher repeats again and again. Christ is the second Adam. He may legitimately be considered as the human consciousness of God in its perfect form, as the final stage of the development of a principle embedded in our nature (§89). The essential point is not the movement by which God manifests himself to us in Jesus, but the contrary movement by which the creature fulfils itself in him (§92). Here again the perspective is clearly subjective, i.e., humanist. The achievement of humanity is the main point. Jesus has realized the true idea of man (§92). He has revealed the perfect ideal of humanity and perfectly realized it (§93). In what consists this perfection of the human, this ideal? It consists in a man who has full consciousness of God. Without God, man is

not himself. To attain to his true stature, he must go through a long process of development until he reaches this perfect association with God. But this is the man presented to us. He is man in full truth because he is the living manifestation of the consciousness of God in all its purity (§93). He expresses the full reality of the species. This being the case, one may discern in him a divine and human unity, since such a conjunction belongs to the essential nature of perfect man. From this angle, it is possible to adopt the traditional affirmations concerning the divinity of Christ. These imply that the consciousness of God in all its sanctity dominated exclusively every moment of the career of Christ, or that God indwelt him and constituted his true being (§94). Intrinsically this is nothing out of the ordinary. It is proper to the true nature of man to be in this full relation to God. Nevertheless, it is a miracle (§95) to the degree that actual man is excluded from this fulness by sin. What ought to be, but is not achieved in any of us, is effectively produced in Christ; hence his significance. He is the ideal of man because he lives in total unity with his Father. Jesus demonstrates in his person the consciousness of God or the immanence of God (§94). He is an exceptional being because he possesses the consciousness of God in an absolute manner. In other words, he possesses the immanent being of God. Yet this is not achieved at a single stroke. It is for this reason that we should not speak of his pre-existence. In fact, this consciousness had to go through a development such as takes place in us. It has to be shown that the nature of the Saviour has undergone a development analogous to ours, that, in particular, inferior functions were manifested in him prior to superior, though without communicating to him the legacy of sin (*ibid.*).

The well-known definitions of Secrétan and Bouvier which seek the divinity of Christ in the perfection of his humanity are fully in the spirit of the master. As Schleiermacher saw it, the nature which we see in Jesus Christ is our own. We maintain that he had it in the most perfect sense (*ibid.*). It may be readily perceived that the classical formulations, especially that of Chalcedon, no longer fit this perspective. Strictly speaking, there are not two natures. There is perfect unity, almost natural or at least quite normal. For it is proper to humanity to reattach itself to divinity, to carry within it, in the consciousness, the immanence of God. Why should we distinguish and separate when the association is so logical and appropriate? The Word is God under the form of the consciousness, and the flesh denotes the material envelope (§96). If we are prepared to accept this new orientation, we may adopt the ancient statements that 'God was in Christ' and that 'the Word was made flesh'. All that is needed is to translate them into a suitable form, namely, that the consciousness of Jesus reached such a stage of development that it was God in him, the divine element forming the principle from which existence derived and the human the organism which contained it (*ibid.*). The two elements thus combine without difficulty, though the term nature, quite apart from the serious rational difficulties which it involves, is not adequate to describe this new association (*ibid.*). In fact, the two elements are so closely conjoined that it is futile and misplaced to try to draw between them limits and subtle distinctions like those of Chalcedon. The adverbs used by the fathers simply destroy the unity of this person (§97). In Jesus everything is perfectly united, not by confusion, but by spontaneous association. Everything proclaims the man, demonstrating the unity which subsists in the series of instants of which each is motivated by that which precedes and each motivates that which follows; and yet everything declares and presupposes God, without whom nothing can be explained (*ibid.*).

In accordance with the subjective spirit of his dogmatics, Schleiermacher has thus overthrown the traditional perspective, adopting a new point of departure. We can no longer begin with the personal incarnation of God in Christ, claiming that God is present himself in this man even though he remains a true man, and trying to understand this encounter as best we can. The theologian has now discovered a better foundation in the formula which he prefers, namely, that the creation of man is accomplished in Jesus Christ (*ibid.*). In other words, we must begin with man—and not with the work of God—to discover that his nature is fulfilled quite naturally in the full consciousness of God which is his divinity. We do not begin with the deity of Christ, for this would be to suspend the dogma of Jesus Christ on the dogma of the second person of the Trinity, which would be quite illogical (*ibid.*). We begin with the man who is supposed to have attained to such a fulness that in fact God is in him, in his consciousness. On this perspective the miraculous birth has only a very attenuated sense, since the transition from the human to the divine is made without the slightest difficulty (*ibid.*).

2. This approach to Christology is the result of a conception of man and his situation and capacities which is perhaps the most pro-

found and decisive presupposition of the author of the *Christliche Glaube*. Both his subjectivism and his theory of experience, his method and dogmatic results, derive in fact from a general anthropology which dominates his whole theology.[1]

Now in the *Christliche Glaube* the conception of man is plainly optimistic. Sin is whatever hampers the free development of our consciousness of God (§66). Strictly speaking it is not revolt against God. It is an obstacle to man's Godward development. It is both original and actual, but in neither case does it destroy man's original perfection. Sin as analysed by Schleiermacher is a derangement or disorder, but it does not overthrow the original perfection. It gives a feeling of uneasiness due to our being out of order (§68). The consciousness of God within humanity is capable of continuous development from its first beginnings to its perfect form. Sin is simply an accident which disturbs the normal course of existence. The quality of Redeemer is to be perceived in him who possesses and can give to us the spiritual life in all its purity (*ibid.*). Schleiermacher's concern is not at all with a righteous God who condemns sin and yet who saves us by accepting the debt in our place. He does not take up his position here. Instead, he turns first to man rather than to God. He allows the imperfection of our sense of God, the poverty of our spiritual life, the primitive state of our humanity. He seeks a means to overcome this. Comparing the fulness of Jesus Christ with our inadequacy, he desires a way from the one to the other. Redemption is this transition from the minus to the plus. The goal of the religious life is the development of the consciousness of God (§62). Now this development will come about by the communication of a new life which in the true sense constitutes redemption. Jesus Christ possesses perfect sanctity. Imparting it to man, he commences the new life and effects redemption (§88). Thus man attains to a state of soul in which his being is associated with God (§13). The Saviour possessed consciousness of God. Living, he poured out his life. To introduce believers into this atmosphere, and to saturate them in it, is redemption in the true and proper sense (§100).

We shall return to the methods used to attain this end. For the moment our task is to show that man is capable of this ascension

---

[1] Methodologically, a striking parallel may be found in Calvin's *Institutes*, II, where it is argued with a slightly apologetic intention that redemption must take the form that it does because of the total corruption of man.

because his nature is good and sin has led only to diminution. To be sure, he cannot do it alone. He needs the influence of Jesus. But he has the power to receive this external influence and to co-operate with it in self-elevation. While the incapacity of man is affirmed, we must not deny his capacity to receive the work of the Redeemer. This is the minimum of original perfection which must be maintained. If we take it away, we take from man his human nature. Even if this were possible, what would then become of faith in redemption? (§70). This question is surely a very strange one. Is it not written somewhere that what is impossible with man is possible with God? But this divine possibility is the miracle of the Holy Spirit. Here faith is posited as a capacity of human nature. If this is so, it is evident that redemption cannot have its classical form. It is no longer the creation of God; it is an adherence of man. Schleiermacher goes on to clarify his position in the same section. If I cannot appropriate it, he maintains, it has no intimate effect on me—as though the efficacy of God's work depended on my capacity to receive it—and sanctification becomes no more than a *flatus vocis* which can be preserved only if we suppose that God gives us powers so new that he creates us a second time (*ibid.*). The newness of the Gospel, though often displayed, is not such that it can convince us of the total impotence of man. Later on we shall see that sanctification is supremely the work of man acting under the influence of Jesus, his true ideal.

Man has thus a big part to play on this view. He has the ability to unite himself to God. Though human nature cannot produce the divine from within itself, nor even attract it, it does have the gift of uniting itself with it, and the race has maintained this gift even though subject to sin (§97). A little lower down he describes the manner of this co-operation rather more precisely. The word by which Jesus addresses himself to man cannot penetrate without the help of man which is dependent on his freedom. This is an ability which we should neither suppress nor exaggerate (§108). There is no strict collaboration, but man offers no further resistance. This is the mode of our being in the presence of Christ (*ibid.*). We have a desire for communion with God awakened by impulsion from above. In these circumstances the significance of election, for example, or of grace, is obviously dimmed. In fact man must be both passive before God, i.e., receptive, and also active, i.e., co-operative. It can all be stated as follows. God, immanent in Christ, transmits the activity.

Humanity receives and continues it. Passivity has thus to be transformed into activity to become personal (§97). Perhaps one ought not to apply concepts adapted to other forms of thought, but it is difficult in this connection not to translate into the language of semi-Pelagianism, synergism or optimism. The power of sin is diminished, the power of man accentuated; the part of God is depreciated and that of man exalted, notwithstanding all the care which the author takes to safeguard the divine pre-eminence.

3. The divine mode of action is hard to define in this framework. The author does not indicate it plainly, and this is only logical since his interest is in the impression which it makes rather than in the cause of this experience. Naturally, the latter is not ignored, but it cannot be the object of theological enquiry if this is careful to avoid the realm of speculation. In any case, the terms used to denote it are themselves sufficiently revealing. The reference is to an influence, an impulsion, a transmission, a communication, not in the sense of a creative word, an instruction, a true act, but rather of an inspiration, or, as one might almost say, an osmosis. This influence produces strict impressions, the development of the sense of God, of consciousness, a climate or atmosphere, a kind of elevation. The task of preaching is to stimulate the inner life by communicating new resources to ensure the blossoming of piety.

One can hardly explain this form of action except by approximating to that which Roman Catholic doctrine attributes to Christ through the sacraments. 'Christ our Redeemer,' writes Bartmann, 'as the Mystical Head causes the gracious forces of supernatural life to flow unceasingly in the members of his body.'[1] The transmission of life is described in terms of flowing. This approximation is not arbitrary. It is in fact inevitable. For once we abandon the fact that God communicates himself through the Word which instructs and creates at one and the same time, and prefer the thought of a mystical influence, we are within the framework of both Roman sacramentalism and Neo-Protestant spiritualizing. The Saviour dispenses life (§100). He introduces a principle of fecundity into humanity (*ibid.*). This takes place through the discourse which is designed to stir the emotions, but also through music or any elements which can create the sweet ambience of piety, as may be seen in *Christmas Eve*. We thus arrive at a definition of redemption which honours this perspective. Deriving its life from that of Jesus,

[1] *Précis de théologie dogmatique*, 1944, Vol. 2, p. 229.

humanity is impregnated, first by an activity which is inspired by the consciousness of God and which is perfectly adapted in every circumstance to every object, and then by the peace which, emanating from the same source, is proof against every trial. When an individual reforms himself in this setting, does he not continue the phenomenon revealed in the person of the Saviour? Does he not seek the furtherance of the power which, to the degree that it is enlarged, diminishes the power of sin? Does he not recover the original destiny of man? Does he not accomplish the whole task of which he is capable? (§101). Thus the human person blossoms and elevates itself under the mystical influence of filial consciousness. Elsewhere it is said that men are attracted to Jesus and come to awareness of their sin through the sympathy which he shows them (§104). It is this sympathy which constitutes vicarious satisfaction. When you consider the passion of the Saviour, you see that he bore it in our place (*vicarius*), for he sympathized even with the sin of those who do not feel any of its anguish, and he was afflicted by evils which are not to be regarded as such by a soul which is truly saintly (*ibid.*).

To exert this influence on man through the consciousness of Jesus, God has no need that an objective event should take place in Christ and change his relationships with the creature. The passion of Jesus is only a secondary element in redemption. It is a sign of his perfect devotion. It has no expiatory value in itself. In fact, the reconciliation does not take place in him but in us. The sufferings of Christ have delivered from punishment inasmuch as in his fellowship we feel evils diminish and in any case no longer submit to them as a punishment. The sacerdotal value of active obedience resides supremely in that which God considers us to be in the Lord, as quickened by him (§104). If we feel that we are quickened, this is reconciliation. But the idea that Christ has won our pardon and satisfied the divine justice by his death is illogical and futile. Similarly, the resurrection and ascension are no longer necessary conditions of the spiritual presence which the Master has promised (§99). Even less so are the return of Christ and the descent into hell. These facts are not indispensable to faith in Jesus Christ the Redeemer. We can venerate him without recognizing them, and accept that God was in him without deducing their inevitability (*ibid.*). And the author curiously adds that if the Christian admits them, it is because they are in Scripture. Thus belief in them is linked with the doctrine of Scripture rather than with that of the person of Christ (*ibid.*). Hence, even though found in the biblical testimony, they are of no importance, since the influence which God exerts on us has no need of them. He can exalt us to himself without these events modifying our relations with him and meriting our pardon. Substitution is completely excluded. If it is alleged that he fulfilled this will in our place and favour, does this imply that we are dispensed from our duty? If so, this is neither a Christian desire nor a moral doctrine (§104). Justification in the Reformation sense, i.e., the declaring just of the believer in virtue of the death and resurrection of Christ, is thus set aside. As in Kant, and for the same reasons, the essential thing takes place in us and not in him, communion and justification being simultaneous (§107, 109ff.) and together constituting the new birth which is our introduction to communion with Christ (§107) by experience of the mysterious attraction which he exerts on us. As for sanctification, it is the employment by the regenerate believer of his natural forces to develop a life analogous to that of the Saviour with whom he is in fellowship (§110).

In short, man aspires to individual achievement, and God responds to his desire by introducing the ideal in Christ and by exercising an influence on us in him, so that our consciousness progresses and triumphs over the obstacles which oppose it, approximating to the divine and human perfection of Jesus. Schleiermacher posits his mystical solution as an intermediary between the magism which concentrates on the work of Christ to the neglect of the 'moral drama' (§101) and the empiricism which denies the supernatural origin of religious phenomena. The former overstresses the extraordinary, the latter the ordinary (*ibid.*). At the centre Schleiermacher unites nature and grace. Putting Christianity within, he advances a subjective explanation of all the classical doctrines. He thus describes, not God's work, but the believer's experience. It need not surprise us that on this basis he has been unable to reconstitute the teaching of the Bible. Experience can tell only what it knows, and in spite of every effort it cannot rediscover what the Holy Spirit has entrusted to the apostolic witness. The Reformers knew this, and that is why they preferred the authority of Scripture to that of tradition (or consciousness). They knew that God had given his prophets and apostles an incomparable wisdom which neither the religious consciousness nor human reason can recreate. In

Schleiermacher we do not have natural theology in the general sense. We have Christian natural theology, i.e., a natural theology which draws on religious experience.

(ii) We remember that Kant, while recognizing that the doctrine of expiation is part of the faith of the Church, rejects it as theoretical in his moral faith, giving preference to man's practical striving after the good. For Sabatier, the distinction is no longer valid. He does not maintain the two possibilities. Although a theologian, he adopts a purely moral faith, declaring that 'the moral philosophy of Kant has succeeded in freeing the modern consciousness in this respect'.[1] What was for Schleiermacher magism and for Kant theory or metaphysics, is now accused of being purely forensic. The author's view is interesting. In a fleeting allusion to Genesis 3 he claims that 'the myth has an original sense and intention quite different from those perceived by ancient exegesis. The notion of a fall in the traditional sense, and the doctrine of transmitted original sin and universal guilt, are quite alien to it. Eating of the forbidden fruit, man no doubt disobeyed; but he still acquired the knowledge of good and evil, which was an incontestable advance on his previous state.'[2]

Previously Genesis had always been understood as a description of the greatest disaster to befall humanity in its desire to put its own morality in the place of God and his commandments. For Sabatier, however, the creature found in the discovery which followed the violation the starting-point of a just and salutary evolution. His whole thought rests on the assumption that morality is the primary human truth. The imprescriptible data of the moral consciousness and of life in society become the criteria of theology (*ibid.*, p. 21). If we add the idea of historical evolution we have the foundations of his study of expiation. After the Reformation, whose work was incomplete, there has fortunately been a new revolution in the nineteenth century. 'It was a matter of moving Christianity from the standpoint of law to that of conscience, of lifting it from legality to morality' (p. 85). This was specifically the work of Vinet and the theologians of the *Revue de Strasbourg*. This 'superior morality' is not that of law but of love, and its principle is the religion of grace.

The history of Christianity may in fact be divided into three periods analogous to those of A. Comte. The first is dominated by

[1] *La Doctrine de l'Expiation et son Evolution historique*, 1903, p. 77.
[2] *Ibid.*, p. 8. On moral autonomy cf. L. Chestov, *Athènes et Jérusalem* (Vrin, 1938) and *La Nuit de Gethsémani* (Grasset, 1923); also Barth, *CD* II, 2.

mythology and the second by legalism. The third 'is characterized by the effort of Christian thought to grasp and interpret religious salvation as an essentially moral fact which is enacted, not in heaven, but in the consciousness' (p. 91). Thus the death of Christ is a moral fact (p. 93). Mediation and satisfaction, which God does not require (p. 101), are replaced by repentance. The work of man is the 'indispensable and adequate condition' of that of God (p. 103). Inward penitence is the only expiation (pp. 104, 106, 107). For this is what destroys sin. The drama of Calvary is human and historical. 'All the magic of sacerdotal ritual and every forensic fiction vanishes; we find ourselves in the reality of the moral life' (p. 110). By these criteria all the older conceptions, both biblical and traditional, are attacked and overcome to the greater glory of the modernist reformation. The work culminates in a declaration of principle which might be applied to describe the method used by all Neo-Protestantism. 'The only privilege is that of faith: to contemplate and follow revelation in the history of its works, and devoutly to hear its voice in our own heart' (p. 115). Unfortunately neither history nor our own heart can give what they do not have. The thought of A. Ritschl was much the same. For him Christianity expresses the ideal of humanity of which Christ is the personification; reconciliation is the change of our will and sanctification is our obedience to the precepts of love.

(iii) The fourth part of the dogmatics of A. Lemaître is entitled 'Jesus Christ', and the introduction states the method of handling this central theme. There is to be avoidance of 'speculations' and of the 'vanity or sterile subtleties of much christological discussion of the past' (p. 215). The synthetic method of orthodoxy is also to be set aside, while liberal theology and dogmatic history will help us to recover the biblical affirmations in their sobriety. 'Our Protestant Christology seeks to attach itself directly to the sources' (p. 216). If it attempts to express the inner facts of experience, these are still based on the witness of the New Testament. Nevertheless, when the author tries to fix his position regarding the traditional dogmas, he does so 'by the light of Scripture and actual conviction' (p. 216). Again, therefore, we are established on the twofold authority of Scripture and consciousness. This method is not inductive alone like that of Frommel, for example (p. 218); it is mixed, following biblical Christology in principle and seeking from the study of Christian experiences only confirmation of the conclusions reached (*ibid.*).

It should be added, however, that the authority of the Bible is not understood in the same way as in the past. The norm, strictly speaking, is no longer the scriptural witness used by the Holy Spirit to instruct us. It is 'what Jesus thought of himself, what the first witnesses experienced in contact with him' (p. 218). These are the 'initial data of revelation' (*ibid*.). We thus remain enclosed within the theology of experience, for the centre of truth resides first in the experiences of Jesus and his disciples and then in ours, which are invoked to confirm them. Thus authority is set, not in the Bible in the strict sense, but in the 'Jesus of history'. Scripture puts us in touch with him, but it is he who binds us. Truly to interpret the Bible, then, we must bring the text into line with our insights into this historical Jesus, and this allows us the greatest liberty, since obviously many passages are incompatible with this religious vision of Jesus. Thus Christology, seeking to be truly biblical, will be 'rooted in the soil of history and in that of the states of soul of the Christian, of which the apostles afford classical expressions' (p. 219). This liberty in relation to Scripture, to the gain of history and religious intuition, leads to very typical conclusions. After briefly resuming the thinking of Paul on expiation, and stating that it is difficult to deny its presence, the author adds: 'We are already far from the Gospel. The God of St Paul does not have the same countenance as the God of Jesus. The doctrine of the imputation of the righteousness of Christ, and that of the divine malediction which strikes the Son of God, have recourse to a vocabulary which is no longer that of the religion of love and which cannot express the most basic thoughts of the Gospel without in some measure betraying them' (p. 255). St Paul, in sum, is the first Christian theologian, but unfortunately he has betrayed in some measure the Gospel and the religion of love. We have thus to adopt another interpretation of the Synoptic Gospels to follow the true Jesus. Affirmed in this way, the authority of the Bible is seriously compromised by an attitude which refers to the four Gospels (though not without serious scruples in the case of John) but explains them in terms of a conception of religion deriving from history and the states of soul of the believer. In interpretation of these texts, we have thus to choose between that given by Paul and ultimately by John on the one side, and that of contemporary theology on the other.[1]

---

[1] Cf. pp. 290f., where John no less than Paul is said to prepare the ground for 'propositions alien to the primitive Gospel'.

To be sure, history cannot explain everything, for Jesus is an exceptional being (p. 233). Nevertheless, it must be our point of departure. Here, too, we must move from below upwards. 'The thought of the divinity of Jesus is the result of the reflection of the believer on what he has been given to experience; it is a truth of the sanctuary, in the phrase of T. Fallot' (p. 285). Yet this high point is not so much the will and wisdom and disposition of God as 'the religious experience of Jesus', 'the consciousness which he had of his divine mission and of his relationship with the Father' (p. 233). 'In things relating to us, we can start neither with the myth of a radical fall, nor with a judicial God who is not the God of Jesus, nor with a doctrine of the metaphysical sonship of a Christ-God, to explain the drama. This drama remains human, determined in part by the freedom of its hero. History and psychology enable us to estimate its significance' (p. 275). Instead of falling into metaphysics, theology should become historical and psychological. 'We do not, of course, cease to speak of an action of God in the cross', for history and psychology cannot give account of the essential feature of Christianity which is the 'sense of sacrifice' (*ibid.*). Hence, in addition to the two disciplines mentioned, there is also religious intuition, and the Bible is the document which forms the basis for this theological method.[1]

The result is that submission to Scripture is not a fundamental principle of this theology. Appeal to its testimony is conditioned by various presuppositions which weaken it even though granting it a place commensurate with the needs of a pre-established religious conception. These presuppositions are those of Neo-Protestantism, particularly on three points.

1. We can still see the results of the Kantian revolution, for the author of *Foi et vérité* constantly reiterates his aversion to speculation. But what is speculation? If he is attacking a dogmatic rationalism, we may rejoice, for a rationalism of the right is no more commendable than a rationalism of the left. But in truth the concern here, as in Kant, is with something very different which relates both to the method of theological reflection and to the content of faith. As concerns method, induction is here preferred to what is called deduction. To know Jesus Christ, recourse is had, not to the work of God, but to history, to psychology, to morality, to the impressions

[1] To take another example, it is argued that 'the moral, religious and mystical life of the soul protests against the exclusivism of the orthodox affirmation that only the resurrection of Christ can bridge the gulf between a holy God and sinful man' (p. 283).

of the consciousness. 'What is normative is already given in history' (p. 219). This supposes that the human and historical, religious and moral consciousness, possess a capacity to teach us concerning God. In place of the classical dogma which recognizes in God alone the power to reveal himself by a special intervention, there is now substituted the conviction that nature holds this power and that we must thus listen to nature to find God. In this conflict between the theoretical or metaphysical and the practical, between deduction and induction, the true point at issue is the serious question whether nature has the power to reveal God. In face of the whole tradition of the Reformation, Neo-Protestantism gives an affirmative answer, and to support itself it launches against all who take a different view the charge of scholastic literalism, of speculation and metaphysics. Now no one would deny that some theologians have developed in too strongly an intellectualistic form the witness which they have sought to bear to the work of God. But it is mere polemics to describe as philosophical speculation all attempts to begin with the Word of God rather than with the work of man, with revelation rather than with nature. The accusation affects the apostles too: 'It is not their intellectual formulae which bind us, but their experiences, reflecting the action of Christ' (p. 219). Thus their verbal witness is of less account than their religious impressions, and in relation to classical theology instruction on the work of God in Christ is less important than the emotions felt in face of it. A human perspective thus replaces that of revelation (p. 311).

This attitude assumes that man's effort, as in Kant, takes precedence of God's gift. Man is placed right at the centre. It is he who decides, chooses, rouses himself, and acts. Aided, no doubt, by God, he yet occupies the centre of the stage: 'The continuity of our inner life alone can associate us with the fervour of the apostles for the person of their Master' (p. 313). We thus see again the main characteristic of Neo-Protestantism from the time of Rousseau in the eighteenth century, namely, an optimistic appraisal of man as one who, though a sinner, has a capacity for God and is divine by nature. Pelagianism, synergism and even a certain pantheism are accepted and applied. In this way the various enterprises of the philosophy of religion and apologetics are justified. There is a smooth passage from nature to grace, not by the miracle of the incarnation, but by man's progressive ascent to God. All schemes which do not follow this ascending path are scathingly rejected.

2. The subjectivism of Schleiermacher is also adopted with enthusiasm: 'It is within the spiritual life and its relationships that we grasp both in Jesus and in ourselves the encounter of the divine and the human' (p. 302). The point of meeting between God and man is no longer in the incarnation, passion and resurrection of Christ, very God and very man, but in our own religious life. Here in us rather than in Christ is the real incarnation of God. The Roman Catholic doctrine of the extension of the incarnation finds fresh illustration in this conception. The extension is now primarily in the consciousness and secondarily in the community. Yet we are on the same ground, for the moment the encounter is not strictly limited to the person of Jesus, in which we are implicated and with which we are associated by the work of the Holy Spirit, it makes little difference whether it is found in the Church, the consciousness, or nature; the principle is the same. Here the decisive event takes place, not first in Christ, but in the inner life of man: 'The human and the divine are grasped in their relation within the religious life' (p. 307). This being so, it is obvious that Christology, i.e., the doctrine of the person of Jesus Christ, has only subsidiary importance. In place of it we find such favourite expressions as 'the irrational', 'the sacred', 'the mystery', 'the ineffable'. 'Paul remained a pupil of the Rabbis. Hence he could never resist the temptation to translate a true religious intuition, the object of which is bathed in the irrational, into concepts which are rational and logical, with the sole purpose of making it communicable. Man's need to know that his sins are covered, the grievous sense of the gap which separates man from the holy God and which his own efforts cannot bridge, the insight that in Jesus Christ it is God himself who comes to remove the gap and to pardon faults—these are thoughts which spring up spontaneously in the inner depths of the Christian life' (p. 253). These facts which constitute the very foundation of our faith are not revelations which God gives us of his intentions and decisions, but intuitions of our own hearts enlightened by the Spirit.

In these circumstances we are sure only of our intuitions, and the work of God, the good news of his intervention, shades into the vagueness of the irrational. 'The image of Christ the Saviour gleaned from the New Testament and Christian experience rests on the facts of consciousness, which are themselves determined by the twofold indiscernible action of the Jesus who lived and of the living Christ' (p. 317). It is known that God has acted and continues to do so, but one cannot grasp clearly either what he says or what he does. Theology, then, is no more than a 'description of the states of soul of the Christian, of the dramas and victories of consciences dominated by the Spirit of Jesus' (p. 319).

3. Historicism also played its part, as may be seen especially in the definition of Jesus Christ. The starting-point is strictly human. The author first asks whence the authority of Jesus derives. One might expect an answer similar to that of Peter, that it is neither of flesh nor blood (Matt. 16). But in fact we are given something very different: 'This authority resides first in his total sincerity, in the harmony of his being, in the force attested both by the generosity of his sympathy and by his solitude' (p. 221), i.e., in his sanctity and active love, in his absolute consecration to God, in his purity, his joyful obedience and his sense of sacrifice. Now he certainly had all these things, but this human ideal has value only if it manifests the sanctity and love of God. Dissociating the divinity and humanity of Christ, Neo-Protestantism has reduced Jesus to the rank of a human, though exceptional, phenomenon. Once more his divinity is simply the perfection of his humanity. 'Jesus, more divine than we are, is not divine in a different sense' (p. 230), as the author wrote in commentary on Frommel. 'Our faith invites us . . . to seek in Jesus the true image of this humanity' (ibid.) and even, in the words of Fulliquet, 'a privileged psychological constitution'. Yet his divinity is not completely exhausted by his humanity. There is still something extra, a kind of 'sacred halo' found 'in the quality of his religious experience' (pp. 232f.). 'Though fully human and historical, Jesus cannot in any respect be simply placed within the human ranks' (p. 233). What, then, is this supra-historical element? It is not his identification with the Father, but his filial experience expressing intimacy with the Father (p. 243). There is a unity of spirit and of will. Real pre-existence in the sense of John 1 is set aside in favour of ideal pre-existence in the mind of God (p. 301). We are in the presence of a man mysteriously united with God and not of God incarnate in order to come amongst us. There is remark-able vigour in the statements at this point: 'Though so penetrated by the Spirit, Jesus does not embody God except within the limits of human possibilities, which should neither be stretched unduly to include full possession of the metaphysical perfections of God nor arbitrarily restricted to exclude a priori the exceptional gifts which could be granted to Jesus in correlation with his mission as Saviour'

(p. 308), and later: 'The hero of the Gospels could not both experience and accept his subordination to the God whom he invokes and to whom he prays, and yet at the same time present himself as very God' (p. 309). In spite of the formal witness of Scripture, Jesus did not feel himself to be such, and 'it is a perilous relapse for an Evangelical church to prefer to the cult of the Christ, Saviour and Lord, Son of the living God, the cult of a Christ-God' (p. 309).

The Spirit is exceptionally incarnate in Christ (p. 309), but, if the Spirit is not God, who is he? Moreover, this cannot be regarded as the only incarnation: 'Radically to isolate this manifestation of the Spirit from all others is both an intellectual and a religious impossibility. . . . The immanence of the living God is variously attested in the world of our experience, in our human prayer, in the prophets, in Christ. Through these manifestations we perceive, not the fatal and necessary development of a divine nature, but successive revelatory actions welling up from the mysterious fount of transcendence' (pp. 310f.). The author is conscious at this point of the distance which separates him from the Reformers, the fathers, and the apostle Paul himself. He marks the difference by distinguishing between the divinity of Christ and the deity. The latter denotes the personal coming of God in Christ, the incarnation of his Word, which is identical with himself. But this is set aside if we retain only the former, which describes a 'functional' relation (p. 301), i.e., an inspiration; Jesus is an inspired man as we may be, though to a higher degree. 'The human person of Christ is the daughter of God raised up and permeated by his Spirit' (p. 302). Thus 'we adore the Spirit who appears in Jesus and who triumphs in him, without being forced either to renounce monotheism or to make of Jesus a second God' (p. 301).

The conclusions which follow logically from these premises should not surprise us. If the formulations of Nicaea are to be retained, they must be adapted at the risk of approximating to the doctrines which they condemn. The incarnation in the classical sense is a myth (p. 302). As for the Council of Chalcedon, it was engrossed in a purely speculative problem which does not really arise (p. 304). The concepts of nature and substance are inadequate, and are Greek in origin.

But is it really a question of terminology? Is there not a fundamental difference? What did the fathers seek to express through these terms? For them, the word 'God' denoted one reality and the

F*

word 'man' another. In saying this they were not referring to a speculative philosophy which was pleased to set a gulf between the Creator and the creature. They were concerned with the gulf between the holy God and the sinful man of Scripture. It is hard to deny that there is a real difference here. In theology, however, we are not simply to repeat the Bible. We are to bear witness to it with the help of human words. Hence the fathers chose the words they did to indicate this difference and distance, often stated in such biblical terms as Spirit and flesh, Creator and creature, life and death. Now it is the distinction or distance itself which Neo-Protestants will not admit. For them God and man are so near and the creature is so elevated that it is very difficult to mark the boundary between them. They must not be separated, much less brought into opposition. They are spontaneously conjoined, not merely in Jesus, but in all men. This is the real objection of Neo-Protestants to the fifth Ecumenical Council. The Chalcedonian definition is rightly seen to be a direct attack on the mitigated pantheism of the modernism which is plainly expressed in a Secrétan or Bouvier but which constitutes in fact the basic character of all new-style Protestantism.

This brings us to the heart of our differences. 'This theory prevails once God and man are regarded as two contradictory terms and are not seen in their living relationship as perceived in the religious consciousness' (p. 305). In the religious consciousness God and man are spontaneously linked, whereas for the fathers they are separated, to be conjoined only in Jesus Christ, the Mediator, in whom they are united by the miracle of his death and resurrection. Now obviously if God is not personally present in Christ Chalcedon is an absurdity. But now everything is changed, a new faith arises. Salvation is no longer an objective act; it is our spiritual and almost normal participation 'in the life brought into history in the Saviour' (p. 326). The cross is only relatively necessary (p. 269) and the resurrection is 'the consummation of creation' (p. 281). Expiation is not an act by which God transforms our situation in the person of Jesus Christ; it is simply a sign that God will bring about this change in us by his Spirit. 'Jesus guarantees before God this transformation of humanity which he will effect by his Spirit. He demonstrates to us the possibility of a life in faith and love capable of transfiguring suffering and death. He does more, for he shows himself capable of winning sinners to this life. He thus assures the Father's pardon to the disciple who by the life and death of Christ is convinced of the power of divine love and is brought by repentance to new life' (p. 272). At the heart of the Gospel we do not have a self-sufficient event reuniting heaven and earth, but a promise that God will perform this act within each one of us. The sacrifice does not really accomplish anything; it simply teaches us that God loves us (p. 275). Thus every 'metaphysical or intra-divine conflict' (p. 276) is set aside in favour of direct spiritual communication.

This review of the principal emphases of Neo-Protestantism has enabled us to bring out certain presuppositions which explain the christological conclusions. Above all, there is a systematic exaltation of man. Man is the centre of concern. He is also the measure by which biblical teaching is partly rejected and partly preserved according to its agreement with the religious intuitions of the believer on the solid humanist and philosophical basis of the Renaissance and the eighteenth century. Religion thus becomes the criterion of revelation, which yields before the deployment of natural theology either in a frankly pagan or a more religious and Christian form. The search for God is always from below upwards. It grasps what it can of the data of revelation, but can never fully endorse the conclusions of the opposite method. The disagreement in formulations does not arise, therefore, from secondary conflicts, from arbitrary choices, from preferences attributable solely to differing and complementary temperaments. It derives from fundamentally different attitudes to Christ, from two divergent conceptions of faith. The Evangelical attitude of the Reformation on the one side and the Neo-Protestant on the other reveal two quite different perspectives which are separated at root by contrary principles and which in the circumstances can find only occasional points of agreement.

2. The Impulses of Evangelical Christology

It is now generally admitted that the knowledge of sin follows rather than precedes that of grace. Jesus reveals our fault by taking it upon himself, i.e., at the very moment when he delivers us from it. It is not so much his judgment as his pardon which defines it, in the act by which he takes our place to suffer its consequences and to spare us. This is where we see the power of evil. Having assumed our condition, Jesus must die. This is the normal end of man as he is.

Here we understand both that God's condemnation applies to us and yet that it is borne by Jesus. The discovery of sin is thus part of grace. It is inseparable from the act by which sin is truly vanquished. It is a gift of mercy and therefore good news, since the fault is taken away the moment it is unmasked. Strictly speaking, this knowledge is part of the description of Jesus Christ. It is thus a christological definition which then becomes a deduction concerning ourselves and therefore an anthropological concept—we are what he became. In this sense, it is part of the knowledge of faith and not just a simple affirmation of our natural imperfections or disobedience to some rule.

The sixteenth century does not seem to have been wholly clear on this point. It was thought that the judgment of God, his wrath and Law rather than his grace and redemptive sacrifice, would establish the gravity of sin. This explains in large measure the plan of Calvin's Christology, which opens with a description of original sin, continues with an evaluation of the powers of man and concludes with his total depravity, thus inviting him the more urgently, as it seems, to seek salvation in Jesus Christ (*Inst.* II, 6, 1). Although this was not the idea of the Reformer, we must say that at this point his Christology depends on his anthropology, as though we had to weigh the capacities of man in order to establish the necessity of redemption and to decide the part played by God in it.[1]

Yet there is a further and more legitimate reason for Calvin's arrangement. He maintains that the Christology of his day is particularly threatened by too optimistic an estimate of the powers of the creature. Now there is no need for God to do for man what he can do for himself. Thus, the moment we think we are justified in exalting the creature, we are inevitably led to underestimate the work of the Reconciler. Calvin sees this, and it is for this reason that, going straight to the point, he opens his study of the efficacy of the ministry of Christ with a vigorous attack on this misleading anthropology. His polemical intention is most instructive. He is speaking against contemporary and past theologians who attribute to man powers which imply an obscuring of the work of God. In fidelity to his principle of *Soli Deo gloria*, even before describing the miraculous intervention of the Saviour, he seeks to demonstrate that man

---

[1] Cf. Anselm's *Cur Deus homo?*, I, 21; II, 17; Schleiermacher's *Christian Faith*, §68. In contrast, v. the christological procedure in Barth's *CD* IV, 1; IV, 2; IV, 3 (cf. *Inst.* II, 3, 6).

has no hope except in God and that it is thus impious to deceive him by giving him grounds for even a little confidence in himself.

In spite of the danger which it poses, this arrangement of the Reformer is interesting for several reasons. 1. It shows us that Calvin was really in the same situation as we are today; as he saw it, his main adversaries offended by excessive optimism concerning the capacity of man. 2. Modern theology does nothing new by basing itself upon similar presumptions; it is simply taking up again a classical position defended from the very commencement of Church history and especially at the end of the medieval period. 3. The realism of Calvin—and of all the Reformers—may be seen from the fact that they do not attack transitory beliefs but ancient doctrines which constantly rise up again with aggressive intent, e.g., against Augustine in the fourth century, Calvin in the sixteenth and Pascal in the seventeenth. From this angle, man's self-reliance is the heresy *par excellence*, the sin defined in Genesis 3. This is why Calvin tackles the deviation so vigorously. Even if his statements and arrangement need revision, his intention is perfectly correct.

Let us consider the various points. He is seeking a knowledge of man which 'will indispose us to every thing like confidence in our own powers, leave us devoid of all means of boasting, and so incline us to submission' (*Inst.* II, 1, 2). His exposition, then, is not abstract. He has an end in view, and this is good, for the dogmas of the Church are never theoretical considerations valid in themselves, but attestations corresponding to a precise intention. Now, if Calvin lays his finger at once on the problem, it is because he is convinced that here is our chief temptation. 'Owing to the innate self-love by which all are blinded, we most willingly persuade ourselves that we do not possess a single quality which is deserving of hatred; and hence, independent of any countenance from without, general credit is given to the very foolish idea, that man is perfectly sufficient of himself for all the purposes of a good and happy life. If any are disposed to think more modestly, and concede somewhat to God, that they may not seem to arrogate every thing as their own, still, in making the division, they apportion matters so, that the chief ground of confidence and boasting always remains with themselves' (*loc. cit.*). And the author continues: 'Then, if a discourse is pronounced which flatters the pride springing up spontaneously in man's inmost heart, nothing seems more delightful. Accordingly, in every age, he who is most forward in extolling the excellence of human nature, is received with the loudest applause' (*loc. cit.*). Philosophers especially glorify man in this way, declaring that 'human reason is sufficient for right government; that the will, which is inferior to it, may indeed be solicited to evil by sense, but, having a free choice, there is nothing to prevent it from following reason as its guide in all things' (II, 2, 3). Philosophers are not so misguided as to deny evil, but they think that man has enough wisdom to be able to recognize and fulfil the good in the strength of his own free will. Unfortunately many theologians have followed pagan thinkers too closely in this regard: 'Among ecclesiastical writers, although there is none who does not acknowledge that sound reason in man was seriously injured by sin, and the will greatly entangled by vicious desires, yet many of them made too near an approach to the philosophers' (II, 2, 4). They thus placed themselves between revealed and natural knowledge, and this partly because they were afraid of being mocked if they deprived man of free will and partly to avoid discouraging those in search of the good. This was why 'they made it their study, in some measure, to reconcile the doctrine of Scripture with the dogmas of philosophy' (*loc. cit.*).

These quotations are sufficient to pose the problem. Out of regard for the world, or, as we might say today, out of concern for apologetic interests, the majority of Christian theologians have abandoned the sole authority of Scripture for an intermediary position between grace and nature, which they bring into association. Calvin shows a fine appreciation of the real root of the problem, and, though we might find some vacillation in his attitude to natural theology, in these passages he decides plainly for the sole authority of the Bible against all the dualisms described in Part I of the present work. In this respect Calvin breaks with the predominant tradition. Yet there have been fathers who, notwithstanding ambiguity in some statements, have maintained the teaching of Scripture on this point. 'They hold human virtue in little or no account, and ascribe the whole merit of all that is good to the Holy Spirit' (II, 2, 9). The reformer again manifests a sure instinct. The Bible attributes to the Holy Spirit what philosophers ascribe to man. When theologians follow the latter, they give evidence of unbelief in the power of the Spirit. Pelagianism brings to light in theology a marked weakness in the doctrine of the Third Person of the Trinity. Protestant Modernism bears a heavy responsibility in this respect, for once man is thought to be able to know God of himself the action of the Holy Spirit is automatically reduced to vague inspiration.

Calvin does not believe that he is here abasing man too much (II, 2, 10), for it is better to trust in God than in oneself. The more one exalts the grace of God, the greater is the profit of man. To exalt man, however, is to cause him to rely less on God and therefore to impoverish him. Hence it is not without reason that Calvin diminishes the part of man almost to the point of suppressing it altogether. He does this in order to dispel the illusions which finally isolate him, depriving him of the love and omnipotence of God. Above all, he does it because Jesus Christ has already accomplished everything, and it would be tragic to neglect this victory in order to turn once again to human works. The much-contested pessimism of Calvin is simply the logical result of his total confidence in God, of his assurance of Christ's victory over sin and of his love for men who, even by the Church itself, are diverted from the only adequate remedy for their evils.

Following this course, Calvin knows that he is a good pupil of the apostle Paul: 'His object . . . is to teach that all are overwhelmed with inevitable calamity, and can be delivered from it only by the mercy of God' (II, 3, 2). He accuses man, not to crush him, but to save him, since that in which he boasts is stolen from God: 'It is, therefore, robbery from God to arrogate anything to ourselves, either in the will or the act' (II, 3, 9). Later he observes that the main fault of this confidence in self is that it prevents us from appreciating the true value of the gift of God and from profiting by it as much as we should (II, 16, 2). Moreover, we are so ignorant of God and opposed to him that the middle position is also to be rejected according to which the grace of God is simply offered and each may accept or reject it as seems good to himself (II, 3, 10). If this were so, we should never receive it.

Properly understood, these indications enable us already to see the true impulses of Evangelical Christology. At a first glance, one might be tempted to see here only a collection of negative judgments which express a systematic scorn of man. But when they are examined more closely we at once see again the disengagement of which we spoke in Part I. There is another dimension concealed behind these definitions, i.e., that of the true objectivity which resides in the work of God. To reach these judgments on fallen man, Calvin begins with positive reflection on the miraculous and wholly sufficient intervention of God. If he expects nothing from man, it is because he expects everything from Christ. If he turns from our works, it is because the person and work of the Saviour seem to him to be so perfect that there is no need to seek anything complementary to them. Fixing his eyes on the victory of God, he rejects every other support lest an alien element should obscure the fulness of the divine achievement. His pessimism concerning man is a necessary consequence of his irresistible optimism concerning the omnipotence of divine love. His doctrine really rests on the second point. For him, grace implies judgment, for God need not have condescended to us if we could have elevated ourselves to him. Even before the Law, it is mercy which reveals and condemns the pride of man. Calvin would probably not have insisted so strongly on man's corruption if his opponents had not enlarged so fully on his supposed abilities and thus rejected the work of God. In effect, the real subject of this whole chapter is not man but the grace of God. The point of the negative propositions is indirectly to emphasize the comprehensiveness of the salvation given.[1]

Having established these preliminary points, Calvin now turns to Christology proper: 'Since our fall from life unto death, all that knowledge of God the Creator . . . would be useless, were it not followed up by faith, holding forth God to us as a Father in Christ' (II, 6, 1). 'Therefore, although the preaching of the cross is not in accordance with human wisdom, we must, however, humbly embrace it if we would return to God our Maker, from whom we are estranged, that he may again become our Father' (*ibid.*). Salvation, like the knowledge of salvation, exists 'only in the expiation which Christ alone completed' (II, 6, 2), i.e., in the 'grace of the Mediator'. For, 'when Christ is called the image of the invisible God (Col. 1.15), the expression is not used without cause, but is designed to remind us that we can have no knowledge of our salvation, until we behold God in Christ' (II, 6, 4). 'Hence it is plain, as we lately observed, there is no saving knowledge of God without Christ' (*ibid.*).

Now Jesus Christ can be known only through Holy Scripture illuminated by the Holy Spirit. It is to this that we must listen. This has been chosen by God as the instrument of the new instruction which will overcome our ignorance and blind compromises. There

---

[1] Cf. Leon Chestov, *La Nuit de Gethsémani*, pp. 98–101. The real issue is natural theology against Scripture, and, like Luther, Calvin thinks that in the main the Church has supported the world against Christ, heresy against the Gospel.

is not the slightest reference to experience or history, to intuition or consciousness. How can the reformer draw on these sources when he has shown how unreliable they are? In place of our impotent insights and hypotheses he sets the full clarity of the divine instruction, the Word of God which miraculously dispels our ignorance. Dare one suggest that in adopting this way he is borrowing from metaphysics, magic or legalism? It has been done. But in fact Calvin accepts the fact that even religious man cannot help himself and that his own efforts are disqualified from the outset. Hence he can rely only on God, if God exists. Calvin does not ask, of course, whether God exists. The fact is there. God has spoken and acted. In Jesus Christ, he is present among us. What comfort to embrace him! Yet not merely comfort, for this is a matter of life and death. Where Calvin, like Athanasius, Augustine, Luther, Pascal and others, sets the whole destiny of man at stake, the moderns have sometimes perceived no more than sterile and arbitrary speculations.

What does the reformer discover in thus accepting the sole authority of revelation in Scripture? Not modernism, but the classical teaching. Nor is this mere conservatism, a lack of boldness due to modesty or logical preference. It is because his life and the life of the Church are here at stake. Theories have not the slightest interest for him. In this respect, he has nothing to learn from modern existentialists. What Calvin seeks is the reality of his own deliverance and that of all men. To ascribe to him other concerns is a serious error. Even in the most searching theological investigations, true orthodoxy has always thought in terms of existence rather than doctrine, as may be seen from the striking examples of Athanasius and particularly Anselm. These men simply went a little further than their detractors in the knowledge of life and of man, and they saw that the attacks against them were not really due to differences of opinion but to more profound reasons which all involve confidence in man himself, i.e., the sin by which he prefers himself to God.

Convinced of human perdition, Calvin places all his hope in the work of God. Unable to find this by his own efforts, he asks the Saviour himself to instruct him on the measures which he has freely taken to meet our insufficiency. Who but God can teach us concerning the initiative which he has taken without consulting us? Subject to the authority of the Word by which God makes himself personally known to us, he discovers the majesty of God's redemptive work. Treating of the Law, he shows that it really discloses our bondage: 'We must be freed from the fetters of the Law, if we would not perish miserably under them. But what fetters? Those of rigid and austere exaction, which remits not one iota of the demand, and leaves no transgression unpunished. To redeem us from this curse, Christ was made a curse for us: for it is written, Cursed is every one that hangeth on a tree' (II, 7, 15). What we cannot do, another does in our place. Expiation and substitution are already implicit in this single phrase.

But who is this other? It must be God himself, for what man, however great, has this power? Moreover our pardon, if it does not imply change in God, certainly means decision on his part. What man, however devout, could cause God to make this decision to lift from us the weight of our sin and of the judgment which it brings? None. It is in God that the event of our acquittal must take place, as is shown by the parable of the unjust steward (Matt. 18.23ff.). 'It deeply concerned us, that he who was to be our Mediator should be very God and very man. If the necessity be inquired into, it was not what is commonly termed simple or absolute, but flowed from the divine decree on which the salvation of man depended. What was best for us, our most merciful Father determined. Our iniquities, like a cloud intervening between him and us, having utterly alienated us from the kingdom of heaven, none but a person reaching to him could be the medium of restoring peace. But who could thus reach to him? Could any of the sons of Adam? All of them, with their parent, shuddered at the sight of God. Could any of the angels? They had need of a head, by connection with which they might adhere to their God entirely and inseparably. The case was entirely desperate, if the Godhead itself did not descend to us, it being impossible for us to ascend. Thus the Son of God behoved to become our Emmanuel, i.e., God with us; and in such a way, that by mutual union his divinity and our nature might be combined; otherwise, neither was the proximity near enough, nor the affinity strong enough, to give us hope that God would dwell with us; so great was the repugnance between our pollution and the spotless purity of God' (II, 12, 1). If in Kantian terms theory is the work of God in Christ and practice the work of man obeying his moral imperatives, we are here in the sphere of theory alone. But on this theory depends the proximity of God and man and therefore the only truly important problem of humanity. In Christ it is God himself who becomes one of ourselves, drawing closer than anything

else, 'inasmuch as he is our flesh' (*ibid.*). His humanity is just as
necessary as his deity, for of what avail would be a distant God?
No more than a Mediator who were not God himself. 'Who could
do this unless the Son of God should also become the Son of man,
and so receive what is ours as to transfer to us what is his, making
that which is his by nature ours by grace?' (II, 12, 2). 'Moreover,
it was especially necessary for this cause also that he who was to be
our Redeemer should be truly God and man. It was his to swallow
up death: who but Life could do so? It was his to conquer sin: who
could do so save Righteousness itself? It was his to put to flight the
powers of the air and the world: who could do so but the mighty
power superior to both? But who possessed life and righteousness,
and the dominion and government of heaven, but God alone?
Therefore, God in his infinite mercy, having determined to redeem
us, became himself our Redeemer in the person of his only begotten
Son' (*loc. cit.*). It was also necessary that 'man, who had lost himself
by his disobedience, should, by way of remedy, oppose to it obedience, satisfy the justice of God, and pay the penalty of sin. Therefore, our Lord came forth very man, adopted the person of Adam,
and assumed his name, that he might in his stead obey the Father;
that he might present our flesh as the price of satisfaction to the just
judgment of God, and in the same flesh pay the penalty which we
had incurred' (II, 12, 3). It will be seen that Calvin does not adopt
traditional formulations or doctrines for their own sake. His attention is fixed on the event of salvation. With no scholastic preoccupation he simply tells the story of our returning to life. This makes his
exposition good preaching. Yet almost incidentally he makes use of
almost all the traditional expressions. 'Finally, since as God only he
could not suffer, and as man only could not overcome death, he
united the human nature with the divine, that he might subject the
weakness of the one to death as an expiation of sin, and by the power
of the other, maintaining a struggle with death, might gain us the
victory. Those, therefore, who rob Christ of divinity or humanity,
either detract from his majesty and glory, or obscure his goodness.
On the other hand, they are no less injurious to men, undermining
and subverting their faith, which, unless it rest on this foundation,
cannot stand' (II, 12, 3). Thus the two natures are an ineluctable
and wonderful reality on which everything in faith depends. There
is no faith except on this basis. To remove the basis is not merely
to mar faith; it is to destroy it. Hardly anything could be more

affirmative, and modernist explications seem strangely hazardous by this criterion. Calvin is not afraid of the term 'nature', whether its origin is Greek or Latin. He thinks it the most apt, in the sixteenth century, to describe the mystery by which we are snatched from death.

The work of God first means incarnation. 'When it is said that the Word was made flesh, we must not understand it as if he were either changed into flesh, or confusedly intermingled with flesh, but that he made choice of the Virgin's womb as a temple in which he might dwell. He who was the Son of God became the Son of man, not by confusion of substance, but by unity of person. For we maintain, that the divinity was so conjoined and united with the humanity, that the entire properties of each nature remain entire, and yet the two natures constitute only one Christ' (II, 14, 1). If the two natures are not conjoined in one person, Christ is not a real being; he is a myth, and our hope is shattered. If they are confounded, we are not dealing with God; we are dealing with a man alleged to be perfect and in this sense divine, and therefore once again he is a myth, for there is no such man, and even if there were he could not assure us of the divine clemency but could only leave us in our isolation. In either case, faith would vanish. Docetism and Ebionitism are thus rejected, and in advance modern Confusionism. Calvin saw quite clearly the practical consequences of these deviations. He saw that they are truly catastrophic for the whole of Christianity. This is why he regards Chalcedon as the key of the whole building. 'Let us, therefore, regard it as the key of true interpretation, that those things which refer to the office of Mediator are not spoken of the divine or human nature simply' (II, 14, 3). 'Christ, therefore, as God and man, possessing natures which are united, but not confused, we conclude that he is our Lord and the true Son of God, even according to his humanity, though not by means of his humanity' (II, 14, 4). He thus approves of the condemnation of both Nestorious and also Eutyches at Constantinople and Chalcedon, 'it being not more lawful to confound the two natures of Christ than to divide them' (*loc. cit.*). It is perfectly clear that in speaking thus Calvin is not defending obscure doctrines of the past but the simple faith which is otherwise lost.

There follow naturally, as the central themes of his preaching, expiation, satisfaction and substitution in the sacrifice of Christ, justification by his blood and sanctification by his work rather than ours. The passion, the descent, the resurrection and the ascension

are not just signs of his victory but the very facts in which our transformation is accomplished. Everything takes place in him, not in us.
Yet Christ has assumed us and therefore we are implicated in the
events through which he passes. What Neo-Protestants remove into
our own inner life here takes place in Christ. This unmasks the
extreme point of modern self-centred humanism. In this it is no
longer Christ who assumes us and associates himself with us; it is
man who draws Christ to himself to make of him supremely the
expression of his own pious experiences. There is identification in a
different sense. Instead of letting himself be apprehended by Christ,
it is man who now takes possession of him.

This short review fully confirms our previous conclusions and
emphasizes the opposition between Reformed and Neo-Protestant
presuppositions. On the Reformed side it is God alone who counts;
in his incarnation in Christ he is the only hope of humanity. The
description of the person and work of the Saviour really fills the
picture. How can his achievement be completed? What can be
added to it? How can his sovereign power be shared by other
authorities? Persuaded that Jesus Christ is the only remedy for our
lost state and that all fulness comes from him, Calvin keeps to this
faith both in fidelity to Scripture and in love for those who derive
from it all they need.[1]

When we turn to Luther, though we cannot discuss him in detail
it is evident that in respect of the basic impulses of Christology he
occupies a similar position. If he comes to much the same conclusions, it is because he begins with the same presuppositions and
criteria. We find in him the same conviction of sin, the same attacks
on Scholasticism for minimizing it, the same acute need of the
decisive intervention of God, and perhaps even more joyous wonder
in face of the reconciliation accomplished in Jesus Christ. Tradition
as such, speculative systems and the technical researches of theology
have, if possible, even less importance for him than for Calvin. His
only real concern is with the relation of the soul and God. Faith is
for him discovery of the blessings which God grants to the creature
in its need, and he finds these blessings in Christ: 'I have had so
many experiences of the divinity of Christ that I have to say:
Aut nullus est deus aut ille est' (*Table Talk*).

---

[1] Though cf. the criticism of Calvin in Barth's *The Humanity of God*, ET, 1961, p. 49,
where it is pointed out that Calvin does not sufficiently grasp what it means that reconciliation is truly accomplished and that in Christ man is thus exalted.

Out of this misery, with this longing, discovery and experience, under the influence of the same victorious grace, he comes back to the great classical affirmations in witness to free salvation. Jesus Christ is true God and true man, two natures and one person.[1] If he were not man, there would be no revelation, and if he were not God, the Lord would not give himself and act in him. Luther sets all his hope on this concrete manifestation of God in Jesus. His intervention alone counts. In describing it, though he has some peculiarities whose underlying intention we should try to grasp, he is not afraid to use the ancient terminology: *Hae duae naturae in Christo non debent separari sed uniri quantum possunt* (*Disp.* 512, 514). *Humanitas et divinitas in Christo constituunt unam personam . . . Non sunt duae personae distinctae, sed sunt distinctae indistinctae, i.e. sunt distinctae naturae sed indistinctae personae* (593). *Unio humanitatis et divinitatis in Christo est una vera persona.*[2] Similarly, in relation to the work of Christ, he emphasizes the satisfaction which the Son offers to the Father by his obedience and death on behalf of the race. Jesus takes our place: *Nu aber ist er an unser stat getreten und von unsernwegen das gesetz, sund und tod lassen auf in fallen.*[3] He mediates between us and the Father, takes to himself our sin and pays our debt.[4]

In all this Luther is not simply preserving ancient doctrines with which he did not have the power to break and which now need to be set aside in a new reforming movement. He believes that the event which the doctrines denote is the only hope of every man. Without this act of expiation, we remain in our lost condition. It is in this act and not elsewhere that the healing of the race becomes a reality.

We now turn to the most prominent Reformed theologian of our own day, Karl Barth, and we again find the same presuppositions and impulses. In greater detail and with a slightly different orientation, the author of the *Church Dogmatics* takes up the classical statements, and just because they have suffered an almost complete eclipse in modern Protestantism, he seeks to give them the stronger emphasis. For the moment we shall not consider the content of the dogmas but certain criteria which seem to have directed their elaboration.

[1] *Werke*, Erlangen, ed., 7, pp. 185f.
[2] 778, quoted by R. Seeberg, *Lehrbuch der Dogmengeschichte*, 5th ed., 4, Part I, p. 225.
[3] *Werke*, Weimar ed., 36, 693.
[4] Cf. esp. the *Commentary on Galatians* at 3.13.

(1) The most notable feature of this Christology is surely the decisive accent which it lays on the achievement of the work of God. That Jesus Christ really rose from the dead is what counts from beginning to end. If Easter is inseparable from Good Friday, it was on the third day that light was shed on the significance of this death and therefore on the whole work of God. The birth, life and death of Jesus Christ, and also his ascension to God and final return, all receive their true orientation from the victory of Easter.[1]

The resurrection is the revelation of God as he is in action.[2] His perfections are here manifested. This event constitutes the sum and recapitulation of the work of God in its totality.[3] Moreover, it is the centre of understanding for every Christian truth, since nothing makes sense unless seen in the light of Easter.[4] Attesting the victory of God over our revolt and over what is visible, this needs to be taken far more seriously than the evidence—and it is the privilege of faith to be able to do this. On the basis of this fact, faith understands the exaltation of man, who is at last delivered from the powers which crush him. It presents itself as an axiom which controls all our wisdom, challenging the most pretentious gifts of natural wisdom. By a complete reversal, it gives a wholly new direction to our thinking. A theology which begins with this event is saved from the hesitations of natural thought and placed beyond the good and the bad, beyond the exigencies of religious or moral feeling, of history and experience, beyond sovereign reason and the infallible Church. It is set at the heart of reality, yet from the standpoint of the divine victory over all that mars it. The new world of divine and human fulness is opened up to it, and it operates on this new territory. In fact, the essential and wonderful task of all true dogmatics is to show the scope of this event.

2. The second feature of this Christology seems to coincide with the constant concern of its author to respect at all points the utter newness of the message.[5] The aspirations, needs and feelings of man, his knowledge of good and evil, his evolution through the centuries—none of these is new. Conversely, if God suddenly presents himself—not an idea of God nor an anonymous providence, but the living Lord—something genuinely new breaks into ou

---

[1] It is significant that in the course of the *Church Dogmatics* Barth increasingly diverges from Kierkegaard and turns more and more to the resurrection as the centre of the Gospel.
[2] *CD* IV, 2, pp. 132f.   [3] *Ibid.*, 140ff., 150, 152, 154.   [4] *CD* I, 2, p. 114.
[5] Cf. in this regard the biblical passages quoted in *CD* IV, 1, pp. 49f.

human world. We are confronted by something other than our own reflection or the expression of our own yearning.[1]

Practical reason, the feeling of dependence, the spiritual evolution of humanity—none of this is new. These things are part of our world. This is why we appreciate them. But that God should stake his honour on coming into the midst of his enemies, not in the form of a sovereign but in that of an infant and of one condemned to die; that he should draw near, not to judge us, but to save us by being condemned in our place; that he should not automatically pardon our offences like an indulgent father but that his righteousness should demand the death of his only Son to make us just; that his love and not his wrath should call for this condemnation and that life should be offered us by the resurrection of this expiatory Victim; that he should be prepared to conclude thereby an alliance with those who hate him and that in face of their revolt he should think it good to become in his own person, for us and in our situation, his own Partner; that he should have chosen this means of solving the human drama and putting an end to sin—all this is so totally new that we are not prepared to accept it. Who does not desire that man should learn wisdom? Who has not felt the presence of a superior being? Such experiences are the common lot. But in what respect do these things approximate to the Gospel of the God-man? In what respect do they help us to receive this and to live by it?

This newness does not necessarily signify reversal, but the irruption of the world of God into our world. To begin with this and to keep to it alone is the only objective and truly scientific method in theology.[2] When this method is followed, the value of Christology does not consist in the impressions to which the person of Christ gives rise in us, but in the decisions which God takes in respect of us. What counts is God's choice, i.e., Jesus Christ. The election, which expresses the will of God to save us through the ministry of his Son, is the keystone in this whole history.[3] The newness is precisely that God is not a distant and unfathomable mystery, but the revealed God. Thus to attain to him we do not have to traverse infinite space;

---

[1] The Neo-Protestant attempt to make Christianity more attractive by secularization has broken inevitably on the rock of human resistance to grace, which the Bible realistically expects; but the Church is slow to grasp the real reason for modern unbelief or for the vehement protests, e.g., of Nietzsche, Kierkegaard and Marx, against its humanized, naturalized and secularized version of the Gospel.

[2] CD IV, 2, pp. 46, 118ff., 367.   [3] Ibid., pp. 31f.

we have simply to receive him where his acts express his being. In all their historicity these events reveal, not the needs of our consciousness, but the dispositions of the love of God. They all attest his presence. He is less concerned with the reasons for our situation than with the plight in which he now sees us.[1]

3. The third characteristic of this Christology is its objectivity, i.e., its attempted submission to the object of faith. The definitions and formulae are of infinitely less account than the event itself, than God's actual coming to save us. What are our ideas, preferences, impressions or experiences in comparison with this fulfilment? The dogmatic formulae are useful to the degree that they help us to receive the Lord, to understand and love him better. The most complicated doctrines are to be judged by the question whence they come and whither they lead. Modern theories cannot escape the question what they are seeking to defend and to show. What values do they espouse? Man, the Church, science, the modern spirit? Are they able to conduct us to the only name by which we may be saved, or do they imperceptibly turn us from it? Dogmatics is of value only if it implies joyful submission to the Word of God.[2]

Objectivity corresponds in theology to a discipline which is applicable to all its parts and which carries with it a threefold requirement: respect for and praise of the sovereign liberty of the love of God; recognition and outworking of all the implications of the well-known Pauline phrase 'in Christ'; the discovery that our life has meaning only because the Son of God took it to himself in his incarnation. Let us briefly examine these three criteria.

(1) Because God is the Subject who determines all else, the Author and Master of his work, he is also the only object to which we must make absolute submission. He is the Master and we are disciples. No reality has either the right or the power to take his place. The authorities of the world immediately become idols if they try to compete with him. Nor can the Church and its traditions, dogmas and experiences, nor even the Bible, make a parallel claim. Demanding total commitment, he brooks no competition. Repentance is the change of attitude in which he manifests his authority by delivering us from all others and subjecting us to his Word alone. Poverty of

---

[1] *Ibid.*, p. 232. Barth brings out the aspect of liberation and alleviation which he thinks is not sufficiently emphasized by the Reformers but which is found in Eastern theology and especially in Athanasius, who rightly saw that Arianism obscured the divine gift and robbed man of his true and only help.

[2] Cf. Barth's appreciation of the objectivity of Mozart in *CD* III, 3, pp. 297ff.

spirit, gratitude and praise are the fruits of this commitment, which carries with it both our freedom and our responsibility. In virtue of his victory, we are put at his disposal. This attitude is a mark of faith but it is also a methodological principle in theological investigation. The object of this study is neither the Church, piety nor the Bible, but the Lord. No intermediary authority should be allowed to arrest us. We deal with invisible things made visible, though still mysterious even in their incarnation. In so doing, we are not so rash as to enclose the object of investigation in our formulae and institutions. We are at his disposal, in total insecurity, yet also in confidence, hope and gratitude. This object dominates us. It is he who both confounds and saves us. We have no shelter from him, and we are careful not to attempt anything which might neutralize him.

At this point we are confronted by an objectivity which far surpasses that which we normally practise. It is no longer a matter merely of the superiority of reason over emotion, of the decisions of the Church over individual opinions, of history over momentary impulses. It is a matter of the sovereignty of God over our presuppositions, representations and desires. He challenges them all that he may reign alone in our life and thinking.

(2) This objectivity implies that we possess nothing in ourselves but that all things are granted to us in Christ. Our life is in him; to him we must look. Jesus is not alone. He does not occupy a solitary place in history as though he were simply a superior individual within the general ranks of humanity. He is, as it were, a recapitulation of creation in his own person and history. On him converge all the lines of our history, the impulses of this fallen race summoned to salvation. The divine fulness is in him. He is thus wholly for us. To the dualism which separates or adds, Barth opposes the total Christ who bears all reality. Nothing exists outside, alongside, or independent of his person. All things are recapitulated in him.[1] It is for this reason that there is no cause to add anything at all to his person or to seek any extension of it. Everything exists already in him. It is thus that he is our Mediator at both poles of the covenant: God for us and we with God. The two come together, as they could not elsewhere, in his being and in the history of his life.

Here again it must be said that we have both an act of faith and a methodological principle. Jesus Christ is not just a man. He is man *par excellence*, in his fall and in his exaltation. Nothing proper either

[1] *CD* IV, 2, p. 60.

to the Creator or to the creature is not found in him.[1] It is thus that he presents himself to us as the Truth, the Life, the Way, so that theology can be no more than a witness to his fulness. He is its unique object of enquiry and also of adoration. It can have no other knowledge than that which derives from the mystery of the God-Man.[2]

(3) The third criterion, as indeed the first, is simply a deduction from that which we have just mentioned. If we are in Christ, in virtue of his merciful will, we cannot speak of anything in theology except in the light of him, if not in the actual mystery of his own existence for us.

He is our election, our righteousness, our wisdom, our redemption and our sanctification.[3] He is also our repentance, our baptism, our conversion, our resurrection, our life. Because all this is true in him, we can participate in it by the Holy Spirit who associates us with his person. Man is not truly perceived except in the humanity of the Saviour. It is here that he is restored to his real condition. Apart from this incorporation man is an abstraction (pp. 270f.). His history is also our history, and the creed thus describes what we usually call our religious experiences, i.e., our participation in what he has accomplished for us. Our consciousness is the discovery that all that happened to him directly concerns us, and that we are associated with his experiences. The Church and the world are in him. One cannot speak of the former except as the manifestation of his own being (pp. 618f.). All institutionalisms, whether of the right or the left, err by according precedence to the historical dimension over the Christological. Thus Jesus Christ carries the true Church in his own person, and he actualizes it by his word. Christ is the Church though the Church is not Christ (p. 655). The world, too, receives its identity from Christ who created and who sustains it. Analogies derive from him, not *vice versa*. It is he who justifies creation, revealing the signification of all that it contains. This perspective revolutionizes our ethics and prevents us from being merely religious.

The objectivity of faith requires that all these elements be examined in him, and because Christ exists for us they receive from him their true *raison d'être* and their relative autonomy. We thus avoid both the subjectivity which takes these elements in isolation

---

[1] *CD* IV, 1, pp. 118, 122, etc.
[2] Dualism of every type not only sets up two authorities but creates a disjunction between Jesus Christ and humanity in place of the *totus Christus*.
[3] *CD* IV, 2, pp. 268f.

and the mystical abstraction which withdraws from them to see only transcendence. In Christ these two aspects are united, but in the right order.

(4) A further essential feature of this Christology is to be found in the importance which it accords to the doctrine of the Holy Spirit. A large part of the exposition of the work of reconciliation is devoted to this doctrine. It takes the place of the Mariological appendix which we shall analyse in the next section, except that it is in no sense an appendix but a constitutive element in Christology.

We may make the following brief observations in this regard.

If the Spirit is the power of God the Father, he is also the Spirit of Jesus Christ, i.e., the presence and action in us of the Lord himself.[1] No separation or division is possible between the three divine modes of being to which the three moments of revelation correspond. On the contrary, they are intimately united, as the dogma of the *perichoresis* emphasizes. It is thus impossible to speak of the work of the Son without referring at once to that of the Spirit.[2]

In emphasizing this novel aspect of consistent Christology, we do not leave the sphere of objectivity as previously defined, i.e., the sphere of grace. The Holy Spirit is the subjective aspect of the work of God, his intervention in us, but since he is the Spirit of God, even within us he is the presence of our Lord. He lays hold of our being, but by full assumption rather than confusion.[3]

Grace thus controls the last phase of our salvation too. It accomplishes creation, then reconciliation and its application to us, and finally the ultimate redemption. Neither the Church nor piety can assure the success of this new enterprise. But the Holy Spirit can, for he is God. He can do it sometimes in spite of the Church and piety. Christology is necessarily Trinitarian, first because God is fully in Christ, and then because the Holy Spirit is our only recourse if we are to know, live out, declare and glorify the decision by which God has transformed our situation.

The Holy Spirit thus points to a new intervention of God by which he causes us to know that all things have been effectively accomplished in Christ. He shows that we are implicated in this

---

[1] *CD* IV, 2, pp. 322f.

[2] The Spirit brings us to Jesus (*ibid.*, p. 44). Pelagianism of every kind necessarily reveals weakness in the doctrine of the Holy Spirit.

[3] The true approach to Christian experience is from this angle. Christian experience is the Holy Spirit in us, distinct, yet united. There can be no question of co-operation or of independent validity.

history. He helps us to see that our participation in grace is already secured by the fact that the grace is for us. Faith is this discovery. The stages in the life of Jesus are those of our own existence, so that by an inner illumination we realize that we are effectively translated into him.[1]

On this perspective the role of the Holy Spirit is described far more precisely and narrowly than is generally the case. Strictly speaking, he does not help us to receive more profoundly the influence of Jesus, to understand the Scriptures better, to pray better, to develop our faith and to be more conscientious in our obedience to the commandments of our Lord. He simply brings us to see that our justification, our sanctification, our full incorporation into God, and therefore our perfect obedience, as also our joy and praise, are fully achieved in Jesus Christ, and that our participation in his life is a reality already accomplished. We are in him because he has taken us up, not because we shall raise up ourselves to his perfection; we have only to apprehend this for the reality to become ours by his power, and this for the simple reason that it is objectively true even for those who do not yet know it. The Holy Spirit does not add anything. He simply permits us to grasp it and to live by it.[2]

(5) Finally, reference should be made to a fifth characteristic, which consists in the movement observed by this Christology in every phase of its description. Nowhere in the Gospel do we have simple notions, set realities or fixed situations. At all points there is movement, history, operation. Even in detail the author attacks all the forms of static thinking which have marred this central sector of the faith, laying emphasis on the conflict which is waged, on the action which unfolds, on the tension between life and death.[3]

This movement, of course, is not that of a progressive conquest of divinity by man.[4]

[1] In the work of the Holy Spirit our own separation from and even hostility to Christ is revealed. It is overcome, however, by his associating us with the death and resurrection of Christ, so that what is true and actual in him is made true and actual in us. The implied dualism is resolved, not by synthesis and co-operation, but only by tension and mortification.

[2] The meaning of repentance in Matt. 3.2 is decisive in this regard. It signifies a change of heart and mind in view of what God has done and by the gracious miracle of God the Holy Ghost.

[3] His main criticism of Chalcedon, which he generally endorses, is that it separates the person of Christ from his work (CD IV, 1, pp. 123ff.; IV, 2, pp. 106f.). Cf. also his criticism of Lutheranism (IV, 2, pp. 51, 66, 79) and of the classical doctrine of the two states (IV, 1, pp. 132ff.).

[4] The twin errors of Neo-Protestantism and Roman Catholicism at this point are (1) to make religious man the subject and (2) to abstract from man altogether. The

The movement at issue in Barth is in the first instance that of the living God who comes. 'God with us', Emmanuel, is the central Christian message. This phrase describes a divine act. But this act is God's very being in action. God gives us what he alone can give, namely, himself. What is meant is that God comes and is found among us in spite of the opposition we raise against him. To do this God humbles himself and takes flesh. This is the story of his love fulfilled in Jesus. This movement, this event, this history, constitutes the essential thing without which nothing makes sense. Jesus Christ does not represent a static datum, nor does his work. He represents a history, that of reconciliation, which precedes all other history and constitutes the only history that really counts. This is the history of the humiliation of God and the exaltation of man (IV, 2, p. 106). It is past history, yet it does not cease to take place and it is thus actual event. One should here speak, not of phenomena, but of operations, for we are everywhere dealing with God himself in action.

The first movement carries with it a second, the 'God with us' a 'We with God', i.e., our own elevation. This is not a parallel or rival process. It is the necessary effect of the first action. If God gives himself, it is to take us back to himself. Otherwise his intervention would be meaningless. The movement of God to us produces that of our own ascension. It is not that man takes God's place as a result of the incarnation. It is rather that he recovers his own quality as true man. This transition takes place in Jesus for us, for etymologically reconciliation means exchange.

There is movement, too, in other aspects of the work of redemption, especially in the attitude of man. The notion of sin must also be purified of static conceptions. The creature is not neutral in face of the Creator. On the contrary, it is active. Where God stoops down to take it to himself, it continually ignores this appeal and tries to exalt itself in its own strength. In face of the abasement which God accepts, sin takes the form of a passionate, titanic and desperate movement on the part of man to achieve his own deification. The two histories of the humiliation of God and the presumptuous ascent of man meet in the cross of Christ. On the other hand, where God sovereignly elevates his creature in the resurrection of his Son, we

former course leads to a secularized subjectivism and the latter to an objectivity of the cloister. Either way, the result is a form of mysticism (individual or sacramental), and Christ is understood only in terms of the believer or the Church (cf. IV, 2, pp. 8, 12f., 57ff.).

see man fall victim to the contrary movement. He refuses this appeal; he lets himself fall; he sinks instead of grasping the hand held out to him.

The work of redemption thus presents itself, not as a collection of ideas or a simple communication of truths, but as a living drama, a clash of various contradictory movements, a victory. Jesus is the setting of this drama which implies the condescension of God, the revolt of man, death and resurrection, the triumph of God and the ascent of his creature. No dogma has the right to reduce this epic drama to a collection of ideas or symbols.[1]

3. The Impulses of Roman Catholic Christology

As distinct from the Neo-Protestant Christology which we have already rejected and which is marked by the predominance therein given to the religious experiences of believers, Roman Catholic theology seems at first sight to give an impression of remarkable solidity and plenitude. Based on John 1.14, it respects the principal articulations of the event of the incarnation. As regards the deity and humanity of Christ, it endorses the essential features of the fourth- and fifth-century formularies. As regards the hypostatic union, it maintains the established features of the Chalcedonian definitions. Though preoccupied with the sacerdotal function of Christ, it does not ignore his prophetic (or teaching) office, nor his kingly. It thus accepts the three main aspects of soteriology. To say this gives legitimate satisfaction. We are here in a very different atmosphere.

Nevertheless, certain errors which might seem small at a first reading will not fail to strike the attentive student. The main one is the emphatic separation between propositions which concern the person of Christ, here treated in isolation, and those which concern his work. The former constitute Christology, the latter soteriology. If we seek to distinguish too sharply between these two aspects of the same reality, we run the risk of freezing the person of the Saviour in an abstract majesty and of detaching from him the results of his coming. Such classifications lead to static conceptions. The living Lord is too easily enveloped in a series of formulae. The attempt is made to describe him as a mere object instead of attesting his lordship in the movement of his condescension, conflict and triumph.

[1] The fact that this is God's history means that the categories of historicism are inadequate to describe it. In isolation they can even become quite unhistorical, for they cannot allow for the specific historicity of this event and in their attempt at objectivism and realism they are in danger of finishing up with an abstraction or fiction.

Jesus Christ is thus presented as a kind of 'deposit' on which the Church reflects and which it transmits, so that the truth is no longer a living person but a collection of related dogmatic and authoritative formulations.

These reservations cannot, of course, veil the true grandeur of a Christology which is attentive to the two main lines of biblical witness, namely, the presence of God at the heart of history in a man who in all things resembles us except only for sin. We shall not develop this aspect at the moment, since in itself this Christology bears such a strong resemblance to that which we shall be expounding later.

Unfortunately, however, this doctrine is not content simply to describe the one name given to men whereby they might be saved. It feels obliged to add an appendix to its more or less correct exposition. What is this adjunct, which is usually treated in the same chapter? The answer is plain; it is Mariology. 'From the person of the Redeemer, one must distinguish absolutely, but one cannot wholly separate, the mother of the Redeemer.'[1] There is so little separation that the figure of Mary occupies a place within Christology immediately after that of Jesus.

This would not be so serious if we had here no more than an appendix. In fact, however, Mariology assumes such importance that in practice, and in spite of the energetic denials of its better defenders, it does not merely accompany Christology, but gradually, by invincibly drawing attention to its own dogmas, it overshadows christological statements in the stricter sense. Our task is to show the significance of this singularly militant adjunct. We shall do so in the form of brief observations, since it is hardly possible to give a full analysis of this doctrine which has recently undergone such a disproportionate, if logical, expansion. To do this would deflect us from our true theme. We must be content, then, to indicate the profound impulses behind this prodigious excrescence and to determine its influence not merely on Roman Catholic Christology but on the whole of Roman Catholic theology.

1. *The significance of Marian doctrine*

Whether it be regarded as an adjunct to Christology or as a part of ecclesiology,[2] all Roman Catholics are agreed in according to

---

[1] Bartmann, *Précis de théologie dogmatique*, 1944, Vol. I, p. 456.
[2] Cf. C. Journet [Professor of Catholic Theology at Fribourg], *Esquisse du développement marial*, Paris, 1954, p. 63.

Mariology a pre-eminent role not merely in the piety but in the total life and especially in the doctrine of their church. If there are certain sentimental reasons for this, we should be wrong to regard them as primary. In fact, Mariology is important because it illustrates and expresses the most characteristic positions of Roman Catholicism, whether in regard to the power of man or to grace, to the doctrine of the Church or even to that of Holy Scripture in relation to tradition and the teaching office.[1]

2. Mary the type of humanity receiving grace

It is well known that the Council of Ephesus proclaimed Mary the 'Mother of God'. 'This is the concept on which the attention of the Church is infallibly concentrated and from which all the privileges of the Virgin derive, not by fragile arguments of convenience, but by authentic development.'[2] It should be noted, however, that originally the *theotokos* did not correspond to Marian preoccupation. The real concern in according her this title was not to exalt Mary but to defend the unity of the person of Christ against the tendency of Nestorius to disrupt it. To bring out the unity of deity and humanity in him it was argued that the mother of Jesus must have been the mother of the Son of God, since Jesus and the Son of God are one and the same. Opposition to the formula could come only from those for whom Jesus was not Emmanuel, i.e., God himself among us. It could come only from the Nestorians who divided the person of the Saviour.

Marian preoccupation did not come till later. It rests primarily on an interpretation of Luke 1. Once this is understood, the rest follows logically. The interpretation is quite clear. Mary is not just an object of unforeseeable and victorious grace. By her inner virtues, her purity, thanks to the influence of a prevenient grace, she is already worthy in herself to receive this grace and able to consent to it. Her merits enable her, not merely to cleave to grace on her own initiative, but actively to co-operate with it in bringing the Saviour into the world. By her own intrinsic human dignity she thus participates in the event of the incarnation. In her more clearly than any

---

[1] For some recent estimations of the place and importance of Mariology, cf. H. de Lubac, *Méditation sur l'Eglise*, 1953, H. Rahner, *Marie et l'Eglise*, 1955, and on the Protestant side P. Maury, *Le Protestantisme et la Vierge Marie*, 1950, p. 47, and K. Barth, *CD* I, 2, pp. 138ff. In Roman Catholicism Mary, as the symbol of the Church, emerges as the centre of the world and the virtual source of all truth, since it is she who gives birth to Christ himself.

[2] Journet, *op. cit.*, p. 62.

others one thus finds proof of a collaboration between grace and
nature, each of which contributes to the work of salvation. Nor is
this in consequence of grace properly speaking, but as the result of
a prevenient grace, i.e., a grace anterior to the action of Jesus Christ
himself, though linked with it. This ability of Mary constitutes the
first aspect of Mariology, which fully corresponds to the synthesis
established on the basis of the analogy of being between man's
part and God's in the work of salvation, and therefore to the doctrine of merits and to the whole dualism which characterizes this
theology.[1]

There results a kind of elevation of Mary, not to put her at the
side of God, but rather to express in her the powers attributed to
nature. By this motherhood she has acquired an internal dignity
which resides in her virtues. 'Mary has acquired great merit in
relation to the redemption of humanity by accepting without hesitation, as a handmaid of the Lord and in faith, the task which God
proposed, and by accomplishing it with obedience. Her personal
and active participation in the divine work of salvation commences,
according to the fathers at the incarnation, in which she believed
personally and to which she rendered personal service.'[2] In all this,
no matter to which author we refer, emphasis is freely placed on the
work of Mary, on her moral and personal participation, and not
solely or primarily on her charismatic situation. In plain terms, what
is underlined is the part of man, of the nature of the believer, in the
work of salvation. This is carried so far in the case of Mary that she
does not merely accept grace but she draws it upon herself, and, by
her obedience, upon the race.[3] This is the starting-point for her role
as corredemptress, with its suggestion that she has made a 'subjective co-sacrifice'.[4]

In this way Mariology finds its way to the very heart of the
doctrine of grace to bring into it the classical response of Roman
Catholicism. It attests in fact the twofold mysery of the incarnation
and of human co-operation. Many theologians of this confession are

[1] For the understanding of Luke 1.28 which is the basis of this aspect of Mariology
cf. Thomas Aquinas, *ST* III, 27, 5; Bartmann, *Précis*, I, pp. 472ff.; Rahner, *Marie
et l'Eglise*, p. 63.
[2] Bartmann, *op. cit.*, p. 475.
[3] Journet, *Développement marial*, p. 110.
[4] Bartmann, *op. cit.*, p. 476. Against the Protestant view of Luke 1.23, namely, that
Mary is shown grace rather than full of grace, Congar appeals from philology and
exegetical science to the Church (*Vraie et Fausse Réforme dans l'Eglise*, 1950, p. 487).
Cf. also C. Brütsch [pastor at Borne], *La Vierge Marie*, 1943, and Barth's discussion of
Scheeben, *CD* I, 2, pp. 140ff.

now seeking ways to minimize the difference which separates their attitude from true Reformation witness. They are prepared to accept the *Soli Deo gloria*, which to them is completely safeguarded by recourse to prevenient grace. They energetically affirm that 'neither Mary nor the Church replaces . . . in the very least the humanity of Jesus Christ'.[1] They bring the counter-charge that Reformation theology professes a grace which does not come down to man, or which at least remains always outside him. They thus cause the most regrettable misunderstandings both for the cause of faith and for that of Christian unity.[2]

The Roman doctrine takes up the whole of human nature, sick but not entirely corrupted, into alliance with God. The encounter between God and man no longer takes place exclusively in the humanity of Jesus Christ, with which we are associated by our death and resurrection, i.e., against ourselves and against the flesh of sin which is summoned to disappear. On the contrary, there is an assumption of this flesh, which is not replaced by the new man, but itself converted, exalted, even divinized in some respects. This is the basis of the strategy of the Roman Church, which incorporates nature into theology and into its apologetics, into its ethics and into its politics in the stricter sense. At this point it always shows itself to be ready, especially in Christian parties, to embrace human values which it judges to be in conformity with the work of creation. It thus weakens the significance of the rupture produced in the death of Jesus Christ and also the necessity of a resurrection of the dead, substituting for man's revolt against the Lord a serviceability, an openness, a good will towards him, which renders the miracle less costly and the gratitude less profound.

Moreover, this doctrine follows the same movement as that later followed by Neo-Protestantism, transferring to ourselves the emphasis which Scripture places on Jesus Christ alone. The totality of salvation no longer takes place in him alone for us, but simultaneously in him and in us. The objectivity of the Church cannot mask the subjacent subjectivism whereby religious man becomes the second pole of faith. The essential Evangelical truth that our righteousness and satisfaction are won in Christ and are attributed, yes, truly accorded to us by the Holy Spirit, is here veiled in favour

---

[1] De Lubac, *Méditation sur l'Eglise*, p. 241.
[2] The only point of the innumerable distinctions in the Roman Catholic concept of grace is surely to keep a place for man's co-operation in his own salvation.

of our inner religious life or of the ecclesiastical institution symbolized by Mary. We are no longer called upon to die when Christ himself becomes our life. Our nature, elevated by grace, undergoes an inner transformation which makes it worthy of association with Christ. In short, God no longer answers in our place to unite us with him. He makes us capable of answering on our own account. Mediation strictly speaking is no longer the act of Jesus alone; it is also that of the Church and finally of the Christian too. Thus the work of Christ finds extension in that of the Church and the believer, who join themselves to the humanity of Christ instead of recognizing that they are implicated in it.[1]

3. Mary a type and recapitulation of the Church

Mary represents the Church as well as the co-operating creature. Now she does this for Protestants, too, namely, in her humility and lack of pretension. In Roman Catholicism, however, the Church is exalted to the same extent as Mary. The marks of its dignity correspond to the acknowledged qualities of Mary.[2]

The parallelism between Christ, Mary and the Church may be regarded as the underlying reason for the progressive development of Marian dogma, the stages of which we shall briefly review.

The expression Mother of God is diverted from its original purpose of safeguarding the unity of the person of Christ and becomes the sign of the dignity of Mary and of her positive and even creative work: 'The motherhood of the Virgin is an exact image of the motherhood of the Church.'[3] As Mary gives birth to Christ, so the Church brings believers into the world. It has a power hitherto reserved for Christ and the Holy Spirit alone. It becomes in effect the 'mystic Christ' which, 'in virtue of the sacramental power transmitted to it by Christ, brings into the world for eternal life the members of this body which is the total Christ'.[4] The depository of grace, it transmits it and thus leads men to God. Just as the assent

---

[1] Cf. L. Bouyer, who in his Du Protestantisme à l'Eglise, 1954, pp. 46f., 158, argues that what is good in Protestantism is truly Roman Catholic, so that Protestantism can come to fruition only in the Roman Catholic Church. Like Neo-Protestants he accuses the Reformers of too strong an emphasis on the divine sovereignty and argues also that the Evangelical doctrine of justification is too forensic, finding nothing real in man himself. Apparently the work of the Holy Spirit is not real, since it is only from God and not from man. (On the Neo-Protestant side, cf. Lemaître, Foi et vérité, pp. 23, 31, etc.)
[2] Cf. de Lubac, Méditation sur l'Eglise, pp. 245f.; Journet, Développement marial, p. 66; Rahner, Marie et l'Eglise, pp. 24f.
[3] De Lubac, op. cit., p. 246.   [4] Rahner, op. cit., p. 48.

of Mary 'made possible the irruption of divine grace into the whole of humanity, mediating the incarnation of God' (*ibid.*, p. 58), so the presence of the Church makes possible the return of men to God. It is thus a condition of salvation. 'As Eve was a cause of death for the whole of the human race, so Mary was a cause of salvation for the whole of the human race. It is only another step to the explicit affirmation that Mary is the mother of all men in the supernatural order as Eve is the mother of all men in the natural order. . . .'[1] From Mary this power passes to the Church. It is the 'motherhood of grace',[2] in accordance with which it is declared capable of converting and saving in full association with, and even in place of, the Word of God and the Holy Spirit. Roman Catholic sacramentalism finds here its distinctive force, for it is the means by which the Church transmits the grace which it possesses and makes men Christians.

The miraculous birth, which is placed at the beginning of the Gospel precisely to show us that everything here proceeds from the grace of God attested by the Holy Spirit and incarnate in Jesus of Nazareth, is interpreted in exactly the opposite sense, namely, that everything comes effectively from God, but with the co-operation of nature and the Church. Dualism is thus established with far greater subtlety than in Neo-Protestantism, where this witness is simply discarded. But the result is the same, for in both cases there is concern to safeguard the participation of man, however modest.

The perpetual virginity of Mary, which is not without exegetical difficulties (Matt. 1.18; the brethren of Jesus, etc.) is of primary importance, first because the incarnation of God could not take place in flesh which was not perfect, and then because virginity is a sign of the purity of the Church itself. The idea is ancient and probably goes back to the seventh century, for in 649 a Lateran Council pronounced anathema on all who denied it. De Lubac (pp. 246f.) quotes a clear statement of Honorius: 'The glorious Virgin Mary represents the Church, which is also virgin and mother: mother because, made fruitful by the Holy Spirit, it daily presents new sons to God by baptism; yet also virgin because, inviolably preserving the integrity of the faith, it does not allow itself to be corrupted at any point by the stain of heresy.' In the

---

[1] M. Besson, *La Sainte Vierge*, quoted by Brütsch, p. 109.
[2] Journet, *op. cit.*, p. 112.

case of Mary, as of the Church, virginity denotes purity, and in the case of the latter it denotes the sanctity which no heresy can sully.

The immaculate conception, proclaimed in 1854 by the bull *Ineffabilis Deus* of Pius IX, completes the previous article in expression of the infallibility of the Church. Already in 1870, like many before him, Scheeben could point to 'a rich and striking analogy between the dogma of the immaculate conception, the absolute purity of the *fides sapientiae*, and the dogma of the infallibility of the Holy See, the absolute purity of the *cathedra sapientiae*'.[1] We need not tarry on the exegetical and systematic demonstration of this dogma. The essential point is its intention. The process of development imposed this decision, as it did later that of the papal infallibility, not in the interests of Mary but in that of the power which the Roman Church thought it should assume. 'The bride which is such because it has no spot or wrinkle or any such thing, but is pure and immaculate, is the Church, considered not in the stains of each of its individual members but as a totality, a collective which stands outside the stains of its sinful members. It is as such that, though not without sinners, it is without sin.'[2] The institution thus rises above its members and declares itself to be incapable of sinning, to be like Christ in its purity, to be infallible through the voice of its head. It will be noted that this decision, like that of the assumption of the Virgin, was reached under the pressure of the consensus of the Church, i.e., by the consent of the faithful rather than by scriptural revelation, according to 'the ancient maxim of Augustine and of Lerins': 'In the Catholic Church there must be scrupulous concern to keep only to what has been believed everywhere, always and by all.'[3] The criterion is no longer revelation, but the faith accepted in the Church, and the breathing of the Spirit in one sense or the other. The bull *Ineffabilis Deus* 'also insists primarily on the consensus of the Church in relation to the doctrine of the immaculate conception'.[4]

It follows from these observations that the Church, like Mary, is a

[1] Quoted by de Lubac, p. 250.
[2] Journet, *Développement marial*, p. 68.
[3] Journet, *op. cit.*, p. 19; cf. Brütsch, *La Vierge Marie*, p. 106.
[4] Journet, *op. cit.*, p. 18. Lemaître would agree that the norm is not the Bible. For him it would be the Gospel, but this is, of course, defined in terms of experience and there is thus approximation to the Vincentian Canon. There seems to be an instinctive religious need to put confidence in the Church, and it is to this that the Roman Catholic doctrine appeals. Neo-Protestantism makes a similar appeal, though along different lines.

mediatrix of graces and is associated with Christ in the redemption of humanity.[1]

The assumption of the Virgin 'is the mystery of its own consummation which the Church thus elucidates; by it is revealed what will be the portion of the whole Church',[2] i.e., its own elevation and ours. The ascension of Christ is no longer adequate to assure us of our return to God. The ascension of the Virgin and that of the Church have become the indispensable guarantees: 'What takes place sacramentally for the Church and its children regenerated by baptism is ascension into the blessed desert of solitude face to face with God. With eagles' wings it is to fly up out of this fallen world. In Mary there is already realized what will be accorded to the human nature which is ours and which we have in common with her.'[3] Why in Mary and not in Christ? Because in Mary our humanity is taken up in some sort in its weakness and our flesh is assumed, whereas in Christ it is cursed. In Mary the gate is less narrow, the judgment is less rigorous. She is nearer to us, more compassionate perhaps, more close to our actual condition. In her our nature is simply healed and then elevated and associated with God, as in the Church, which does not demand so total a renunciation as the crucified Christ in order to take us up and to present us to God. A theology of glory arises out of this Marian redemption which is apparently designed to facilitate our access to the heavenly mansions.

The assumption, then, is simply the consummation of the progressive glorification of the Church by successive developments in the 'night of faith'. It confirms all that precedes, presenting us with a Church which is pure and holy, which is glorious and infallible, which has the majesty of a virginal figure which possesses all grace and all truth. It is fortunate 'that at the moment when the myths of materialism threaten to destroy the life of men' we should receive this good news of the serene perfection of the Roman Church in its divine plenitude. Already it finds itself set above the human condition, in all things superior to it, the present realization of the kingdom of God, heaven upon earth. 'Mary escapes the common law which defers until the end of the world the hour of resurrection and glorification. . . . Mary can thus rise again and be glorified before the end of the world.'[4] If we apply to this sentence the method

---

[1] On the title 'Co-redemptress' as applied to the Virgin cf. Bartmann, Vol. I, pp. 479f.; the encyclical *Mystici corporis Christi* of Pius XII, quoted in Brütsch, pp. 108f.; and especially Journet, *op. cit.*, pp. 67, 146.
[2] Rahner, *Marie et l'Eglise*, p. 116.   [3] *Ibid.*, p. 123.   [4] Journet, *op. cit.*, p. 144.

extolled by the most prominent Roman Catholic theologians of our own age, who see a complete parallel between the Virgin and the Church, even in the most minute details, we shall quickly discern the profound and implicit meaning of the proclamation of the assumption of Mary. The Church is declared to be invested already with eternal plenitude even before the return of Christ and the end of time. As the resurrection and ascension of Christ are signs of his deity, so these events ascribed to Mary reveal that the Church has already attained here below to the perfection promised hereafter. The history of the salvation of humanity is achieved in it in such a way that celestial plenitude is already presented to our astonished gaze. The point of the assumption of Mary is 'to manifest before all eyes the sublime end to which our body and soul are pre-destined'.[1] The Church already prefigures and even realizes in advance the new earth promised in the last days.

4. The justification of this doctrine

It is most interesting to see finally how it has been possible to justify this prodigious development by the criterion of Christian truth. To do this, Journet elaborates an illuminating norm which puts the Church in a position gradually to discover and to teach the full truth of God. This norm is the 'deposit of the faith' as defined at the Vatican Council.[2] But what does this mean? 'The revealed deposit is the mystery of salvation with all the divinely guaranteed truths which declare its sense and thanks to which theological faith adheres integrally to this mystery.'[3]

We may first observe that revelation here is no longer the living Word which the living God addresses personally to the Church. It is a deposit which is transmitted to the Church, which the Church bears within it, and which it is to pass on. This deposit consists of a collection of established truths, i.e., of concepts and notions rather than divine communications. There is also reference to a 'primitive' deposit (p. 15) which, to become actual, needs the historicity of the Church. The gulf which separates us from the prophets, Christ and the apostles is no longer bridged by Christ himself eternally present, nor by the Holy Spirit continually giving life to testimonies which are historically ancient but which are always actual because they are the instrument of a personal and therefore a present intervention

---

[1] Pius XII, quoted by Journet, p. 146.
[2] Sess. 4, chap. 4, Denzinger, 1836.   [3] Journet, *op. cit.*, p. 14.

of God. This historical distance is now overcome by the presence of the Church, which continues the work of its Lord. In this historical conception the Bible is relegated to the distant past, and in practice it yields to the only word which is truly actual, namely, that of the Church. The intervention of God, whether past or present, is thus reduced to a minimum. It is more important to attach oneself to 'what the apostles held in relation to their faith'.[1]

It is not contested that the apostles enjoyed full knowledge of the mysteries of God. Unfortunately, however, they could not give an integral transmission of their vision of God. What they saw, 'with the clarity of an infused prophetic light', 'it was impossible for them to transmit as such to those around them. They had thus to pass on this mystery to the faithful by a living and progressive attempt at conceptualization and formulation conditioned by various historical circumstances' (p. 26). There were thus things which they saw without being able to state. Furthermore, it is obvious that not everything was written. The early Church received the truth by the twofold path of Scripture and oral tradition. One should not unduly separate these paths by setting them in juxtaposition. It is more correct, argues the author, to insist on 'a certain transfusion of tradition into Scripture' (p. 31) by simply saying that the Bible, 'especially as it neared completion, was seen to contain explicitly, certainly not all the truths of the revealed deposit, but at least the essential truths, the principles, the articles of faith, on the basis of which the whole of the revealed deposit might subsequently be brought to light with the assistance of the Holy Spirit' (p. 36).[2]

In this way the Bible is much more fluid and malleable, and the only remaining task is to define the teaching office. This is quite simply to unfold and to bring out what is undoubtedly implicit in the first part of the revealed deposit. Its role is 'to declare irreformably that a certain truth is truly included in the primitive deposit either explicitly or implicitly' (p. 43). The Holy Spirit alone can no longer lead us into all truth; he needs the teaching office, which with his assistance can confidently reveal, not merely what the apostles saw but did not state, what the Bible contains without expressing, but also what the primitive Church did not have the privilege of

---

[1] *Ibid.*, p. 26. As in the Neo-Protestant theology of experience, the centre of gravity lies here, not in the divine instruction, but in the subjective experience of the apostles.
[2] Thus Paul in I Corinthians discusses marriage, the Lord's Supper, idol meats, etc., but he might just as well have made explicit the teaching concerning the immaculate conception and left the other topics for explicit development later (cf. p. 27).

G*

discovering. 'Hence one might say that the early Church "did not know" explicitly some of our actual dogmas; yet it did know explicitly others in which these are implicitly contained' (pp. 47-48).[1]

In this conception the norm of truth no longer resides in the two classical courts of Scripture and tradition; the teaching office is included in and added to tradition. In reality the two courts are now tradition on the one side, which comprises what God communicated to the apostles and then what they transmitted to the early Church both orally and in writing, and on the other side the teaching office which within the post-apostolic Church discovers 'new developments of the deposit of faith once for all delivered to the Church by Christ and the apostles' (p. 45).[2]

One should not neglect in this regard to refer to the impressive analysis given by Barth.[3] It is shown here how the evolution of Roman dogma has led progressively to an absorption of Scripture by tradition and of tradition by the teaching office, so that in effect the only ultimate authority is the Church concretely identified with revelation (pp. 56of.). Recalling the main postulates of Neo-Protestantism and comparing them with the fulfilment of Roman doctrine at the Vatican Council, Barth is able to demonstrate full correspondence between the two attitudes. Whether revelation is identified with the Church or with the religious consciousness which also issues in the community, in both cases it is assimilated to an immanent religious reality and it is man who becomes the ultimate criterion of truth.[4]

We are now at the crucial point in closest proximity to the Chalcedonian doctrine. For the Reformers, the Word of God, while it comes to man, is not confounded with religious capacity or ecclesiastical power. It maintains its integrity, uniting itself with man and the Church, but ruling over them by the grace of its judgment and salvation. Man and the Church are already implicated in the humanity of Christ, which needs no extension since it already contains everything within itself. Roman Catholicism and Neo-

---

[1] Thus infant baptism is developed from what is implicit in the Bible. It is interesting that Neo-Protestantism gives to theological scholarship a task not wholly dissimilar from that of the teaching office in Roman Catholicism.

[2] There is thus a twofold prophetic light, the apostolic to state what is explicit and the post-apostolic to bring out what is implicit. Along these lines, whether in Roman Catholicism or in Neo-Protestantism, it is possible to make anything biblical.

[3] CD I, 2, pp. 544-72.

[4] The basic identity may be seen in Moehler, in whom we have a synthesis of Hegel, Schleiermacher and the developing Vatican theology (ibid., p. 561).

Protestantism turn things upside down, not placing Christ directly at the centre, but our individual and collective consciousness. Far from doing justice to the mystery of the incarnation by a supposed complement, they conceal it, substituting other authorities. This excrescence is nowhere envisaged by the terminology of the Council.

On this view, the Church is naturally of great importance. It is the society which mediates the truth and authority of the Christian religion, and Christ is not truth or authority for us except by means of it.[1] The presence of the living Christ and his Spirit makes the Church humanly infallible, since, for us, the divine element does not exist without a human counterpart to transmit and express it.[2] There is thus a human element which is infallible, pure, holy and divine. Nor is this just the Holy Spirit in us. It is our own consciousness of God, our merits, the Church. And this element, which is strikingly asserted in Mariology as in the theology of experience, becomes a condition of the efficacy of the Word of God. A real alliance is concluded between God and religious man which constitutes, as it were, a second incarnation, or, if one prefers it, an extension of the incarnation of Christ. On this foundation, it is quite logical to work out a Christian natural theology, since the Church and the believer have real capacities to know God spontaneously and to respond to him. It is also quite normal that different instruments of revelation—Scripture, tradition, religious consciousness, the teaching office, the consensus of the Church and those who represent it, whether the pope on the one hand or believers and especially professors of theology on the other—should merge into a single authority which is the Church itself, the company of the faithful.[3]

What real difference is there between the intuition of Schleiermacher and the more ecclesiastical intuition of Moehler? What real difference is there between the religious impression which the believer expresses in his theology of experience and that which the Church expresses in its tradition? We see the same development at this point in both Roman Catholicism and Neo-Protestantism. First there is tradition associated with Holy Scripture as a simple confirmation, just as the initial Neo-Protestant appeal is to reason, sentiment, moral obligation or history in a purely auxiliary capacity.

[1] Cf. Moehler, quoted in *CD* I, 2, p. 561.
[2] Moehler, *Symbolik*, p. 336; *CD* I 2, p. 562.
[3] Cf. Moehler, *loc. cit.*, quoted in *CD*, *loc. cit.*

Then these various authorities—Barth lists no less than twelve—take on equal importance with Scripture. Finally they dominate the Bible, which is absorbed by them. The result was reached at much the same time in the two spheres, for Roman Catholics at the Vatican Council, where Pius IX replied to an interpellation: 'I am tradition',[1] and for Neo-Protestants when Schleiermacher, Kant, Lessing and their successors deliberately, as we have seen, placed their own criteria above the Gospel. Strauss clearly perceived the development and its climax: 'Moehler could derive the sole redemptive Popish Church with no greater difficulty from the Christian consciousness than Schleiermacher could his Redeemer. He could give the Christian consciousness a form, in which it seemed interchangeable with the modern principle of progress.'[2]

To contest Modernism and Protestant Liberalism, the Vatican Council comprehends them and orders them within its own system. This statement is not so paradoxical as it looks. The basis of all three positions is exactly the same. Mariology expresses what we may now see to be the heresy *par excellence*, not merely of Roman Catholicism and Neo-Protestantism, but of every Christian doctrine —and where the Church is present, how is this to be avoided?—in which the religious man appropriates the Word of God to judge, formulate and proclaim it according to his own consciousness instead of letting himself be judged and transformed by it. When it does this, the Church is simply listening to itself. From this standpoint, although Mariology is formally only an appendix to Christology, in fact it threatens it at its very heart. In this respect we must allow that Neo-Protestants display a more realistic logical coherence. Aware that their system implies rivalry between the incarnation of God in the humanity of Christ alone and his incarnation in the human consciousness, they openly prefer the latter and dismiss without regret the speculative formulations of Chalcedon. Here the situation is quite clear. God speaks directly in human evolution, in the categorical imperative, in religious feeling, and if he speaks also in the man Jesus it is only because Jesus is a specific instance, highly remarkable no doubt, of a far more general revelation. Hence one cannot maintain the Chalcedonian exclusivism which postulates only one point of meeting between God and Man. Roman Catholic thinking avoids extremes, and especially this one. It will preserve Chalcedon, but will add an extension which apparently only com-

[1] *CD* I, 2, p. 572.   [2] *Ibid.*, p. 563.

pletes Christmas but which in reality seeks to replace it no less radically. The Church is now the true place where God becomes flesh and blood. It is not only carried by the Word; it also carries the Word. If the Chalcedonian formulae apply to Jesus, by extension they are also true of the Church, even though it is difficult, as we shall see later, to give them their full sense as thus applied.[1]

The co-existence of a correct Christology with Mariology is thus a mere formality. Or, to put it less bluntly, at this point of development both Christology and Mariology have simply become appendages of ecclesiology. There is a reversal of roles. It is no longer Christ who commands the Church and religious consciousness. Christology now constitutes a special chapter of religious thought in which are expressed the intuitions of the believer or the community, of the teaching office or the ecclesiastical consensus, concerning Christ. This chapter includes not only what Scripture teaches about him but also what the Church and believers think about him, as we have seen both in Kant, Schleiermacher and Sabatier and also in consistent Mariology.

Protestants will no doubt feel surprise at these developments. They can achieve some understanding of other points in Roman Catholicism. But here they cannot but be firm. Devotion to Mary wounds not only their faith but their profoundest instincts. They freely accede to the caustic criticisms of Vinet: 'In a Christianity which is already weakened, the cult of the Virgin has weakened what remained of Christianity.'[2] 'As concerns my aversion to the cult of Mary, it is no less vigorous than well-grounded. This corruption of Christianity is in my view one of the most tragic inventions of the spirit of evil. It now bursts all limits. The great Catholic doctors of the seventeenth century would have been astounded at it' (*ibid.*). 'A Gospel which adores Mary, which gives her a part in the mediatorial power and in the divinity of the Messiah, is another gospel than that of Jesus Christ' (*ibid.*). Another gospel! Why? Vinet sees the heart of the problem, even though he does not draw all the relevant consequences: 'To set up an idol in place of the true God? This is what we do. The only point is that sometimes the idol

---

[1] M. Thurian in *Verbum Caro*, V, 1950, pp. 2–41 shows that the tendency to transfer emphasis from Christ to Mary goes back to as early as Cyril of Alexandria (cf. also de Lubac, *Méditation sur l'Eglise*, p. 282; Rahner, *Marie et l'Eglise*, p. 64). There is a corresponding Neo-Protestant movement to get closer to Christ by stressing his presence in our consciousness.

[2] Quoted by Astié, *Esprit d'Alexandre Vinet*, I, p. 317.

has a name and sometimes not. But either way it is our own heart. Yes, it is his own heart, his own carnal heart, which the deceived Catholic adores under the name of the Virgin. It is to a weakness, to a relic of unbelief, that he unwittingly pays homage. All forms of adoration, except of God incarnate in the flesh, contain this idolatry. All prostrate us before an altar of which our ego is God. If God alone is not worshipped, everything will ultimately be God except God himself.'[1]

'This is what we do.' In fact, Mariology expresses three temptations: (1) to elevate human nature, which is assumed to be capable of responding to God and co-operating with him; (2) to elevate the Church, with confidence, not in the Word of God alone, but in itself, i.e., in its piety, experiences or tradition; and (3) to comprehend Scripture within the fulness of the believer as attached to a religious collective. These three impulses correspond exactly to the presuppositions of Neo-Protestantism as we have already expounded them: (1) optimism concerning man; (2) confidence in his religious experiences; and (3) the absorption of the Bible in the moral or religious impressions of the believer or in the findings of history. Religion takes precedence of revelation, and this explains in both cases the gigantic development of natural theology, the Pelagianism inherent in both systems, the refusal of both churches to allow themselves to be questioned by the Word of God, in short, the sovereignty of religious man in place of the sole sovereignty of Jesus Christ.[2]

Conclusion

In their search for an adequate formulation of Christology, the Reformers were impelled by a number of concerns of which the following are the chief. (1) Christian truth makes no sense unless it is the living, personal and decisive communication of God himself; otherwise it is no more than a myth or an illusion. As they see it, it is not dogmas that count, but supremely and uniquely the risen and

---

[1] *Etudes sur la Littérature française*, Vol. III, 1851, p. 311.

[2] What Neo-Protestantism really needs to understand is that Mariology also expresses its own defection. No true ecumenicism is possible unless this underlying error is exposed and eradicated (cf. *CD* I, 2, p. 146). Yet some Roman Catholics are aware of this, esp. U. von Balthasar (*La Théologie de l'Histoire*, Plon, 1955, p. 67), who seeks to incorporate Mariology into Christology (p. 109) and thus to achieve, as he hopes, a more comprehensive and balanced Christology than that of Barth (*Karl Barth. Darstellung und Deutung seiner Theologie*, 1951, pp. 253ff.).

living Christ. In him God comes to us personally and triumphs over our vanity. Apart from this everything is drab and uninteresting. (2) But God is perfectly free, which means that it all depends on his initiative. We cannot provoke his intervention, nor even foresee it. We can only recognize it as a prevenient fact. This liberty also implies that if God does intervene and draw near to us, nevertheless he does not cease to be himself. He does not confound himself with us, but remains the Lord even in coming to us. This principle also emphasizes the fact that grace is never in any sense a capital which we control and which is identical with our religious life. To live by the grace of God alone is to live by his faithfulness, i.e., by the renewal of his interventions, not by an ecclesiastical or religious extension which, referred though it is to grace, has yet a certain power of its own. (3) In this sense the third Evangelical concern is to safeguard in detail the sole authority of this grace, even in the response which man is summoned to make to it. Man's obedience will never be the product of natural adherence. It will always be the victory of God over the forms, even the religious forms, of his rebellion. (4) At this point Evangelicals expressly emphasize that man is not well-disposed to God. He is not even neutral. He manifestly rises up against him in opposition to his grace. He is a rebel even in his piety. He is closed against God's action. Only a divine miracle can overcome him. His dispositions, far from constituting a kind of preamble, a field ready to be sown, a point of contact offering an appropriate response to the miracle, represent instead a negation of revelation. This realism derives directly from contemplation of the cross. (5) Thus the supreme point of the act of faith is recognition in Jesus Christ of the unforeseeable coming of God himself to manifest his power in a rigorous judgment of our condition and a literal resurrection of our being, which is otherwise doomed to perish. Taking account of these two elements, faith discovers the true dimensions of the event declared in Scripture, and also the necessity of placing confidence and hope in this event alone.

Neo-Protestants, faced by the apparently less urgent but no less genuine need to formulate the truths of their faith, follow very different impulses which we may nevertheless compare with those which precede. (1) The existence of God, which is for them a less essential question, is found to be directly proved by reason, by the sense of the infinite, by history or by the consciousness, and once they discover this proof they are unfortunately less disposed to emphasize the revelation of a God who is already known in part. The prior assurance which they have of him relegates to secondary rank any concern for his miraculous intervention. While they do not ignore this aspect of the biblical message, they are impelled to attach greater importance, if only for apologetic reasons, to the spontaneous knowledge of God which man is privileged to enjoy and which reunites the divine appeals perceptible in nature and in the Bible. (2) Although this school recognizes the liberty of God, it gives to it a very different interpretation, the accent being incontestably placed on the freedom of man. This is what must be asserted and defended unceasingly and at all costs. In spite of sin, man still has essential liberty before God. Underlined continually, sometimes imprudently and unreservedly, sometimes with greater caution, this basic intuition seems to be the common denominator of all Neo-Protestantism. Free to return to God, to obey him, to imitate him, or simply to say Yes or No to him, this man is subject to the divine appeal, but his salvation is conditioned by his own response. The final decision is not with God. It is with this responsible man who may welcome or reject grace and thus ultimately decide his own fate. It need be no surprise that a dogma like that of the election of grace should be the subject of resolute and passionate protest in this sphere. (3) In these circumstances it will be seen without difficulty that the major concern of these theologians is everywhere and always to safeguard this spark of divinity in man and therefore his co-operation with grace, which decides its efficacy. This is particularly apparent in the field of Christology, from the miraculous birth to the empty tomb and the ascension. (4) On this view sin is necessarily minimized. Nothing must be allowed to threaten the part of man, since his dignity resides in the power which remains intact even after the fall. The well-known charge of pessimism constantly brought against the Reformers springs from genuine distress: How can they be so pitiless in relation to man? Far from helping, they crush him. For those who do not know the unheard of succour there is in grace, Evangelical realism may well seem to be despairing, but only for them! However that may be, free will, the participation of man, in a word, the anthropocentricity of all these systems, which necessarily leads to the co-operation, if not of natural, at least of religious man, corresponds to a defensive reaction which will not accept God as man's sole Protector, which demands that man should be self-reliant, which feels that otherwise he is plunging into a bottomless abyss. This is the source of Neo-Protestant optimism. It indicates a lack of confidence in the work of God at the expense of that of man. (5) The act of faith thus refers both to God and to man directly associated in the progressive elevation of the human race. All dogmatic formulations must respect these criteria, and dogmas which are in conflict with these basic principles are vigorously rejected as inhuman.

As concerns Roman Catholicism, we have seen that its attachment to Jesus Christ, which is expressed in a more or less correct Christology, is submerged under Mariology, by which this church irresistibly seeks to defend a certain equilibrium between God and man and to protect its own laboriously elaborated structure. The traditional truths naturally form a part of the whole, but the development has constantly added to them new implications which control their interpretation. Thus by means of later developments the older dogmas are encircled by new decisions which both complete them and also bend them in a modern sense. In spite of the early councils and the main line of authentic tradition, the principal themes of Neo-Protestantism thus gain a voice in this system and lead the totality into a dualism of which the Vatican Council has become the official expression. (1) Revelation is deservedly honoured in this framework, but it finds additional incarnation in the Church which is its depository and norm. The personal God expresses himself through the Church, i.e., through its teaching office, hierarchy, and sacramental powers. (2 and 3) The liberty of God is respected in the authority of his earthly representative, who infallibly transmits his decrees and gives them visible and concrete form. In relation to the world the liberty of God is thus identical with the power of the Church, nor does it retain the least margin in relation to the actual institution, which has appropriated it once and for all with serene assurance. (4) The co-operation of man is safeguarded in this admirably balanced system which allots to each his own part in an arrangement which is sometimes extremely subtle. Carried over to Jesus Christ and the Church, the alliance between nature and grace is here more open and more attractive. (5) On this view faith necessarily becomes more ecclesiastical than biblical, and it can encompass humanist elements without challenge to the religious framework. In the synthesis which the Church represents between the divine and the human, there is no place for even the slightest rivalry between them, in contrast to Protestantism, which seems to oscillate between exaggerated emphasis on either the one or the other. Nevertheless, the fact that alongside Mariology Roman Catholicism does profess a rich and profound Christology helps us to understand why one can find in its members a sense of the mystery of Christ which is often far more developed than in many Protestants, for whom Christology is completely overlaid by various religious or humanitarian additions.

   In the three cases, the accent falls on the points where the interest is most acute—revelation, experience, or the Church—and everything else in the theology and life of the Church follows from this primary concentration. 'For where your treasure is, there will your heart be also' (Matt. 6.21). The dogmas illustrate in the three theologies the perspective which has imposed itself as the main concern, and they all seek to defend the basic insight. Can one say that these insights are all on the same plane? It is hard to choose between them unless one is constrained by Scripture itself, so that the insight preferred is no longer a hidden impulse but a clear confession of apostolic truth.

5

The Person and Work of Jesus Christ

As WE now turn to Christology proper, we cannot hope to deal with the whole subject in a single chapter. The plan of the present study imposes rather a different task, namely, to single out the main articles and to show that the conclusions adopted in relation to them correspond at all points and by an irresistible movement to the presuppositions on which they rest. There is here no question of chance. It is pure illusion to think that we can begin with Neo-Protestant assumptions and finally arrive at the Chalcedonian dogma. The converse is also true. Though some restatement may be necessary, Chalcedon is inevitable for those who adopt the Evangelical starting-point. Better than any arguments, these dogmas unmask the ultimate conceptions.[1]

We shall group the articles under the two great themes corresponding to the classical division, the incarnation and reconciliation.

1. *The Incarnation*

Emmanuel, God with us: this event is described in many ways in Scripture, especially in the Prologue to John, the opening verses of Hebrews, the epistles to the Ephesians and Colossians and the Nativity stories. The most succinct yet comprehensive testimony is to be found in the well-known verse John 1.14: 'The Word was made flesh.' The dogma of the incarnation has to give account of these three elements: the origin of this story of the coming of God amongst us; the occurrence; and the movement which animates it.

(i) In the first instance there is little need to define the term

---

[1] They were undoubtedly designed with this in view. Hence, although condemned by Neo-Protestants as speculative, they serve the very practical purpose of forcing us to decide, not between these dogmas and no dogmas, but between true dogmas and false.

'Word' as we use it today. Far more important is to find its meaning in the passage as illuminated by the canonical context. Now the Word in question here is that of God himself. Whatever our doubts concerning the notion as applied to God, we learn from the text that there is a reality which emanates from God and yet of which we must say that it is itself and distinct from him (John 1.1). The Word of God is his being, his act, his expression, in a word his person with an outward reference. Before considering the signification of the term, we may note that in any case it denotes a personal intervention of the Creator. What is at issue in one form or another is his own initiative.

But this intervention is also identified with a visible, historic person, namely, Jesus Christ. The apostle does not stop at the contemplation of an intradivine hypostasis. He does not attempt an abstract definition of the reality to which he applies the current concept of *logos*. On the contrary, he hastens to affirm a twofold identification which is more eloquent than any theory. The Word is God, and the Word is Jesus Christ. This is his definition.[1]

This twofold identification is in no sense qualified, and at a single stroke it reveals a truth concerning God and this man, namely, that from one aspect at least they are the same. There is thus in God an essential disposition, a decision, an overture, an activity, which, while it is his own true essence, is sufficiently distinct to be assimilated to a man, and which the Bible calls the Word or Son. We do not know this reality. We cannot conceive of anything to which it might correspond (John 1.18). But it is revealed to us in the existence of Jesus. When he speaks thus, John is not allowing himself to be entangled in speculation. He is affirming something quite concrete and tremendous. God is this man, and this man is the very being of God, who has overcome the distance which separates us from Him to be amongst us and with us. The Lord has become a historical reality (John 10.30). Whether the unity be seen from above downwards as John prefers, namely, that the Word of God is this Jesus, or from below upwards as in the Synoptists (Paul has both), namely, that this Jesus is the Word of God, the result is the same. The starting-point of the incarnation is not man, as Schleiermacher desired, but the decision of God. There is here no primary question

---

[1] The Word is also the Son, who again is both God and Jesus Christ. The reality does not derive from the words used, but the words from the reality. Other words might have been chosen at a pinch, but these are the most apt.

of an exaltation of man under the influence of a vague divine inspiration, but of the free initiative of God.

The biblical writers do not begin with a preconceived idea. They do not invent a God who will become man or a man who will raise himself up to God. For what credit could be attached to such a hypothesis? More prudent and self-effacing, these witnesses are content to give an account, as well as they can, of an event over which they have no control and which they do not pretend to prove, but which has astonished them. If it had not taken place, there would be no rhyme or reason in it. But if it has really happened, it is adequate of itself to impose itself, and its witnesses must declare it with a minimum of pretension and in full expectation of the offence which their declaration will cause.

The Word or Son, therefore, denotes this event, which may be regarded from two angles. From God's side the words mean that the Lord goes to work in person, in the fulness of his being, to take upon himself our nature and to put himself in our place. It is hard to see what is the value here of subtle distinctions between the divinity of Christ and his deity, his essential divinity and his functional. Is there then another alternative as between God or not God? At root, the Trinity is in no sense a speculation. It is demanded by the most elementary faith, which attests an encounter with God himself in this Word, in Jesus. As a human expression of the discipline of the Church, the doctrine of the Trinity is designed to guarantee the twofold discovery that God is with us in this man and that this man is the personal presence of God for us. It respects both the necessary distinction and the unity, for if God were not personally present in these two elements, what benefit should we draw from this description? That revelation may be a decisive fact, it is essential that God should be the same in his proximity and in his remoteness. In addition, the Trinity postulates that when God comes into us to open us to his presence in Jesus, it is again God himself who acts and abides in us, namely, the Holy Spirit.

In these circumstances the Word is God coming to us without ceasing to be himself in his eternity. The term denotes a second manner of being on his part. After creation comes reconciliation, i.e., a new intervention by God in very different conditions, sin having arisen in the meantime. In this second movement to overcome our revolt, it was necessary for God himself to act, but this time in a different situation, in our situation, to overcome our perdition.

Being God, the Word is necessarily eternal. We learn thereby that even before creation God desired in himself to have alongside him one to sing his glory and to mirror his perfections. The Word is in God his love evoking this other. It is in the bosom of the Father the image of the creature which will be born to praise the Lord. It is both its necessity and truth. We may thus understand why at the moment of reconciliation it is this Word which intervenes, not merely to start again the broken dialogue, but victoriously to affirm its own intention, which in part at least is the reason for its existence and which is momentarily destroyed by sin. The terms Son and Word are not chosen at random. They denote a living relationship in God which by the very fact that it exists seeks extension in creation. Checked by the fall, it now seeks to re-establish itself both in restitution of the integrity of the divine impulsion and also for the good of the creature itself.[1]

Thus Jesus himself is the history in which God comes to us. The dogma of his deity is in no sense a metaphysical description of his nature. It is the simple pronouncement of three great affirmations: (1) that this movement of God has really taken place—the basis of all our assurance; (2) that it has taken place in this man—the unanimous declaration of all the biblical witnesses; and (3) that we thus encounter in this man the Lord who accomplishes this unheard of miracle. It was necessary for God, for the unknown God, to draw near to us, and the point of the doctrine of the deity of Jesus Christ is simply to affirm that he has actually done so.[2]

Finally, in answer to *kenosis* teaching, we maintain that there are no legitimate grounds for supposing that this Word, when it became incarnate, ceased to remain itself. To be sure, it abased itself, but how can we agree that in this movement it underwent a diminution in its true being? And what profit would there be if it did, seeing we should no longer be dealing with it in this encounter if this were so? If we are not certain that God has come in person in this Word, we can only fall back on religious feelings and on man's own powers to bridge the gap left by what has now become a purely hypothetical revelation.

---

[1] The incarnation cannot be understood except in terms of the Trinity, nor can it be justified except as a confirmation of the necessity essential to the inner perfections of God, i.e., to his love.

[2] The great heresies have all substituted rationalist considerations for the gratitude of faith. Thus the Neo-Protestant Christ is a special instance of general revelation, and his divinity of the divine immanence. No place is left, therefore, for uniqueness or for true deity.

(ii) That this Word has become flesh emphasizes first the great sweep of this identification. The Word has become truly human, for the term 'flesh' is the most concrete possible term for man, for humanity, for created nature as we see it and as God judges it by assuming it.[1]

The word 'flesh' denotes humanity in that which distinguishes it from God, angels, nature and animals. Without ceasing to be himself, God has become a member of our race, assuming its characteristics. But the term is even more precise. It denotes this humanity in its actual condition, i.e., under the dominion of sin and therefore the judgment of God. It is thus equivalent to 'ourselves'. But if the Word takes our condition or nature—and why avoid a word which merely sums up the features of our species as compared with God or the animal kingdom or matter?—it does so in a different manner. In sin, Jesus remains without sin. The Bible is equally insistent both that Christ is sinless, i.e., that he maintains his relation with God, and also that he has become sin. Because he remains the Word of God, even in abasing himself to our level the Son incarnates the perfect man in full relationship with God, and yet he also incorporates himself into our sin by placing himself, the Righteous, in the gap. Though he does not take part in the revolt, he overcomes it, so that we see in him both the truth which unites and the tension of the fall which he reveals by assuming and conquering it. In this way he reflects as in a mirror the attitude of God himself, who is both righteous and free, who is compassionate to the point of entering into our misery, and who is resolved to overcome it.

The incarnation is decisive only if undertaken by God himself in manifestation of his intentions. It is accomplished by the whole being of God in this tragic solidarity. This is what is implied by the word 'flesh'. God is concealed in this dramatic history of a man both pure and true on the one side and condemned and cursed on the other. And this flesh attests the judgment which God applies to himself, fighting in his own 'body' the chaos which could touch him only in his creation and triumphing over a power which he had always resisted in himself but which had succeeded in arresting his grace in his children. He whose deity is never in question but whose heart bleeds to see the creature's ruin is willing to incorporate

[1] Lemaître's charge that the deity of Christ increases the distance between him and us and makes it impossible to understand the Jesus of history (*Foi et vérité*, p. 310) is meaningless in face of the actual incarnation and consequent historicity of the Word (John 1.14).

himself among the victims of the drama and to give himself to the titanic conflict as if he were himself at stake. The conflict shifts. God in person becomes the centre in this man and for all men. The conflict will now be waged in a very different dimension.

(iii) The future of the whole universe depends on this identification, i.e., on the movement to which God submits himself in order to reach the heart of the conflict. The verb *egeneto* which links the two terms in the identification guarantees the movement in this inconceivable history. In itself the identification might give rise to error if this verb did not protect the difference between the two poles and their meeting. What would there otherwise be to prevent the Word from being understood as a simple reality in the world in virtue of its solidarity with us? Conversely, what would there otherwise be to prevent an immediate divinization of flesh in virtue of its identification with the Word? Either way, the incarnation would lose all its value. Imprisoned in this man, God would be confounded with his perfect holiness, or, as in Schleiermacher's *Christmas Eve*, the incarnation would declare the elevation of the creature to divinity, the essential point being that flesh has become the Word (pp. 69ff.). This twofold confusion respects neither the deity of God, the perversion of man, nor the truly miraculous character of the unity breaking in like a victory over death. The verb underlines both the distance which separates the two magnitudes, so that they cannot be confounded, and also the movement which brings about their meeting, so that they cannot be separated. Essential to a proper definition of the event, it contains within itself already the well-known Chalcedonian adverbs. Its significance may be briefly described as follows.

(1) God is not this man; he becomes this man. What predominates here from first to last is the divine Subject, his decision, his initiative and his act. The God of the Gospel is the living God. Even in his love he is strong. In himself and in all his doings he is free and sovereign. One cannot speak of him as of a reality which lets go of self and easily combines with our institutions and needs. The witness of John 1.14 is not to a facile synthesis of God and man. Everything depends on the good pleasure of God. The vital point in the message is that he has decided to act. We may and should be hesitant in face of this news until he imposes himself upon us by his personal coming.

(2) The divine sovereignty and liberty alone can guarantee the

authenticity of the event. What value would there be in assuming it or even in placing it at the heart of our faith if God did not truly reveal himself in it? The incarnation makes sense only in relation to its origin. If God has become man, everything is changed. But if this formula merely expresses our own yearnings and false securities, what weight does it carry? All systems are here put in their proper place, for the event has value only because it is extraordinary. Hence the verb controls our whole attitude in faith. It shows us that faith is always and at every moment the incredible discovery of the personal and glorious coming of God which is in no sense facile or automatic but in which everything is miraculous and decisive.[1]

(3) *Egeneto* thus establishes a hierarchy in John 1.14. The Word dominates, judges and decides. This is why the unity makes sense. It is the work of God. It is an alliance, not a mere association in which the terms might be more or less interchangeable. It is a miracle, i.e., the exceptional result of the will of God to present himself as Lord in this form of a servant. The meeting takes place in a definite order. The man is assumed and subordinated. He finds his liberty in this dependence. He is taken, judged and subjected, and his felicity derives from submission to omnipotent grace.

(4) The event of the incarnation is determinative only as it is animated by the life of God. It cannot be reduced to mere truth. It is the sovereign act of the Master disposing according to his wisdom, holiness and benevolence. A creative act, it calls, constrains, quickens and transforms. It never loses its vitality. In the present circumstances of humanity, it is a perilous story of conflict, of titanic confrontation, and of victory. The elements are against it, as the biblical records abundantly testify. The cross is already near and the resurrection is present within it, since nothing can stop the love of God, resolved to conquer by submitting to the dominion of chaos.

This 'becoming' of God thus expresses all his perfections as they are set in motion by the drama which we experience, and it emphasizes the grandeur of a gesture which recapitulates in itself creation and universal history and which already intimates the final redemption. Before this fact, we can only tremble, accept and adore, and in our turn we are transformed and brought into action.[2]

[1] This insight must be respected at all points in our theology. Thus the Bible is God's Word only because God speaks, and the Church is Christ's body only because God makes it such. The glory is all God's because everything depends on him.
[2] Striking descriptions of this event may be found in Ignatius, *Eph.* 13, 3; Polycarp, *Phil.* 7, 1; Irenaeus, *Haer.* III, 18, 2; Tertullian, *Adv. Prax.* 213, 18, 2; Origen, *De*

On the details of this meeting between God and man in the incarnation, classical theology has offered several definitions which have given rise to no little discussion. Various dangers must be avoided. (1) Our way of envisaging the meeting must not convey even the slightest suggestion that the presence of God is not fully real in this man, nor must this presence be so strongly affirmed that the humanity is absorbed and becomes a mere appearance. The incarnation takes place in such a way that it prejudices neither the divinity nor the humanity. (2) It must not be suggested that the presence of the man in this union is incomplete, nor must there be attributed to this humanity powers which make it no longer similar to ours. Although righteous, this man represents us in this meeting with God. (3) Care must be taken not to conceive of the God-man as a kind of third reality intermediary between the Creator and the creature, but neither truly God nor truly man. For how can there be mediation if Jesus does not incarnate and therefore unite the two in question? The only way to avoid all these dangers is to establish carefully the true deity and the true humanity of Christ, and also their unity, though without confusion or division.

The following general thesis is thus to be respected. God in the fulness of his deity personally assumes, in his mode of being as the Son, the being and becoming of the creature, so that this humanity is associated with his divinity in such sort that they can neither be separated nor confounded. This unity is, of course, the result of a victorious conflict and not a mere state. It constitutes for us both the most unexpected event and the most unforeseen mystery, since we ourselves exist in division. This is why, if it is authentic, it must be revealed to us as a truth which contradicts our actual situation and completely transforms it. It is a power on which depends our salvation and our life.

In this regard the Chalcedonian fathers did not invent anything. They simply established certain generally accepted guiding lines by which to combat the deviations which were becoming an increasing menace in their day. We may briefly examine the conclusions of the council.

Princ. in Ench. patrist., 445, p. 164; Athanasius, De Incarn. Verb. 8; Cyril of Jerusalem, Catech. Or. IV, 9; Gregory of Nyssa, Cat. Disc. XIII, 2; XXIV, 6; John Chrysostom, Hom. de Incarn.; Augustine, Enchiridion 35; Anselm, Cur Deus Homo II, vii; Bonaventura, Meditations on the Life of Christ; and the Reformation confessions. In contrast, cf. the rather weaker statement in Vinet, Nouvelles études évangéliques, 1851, pp. 429f. and the humanistic reversal in Harnack, What is Christianity?, ET, 1901, pp. 63ff., and Sabatier, Les religions d'autorité et la religion de l'Esprit, 1904, pp. 456f.

The preamble to the definition states clearly that what is at issue is not an abstract conflict but a problem of piety.[1] The 'preaching of the truth' is in question. The rejected formulae are an expression of evil and threaten the 'seed of piety', introducing novelties contrary to the truth. We may deplore the ensuing reference to the emperor as the envoy raised up by God, along with the hierarchy, to 'preserve the flock of Christ from falsehood and to nourish the plants of truth', but the authors of the work and the circumstances in which it was composed are of less importance than the contents. What matters is the authenticity of the witness it gives and not the difficult and in many ways unedifying circumstances in which, on account of our sin, it came into being. The council then confirms the conclusions of Nicaea, Constantinople and Ephesus (431), and it adds the significant remark: 'These two symbols (Nicaea and Constantinople) were for many years sufficient to make known the faith and to strengthen true piety, for they teach all that is necessary regarding the Father, the Son and the Holy Spirit, and the incarnation of the Lord, to those who receive them with faith; but certain men, seeking to suppress the preaching of the truth, have imagined frivolous expressions because of their errors, and have dared to disfigure the mystery of the incarnation of the Lord and rejected the expression "Mother of God", or else they have introduced a kind of confusion of the natures, their monstrous dream being that there is only a single nature of the flesh and the divinity, and that the nature of the only-begotten Son by the admixture of humanity, has become capable of suffering.'[2] These are the heresies which have made the council necessary, not to satisfy a desire for disputation or abstract speculation, but in defence of the faith. If they had been silent, the fathers believed they would have betrayed the cause of Christ. If they spoke, it was simply to confirm the decisions of previous councils, with no pretence at originality.[3]

Coming now to the heart of the problem, the council excludes both those who seek to divide the mystery of the incarnation into a duality of the Son . . . and those who imagine a mixture or confusion of the two natures in Christ. More positively, they all unanimously teach 'one and the same Son, our Lord Jesus Christ, at once complete in Godhead and complete in manhood, truly God and

[1] Hefele-Leclercq, *Histoire des Conciles*, 2, 2, p. 721.
[2] *Ibid.*, pp. 721f.
[3] It is thus difficult to understand why Lemaître among others should find Nicaea more acceptable than Chalcedon (*Foi et vérité*, pp. 303ff.).

truly man, consisting also of a reasonable soul and body, of one substance with us as regards his manhood; like us in all respects apart from sin; as regards his Godhead, begotten of the father before the ages, but yet as regards his manhood begotten, for us men and for our salvation, of Mary the Virgin, the God-bearer; we confess one and the same Christ Jesus, Son, Only-begotten, recognized in two natures, without confusion (ἀσυγχύτως), without change (ἀτρέπτως), without division (ἀδιαιρέτως), without separation (ἀχωρίστως); the distinction of the two natures being in no way annulled by the union; but rather the characteristics of each nature being preserved and coming together to form one person and hypostasis; not as parted or separated into two persons, but one and the same Son and Only-begotten God the Word, Lord Jesus Christ, even as the prophets from earliest times spoke of him, and our Lord Jesus Christ himself taught us, and the creed of the fathers has handed down to us.'[1] The text concludes with a warning that none is allowed to propose any other belief. The formulae serve the faith. They have only auxiliary value. Yet the fathers realize that if the Church derogates from this statement it will stray into another faith and another religion. This is the disaster which they seek to prevent.

The main points in this definition are the unity of the person of Jesus Christ, both Son of God and Son of man, and the two natures or substances which can neither be separated nor confounded. The terms which attract such censure are not essential in themselves and the definition itself explains them. They denote that in Jesus we are dealing personally with God himself, the Word being simply his being in all its divine fulness. He is thus true God and not a symbol of divinity, a vague inspiration, an idea of perfection, an ideal of humanity. He is the living God in person, consubstantial with the Father. This assertion establishes revelation and redemption. On the other hand, he is truly and fully man, consubstantial with us apart from sin. If this were not so, the incarnation would be suspended above us. God would not really have overcome the distance which separates us from him. He would not have assumed our condition nor cancelled it by his death and resurrection. In fact, however, he is the new Adam who succeeds fallen man and in whom we see what separates us from him, what we should be and the accomplishment of our reconciliation with God. It is hardly possible to bring these

---

[1] Hefele-Leclercq, pp. 723–5; Bettenson, *Documents of the Christian Church*, 1943, pp. 72f.

two affirmations into a synthesis, and the fathers are not concerned
to make them logically coherent. They maintain that both are
essential to the defence of the Evangelical faith, and they simply see
in them the basic facts presented in Holy Scripture.

As to the mode of this union, it is more precisely defined in the
famous Greek adverbs: without confusion, change, division or
separation. Here again autonomous reason has difficulty, but what
can it do at this point? The fathers use their reason within faith and
not in the sphere of supposedly free thought. Their terms are not
meant to elucidate the mystery but clearly to mark off the limits.
In the last resort they are simply warnings. They are a kind of
discipline for the testimony of the Gospel. If we confound the two
natures, we fall into pantheism, God and man being simply two
aspects of the one reality. If we allow the changing of the divinity
into humanity or *vice versa*, we reach the same result. If we divide
the person of Christ, we annul his mediation. If we separate the
natures, we destroy the mystery of the full reunion of Creator and
creature in Jesus. All these errors derive from sin, whether in the
form of man's seeking to be equal with God (confusion) or of his
remaining in separation, which is the very definition of sin. In
either case natural theology takes the place of the revelation correctly defended by the fathers.

It must be recognized that this definition, which is extremely
simple in its intentional sobriety, is a good commentary on John 1.14
and a good safeguard against the deviations which constantly arise
afresh in relation to the various terms. It is now wholly free from
criticism. Centred on the definition of the person of Christ, it does
not sufficiently emphasize the movement which results in the union
of God and man in him. This failure deprives the declaration to a
large degree of the dynamism which animates the text of John. Jesus
himself seems a little artificial. There is no mention of his work.
Only his person is taken into account. In fact, however, Jesus is
also a history, a movement from Christmas to Good Friday, Easter
and the Ascension. He goes through a number of stages conformable
both to his being and to his mission. Nevertheless, so far as it goes
the definition is quite correct, and we may say that it is one of the
essential criteria of true adherence to Christian truth as a whole.[1]

---

[1] The real reasons why Neo-Protestantism dislikes Chalcedon are to be sought in
its doctrines of immanence, of a general incarnation and of the unity of God and man.
These reasons are usually disguised behind various accusations, e.g., of abstraction or

The description of this unity has been further investigated especially in the discussions between the Reformed and the Lutherans. The former insisted on the personal union between God and man in Christ according to the Latin tradition, whereas the latter emphasized particularly the union of natures as in the Greek tradition. Both conceptions are right, but there is a shade of difference between them which can have serious consequences. The point of the Reformed understanding is to stress the origin of the movement and the fact that, if Jesus Christ is a historical personage, the heart of it all is to be found nevertheless in the personal incarnation of God in him. The accent is thus on God intervening and giving himself. The Lutherans for their part are more concerned with the result of the movement in the person of Jesus conceived as the union of two realities in the same person. The temptation of the Reformed is to insist on the movement at the expense of the result. In other words, there is the danger of a Nestorian trend which cannot really do justice to the full unity of Christ. The Lutherans are threatened by the contrary error. By insisting on the result of the movement, they run the risk of missing the point of departure and of slipping into a mixture of the natures which perpetuates the Eutychian heresy. The classical Lutheran position undoubtedly opens the door to more serious dangers than the Reformed attitude. Directing attention to a state rather than the event, it is in danger of transforming the revelation of the living God into a datum, a principle, an autonomous reality, which in extreme form may ultimately become an immanent truth, a property of sanctified nature. Extensions of this kind have a fatal inclination towards institutionalism, which believes that there are human realities capable of bearing and conserving the truth apart from new interventions on the part of God. In other words, they tend towards the modified pantheism of modern Protestantism and the Roman Catholic view of the extension of the incarnation, both of which are convinced that grace can be possessed, whether in the consciousness or the Church. It is true that Lutherans of the classical epoch did not go to these extremes. Yet it is also true that their doctrine, though correct in many

speculation. In fact, however, Chalcedon exposes every kind of synergism, whether mariological or humanistic. In its concentration on Christ alone as Saviour it is fully in line with the true orthodox position seen, e.g., in Irenaeus, *Haer.* III, 18, 7; Tertullian, *Adv. Prax.* in *Ench. patrist.* 379; Gregory of Nyssa, *Catech. Or.* XXXVII, 8–9; Athanasius, *De Incarn. Verb.* 20; Augustine, *De Trin.* I, 11; Leo, *De Incarn.*, Denzinger 143f.; Anselm, *Cur Deus Homo.* I, 8; II, 16.

respects, does not provide adequate safeguards against these unfortunate developments.

There is thus need of greater precision to avoid the risks indicated. The expressions *anhypostasis* and *enhypostasis*, the content of which is very ancient, were adopted with this intention. The first of these signifies that the humanity of Jesus Christ cannot be isolated from his deity as though it had an existence in and for itself. The second lays positive emphasis on the fact that the humanity is strictly dependent on the deity. Using person for hypostasis, some modern writers have suspected in these ancient formulations a tendency to deny the human personality of Jesus, and they have thus brought against them the charge of Docetism. This mistake, like many others, rests on ignorance of the use of terms. When the fathers introduced these terms, they had no intention of mutilating the full humanity of Jesus. Their concern was to stress the perfect unity of his humanity with his deity in the correct order. This humanity receives its fulness only in its dependence with regard to the Son who has assumed it (*enhypostasis*); separated from it (*anhypostasis* with an 'a' privative), it is no longer the humanity of the Son of God but an independent creature. Now the humanity is not truly itself except in its unity with God. To separate it from the personal presence of God is not merely to break the unity but also to rob this humanity of its true nature. Sin consists precisely in this separation and in the fatal humanity of man which results.

These more precise statements are essential if we are to avoid at the heart of the mystery not merely deficient formulae, but sin itself insinuating itself into these profundities to destroy the work of God and to express the preferences of our fallen minds in place of the revelation of the risen Christ. The two terms simply indicate that the humanity of Jesus receives its fulness from strict dependence in relation to the divinity. In this union, the divine nature predominates. It is this nature which commands and which provides what is necessary. The human nature receives. It is set in motion and becomes active under the influence of the first. This order prefigures true co-operation between God and man and already expresses a correct relation between faith and works.[1]

The *communicatio idiomatum* has been particularly defended by

---

[1] Rejecting Chalcedon, Neo-Protestantism concentrates on the humanity of Jesus, but wrongly seeks to understand it in terms of our humanity rather than as the humanity of God known only by revelation.

the Lutherans, who intend thereby to emphasize the perfection of the unity. Whatever happens to Jesus Christ concerns both the Word and the flesh. If the Son of Man is also the Son of God, we cannot attribute certain events to his humanity alone and certain other aspects of his work to his divinity alone. It is the Saviour in his divine humanity who comes and goes, preaches and heals, suffers and dies, with no breach of the unity of his person. Thus, even though the two natures are distinct, there is between them a real communication of their proper attributes. To heal the sick, Jesus is endowed with divine power, while in his death his divinity does not leave him but submits to the laws of nature. Sometimes he is exalted, as at his transfiguration and above all his resurrection. Sometimes he is abased even to the point of momentary ignorance of the intentions of his Father, with whom, of course, he is so intimately united that when we contemplate this man it is the Father whom we are given to see. These various points in his history all affect his whole being, and his life is a perpetual exchange in this unity.

The Reformed do not reject this proposition, which is wholly in keeping with the teaching of the Gospels. But the Lutherans, in their legitimate desire to stress the real presence of God in Christ, go to extremes in postulating, in consequence of this exchange, a kind of elevation of the human nature. By its relation with God, and by the communication of some of the attributes of God, it has become capable in itself of divine acts, as if the power belonged to it. There is here a certain transubstantiation; nature is lifted above itself and partially divinized. Instead of simple communication we have an attributing of divine properties to the humanity, which is thus regarded as superior to itself. The result is unacceptable because it leads to a partial sacralization of nature and then to institutional confusion. Man is presumed to be endowed with a religious power which elevates him above his condition and which allows him both to possess the truth in himself and to co-operate with grace. All attempts at Christian natural theology find justification here, as does also the idea of an intrinsic continuity in the Church and the Christian consciousness. In truth, however, human nature remains just what it is. If at times it is endowed with powers which are beyond it, this communication is not of itself but by the grace of God. It is God's work in man, who participates in it without being thereby lifted above himself.[1]

[1] Though Christ differs from us in virtue of his union with God and his sinlessness,

The *extra calvinisticum* corresponds to the concern of the Reformed to safeguard the sole glory of God and to avoid its admixture with human pretensions. Without weakening the real presence of God in the flesh (the *intra carnem*), but seeking to stress the fulness of the divinity, the Reformed follow several fathers in declaring that the divinity cannot be imprisoned in Jesus. It is hidden in him, but it also remains in heaven. Here, then, as in their forensic grace, they do not minimize the divine intervention but they do not allow it to be confused with transformed human elements. They thus champion the divine liberty fulfilled, of course, in the divine self-giving, in the divine love. This further refinement is a confirmation of that already mentioned. Calvin has formulated it in irrefutable terms: 'For although the boundless essence of the Word was united with human nature into one person, we have no idea of any enclosing. The Son of God descended miraculously from heaven, yet without abandoning heaven; was pleased to be conceived miraculously in the Virgin's womb, to live on the earth, and hang upon the cross, and yet always filled the world from the beginning.'[1] Athanasius had already defended it: 'For he was not circumscribed in the body, nor, while present in the body, was he absent elsewhere; nor, while he moved the body, was the universe left void of his working and providence; but, thing most marvellous, Word as he was, so far from being contained by anything, he rather contained all things himself.'[2]

Gregory of Nyssa, Augustine, John Damascene and Thomas Aquinas have emphasized the same truth. Even Luther did not completely ignore it. The intention behind it is to safeguard the essence of the faith, namely, the dynamism of the incarnation, the sovereignty and initiative of God, the distinction between the Word and the flesh, their unity without confusion, in short, the Gospel of the coming of God among us to take to himself our distress and to rescue us from it.

Why did God have to act in this way? Could he not save us by some other means? *Cur Deus homo?* This classic question claims our attention. It is not speculative. It is not meant to be in either Athanasius or Anselm. It arises within faith and not at the philosophical level. Far from speculating on an eventual intervention of

he does so as authentic man and not as the transubstantiated or consubstantiated man of Roman Catholic or Lutheran Christology, with its dangerous ecclesiastical, liturgical and pietistic implications.

[1] *Inst.* II, 13, 4.   [2] *De Incarn. Verb.* 17.

H

God, Athanasius and Anselm both consider the question in sub-jection to the given fact of this intervention. The hypothesis that God might have acted otherwise falls before the decision which he took to act in this way. Hence we cannot question the act. We can only seek to understand it. We have thus to plumb the motives behind the decision as displayed in revelation itself. The wonder of faith thus precedes and conditions the investigation. But it also demands it, for we are called upon to descry the reasons for this event. We thus discover that in the form in which it is presented this work corresponds no less to the perfections of God than to the aim in view. God's righteousness, love, patience and glory are satis-fied by this act, so that the person of God is fulfilled in it. On the other hand, it is fully commensurate with the demands of our human drama. If reasons are asked, we may thus reply that this intervention corresponds to all the factors in the divine and human problem posed by a creation which is fallen but which is also called to reconciliation.

That the unknown God should be known by us, it was necessary that he himself should overcome the distance dividing us. This act is superfluous only if we know him already. Drawing near to us, God shows us who he is, for what do we really know of his per-fections apart from his humanity? By his presence he also brings to light our own situation. Here humanity is measured by another standard than its own. In our place he then decides for us. It is he who now fights and suffers in our condition and for us. This leads us to the heart of the debate. Who accomplishes our salvation, he or we? There seems to be no third possibility. Jesus is either our Saviour or our Example. Moreover, he causes to rise up among us a new man who is freed from his chains and impotence and who is restored to life. Who but the God-man can face death and defeat it? This act is necessary if we are to have complete assurance.

The aim of these propositions is thus to protect the elementary requirements of faith and to ward off the theories which endanger it.[1]

The dogma of the incarnation is completed by two further state-

[1] Other attempts at explanation all resolve themselves into variations of Docetism on the one side and the complementary Ebionitism on the other, or less crudely Nestorianism on the one side or Eutychianism on the other. In spite of their antithetical character, these heresies have a common origin in the resistance of sinful man to the fact of the incarnation, and they shade into one another in their implications, and particularly in their final exaltation of humanity. In face of them, whether in ancient or modern form, we can the better appreciate the firm and clear-sighted work of Leo and the Chalcedonian fathers.

ments adopted from the creeds of Nicaea and Constantinople, namely, 'conceived of the Holy Ghost' and 'born of the Virgin Mary'. These expressions denote the mystery of Christmas and already contain implicitly the definitions of Chalcedon. They show us that Jesus is a man in the full sense, the son of a real mother, and yet that there is in his birth a mysterious element which points us continuously to something else, i.e., to the Holy Spirit. He is truly flesh, yet, slight though the biblical testimony is on the point, it plainly seeks to warn us that this truly human birth had also and at the same time another origin. This is not now denoted by the term 'Word', as in John, but by reference to the Holy Spirit. Now for all the biblical authors the Holy Spirit is God himself, the Lord of lords. Here again we have the identification with distinction noted in John with respect to God and the Word. The cause of this birth is not to be found in man, nor in a vague general providence in which the Creator is regarded as the more or less distant basis of all procreation and in which children are in some sort viewed as gifts of his fatherly goodness. No, the disciples are at pains to make it clear that the conception of this infant is the result of a direct intervention of God. Sometimes the witness is negative in terms of the exclusion of Joseph, sometimes positive in terms of the intervention of the Spirit, but either way it is affirmed that, though this infant has all the features of full humanity through his mother, yet the direct cause of this event is God himself coming in the form of the Holy Spirit in Mary. This does not mean, as some have thought, that there was a kind of conjugal union between the Holy Spirit and the mother of Jesus. At this point the Bible makes it perfectly plain, in harmony with its whole teaching, that if Christmas celebrates the birth of the infant Jesus, it proclaims above all the intervention of God, the movement by which he himself comes into our midst to bring about this event, acting among us in place of man. God is the true Master of this event in which he himself is present. For the action of God cannot be separated from God himself personally active and therefore present in his activity. Though it is not a full definition of the incarnation, the twofold credal phrase is thus a kind of advance notice to the reader. This infant is the product of a special intervention of God making use of Mary to bring into the world a being who is both like us through his mother and different from us in virtue of his divine origin. This event is historical and yet it is also supra-historical, for the initiative is not with man but with God, who is its chief and indeed its only author. These are the elements which the doctrine of the incarnation must always respect.

The sovereignty of God in this act is also emphasized in the judgment which the records therein pass on man. At the commencement neither Joseph nor Mary is truly active. The exclusion of the former is an indication that the supposedly powerful element of sex, the most resolute and enterprising representative of human pride and pretension, has here to give place to God. Grace alone must act, and man's effort can only disannul it. The same phenomenon is found in Mary, who represents the human creature without either power or will, without creative or sovereign strength. In both cases the Holy Spirit alone is truly active, and he subsequently makes Mary active in her turn.

This description tells us what happens in the incarnation and then more generally in the work of grace. Against the false doctrine of a preliminary co-operation of nature with grace as seen both in Roman Catholicism and in Neo-Protestantism, the two biblical expressions of the ancient creed give us a picture of the true co-operation which follows the work of grace. 'Human nature possesses no capacity for becoming the human nature of Jesus Christ, the place of divine revelation. It cannot be the work-mate of God. If it actually becomes so, it is not because of any attributes which it possessed already and in itself, but because of what is done to it by the divine Word, and so not because of what it has to do or give, but because of what it has to suffer and receive—and at the hand of God. The virginity of Mary in the birth of the Lord is the denial, not of man in the presence of God, but of any power, attribute or capacity in him for God. If he has this power—and Mary clearly has it—it means strictly and exclusively that he acquires it, that it is laid upon him.'[1] Man thus comes to co-operate with God only under the impulsion of God himself. His good works are the result, or fruit, of grace, not a meritorious contribution of his own.

This is why the Holy Spirit is mentioned in this connection. He alone is our capacity to receive the Word of God, to respond to it and to obey it. He comes into us to overcome us, to open us to the completely new reality of the divine intervention, so that our faith and obedience—and the Church itself which responds to its Lord and adores and serves him—are in fact miracles of God, the creation of his free initiative. Woman is here presented as nature enabled by

[1] K. Barth, CD I, 2, p. 188.

God to receive the gift and power of his Word through the intervention of his Spirit, i.e., through his own presence in it. She is also a figure of the Church which lives by the Word of God alone, not simply remaining passive, but called into action by its Lord. The Holy Spirit indicates both the incapacity of man for God and the irruption of the divine love which itself constitutes within us the capacity to love and serve him, though not by confusion with our own fallen nature. The fact that we may receive and serve is already the work of God within us.

Like John 1.14 these two phrases magnify the grace of God alone, like the many declarations of the apostle Paul that if it is of grace it is no longer of works (Eph. 2.9; Rom. 3.20; Gal. 2.16, etc.).[1]

The story of the incarnation is thus the story of the unfolding of the divine action which is the expression of the divine being. God abases himself in his Son to the level of condemned sinners to raise us up to the liberty, peace and truth of creatures who are fully reconciled to their Creator and who find their destiny in this association. The abasement and the elevation are more specifically accomplished in the second phase of this story, the work of Good Friday and Easter.

2. *Reconciliation*

The man whom we have briefly described in respect of his origin, of the movement which causes him to be born and of the divine and human fulness in which he lives, now goes on to effect our reconciliation with God. His work will express his person and bear all its features. These two aspects of his existence are indissoluble. They are linked by a perfect correspondence. His being accomplishes his acts and his acts manifest what he is. The same features which occur in the definition of his person are thus found again in his life. Together, the two form his history, which is at the same time that of the intervention of God among us and for our salvation. It is in living thus that he fulfils the will of God and our reconciliation with him. It all takes place in him; it is all achieved in his existence. His words are acts and his acts are the Word of God addressing us. We must be equally careful not to separate from his person our

---

[1] These expressions render a divine-human synthesis impossible, and therefore both Neo-Protestants and Roman Catholics try to evade them, the former by rejection, the latter by reinterpretation. It should be noted that the phrases do not negate human co-operation. Grace enables man to do what previously he could not. It thus liberates him for full and responsible co-operation.

participation in his work, i.e., soteriology, since we shall see that this, too, is implicated in his history. Thus everything is focused on his name, i.e., on his person and work, in which the work of God and our restoration are fully and definitively accomplished.

If, then, we are to know the divine decision concerning us, we must simply follow the various movements which constitute the life of this man in his short history. Like everything which concerns him, this history has a double dimension. He acts as Son of God and as man. His work is that of the Word made flesh. To his two natures, or, if we prefer it, to the two aspects of his personal fulness, there corresponds a history which is both twofold and yet one, God's action taking place in human and earthly events. The tension which rends the creature is reproduced in him, so that sometimes his deity seems to be set in the shadows. At other times it asserts itself triumphantly. It is thus that as man he relives our drama in confrontation with God. All phases of the conflict reveal God at grips with man and man wrestling with God. But always God is there to conquer. This meeting and twofold presence, in a living unity which does not exclude conflict but results in reconciliation, constitute the two aspects of his history, which is at one and the same time that of God and that of man in direct confrontation.

The incarnation sets us before a compound work where God's action is linked with man's. It sets us in a full union of history and supra-history, without confusion or separation. In this man we take part in a dramatic recapitulation of universal history in which God and man confront one another directly to re-establish peace between them. It is this meeting which itself constitutes the event by which God comes to end our tragedy.

Before examining this mighty enterprise, we may first make three more general observations.

(1) The many terms used to describe the work of reconciliation are not essential in themselves. From the very first we find such words—usually based on the Bible—as ransom, debt, sacrifice, mediation, substitution, satisfaction, merit, redemption, propitiation and expiation. To build a doctrine of salvation on mere discussion of these terms might give a balanced system, but it would also be to deprive it of life. Here more than anywhere what really counts is the person of Jesus Christ in his movement. In this regard, it is worth noting that several passages in the early fathers give more solid insights even in their lack of precision and by their very

THE PERSON AND WORK OF JESUS CHRIST   231

omissions than many of the later more rigorous and self-enclosed expositions. The closer the dogmatic discussion, the more the living person of the Saviour seems to withdraw. Instead of being simple witness the dogma finally claims to be the enunciation of the truth itself. The primary concern here is not with correct expositions; it is with our life and death, with our encounter with the living God, and therefore with our ultimate destiny.[1]

(2) The work we are to describe has both an objective and a subjective bearing. Now in the history of the doctrine there has often been tension between these, and innumerable misunderstandings have resulted. Since Trent, Roman Catholicism has constantly charged the Reformation with undue objectivity. Seeking a middle path, it has opposed both what it considers to be the extremes of pretended orthodoxy and also the integral subjectivism of the humanists. Neo-Protestants have brought the same charges, but they embrace Roman Catholics as well under the accusation of theological objectivism.[2]

But surely these tensions and misunderstandings derive from a deficient doctrine of the Holy Spirit. In the last resort, is not the part of man, which some seek to preserve at all costs and which they accuse others of neglecting, the work of the Holy Spirit? If the Reformers had really left us outside the work of God, they might well be accused of undue objectivism. But this is not so. The participation of man is for them fully assured by the miracle of the Spirit who unites us with Jesus. The fears of Roman Catholic theology are thus without foundation. Indeed, they seem to be simply a pretext to safeguard free will. As for Neo-Protestantism, if it really wished to stress the part of man—in face of a certain type of orthodoxy which ignored it—would it not have done better to examine the work of the Spirit instead of reducing it to a vague inspiration and thus leaving no option but to emphasize out of all proportion the capacities of natural or religious man?

Placed under the authority of revelation in its three aspects, objectivity is surely correct as a definition of the work of God in its fulness and as a description of grace, which alone is truly decisive, in all the stages of salvation. Authentic subjectivity is comprehended

---

[1] True theologians have always seen this. Cf. H. F. Kohlbrügge, *Die Lehre des Heils*, 1903, Qu. 232; also such early fathers as Irenaeus, Origen and Gregory of Nyssa (in spite of the pedestrian criticism of Fulliquet, *Précis de dogmatique*, 1912, p. 48).

[2] Cf. J. Rivière, *Le dogme de la rédemption*, 1931, pp. 496ff., 553; Sabatier, *La doctrine de l'expiation*, 1903, p. 107.

within objectivity. Hence if it is ignored, the fault lies not so much with too abstract a definition of the mercy of God as with an incorrect exposition of its realization in Christ, which carries within it our response.

The true Catholicism of the early Church grasped this perfectly well, whereas Roman Catholicism and Neo-Protestantism have unfortunately misstated the whole problem. These two movements seem to be perpetually concerned to protect man against God, as though he were in danger of being crushed by grace. A kind of rivalry is established to save him from the absorption which in fact is alone able to liberate him. On this view, subjectivity is simply a fresh assertion of the natural man who is loathe to die. This man's religion becomes an independent value. Before God, he thinks that he is a useful partner in virtue of his own piety. He does not realize that it is by completely renouncing himself that, through the strait gate, he will find again his true destiny. Hence the Holy Spirit must make him die to this subjectivity in order that in Christ alone he may find his true nature, freedom and responsibility. He will become true man only as he ceases to be and begins a new life in the Lord. This assumption of man in Christ is his only chance of alliance with God, and since grace operates only through this death and resurrection, the more we insist on its objective action the more chance there is of seeing the birth of this new human subjectivity which is fully assumed by God. This is why the Reformers sometimes give the impression of neglecting man. By insisting so much on the work of God, they offer man his only hope of truly participating in grace. When God begins to work, man can only die and rise again. It is thus better to speak of the power which accomplishes this than to talk incessantly of man at the expense of that which can heal him. In the last analysis, the life of this man, his experiences, his being and action, are simply his being in Christ, not as a permanent endowment, but as a constant gift of grace, i.e., as a judgment, death and resurrection. Man seeks to be something in his own right, but the Word of God condemns and rehabilitates him. Thus strictly the subject exists only in the object, in which it finds also, in the right order, its legitimate autonomy.[1]

In this exposition we shall seek to give as objective a description as possible. This does not mean that we neglect our own participation in the mystery of life. It means rather that we wish to emphasize

[1] Cf. Augustine, *Enchiridion* 53.

it as the fruit of the grace which triumphs over our own lamentable tendency to autonomy.

(3) It has been alleged and repeated that the classical doctrine of expiation rests primarily on passages in Paul, and that the teaching of Paul differs from that of the Gospels. Now there is, of course, no doubt that the Pauline Epistles are an inexhaustible source of references to the redemptive death of Jesus Christ, not only in the well-known passages, but also in the profound movement of the apostle's doctrine.[1]

But Paul is not the only one to develop these ideas. Though they are more historical in the preceding sense of a history in two dimensions, the Synoptic Gospels contain similar indications, some of which are quite plain, some rather more mysterious. The same is true of other New Testament books, where we find much the same kind of statement, often under Old Testament influence.[2]

The difficulty is that we may become so entangled in ready-made doctrines that we do not find in this mystery the assurance of our own life as it is snatched from death, and therefore our most certain hope.

Perhaps **we** shall find greatest help at this point in a linguistic consideration of the relevant Greek words *allasso, antallagma, apallasso, dialasso,* and especially *katallasso, apokatallasso* and *katallage.*[3]

The chief moments in the history of God and men are indicated by these various compounds, all of which relate basically to the idea of change or exchange. Men have changed the truth of God into a lie. But God also changes his wrath into pardon. By a specific action he modifies the situation of man, changing his state from that of a sinner to that of a son. The process which transforms the relations between creature and Creator, and also between one creature and another, thus transfiguring the whole universe, is worked out in Jesus Christ, and especially in his death and resurrection, i.e., in the revolution whose author is God and which Scripture specifically calls reconciliation.

---

[1] Cf. Rom. 3.21f.; 4.25; 5.6, 9; 6.3; 8.3; 14.15; I Cor. 1.22f.; 2.2; 6.20; 7.23; 15.21f.; II Cor. 5.20ff.; Gal. 1.4; 2.20f.; 4.4f.; Eph. 2.4f., 13; 5.25f.; Col. 1.20; 2.10; I Thess 4.16; 5.9; I Tim. 2.5; II Tim. 1.9; Tit. 2.14; 3.3f.

[2] For the Synoptic Gospels, cf. Mark 8.31f. and par.; 9.12; 10.45 and par.; 14.22ff. and par.; 14.36f.; 14.61 and par.; Luke 24.44ff. Cf. also John 1.29; 3.16; I John 4.9f.; John 10.10f., 15; I John 2.2; Acts 8.28–36; I Peter 1.18–21; 2.21–25; 3.18f.; Heb. 7.26f.; 8.6; 9.15; 12.24; also 2.17; 9.5; 9.26; 10.10, 29; 13.20; Rev. 1.5f.; 5.9; 7.14; 22.14.　　　　[3] Cf. Büchsel in *TWNT* I, pp. 252–60 (*TDNT* I, pp. 251–9).

H*

We shall now examine certain elements in this change or exchange in the light of some basic concepts which recall both the presence of God in Jesus, in the history of his love, and also the presence of man in the drama of his fall and elevation.

(i) *Jesus Christ is the covenant between God and men*

The idea of a covenant denotes in both the Old and the New Testament a relation of perfect unity between God and the creature according to the reciprocal requirements of their respective natures. It thus presupposes two partners perfectly associated in the order befitting their status. It is most simply described in Lev. 26.12: 'I will be your God, and ye shall be my people.' The question arises, however, how this is to be achieved. The Bible unhesitatingly replies that it can be achieved only at one point in history, in the person who bears the name of Jesus of Nazareth. Everywhere else it is shattered. This is the central message of the Gospel.

The covenant concept was not greatly exploited by the early fathers but was strikingly emphasized by seventeenth-century Protestant theologians. When strictly applied to Jesus Christ, who is its true content, it may be divided into three essential elements. It implies (1) the real presence of two partners associated in this man; (2) the history of a drama and victory which re-establishes the contract between the two partners; and (3) a miraculous revelation concerning this person who incarnates all the forces concerned. We shall now consider separately each of these three aspects of God's covenant with us.

(1) A covenant means encounter, mediation, mutual openness and spontaneous knowledge, faithfulness on both sides. Where there is elsewhere only competition and strife, here peace is attained in a perfect adjustment of the two associates. There is no more question of wrath and judgment on the one side or revolt and indifference on the other. God is seen in all his kindness and glory as the one who loves and evokes the response of love. Man for his part reflects this perfection according to his vocation as a creature. Not merely is he well disposed to the Creator but all his constituent qualities correspond perfectly to those of God. Within the limits of creation, he may be defined in terms of this resemblance. His humanity responds to the divine fulness as the image reflects the figure which faces it.

This analogy, to which we must refer already, legitimates the meeting of the two partners, their close co-existence, and the exchanges which constitute their common life and perfect unity. In this association they are wholly present the one to the other. In all the fulness of his being God is incarnate in this man to re-establish with him the unity which was the goal of creation. By a miracle of condescension he is truly there, united with this man. Conversely, this man, at this point in history, is truly linked with God.[1]

If, however, this meeting implies a presence, namely, that of God in all his perfections and that of man as God willed and created him, it also carries with it a judgment. Why is God's presence actual here and not elsewhere? Except at this one point in history, it is not received. God is Lord of his creation, but his presence is as it were effaced and denied by those who should profit by it. The fact that God comes forward to unite himself with this man shows the gravity of his absence elsewhere. Since they no longer live in this correspondence, other men are not qualified to take part in this covenant. They can no longer give the response which God expects in order that his perfection may be mirrored in that of his partner.

We thus find ourselves in face of a unique event. In this man we realize that God and man are fully associated, living in a perfect reciprocal knowledge, in a love without opposition or shadow, in a permanent dialogue which never ought to have ceased between Creator and creature. God is personally present and this man who responds to him bears all the features of an authentic creature. Elsewhere things are very different.

(2) This serene vision of full correspondence between man and God cannot exhaust the significance of the covenant personified in Jesus Christ. In itself it is not a peaceable state. It is a tumultuous history which comprehends both this basic element and yet also the rupture of the covenant and its re-establishment by a striking victory. In Jesus, God and man are ready to go through together all the phases of the history of the race, from its perfection to its fall and redemption. Hence this man does not restrict himself to living in covenant with God. He elects to bear the tension which destroys the covenant, and thus to re-establish it.

As we follow the stages of this history, we first find in him the perfection which obtained at the outset. But at once we see even this man fall victim to opposition and suffering. He identifies himself

---

[1] It is as difficult to conceive of this meeting as it is for one born blind to describe what he has not seen. It is something new which we can know only by special illumination.

with our situation. Though perfect man, he becomes the malefactor of Good Friday. 'If he were not a malefactor, we would not have delivered him up unto thee' (John 18.30). This is what the religious leaders of the Jewish nation say when they bring him before the representative of the Roman state. Apart from sin—and in this respect we cannot retract what we have already said—he becomes the man of corruption, bearing our sins in his own body (I Peter 2.24). He thus passes from the one state to the other, revealing our own history, making himself like us to bear our curse (Gal. 3.13). In this second situation he shows us what we really are.'[1]

In 'his *status exaninationis*, to use the ancient term—though strictly one should not speak of a state but of a stage in the movement which leads from the perfection of his humanity to his ruin and then back to his former glory—Jesus shows us the actual position of the man who has broken his covenant with God. In spite of his true or pretended greatness, he has become a malefactor who stands under the wrath and malediction of God, who is condemned to death, to definitive destruction. The negation of the covenant deprives him of God and of life. God still loves him, but when his love is repulsed it necessarily reproves that which contradicts it and thus manifests itself as judgment and wrath, as the judgment, wrath and reprobation of this love which cannot, without denying itself, either cease to reign or let go its object.

In thus abasing himself, Jesus descends by a fall similar to our own into the depths of disobedience and revolt. He does not take part, of course, in the rebellion. He voluntarily gives himself up to it in order that from within he may overcome this movement of self-destruction. He even goes to the point of acknowledging his dereliction (Matt. 27.46). From the perfection of complete harmony with God he abandons himself to the darkness of our solitude, drinking to the very dregs the cup of the wrath of God (Jer. 25.15). In this respect, too, the second Adam imitates the first, although in very different circumstances.

The history does not end with defeat. A third stage follows. This is the resurrection, of which three aspects are particularly striking in the present context.

(*a*) On Easter Day we see in him for the first time a man who

---

[1] Observation alone cannot show us our true state; it can show us only the ambiguity of our nature. We know the fall only in the light of Scripture, and specifically of the incarnation.

triumphs over death. The faithful and victorious servant replaces the unfaithful and fallen. In the same situation as Adam and facing the same enemy, he resists and comes through unscathed. We no longer hear the voice of the tempter nor that of the first man. The murder of Cain, the revolt of the chosen people, the verdict of the Sanhedrin, the treachery of Judas, all these crimes are overcome, and with them the clamour of unbelief. Here man lives. He has found again his liberty, his ability to praise his Lord, and therefore to escape nothingness. At Easter the creature appears before us as God willed it and in the dominant situation which God attributed to it.

(*b*) But if this man is actually in this position, it is because God himself has intervened for him. What creature could regain its integrity of itself? God has triumphed in this man for him and for all. Otherwise the victory would be only an illusion. To be a true human victory, it must first be God's victory. The two aspects are complementary. Man is restored because God snatches him from ruin, but God wills to gain the victory, not in heaven only, but in the very man whom he restores.

(*c*) Thus God and man are at one in this struggle and victory. And this is the meaning of the covenant. It is no frigid alliance, but a living union for better or for worse, a mutual submission to the requirements of truth, an effort in concert. The covenant is here a drama, but one which comes to a happy end, just because God has chosen to ally himself with man to the point of solidarity with his destiny. The covenant is reconstituted in this man for all humanity.[1]

All these exchanges lead to a final substitution. One world is excluded, rejected and condemned, and it is replaced by another in which God reigns and man serves him. This twofold restoration—of the Son of God and of man in the same act—marks the end of the drama. At this unique point in history the past is rejected and a new situation definitively established. Objectively, the fact is already in force for all humanity, since Jesus represents us all before the Father in the newness of his being which has triumphed over death. We have only to grasp this by the inner illumination of the Holy Spirit and the benefits of this work will be applied to us.

(3) Finally, this history sheds a vivid light on the identity of the

[1] It is part of the significance of the empty tomb to show us that our concern is not merely with the soul but with the whole man. Rather strangely, the supposed champions of true humanity have been the most eager to deny the bodily resurrection and thus to lose their grasp of real man.

one who lives it. What man can so deliver himself from the domination of sin as to be completely free from it and able moreover to put it on without participating in it, to subject himself to its effects and to triumph over it? We may say quite confidently that the race has never produced such a man. If we affirm nevertheless that one has done this, we must call this one exceptional. Any diminution of his person will inevitably involve a modification of the service which he renders. But in what sense is he exceptional? In his twofold qualification. The biblical witnesses define his person in terms of the benefit derived from his work. They declare that God alone has the power to accomplish this restitution and yet that it is necessary that the victory should be won by a man. These two requirements are both equally urgent. If the first is not met, the covenant is not sealed with God; if the second is neglected, man is absent from the meeting. We are thus faced by two essential conditions if the action is to be valid.

God alone can become such a man. He alone has the power to resist temptation and to incarnate himself in a being free from the consequences of the fall. He alone can validate the sacrifice of the cross and give to it its redemptive significance. For what death other than that of the Son of God can satisfy justice and substitute blessing for cursing? In other words, in spite of the intuitions of integral subjectivism, an act of God was necessary for the Lord to become propitious to us again. It was necessary for several reasons, first, because the power of sin was so great that it could not be overcome by anyone else, then because he could show us the nature of his love only by himself suffering the injury done to his honour and sparing us the punishment, and finally because the victory had to be real and not illusory. Moreover, there is an element of grandeur in this struggle of God against Satan when all creation had been conquered and subjected by this enemy. It is the more extraordinary in that God does not come with the glory of an avenging verdict but in the humiliation of the Son as the Servant of all, as the Lamb led to the slaughter. This mystery is worthy of God, and the more we study it the more we are compelled to admire the lofty wisdom and unfathomable mercy therein revealed. This object is surely more glorious and more worthy of our admiration than the intuitions of our consciousness and the imperatives of the moral law.[1]

[1] Though many of the objections to the substitutionary nature of Christ's work seem to have some cogency, e.g., the personal aspect of responsibility, the difficulty of one

The cross is thus the expression of a permanent suffering in God. Far from being a momentary act, it reveals a wound which God bears in himself from the beginning and which is here written into our history. Surely God must have suffered on account of sin from the very moment of its appearance. Surely he must have been tortured by this revolt against his grace and this disavowal of his love. Sin does not affect man alone, so that it is enough merely to correct its results in us. It carries its negation into God himself, who overcomes it both for his own glory and for our deliverance. Calvary reveals the state in which God finds himself in consequence of our disobedience. It lays bare the heart of God and the means which he selects to end the drama which tests him no less and perhaps more than us. Once we see the twofold reach of this suffering, we can no longer speak as if it concerned only man or only God. The two partners are together. They are engaged in the same adventure. And when we can no longer count on man finding the solution, we must praise God for the decision which he takes to end this tragedy.

The God of the covenant is thus a very concrete God. Before picturing him in heaven, we must first see him alongside us, fighting with us, sharing our lot, as if his own existence depended on it. What concerns us touches him. He does not merely present us with an abstract image of what we should be from the lofty distance of his divine throne. He sets before us in himself all the aspects of our own situation. Jesus incarnates them successively right up to the ultimate victory. God is fully there in Christ, participating in our condition in order to restore it.

In this situation, he plays both his own role and ours. The fault must be remedied by the guilty, and when he cannot do it God himself takes up the role of the defaulting creature. Man is powerless, and therefore God comes to answer for him. In his Son, he becomes his own counterpart, his own effective partner, in place of the defaulter. Nor does he do this merely in the bosom of the Trinity. He does it in creation too. The Word which was the instrument of creation now becomes the organ of its rehabilitation. Laying aside his majesty, he accepts the role of the fallen creature, personifying in his existence the whole of creation now brought back into

suffering for all, etc., they break against the fundamental truths of the incarnation and of the indissoluble union of God's love and righteousness, of all his perfections, in this act.

covenant in him. In face of the absence, or silence, of man generally, and the even more serious unresponsiveness of his chosen people, God himself comes in his Son to incarnate humanity in its different stages and to restore it to himself.

He becomes both the Master and the Partner in the covenant, both the God who remakes contact and the man who accepts it. In Jesus Christ God is real and close, but so, too, is man: real because he responds to his Creator, which is the only guarantee of life; and close because he overcomes the perversions which alienate us from our true being. Here God is both. For he substitutes himself for us in order to make response for us and by his work to lead us to make this response again in him.[1]

The covenant thus concluded in Jesus Christ reflects that which obtains between the Father and the Son and it also reproduces that which was constituted by creation. It is effected in a series of exchanges which bring us back into fellowship with God. The Son exchanges his glory for the humility of the servant. God exchanges his justice for justification. Jesus exchanges his human perfection for the curse which falls on the sinner. Man in him exchanges his foolish independence for restored obedience. Life takes the place of death. All this takes place in him for us. In his life it is we who triumph over ourselves, thanks to the fact that he has disguised the divine omnipotence in this humanity and that restoration is thus made possible. Easter is in the first instance a human victory. It is possible only because God is in this man. Yet its significance is not just religious; it is more broadly human. This is our own victory in him and by him for us.

Thus the covenant is not merely concluded in him. In his person it is already fulfilled for all creation, as the Holy Spirit enables us to see. Jesus, then, is the only Mediator between God and men (I Tim. 2.5). He is the Mediator of a more excellent covenant (Heb. 8.6), of the new covenant (Heb. 9.15; 12.24) which is personified and achieved in him.[2]

(ii) *Jesus Christ the Mediator*

Since this event has taken place, we can no longer speak of grace as though it were a vague and distant influence, a general and

[1] Substitution does not exclude us. It rather includes those who are self-excluded by sin. What is excluded is our co-operation in achieving salvation.
[2] Cf. the precise definitions of this pact in seventeenth-century Reformed theology (Heppe, *Reformed Dogmatics*, ET, 1950, pp. 371ff.).

mysterious benevolence descending from highest heaven, an inspiration which is beneficent but which is so diffuse as to be void of precise content. Grace is now a sharply defined and concrete reality. It is this man in all the stages of his history. It is the restoration of the covenant as accomplished in his person.[1]

To give content to the term, therefore, we have only to consider this man. Grace is certainly the divine mercy. But it is this mercy manifested in the gift which he makes us of himself. It is thus his presence, suffering and victory in Jesus Christ. It is his love, though not merely in the form of a vague paternal sympathy. This love is action. It does things. Far from being mere sentimentality, it is the event of the radical transformation of our condition in this life and death and resurrection. It is God's righteousness and holiness at work, not in the form of a terrifying and definitive condemnation of our sin, but in the judgment of this crucified man who at the very moment when he submits to it delivers us. His righteousness is thus concretely the act by which he justifies and pardons us, and his holiness is the gift which he makes us of his own perfection incarnate in Christ for us. His omnipotence is displayed in this victory and his patience takes on a new significance in this event. A supreme impatience with sin, it is infinite patience with us even in God's very rigour against himself. Grace is thus his being imposing itself and triumphing in this history by which he takes charge of our disgrace, sacrifices himself and thus makes redress. Its content is the series of events which constitutes the life of Jesus Christ. It is also the elevation which results for us by our participation in his victory as inscribed in the very acts of this person. This transformation is grace because it is effected in Christ, i.e., not in the first instance in us, but in him for us, as an implication and as the true goal of this movement.[2]

From this angle grace is the mediation of Jesus. It is the presence of God in this man to relive the stages in our drama by absolute identification with us. It is this person in which God and man are at grips because they are together even in their conflicts and are reconciled by the triumph of life over death and by the restoration of peace between them. That this man is truly God in the radiance of his perfections and the acceptance of our plight; that he is also

[1] Cf. Ignatius of Antioch (T. F. Torrance, *The Doctrine of Grace in the Apostolic Fathers*, 1943, p. 59).
[2] The main fault in a doctrine of merits is not to put false confidence in man but to fail to trust in the finished work of Christ.

truly ourselves in our nature, fall and resurrection—this is the whole reach of grace. We can speak of it only by describing the God-man, the covenant, the Mediator, the Reconciler. In this event we are already reunited to God even though we do not realize it. We are heard even before we ask and restored even before we express the desire for it. All our religious needs are here met in advance. Everything is accomplished, acquired and fulfilled in him. Grace is the achievement of our salvation, already actual and complete in Jesus.[1]

Jesus Christ incarnates both Creator and creature. This suggests the term 'Mediator', on which the formulae of Chalcedon are ultimately only a commentary. He is not merely between the two; he is the two together. His mediation is not merely that he represents them both; it is that he brings them together in an act which is synonymous with reconciliation.

Like Moses, Jesus stands between the Eternal and us (Deut. 5.5; Gal. 3.19), an intermediary declaring to Israel the intentions, judgments and promises of God and presenting to God the appeals, faults and prayers of his people. Jesus is placed in the same situation and yet he is more than Moses, or a prophet (Matt. 11.9), or Jonah (Matt. 12.41), or Solomon (Matt. 12.42). What is the difference? The difference is that he is not a third party between the others. He is the immediate and total meeting of the two (I Tim. 2.5; Heb. 8.6; 9.15; 12.24). In him the unity of the two is realized, so that his mediation is of infinitely greater significance. The term here denotes far more than mere interposition or juxtaposition. It denotes the mutual representation of the one by the other, i.e., mediatization. God does not come to us directly. He is present and accessible in this man. His presence is mediatized by him and communicated by his concrete existence. Similarly, the humanity of this man is not directly accessible. His humanity is authentic because it is that of God. Hence it is not ours in its actual situation. It is a condition which we do not know and which has to be revealed to us, since it does not bear the stamp of sin. God by his presence is the means of this revelation. His deity is the mediatization of his humanity. To know the man Jesus we must know the God whom he resembles. It is by beginning with the revelation of God in Christ that we can

---

[1] Cf. at this point the distinctions of grace in Roman Catholic theology (Bartmann, *Précis*, II, pp. 22ff.), which might be defended if construed as effects of grace rather than grace itself (cf. Thomas Aquinas, 1a–2ae, qu. 111, art. 2).

discover in what consists the humanity with which he has associated himself from the commencement.[1]

Thus mediation first signifies that all the elements of creation are as it were recapitulated in Christ. It then attests that the man Jesus incarnates God in his humanity, which becomes the means whereby the Lord reveals himself, and reciprocally that his humanity is manifested in its true features by the definition which God himself gives of his will in making himself known. This leads us to a third and, if possible, even more important point. A mediator is one who comes between to bring about accord or agreement between two or more persons. Jesus is not a third party. He personifies both partners. Yet this does not alter his role. He is effectively commissioned to bring about an agreement or covenant between the two concerned. The mere fact that this task had to be undertaken by someone indicates the actual situation between them. If agreement must be reached, some opposition must have estranged them. This is the first conclusion to which we are led by the presence of Jesus in our history. Would God have sent his Son among us if the situation had not demanded it? The decision which he takes and the remedy which he chooses have three implications in respect of the relations between God and man: 1. that they are opposed, since there is need of reconciliation; 2. that man, entangled in his revolt, cannot arrange the agreement in question; and 3. that no man can mediate between the two adversaries, since to do so successfully he would have to espouse both the cause of God and that of man and arbitrate between them. God alone is able to deal with this situation. As man, even Jesus cannot bring about the agreement unless he is also God. And what are the conditions of accord? The main need in any arrangement is to set aside the causes of conflict, namely, the reprobation of God and the sin of man. But how are these obstacles to be overcome? An intervention is necessary to overcome Satan, to re-establish the truth and to reconcile the two parties.

The Bible proclaims the good news that this sovereign act has taken place. 'The good shepherd giveth his life for the sheep' (John 10.11). We must now describe the main aspects of this divine intervention in all the simplicity of faith and gratitude.[2]

There are three main components of the act, namely, the gesture

---

[1] This demands the 'very God—very man' of Chalcedon. Otherwise we have neither God nor man. There is real revelation only if God is revealed in this man and if man is revealed by the knowledge which God thus gives us of himself.

[2] Cf. Calvin, *Inst.* II, 12, 4, 7.

which God consents to make, the result which he achieves and the means which he adopts to reach it.

(1) As concerns the gesture, the Bible emphasizes above all the gift which Jesus freely makes of his own life. 'I lay down my life . . . no man taketh it from me, but I lay it down of myself' (John 10.17f.). Earlier Jesus had said that he came down from heaven to do the will of him that sent him (John 6.38). He is thus free to dispose of his life and yet also subject to the will of his Father. He is free because he is associated with the Father in love. He gives up himself to death (Gal. 2.20; Eph. 5.2; Isa. 53.12), and yet it is God who delivers him up for us all (Rom. 8.32; Acts 2.23). The Father and the Son are together in this act which has always a double aspect, the will of the Father on the one side (Rom. 3.25; II Cor. 5.18, 21 etc.) and on the other the free disposition of the Son spontaneously sharing the intentions of the Father (Matt. 26.53f.; John 18.11). In the act of Jesus it is God himself who ordains. It is he who reconciles us to himself by the death of his Son (Col. 1.22; II Cor. 5.19).

The work of the Son thus reveals a decision which was taken in God himself and which corresponds to all his divine perfections. God suffers from this situation which affects him at the very heart. He demands justice and yet, faced by the failings of his children, he decides to pardon. He comes down to enter the struggle in person and to bear the fault. He humbles himself and gains the victory. The Gospel is that he chooses this means of solving our drama, taking responsibility for our acts even to the point of submitting to their penalty. It is the Just One who absolves us, who amends the situation to his own hurt and to our profit.

At this point we should speak of a sacrifice. Jesus lays aside his divine glory, is incarnate, and gives his life: 'He hath given himself for us an offering and a sacrifice to God for a sweet-smelling savour' (Eph. 5.2), and he has abolished death by his sacrifice (Heb. 9.26). Even if the Old Testament had not laid such stress on animal sacrifices, this word would apply quite naturally to the consent of the Son of God to his voluntary destiny, and therefore to the attitude of God himself whose history is here attested. The cross is in any case a sacrifice. Instead of imputing our sin, God takes charge of it. The context of sacrificial ceremonial simply enables us to imagine a little better the mystery of the divine abnegation.

The term 'mediator' is equally apposite. He who dies is obviously

a man. Yet he is more. If he is God, he must be the Son, for the
Father cannot die. He thus incarnates the two opponents, fighting
as it were between the two armies, like David against Goliath.

Substitution is also unobjectionable in this context. The death
which he suffers is a condemnation, for it is the wages of sin and sin
is accursed (Rom. 8.3; Col. 2.14; Gal. 3.10–14). But he is innocent.
For what death is he condemned, then, if not ours? He submits to
the chastisement merited by the guilty. There is thus a displacement
in relation both to the victim and also to the resultant benefit, life
taking the place of death. How else can we interpret the many
passages which attribute to the death of Jesus the power to give us
life (Rom. 5.6; I Cor. 15 etc.)? But this exchange does not imply
passivity on our part; it emphasizes our participation. He dies for
us, so that our humanity is done away in him. He has taken our
condition, and it is as our representative that he dies. In so doing,
he diverts from us the supreme punishment, which now falls on him
alone. By the fact that he dies, our death, which is real in him,
becomes in reality our life. Thus sin is effectively done away, and
yet we are not involved in its destruction, since another has come
forward as guilty in our place.

All these terms are in keeping, therefore, if we are to give a profound and balanced description of the work of Jesus.

(2) The action has a twofold goal which is virtually one and the
same, namely, the vindication of God and the salvation of man. To
explain God's intervention, attention has been drawn to his concern
for his honour, to his love and to the demands of his righteousness.
In fact, these three reasons express the same idea. The first has been
disputed since it seems to imply an unfavourable view of the divine
honour, as though God had to show himself pitiless in order to
preserve his dignity or even his reputation. The same misconception
may be seen in relation to the divine justice, which some regard as a
tyrannical imposition, and the satisfaction of which, in contrast to
love, is supposed to be in favour only of him who claims his rights.
As for love, it is dissociated from holiness and thus becomes a kind
of general benevolence.

Now the honour of God expresses his basic requirement to be
recognized as God. There is no question of arbitrary pretension.
Since God exists, all things must correspond to his being. No reality
can harm or contradict the least of his perfections without being
condemned to perish. This expression simply denotes the right

deployment of all the divine qualities, their fulfilment without shadow or resistance and therefore the praise of all creatures. God's name is honoured when his person is fully radiant. Hence the satisfaction of his justice is inconceivable without the full realization of his love, nor can his holiness impose itself to the detriment of his patience or his grace. The true reason for his intervention is the pure outshining of his being in the just combination of his attributes. Whether we call this concern for his honour, for his justice or for his love, the meaning is the same.

As for the second objective, it is comprised in the first, for only man's perfection can satisfy God. Far from rejoicing in our suffering and death, God is concerned only for our regeneration, life and felicity. Thus the honour of God, as we employ the term, demands and even passionately calls for our rehabilitation.

This work will both reflect the being of God and also provide an adequate remedy for what we have become. The wisdom or truth of the intervention is to be found in its twofold adequacy. Whatever term we use, God has only one aim in acting as he does, namely, to love in the truth and for the truth. There is no other love, justice or honour than the love which proceeds from the truth of God and which rehabilitates the truth of man.

It is thus quite appropriate to speak in terms of ransom, redemption, resurrection, renewal and elevation. Man is to be freed from the tyranny of sin, bought back from his vain manner of life, preserved from judgment, snatched from death and restored to life. This work of salvation is demanded by the simple fact that God exists and that in accordance with his being he has decided 'to visit and redeem his people' (Luke 1.68).

(3) The means of accomplishing this restoration is clearly attested in Scripture. Jesus is the One who does it. He is Author, Instrument, and Accomplishment. The work focuses on him alone. But how does he do it? He does it first by his incarnation, without which the story told in the Bible would be unreal. He does it by his teaching and miracles. But are these enough in themselves? They would be if we had the capacity to discover who it is that does them and to obey his instructions. In this case Christianity would be a new wisdom, another moral system, based on the admirable sayings of a great initiate in whom is such sanctity that he may well be called the Son of God, and who controls a mysterious power not uncommon in men of his type. But the Gospels prohibit this kind of understand-

ing. When they have finished recording the ministry of Jesus, they enter the phase of his martyrdom, and this is so important that we cannot simply regard it as an unjust end. For our salvation more is needed than example and instruction. The death and resurrection of this man are necessary to gain the victory, in spite of the scandal which they cause, or perhaps because of it.

But why his death? Because death is the key to the drama. Not just physical death, but nothingness, falling away from God. The creature is not threatened by a superficial or temporary disorder. It is struck to the quick. It may well perish, or, which is worse, continue in separation from God and therefore without life. God's problem is in relation to the future of a creation which is actually subject to the last enemy, i.e., to death (I Cor. 15.26). He must meet this power. But why does he choose to overcome it by subjection to it? We have seen already that this fight must be waged in our condition, and this means where death is rampant. There is the further consideration that chaos, which is a force, derives its efficacy only from consent to it. It is a temptation, an assault, which produces rebellion and the desire for power. To overcome this force, it is necessary to experience it. It is necessary to undergo it and resist it, i.e., to refuse it inner consent. To expose oneself to its attacks without being conquered is to annul it. For chaos is real only in virtue of the success which it enjoys. It dissipates when it is opposed. In this sense one may say that Jesus has already overcome death when he can oppose to it a heart which is quite impregnable against its assaults.[1]

This death reveals the power which crushes us, the wisdom with which God decides to neutralize the enemy, and his will to re-establish his rule. This attack alone can be successful, for it goes to the very heart of the drama. It thus constitutes the essential part of the ministry of Jesus, without which the Gospel would be a myth.

As regards the resurrection, it bears witness to the victory of God, confirms the hidden meaning of the history which sets the Son of God at grips with the powers of nothingness, and constitutes the greatest victory of man. The triumph proves who he was, why he came and what results he attained. It is now quite clear that the enemy is destroyed and that we belong to the Victor who has acquitted us and received us to himself. The past is wiped out and

[1] Here is the truth in the patristic conception of the outwitting of the devil by apparently yielding to him.

the future is assured. We live in expectation of his glorious coming.

This decisive act is identified with the destiny of the Mediator who has united all things in himself. (Eph. 1.10). It thus takes place outside us and yet with us and for us, since Jesus represents us, takes us to himself and delivers us. Our own drama finds in him its solution. But what is meant by the phrase 'for us', which is so common in the Gospels? It may be interpreted in three senses.

(*a*) It first means 'because of us'. Although the Son comes and sacrifices himself in response to the will of God, it is on our account. Jesus dies under the blows which we give him because of our sin, the true nature of which is here manifested. He submits to the judgment of God, who chastises in him our revolt. Our opposition to him is not just historical, as though the wild crowd gathered to demand his crucifixion represented us. It is more fundamental than that. The death of Christ illustrates concretely the story of the fall. Although children of God, we have become his enemies and even his murderers. Our ambition is to suppress him and to reign ourselves. This, then, is no accidental death. It is inevitable. There is no question of a simple repulse. After the fall God could expect no other reception on our part. The attitude which we have taken up in relation to him is not just a lack of interest in him. It is an obstinate refusal which necessarily leads to the putting to death of his Son. Surely God foresees this. We alone are blind to the risks of the incarnation. Inveterate idealists, we always think we can play down the drama. But the death of Christ brings out our basic attitude to God. This is neither indifference, negligence, nor carelessness. It is virulent hostility, the irresistible urge to kill him. Jesus meets this power knowing full well what he is doing, and events work out in accordance with the basic factors in the problem.

(*b*) 'For us' also means 'in our place'. Jesus enters into our condition. Recapitulating in himself the stages in our destiny, he presents himself before God as a representative of the creature. God seeks his children, and no one replies. They have all become deaf and dumb and blind before him. He thus decides to send among us an authentic man who can make this reply. This man takes our place as one who can make a valid response and who is worthy of his vocation. But sin attacks him too, and he is ready to be swallowed up by it in order to overcome it. Here again he enters into our situation. He then recovers for himself and for us the legitimate role promised to the creature. He is thus in our place as faithful man, then as victim of sin, and finally as conqueror of Satan. In all three states he is the representative of humanity.

(c) Finally, 'for us' means 'in our favour'. The fact that the Son of God becomes man does not mean that when he takes our place he chases us out of our domain. It is rather to put us back there that he comes. He assumes rather than replaces us. The word 'solidarity' is most apt to describe this event. The Son of God comes to take part in our tragedy, fighting with us and for us. He associates himself with us, so that we are all together with him under the judgment of his Father. The solidarity is complete, and yet for a moment it ceases so far as we are concerned, for he alone is condemned and this condemnation of one suffices for all. Thanks to it, we are acquitted in spite of our real guilt. We are no less culpable because he is the victim. But he suffers the punishment, and it is thus lifted from us. Nor is this surprising, since he willed to be man *par excellence* even as God, and the aim was not to destroy us, but to heal us. This free and unexpected solution attests the greatness of his concern for us and also his wisdom, for it is both in keeping with all his perfections and also fully adapted to the circumstances. His death, therefore, is enough to deliver us from our condemnation. This gift is the most precious thing we can receive. No further obstacle separates us from God. The risen Christ is the new man, victorious over the fall. In God he is restored and free again in every respect. 'In our favour' finds its ultimate significance at this point. In him, the glory of the Creator shines anew on us, and we already reflect it. The cycle is ended and order is re-established, in him, for us, and in us by the Spirit and in hope.

Various images will again help us to understand this achievement. His broken body shows us the effect on us of sin, which has broken us, divided us, separated us from God, from ourselves and from others. At the same time, it reveals the pressure of demonic forces on the Son of God. Yet it also denotes the remedy for this tragic situation. Because he is willing to be broken for us, he takes charge of our disintegration and restores our unity. His brokenness can overcome that from which we suffer. When communicated to us, this divided body reconstitutes another body which we now form and which arises out of our divisions. Again, his shed blood indicates that he gives his life to give us life. It implies both purification and resurrection. He washes us from the sin which is the reason for his death, and he clothes us with his own new life. The importance of the image lies in its connection with life and death. It raises again the thought both of the sacrifice of the Messiah under the judgment of God and also of our resurrection. By this means we are delivered from our vain manner of life (I Peter 1.18) and redeemed as a slave could be from his master to be set at liberty. The price paid, or the ransom demanded, is enormous. It is the punishment of the innocent. There is perfect equivalence between the sacrifice of the just and the ransom of the unjust. This thought is everywhere present in the Bible, whether in juridical or financial images: 'Ye are bought with a price' (I Cor. 6.20), and this price is 'the precious blood of Christ' (I Peter 1.18; Rev. 5.18), who has redeemed us both from the curse (Gal. 3.13) and from our own iniquity (Titus 2.14). Thus our rehabilitation does not depend on our attaining perfection or on our acquiring a dignity which now escapes us, but solely on his death and resurrection. The Lamb slain brings about this change in the situation. He is both a propitiatory and an expiatory victim. He makes God favourable by removing the obstacles to our union with him. He thus expiates and cancels sin. It cannot be questioned that justice must be satisfied in this way, for the act would be worthless if it did not meet all the requirements. Christ thus accomplishes justice along the lines of Rom. 3.26, i.e., in such a way that he is both just and the Justifier. Justice seemed as though it could not be met except by the death of the guilty. But it is met by the equivalent chastisement of the Innocent who is also the Judge, so that the guilty are acquitted by an act which is not arbitrary but which is in keeping with both righteousness and love. Justice is more fully satisfied indeed by the rehabilitation of the guilty than by his death, for thereby a right relationship is established between the partners according to the original intention. Vicarious satisfaction naturally follows from a substitution which lays on the Son a penalty adequate to compensate for universal sin. Reconciliation is the final result. Hence all these various terms have their own value in a description of the event in which our life is at stake.

It is common knowledge that Reformed theology has seen in the Mediator the three offices of Prophet, Priest and King. In brief, this definition makes it very plain that without the incarnation of the Son of God and his earthly ministry as very God and very Man we should firstly be without revelation, i.e., without the knowledge of God and therefore without God. Unable to apprehend him in our own strength, we should have remained in ignorance if he had not drawn near. It also makes it clear that secondly we should be without reconciliation, and therefore at war with God and ourselves. Nothing new takes place under the sun, and we should not be able to think of any remedy. Finally, it makes it evident that thirdly we should be without any real assurance, since there would be no control over the forces of chaos. Sin, sickness and death would reign as masters, and far from conquering them we should be hopelessly at their mercy.

Conversely, to receive the good news of this mediation is to receive, first, the Word—and act—which we need to find again our Creator and Father and in him to regain possession of ourselves. Secondly, it is to receive the deliverance which we desire with all our being, since one thing which all men want is to know their return to life by the defeat of the powers of death. Finally, it is to receive the assurance that the power of God is put forth on our behalf. This means that we obviously have all things in God. We do not have them in a distant and hidden God. We certainly do not have them in a man of superior holiness and devotion. We have them in the God-man who is both near and sovereign, both compassionate and righteous, and who of his pure mercy reconstitutes unity between himself and us by living it out for us in this man.[1]

(iii) *Jesus Christ our righteousness and sanctification*

In face of this tremendous achievement, and having contemplated it, we are continually tempted to come back to ourselves as though Jesus had not sovereignly decided our future. To be sure, we accept his help. But there is as it were a gravitational pull back to self. We also allege that we must maintain the right to participate actively in the management of our own affairs. We will not admit that he is more than a helper. This remnant of autonomy within the trust we

---

[1] In the history of the dogma, exaggerations are less important than the general orientation or emphasis. The fathers stress the objective work of God, e.g., I Clem. 49.6; Ign. *Smyrn.* 6, 1; Iren. *Haer.* III, 18, 7; Orig. *Hom. on Num.* 24.1; Athan. *De Incarn. Verb.* 9; Hilary of Poitiers, *De Trin.* in *Ench. Patrist.* 873; Cyril of Jerus. *Catech. Or.* XIII, 33; Greg. of Naz. *Orat.* 2 (*Ench. patrist.*1 016); Greg. of Nyssa, *Catech. Disc.* XXXII, 3; John Chrysostom, *Homily on the Cross*; Augustine, *Serm.* in *Ench. patrist.* 1500; *Confess., ibid.* 1595; *Epist., ibid.* 1857; Leo, *ibid.* 2188); Anselm, *Cur Deus Homo*, II, 17; cf. Harnack, *Dogmengeschichte*, 3, II, pp. 50f. In this they are followed by the Reformers and seventeenth-century orthodoxy. On the other hand, Neo-Protestantism renounces the classical understanding (e.g. Frommel, *L'Expérience chrétienne*, III, pp. 136ff.; J. Bovon, *Dogmatique chrétienne*, II, pp. 24f.; A. Lemaître, *Foi et vérité*, pp. 258ff.) and suggests a psychological and moral interpretation (Lemaître, *op. cit.*, pp. 264ff., summarizing the views of Schleiermacher, Ritschl, Fulliquet, Vinet and Secrétan). For this school, the real event of reconciliation takes place in us under the influence of Christ.

still put in him makes us hesitant, since we make a division between his work and ours. What we have to realize is that everything has now been transferred to him, so that his history is ours, his death is our end which takes from us all self-concern, and his resurrection is our restoration. The truth is not in our hearts, but in his life.

The Christian mystery cannot be thought of in terms of two poles, the above and the below, the below and the above, which have to be brought into relationship as though they had not already been united. This attitude lies behind every dualism. Revelation, however, presents us with the full realization of our wishes. The covenant is concluded. We have now to think and act, not in terms of disjunction, but in terms of this victory accomplished, this reconciliation effected. By faith we find a place where God and man are no longer two but one, where the wall of separation has been broken down 'to make in himself of twain one new man' (Eph. 2.14ff.). Here the part of God and that of man are reunited, without division or confusion. A full co-operation is established between them in freedom and gratitude, as in the voluntary participation of Jesus in the work of his Father. The privilege of theology, as of all Christian witness, is to be able to talk of both God and man only within this meeting and in the light of it.[1]

This is the fulness of the total Christ in whom we find all the promised blessings. The first of these is righteousness. By a natural association of ideas this might first suggest the accusations which God could justly bring against our disobedience and unfaithfulness. It is very hard to think of these judgments falling on Christ crucified. If he has been delivered up for our offences (Rom. 4.25), however, this means that the judgment falls on him. In this case, it is he who is guilty and condemned. Justice strikes him in our stead. The thought of righteousness should thus evoke, not the sense of our own condemnation, but that of his. The content and application of this verdict are the death of Jesus. We are directly affected, since he represents us. But the essential point is the displacement which modifies radically the concepts both of judgment and wrath on the one side and election and salvation on the other.

Though Christ submits to judgment, he does not succumb. He satisfies it, but he is not made captive by it. By his resurrection he triumphs over chastisement. He rises again for our justification

---

[1] The truth is not in heaven, nor in a metaphysical order, nor in ourselves, but in Christ.

(Rom. 4.25). His death was liberating, since it took the place of ours and thus constitutes our ransom, averting punishment from us. But if his defeat was liberating, even more so is his victory.

In this case, the aim of God's righteousness is obviously not to condemn us but to crush him in order that we may be righteous. In this history his judgment is identical with his pardon which restores us. It is reparative rather than destructive. Thus God's judgment has a positive significance in spite of our natural instincts. The sense is revolutionized. God judges to save. He saves by judging in this way. This is why the Bible identifies the righteousness of God with the Gospel (Rom. 1.17).

The revolution is effected in a history, which is that of this man. The demand of God accuses us, but it then falls on Jesus, so that, satisfied by his death and especially by his victory over rejected chaos, it becomes our pardon and justification. In this light, there is no more question of chastisement but rather of restoration. The righteousness of God is appropriately realized through his suffering for us. Judgment is now synonymous with salvation rather than condemnation, with pardon rather than punishment, with resurrection rather than destruction. It is so with the truth guaranteed by Christ in every respect. Because of this event, the righteousness of God exists only in the form of his love. In other words, when we could not become righteous again by obeying the Law, God made us righteous by this obedience, i.e., by the obedience of his Son, which wholly changes the situation. This righteousness is imputed to us because it is his and not ours. It is the righteousness of faith and not of the Law (Rom. 10.5f.).

How are we to explain this distinction? The righteousness of the Law is intrinsic. It consists in the conformity of our thoughts, feelings and acts with the will of God. If we could attain once more to this agreement of our being and acts with the divine requirement, we should not need redemption. We should be righteous by our own movement, possibly with his help. But the Gospel sets aside this possibility. So, too, in practice do reason, experience and history. Another solution must be found. This righteousness must come from without. It must be imputed. Our inability to practise it must be overcome. This imputation assumes (1) that Jesus Christ has attained this perfection in our condition; (2) that God, accepting his mediation, attributes to us the benefits of his work; and (3) that finding this judgment of God by faith, we are effectively clothed in this righteousness and conquered by his sacrifice and victory, even though in ourselves we are sinners. Thus, in the drama of his abasement and subsequent exaltation he becomes the righteousness of the unrighteous, a surety for the wicked, our regained truth and integrity, both before God and before men. To put on the new man is to receive for ourselves the judgment pronounced on him. God imputes to us, not the sin which always persists, since disobedience to a single commandment means full revolt (James 2.10), but the righteousness of his Son which is already protected from corruption.

This righteousness, although imputed, is not outside us. On the contrary, it takes the place of our unrighteousness. It replaces it. It comes to dwell in us. Already it is more real than our unrighteousness. Our being and life are his person and life. We have to see with astonishment that he has become our true reality, more authentic than what we see ourselves to be with these eyes of flesh. We become one plant with him. Thus all that is his is given to us. Moreover, this life, this righteousness, this pardon, this dwelling in us, are eminently active. Their power is greater than that of chaos, which continues its work. We are here in the realm of mystery, but it is more real than appearances. Eternal life embraces us more surely than the shadows of revolt. By faith we can set ourselves alongside God and against ourselves, alongside the victorious mystery and against what is visible, which is robbed of its power. Progress in faith means the continuing increase of this light in us. And we can be confident that this imputation acts far more surely than any works of ours to place us in this new situation and to confirm us in it. It is this which can evoke in us works which attest even though they never completely prove it.

Grace is this acquittal, this invasion by Christ's righteousness. Everything seems to contradict it, but it could not be more true. Jesus is not guilty, and yet he is condemned. We are guilty, and yet we are righteous. We are no more perfect than Jesus was a sinner, and yet he was made sin and we are made righteous. This attributed righteousness results from his condemnation, which includes ours, and from his victory, which implies our rehabilitation in the truth of God and man through our reconciliation with him. This righteousness is guaranteed by the ascension of Christ, who represents us before God as children of God. The Holy Spirit invests us with it, and none can take it from us.[1]

[1] The doctrine of free justification was not too clearly stated in the early centuries

If he is our righteousness and pardon, Jesus Christ is also our sanctification. He is 'the completed fact of our sanctification'.[1] The problem here is more delicate than that which precedes. One might freely admit that pardon is wholly gratuitous and yet argue that, once we are clothed with this imputed righteousness on the basis of the expiatory work of Christ and under the impulsion of the Spirit, our task is to conform precisely to the will of God, to obey him, and through his empowering to achieve the sanctification which he has promised. If this is so, salvation consists of a double movement with at best a common origin in God. Jesus achieves our reconciliation with the Father and then, loaded with his blessings, we advance progressively towards sanctification. This idea need not involve meritorious works. It may rest on an apparently impeccable doctrine of grace as the only determinative factor. It may attribute man's co-operation to the work of the Spirit in him. This man goes in the right direction because grace has vanquished and transformed him. Works do not precede faith; they follow it. Everything seems to be in order. But in fact the most subtle of legalisms is surreptitiously intruded on this view. The question is where our sanctification ultimately resides. Is it the climax of our efforts, evoked and fructified by grace? Or is it in Christ and therefore outside us and before us? Is sanctification an achievement of the believer or a gift of God? Do we attain to it by the faithfulness of our Christian life or by faith, i.e., through grace transcendently at work in the person of Jesus for us?

The full sufficiency of the work of Jesus forces us to choose the second solution. Our sanctification is already achieved in him. He has gained it for us and he gives it to us. We can get it by receiving it from him by faith. It necessarily manifests itself in good works. But these are only signs, not the truth itself.

But how are we to understand this sanctification which is to become ours even though from first to last it is his?

(1) When he releases us from our sin by the victory of Jesus, God

---

(cf. Augustine and the Second Council of Orange). Its significance was first grasped by the Reformers (cf. Luther's *Galatians*, Preface). Trent worked out a compromise which was sharply attacked by Calvin (Hefele-Leclercq, *Histoire des Conciles*, X, 1, pp. 8off.). More recently, Hans Küng (*Rechtfertigung*, 1957, pp. 18of.) has argued that Trent really taught the historic doctrine, negatively refuting Luther's exaggerations but positively agreeing with Barth's restatement in *CD* IV, 1. If this is true, it undercuts traditional Roman Catholic polemics and raises ecumenical hopes. But much historical relativizing seems to be needed actually to find this interpretation in Trent itself.

[1] Barth, *CD* II, 2, p. 777.

causes to appear anew the perfection of his creatures. As yet this is complete only in Jesus. In himself and for us he is the perfect man who takes the place of fallen man.

(2) Whatever may be our actual situation, the Gospel presents us with this restitution in him. Why do again what he has done perfectly? What other man can thus succeed in overcoming sin and regaining his original perfection? It is to be noted that sanctification here denotes, not the sum of human virtues, but our conformity with the will of God. It is not mere obedience to various precepts. It is our return to God, his approbation and the true correspondence established henceforth between him and us. Now Jesus has come to gain this sanctification for us by reliving our drama, and to confer it on us, since we cannot retrieve it of ourselves. He incarnates this sanctification for all men. All are virtually saints in him already, since he represents all before God. For it to become effective we have only to realize this identity and to put it into effect by faith. In other words, he has simply to come and abide in us, and we in him. The more we are in Christ, the more it permeates us. Sanctification is not orientation to good works; it is incorporation in him. By his Word and sacraments, by repentance, prayer and obedience, we are stripped of ourselves and filled with his truth. It is his coming into us which constitutes our sanctification.

(3) This sanctification is not a calm and serene reality. It is a conflict, an exploit. He is holy by nature and he becomes sin to face and conquer it. He thus wins his own sanctification, veiled for a moment by his entry into our condition. At the same time he wins ours. He succeeds where we fail. The fact that his intervention was necessary to destroy sin condemns moralism at the root. If he alone could do it, how can we ignore him and try to wage our own war instead? He fights for us and gives us the fruit of his exploit. Our sanctification is due to his efforts, not ours. We can receive from him by faith what he has won to restore us.

(4) His obedience thus becomes a tremendous promise for us. The fact that there is somewhere a good creature is relevant to all, for this creature assumes us into his own existence. In him man is at last human again. Sanctification is not here a religious value. It is the restitution of humanity, as Calvin maintains: 'The regeneration of the godly is indeed . . . nothing else than the formation anew of the image of God in them.'[1] But how can we agree that this one who

[1] *Comm.* on Eph. 4.24.

alone is holy sanctifies all others? It is the mystery of the divine will to achieve all things in him for us. What he has, he gives to us, and this is the only way in which we may acquire what would otherwise be beyond our reach. Sanctification is God's 'creation of a new form of existence' for man.[1] This is true in him. It is the promise that God truly attributes to us the work of justification accomplished by Christ. Coming to us, Christ communicates to us his holiness, which is already objectively valid in him and the grace of which covers and permeates us.

(5) In other words this sanctification, far from lifting us calmly to perfection, produces a crisis in us, since we are not as he is. It begins by condemning us. Only by stripping us can it take the place of our actual failure. To live in this crisis is to submit to the judgment of God and to grasp his sanctification to cover our infidelities. It is then to let this sanctification work in us to establish in our lives some marks of what he is for us.

Thus, like our justification, our sanctification is perfect only in Jesus Christ during this life. We receive them both by faith. The first declares our pardon, the second brings a complete renewal which bears witness to our adherence to the one who has delivered us. This reality is eschatological in the sense that it is already perfect in him but will not be fully manifested until his second coming. For the moment we live by the promise and in hope of the full manifestation. We are sustained by him, but we cannot reveal all the fulness in our own lives.

Regeneration is the application to our lives of the death and resurrection of Jesus Christ. It is simply his life in us. There is here no question of moral perfectibility. Sanctification is a divine verdict which kills, restores and increasingly incorporates into the fellowship of the one perfect man. It is the action of grace in us rather than autonomous progress to perfection. It is his presence, death, truth, life, righteousness and holiness active in us by his Word. To receive it we must look to him, listen to him and welcome him instead of analysing and forcing ourselves. He will then produce in us something analogous to what he has lived, and this will be our transformation.

As for obedience, this is the result of the new thing established in us. If our being is changed, our acts will change also. They will not become suddenly perfect, but they must express something of this

[1] Barth, *CD* IV, 2, p. 499.

I

new life developing in us. We act in gratitude, to please him who
has saved us by keeping his commandments. We act in the power of
his authority over us, to show that we belong to the Lord who has
taken possession of us. But while this is all true, the real reason why
we act in a new way is that we cannot do otherwise. If faith is real
in us, it cannot possibly be without fruit. As for the nature of these
acts, the main point is that they agree with the work of God in
Christ. This is easy enough to understand, since it is precisely this
work which fashions us. This suggests the idea of imitation. We do
not imitate Christ as a mere example. But we live in him, and,
because we do so, we know his thoughts and produce acts which are
analogous to his, as Calvin said: 'The object of regeneration is to
bring the life of believers into concord and harmony with the
righteousness of God, and so confirm the adoption by which they
have been received as sons.'[1]

Finally, progress in sanctification is growth in faith, i.e., increase
in knowledge and love, or rather the growth of Christ in us, like a
seed which develops. A weak, tarnished and in part erroneous faith
will produce acts marked by many defects, while a strong, deep and
correct faith will renew itself and produce acts which bear the
imprint of the criteria of this new world. The only way to develop
our participation in the holiness of Christ is to listen better so that
we may be the better associated with him. This progress will not
resemble an ascending curve, with no breaks or dips. It is a perpetual contradiction which God opposes to us, a triumph which he
gains over our resistance. As Calvin said again, 'This renewal,
indeed, is not accomplished in a moment, a day, or a year, but by
uninterrupted, sometimes even by slow, progress God abolishes the
remains of carnal corruption in his elect, cleanses them from pollution, and consecrates them as his temples, restoring all their inclinations to real purity, so that during their whole lives they may
practise repentance, and know that death is the only termination to
this warfare.'[2]

(iv) *By the Holy Spirit Jesus Christ himself assures our participation
in his person and work*

Thus far we have commented on the saying of the apostle Paul:
'Jesus Christ is the fulness of him that filleth all in all' (Eph. 1.23).
He is himself our covenant with God, the Mediator who reunites

[1] *Inst.* III, 6, 1.   [2] *Inst.* III, 3, 9.

the two partners in his person, our full and complete righteousness, our perfect sanctification. Objectively we are already contained in him, since he represents us. But how are we to appropriate all these riches? They are ready for us in him, but how are we to take them?

The transition from him to us is first effected by the Word which God speaks. This Word is in effect the personal power of his action. It is personal in the sense that in speaking God gives himself to us and manifests his being. It is active because this Word is not just a discourse but the intervention by which God executes his decisions and creates a wholly new situation. It is powerful because God affirms in it his victorious sovereignty over all opposition. When God speaks, something decisive happens, since all the weight of his person comes into action in the Word which he pronounces. It is by this means that he reaches, judges and transforms us. Hence this Word contains all his love, all his wisdom, and his will not merely to reveal but definitively to realize his intentions.

Now this personal, dynamic and sovereign Word is Jesus Christ himself in his person, teaching and work. He is its manifestation, content and accomplishment. In him God speaks and acts according to his decisions and in conformity with his plans. Moreover, this Word rings out also in the testimonies borne to this man. Why should he have been concerned that the memory of this history should be preserved if not to prolong its effect? The Church which proclaims this achievement also continues to serve this supremely active Word.

When the question of our participation in the work of Jesus Christ is raised, the only possible answer is to refer to this Word of God, to listen to what it says and to submit to its action. Everything is contained in it, and it is also endowed with power to overcome all obstacles. But how can we do this? The Word is hidden. It reaches us indirectly through a man, through human words and actions. And are we not blind rebels before it? How can we accept its dominion? To be sure, we need have little concern in this regard, since it is living, free and even imperious, and it will necessarily reach its goal once it is set in motion. Yet God will not force us. He wishes to associate us with him as responsible and grateful beings. He seeks our adherence. Faith is the knowledge, confidence and obedience by which we respond to his intervention. But by what power can we be made capable of giving to him the response which he expects of us?

This is where the Holy Spirit comes in. He produces in us this capacity to receive the active Word of our Lord and to participate in his work. The Spirit is the power which links us to Jesus Christ and permits us to find in him the fulness of the divine intervention for us. The coming of the Spirit is a new miracle following the miracles of the incarnation and of reconciliation and giving us the freedom to receive what they accomplished for us. The Spirit manifests what belongs to Jesus Christ and what is thus destined for us, and he gives us the power to appropriate it. Though he is wholly free to reach us in any way, he unites himself to the Word, makes it a living Word, and creates in us the faith by which we receive it and thereby receive life and truth.

The following aspects of the person and work of the Holy Spirit may be noted.

(1) The adjective 'holy' is applied to him to indicate that the power in question is that of God himself. This is why the Holy Spirit is personal. In all his manifestations God is in fact acting personally. *Agios* corresponds to *Kurios*. He is the Spirit of the Father coming like the Son, though in another way. But he is also the Spirit of the Son, i.e., the power which enabled him to be and to work, but which is yet to be distinguished from his person. He was always with Jesus, as he is always with the Father. More strictly, he is the link which unites the Father and the Son, the fulness of their communion and common action.

(2) He now comes to lay hold of us in the name of the Father and the Son, i.e., in fulfilment of their work to extend the union to creatures also. He comes to set up in us the reign of the Son and thus to effect a communion analogous to that which characterizes the divine fulness. He is our association with the Father by the Son, the transition which he comes to initiate from us to him. This bond is that of peace and love in truth. It is renewed on the basis of the objective work of Christ. It is first between us and Christ, and then through him with the Father. The Spirit is thus the fellowship, or, if we prefer it, the love which binds the Son to the Father, the creature to its Lord and creatures to one another in this fulness of righteousness and perfection.

(3) But to bring about this harmony, which was broken by sin, the Spirit has to do in us a precise work. He does not simply lift us to the truth. He inscribes in us the death of Jesus, which is God's judgment upon us. By the substitution operative in this death, he

associates us with his victory, which constitutes the miracle of our own resurrection. The Holy Spirit comes to us to break the old man and to put the life and work of Jesus in his place. He applies to us the verdict which God pronounces on us in the death and resurrection of Jesus Christ. Who can bring about this purification in us but God himself? The Spirit confers upon these human words and acts the divine power which can apply them to us and fashion us in accordance with them.

(4) In this action the Spirit reveals himself as the actual work of the truth which he produces in us. Without him we should grasp neither its necessity nor its relevance. He applies the divine decision to us like a sharp remedy. Yet he is also the Spirit of love, not in the sense that he tolerates what we have become, but in the sense that he brings about in us the indispensable transformation. Far from wrapping us in a sweet euphoria, love makes us die, thus destroying what God reproves and restoring us in his glory. He is thus the Spirit of resurrection, for he gives us life by associating us with the Victor over death. In other words, he incorporates us into the movement of the life of Jesus Christ, enabling us to follow all its various stages in our return to God. It is thus that he leads us in the way of our reconciliation with God, and that he concretely authenticates for us what took place in this short life. Moreover, he is the power of our obedience, which flows naturally from our association with him. He is also the power of knowledge, fellowship and service by which we are made Christians, i.e., brought into relationship with Christ. Without this new intervention of God, the work of Christ would have remained external to us. By it we are introduced into Christ's own existence and thus become members of his body. In a word, the Spirit brings into us the truth of the person and work of Jesus Christ as the fulness of the divine decision concerning the fallen creature.

(5) From the preceding points it may be concluded that the Spirit is the power of our rehabilitation. He brings us to our destiny as men by causing us to share in the royal humanity of Jesus. In thus applying to us the act of God which corresponds to his inner life, he does not make us demi-gods. On the contrary, he restores our full humanity. In this work, the Spirit is not just religious inspiration. He is the force which transfigures our humanity after having given it a place in creation and preserving it even in its estrangement. He brings about in man the greatest revolution of all. Those who do not

believe in regeneration naturally look for other means to give man back his integrity, and various new attempts at revolution follow. It cannot be denied that from a distance and impurely, yet truly and usefully, these attest the will of God to regenerate man in his subjection to exploiting powers. Ultimately, however, it is the Spirit of God who incarnates this power of transformation and liberation, and it is he alone who can fully bring about the necessary deliverance.[1]

Thus the Spirit does God's work by restoring humanity to itself through the concrete application of the resurrection of Christ. At the same time he re-establishes in all parts of creation the bond of peace, truth and glory which the fall had broken.

It may be asked what is man's part in all this. Almost all heresies have their origin in a concern to safeguard the partial autonomy of the creature in face of the divine initiative. Is it really impossible, however, to make it clear that the part of man is in fact that of the Holy Spirit? If God defends man in this way, more is surely attributed to him than the creature could attribute to itself. By what tragic unbelief do we refuse the divine offer and turn again to natural powers which have already demonstrated their inadequacy? Before the Spirit the same question is posed as before Christ: Can we really prefer the fumbling attempts of man to the security of the finished work of God? The problem of the sole efficacy of grace is raised again at this point, and sin again consists in putting up man as a rival of God.

Can it be said that the action of God is in danger of crushing man if there is no effort on his part? This is to misunderstand the work of the Spirit. For it is the Spirit who gives to man his full humanity and therefore his freedom and responsibility. Can it not be admitted that the supreme objective of God is to restore to the creature possession of all its privileges? If not, what is the meaning of his love? If God enslaves the creature, nothing makes sense—neither the work of creation, the gift which Christ makes of his life, nor the intervention of the Spirit. But God takes into account our actual situation and therefore our inability to overcome the forces which oppress us. He thus throws in all his resources to restore our integrity. And now we doubt his authority, hoping to find greater assurance of restoration in ourselves, with perhaps a little help from

[1] It would be interesting to consider movements of economic and national emancipation in the light of this will of God to save man from all forms of tyranny.

him if possible. The threat to our freedom is not from him; it is from us. How has it been possible to distort the problem to the point where it is thought we must protect man against the invasion of grace instead of laying sovereign emphasis on grace even against man, and in the last instance for him?

According to his nature God cannot will, nor does he actually will, anything but the crowning of his children. His whole work moves to this end in which his perfections are satisfied and which he fully attains. He thus places man in a situation which is wholly new in respect of his actual state of sin but which was ordained from the very first and which can be summed up in the single phrase, the royalty of man.

This new state implies certain fundamental human qualities of which the following are the chief.

(1) The royalty of man is seen in his due participation in the sovereignty of God. Within his submission, a new correspondence is established. Nor does the dependence do injury to any of the associated elements, as we are naturally inclined to think. It rather enhances them the one by the other, and glorifies them by the interchange of their respective qualities. There is here no competition, but a stimulating accord which is neither forced nor tedious.

(2) From this association there results a total and substantial freedom which is not to the detriment of the other but which remains within a harmony that protects it from its own negation. How can the supreme freedom of man be otherwise defined than in terms of his participation in the freedom of God? It is the mark of truth in the glorious expression of all his capacities. But it is not an unlimited freedom, for it cannot try to take what God rejects without annulling itself. The freedom of God is within a framework provided by his righteousness, his love and his wisdom. Outside this, it is the negation of life. Freedom cannot embrace chaos without becoming an absurd illusion. It is simply the full approbation of life and good. It thus implies a choice. But it is first a quality of being in the truth. Outside this, it falls into illusion. To maintain itself, it has thus to correspond to the freedom which God has to retain to be wholly true to himself. Both for God and for man it is life in accordance with the requirements of the truth.

(3) This royalty also implies the full integrity of man in accordance with his own nature. A creature, he is so only in correspondence with his Creator. It is in this correspondence that everything is in

order and that man discovers his true dimensions. His potentialities are realized in this association, and he now plays the role for which he is destined, both in relation to himself and others, in virtue of this point of reference which puts him at the right place. And it is in the possession of himself, in relation to this God who, without forcing him, but simply by the victory of his truth and love, restores him to his mission, that he assumes again his responsibilities in the sphere assigned to his activity.

(4) Here again there is no intermingling of God and the creature. The unity is without confusion or separation. Each profits by his own nature in a fellowship which stimulates autonomy in this relation and collaboration in this freedom. In this description, how can we avoid the excellent term 'co-operation'? We are forced into it. Free and responsible association produces this common work in which the two partners find their joy and glory. Obedience is no longer servitude. It is natural praise. It is life in this fulness which we would not lose for anything in the world. Freely united with the Saviour, in possession of all our faculties and joyously responsible, we are 'labourers together with God' (I Cor. 3.9). It will be noted that this frequently quoted text occurs in a context which has as its aim the glorifying of God's work. 'So then neither is he that planteth any thing, neither he that watereth; but God that giveth the increase' (I Cor. 3.7). Hence we can talk of the co-operation of man only on condition that we first recognize the pre-eminence of grace. We are thus faced by a double paradox. (1) The participation of man does not become real until the moment when the grace of God imposes itself upon him as the only power of decision. Hence there is no division. The creature finds his powers, his freedom, his humanity, at the very moment when he attributes all power and freedom and sovereignty to grace. (2) The second paradox takes a negative form. Against our expectations, resignation, passivity and resort either to inactive mysticism or to over-enterprising secularization have never accompanied the central doctrines of grace. They have rather accompanied those doctrines which accord a preponderant place to the free will of the natural man. For grace prohibits these withdrawals, of which the believer's desire for independence is the obvious cause. Conversely, the more strongly grace intervenes, the more it demands our action. Those who count on it are projected forwards. Thus the co-operation of man with God is not just an effect of grace; it is implied in it. Sin is what refuses to co-operate,

not gratitude or trust. God triumphs over sin, and the problem disappears. Grace liberates us from this foolish resistance and enables us to participate freely and actively in its work.

Obviously this perfect collaboration is again an eschatological reality. As yet we receive only the signs of this royalty. But by faith we can already consider ourselves clothed with this freedom and integrity, and engaged in this collaboration in the work of God, so long as we listen, receive and give thanks, and are thus set to work.[1]

Conclusion

We thus have all things fully in him (Col. 2.10). With all our powers, therefore, we have to know him and to love him. Our necessary efforts should be steered only in this direction, that his Word may invade and regenerate us and claim us for his service. Our experiences are simply our life in him. Our prayers seek his intervention. The peace which he gives us constitutes our only nourishment, and it is obviously satisfying, consoling and strengthening. Our regard is to him. This is our unique discipline, as it is that of the Church, that his promises may be fulfilled. Our whole Christian life depends on this reference. All things hang upon it. His riches satisfy us. His fulness brings us more than we could ever hope for. In poverty of spirit, in humility and in watchfulness we receive all things from him, to become what he decides.

Moreover, we rediscover creation in him, i.e., the intentions of the Creator and our privileges as creatures. At the same time he teaches us that we actually live under his effective royalty, concealed no doubt, but fully real. Finally, he reveals to us what is to take place at the end of the ages. These three doctrines of creation, of the government of history and of the final redemption should all be related to his person and work, for he is revelation and therefore truth. In fact, creation has often been considered apart from him, on the basis of natural insights. The eschatological promises, when detached from him, have also been debased by current hopes of the immortality of the soul, of progress and of future terrestrial righteousness. This is a theme to which we must return.

[1] If this is what Trent meant by co-operation, it should have put it more clearly. The Reformers certainly accepted this true co-operation, though they saw that the accent must always rest on grace. Neo-Protestantism, of course, maintains a relative human autonomy which makes even the Tridentine formulations seem cautious.

I*

For the moment, our task is to work out some of the implications of this life of the Lord for our own existence, personal, ecclesiastical and public.

6

The Implications of
an Evangelical Christology

IF ALL human realities are already contained in Jesus Christ in a
unity which, far from crushing them, restores to them their freedom,
how can we treat them as though they were still outside him?
Indeed, is it enough to examine them with him merely as their
starting-point? In fact, since he bears them within himself, they can
be considered only in him, in the mystery of his own existence, in
which they are already recapitulated. This is what is required of an
Evangelical Christology and this is the problem to which we must
now turn.

Two dangers are encountered once we leave the sphere of
Christology in the stricter sense and turn to realities which are
supposed to be independent and more concrete. The first is simply
to refuse to discuss them at all, to shut oneself off in a world of piety
with no concern for what lies without and on the pretext of looking
to Jesus Christ alone. It is thus that theology becomes abstract and
theoretical. The desire to look only to Christ is legitimate, but it is
illegitimate not to accept his lordship over all our existence. When
theology does not exploit the full significance of the presence of
Jesus Christ among us, it is betrayed into religiosity or speculation.
This will be the mark of poor Christology. On the other hand, in the
attempt to avoid this, there is the opposite temptation to speak of
these alongside him, as if they had not been assumed into his
existence. Thus man and his works may be considered in the light
of the Gospel but in relative independence of it, as though they
existed on another plane.

To avoid these two dangers, we shall examine some of these
realities in their concrete existence, and for that very reason in their
existence in him. They are not themselves except in Christ, i.e. in

alliance with God without either division or confusion. It is he who bears them and who thus grants them their inevitable significance. The first temptation is Docetic in the sense of an almost exclusive emphasis on the divinity at the expense of the humanity, or even of an absorption of the humanity by the divinity. The second is Ebionite, as if the humanity were to some degree outside Christ even after the incarnation and resurrection.

We use the word 'implication' to show that what we are discussing does not really exist except in Christ and is justified by this very dependence. When we speak of the Bible, the Church, the Christian or even universal history, we are first describing Jesus Christ, for he is their life and truth. The moment he assumes them, he gives them their integrity and freedom and we can thus speak of them as genuine realities. The word 'implication' denotes the richness of the person and work of Jesus, in whom we find ourselves and all that makes up our lives, together with the whole of creation, which to some degree participates in our destiny. On the other hand, the term does not restrict our own responsibility, for this is completely re-established by our communion with God.

The transition which we are now to make is from Christology in the stricter sense, which has the Mediator alone as its theme, to Christology in the wider sense, which deals with creation as it is reconciled to its Lord and as it is considered, therefore, in the One who has restored to it its life and vocation. This transition is necessary so long as it is a description of the fulness which resides in Jesus Christ, since it is in him that we find the truth re-established. Thus, when we discuss Holy Scripture or the Church or personal and social ethics in the analogy of faith, i.e., christologically or in a truly Christian sense, we are still dealing with the same theme. We still bear constant witness to the Messiah. We still disclose his mystery. We are not on another plane but are still engaged in commentary on his work, handling all the problems of faith and obedience as aspects of what he is and results of what he gives.

We naturally do not apply to these human realities that which is true of Christ alone, for if he identifies himself with us, we cannot identify ourselves with him. We are in him, but we are not identical with him. Here, too, we avoid confusion, though without falling into separation. We are called to be like him, but not equal. We cannot apply to ourselves the features which define him alone. Our task is thus to discern the correspondences, the analogies, the implications, which bear witness to the significance of the incarnation. In other words, within Christ we pass from him to us and we find in him what we have become by his work, which is grace. This transfer is what is designated by the words analogy, correspondence and application. For us who live in separation this point is infinitely mysterious. But any dualism annuls in practice the blessings promised by the work of reconciliation. In him there is already unity in difference. This differentiated unity constitutes the mystery of the life from which we are now excluded by sin but to which Christ has reintroduced us.

It is because of our fall from the covenant that we cannot understand how submission to this Lord is the condition of our freedom, how two who are joined together are not really themselves until they become one flesh, how Jesus Christ and his Church are no longer two but one in mutual correlation and in the order defined by their reciprocal responsibilities, how heaven and earth, far from being at odds, are united without confusion, how God can be both three and one, how we are no longer ourselves when the Lord's Supper strictly unites us the one to the other, how soul and body are truly united under the direction of the Spirit without competing with or destroying one another, or how there is necessary interaction between the ecclesiastical community (the Church) and the civil community (the state).

All these interrelationships reflect that which was brought into being between God and man in Christ by the bond of the Spirit. The same bond extends to them. By faith we are set in a new world where unity reigns instead of discord. It is on this new ground that we may now walk, seeing all things from this new perspective which has become actual with the event of reconciliation. We think and act on the basis of the finished achievement and not on that of separation or a mere longing for unity. This means true communion as distinct from the absorption which necessarily implies conformity and tyranny, or distant participation which is afraid of self-offering. In our actual state we oscillate perpetually between over-emphasis on diversity and over-emphasis on collectivization. But balance is now offered to us at the point where God does not crush man and man does not think he must deny God to live.

In face of this mysterious perfection we are constantly tempted to deviate on the one side or the other, opposing grace to human responsibility, the unity of God to the three moments of his revelation, the one nature of Christ to the other, the responsibility of man to that of woman, the body to the soul, the Church to its Head. Everywhere we have sown discord and perpetuated confusion instead of respecting the truth in its integrated unity which assures to each element its integrity in relation to every other. It is thus that God and man are together. Our humanity is in the image of its Creator. It corresponds to it, and all creation is in this nexus of relations. Moreover, the image of God is Jesus himself, so that we shall be in the image of our Creator, in the peace which he gives, when his existence will be reflected in ours. While elsewhere we find only strife and competition, here we have the correspondence of love. To grasp something of this marvellous system of relations, which constitutes life itself, we must begin with the restoration of unity, i.e., with the resurrection of Christ, instead of taking our own point of departure in the sin which refuses this association and which naturally inclines to contest it.

This is why the analogy, if it is to be true, can never be established merely on being or deduced from the relations between essential being and being by participation. This method leads to the fatal result of a dualism in which there is accentuation of the two poles instead of realization of their unity. Or it may issue in confusion, since the analogy presupposes a direct kinship between the two modes of being and this can naturally lead to their partial or total identification. We are thus led incessantly to the paradox of separation conjoined with confusion. The extremes meet. Once truth is lost, the different forms of error are always present even though they may at first seem contradictory. The true analogy is the revelation of what is effected by Jesus Christ. It describes the relation between God and us which exists in him. It is a commentary on the decisive significance of his presence and victory for all creation. It is thus a description of the life which is truly diversity in unity. It is a discovery of faith.[1]

Three criteria must be respected in our enquiry at this point.

1. We must keep strictly to the incarnation of God in Jesus Christ alone, with neither extension nor adjunction. It is in him that the meeting of God with us takes place. All other meetings, whether in the Church or within ourselves, are consequences or implications

---

[1] It is astonishing that in his work on Barth Balthasar does not perceive that this analogy derives from revelation. Anxious to find something ontological in Barth's use of analogy, he apparently misses the point that the only true ontology is in the person of Jesus Christ.

of this unique event. The presence of God in nature, the voice of God in conscience, the providence of God in history—none of these can be put on the same plane as that which has become actual and determinative in the man-God, for it is in him that God gives himself personally to the world, to the Church and to the believer.[1]

2. The second criterion depends on the first. Since relations between God and man are not merely the prototype but already the realization of all other relations attested by the Holy Spirit, the way in which the divine and the human are rejoined in him is the norm of all other encounters. This is why the problem of the two natures takes on such importance in faith. It is not merely a description of Jesus Christ. It is also the rule of what takes place in us, in the Church and in the world. In no phase of history can we find any purer form of association than the union of God and man in Jesus. The disciplinary significance of Christology for all aspects of faith and life is a natural consequence. The relations between the letter and the Spirit in the Bible, between the humanity and the holiness of the Church, between the vocation and the responsibility of the believer, between Church and state—all these correspondences which attest the reconciliation of man with God are reflections of the true association effected in the Mediator. Thus Chalcedon, particularly in its famous adverbs, becomes a rule by which to test the truth of all the other relations created among us by grace.[2]

3. These divergent elements are linked, not by a direct bond, but by a new mediation which even in uniting them closely prevents their confusion. The Holy Spirit himself is this bond of truth and life. By his presence alone he establishes this unity in freedom between the Father and the Son, between Christ and us and between the various members of the body in the Church. He is himself these various relations, the transition from the one to the other, the life and love again circulating in the universe in reconstituted fulness. The system of relations to which we referred above is simply the presence of the Spirit ensuring both the profound integration of the parties and their autonomy in this unity. He is their mutual fellowship.[3]

---

[1] Thus the Church is not an extension of the incarnation except by analogy. Similarly there is no incarnation in religious feeling, moral consciousness, or history.

[2] The other christological dogmas, e.g., the communication of attributes, the *enhypostasis* and the *extra calvinisticum*, have a similar regulative function.

[3] From this angle Docetism and Ebionitism on the one side, Eutychianism and Nestorianism on the other, are sins against the Holy Ghost, either excluding the unity of the Spirit or reducing him to impotence. The Spirit is the miracle and mystery of this communion.

Let us now consider a little more closely the regulative significance of the Chalcedonian Definition. The point is always to avoid confusion or transformation on the one side, separation or division on the other, and thus to receive the unity which the Holy Spirit creates in Christ and then in us. What do the Greek adverbs mean and what is their relevance to our present theme?

I. 'Without confusion' means first that there can be no exaltation of the nature of man or of any supposedly elevating aspect of it in partial or total divinization. God and man remain what they are. Neither loses himself in or is absorbed by the other. God is not transformed into man nor does he intermingle with him to the point of confusion in respect of one or more qualities. He does not become man's consciousness, his sense of duty, or his reason. The Spirit of God is not the spirit of man. God remains himself in the incarnation. Similarly, these human realities, although re-established in their original truth and glorified, do not become attributes of God nor intermingle with his perfections. We nowhere have the kind of union which might be described as fusion in virtue of the transformation of one or other element or their identification. God remains the Wholly Other, not merely in respect of sin, but also in face of his creation. He is perfectly free and true to himself even when he stoops down and gives himself to us. Neither the humanity of Christ, the Bible, the Church nor the Christian becomes divine. On both sides we shall thus avoid transformation, intermingling or confusion in any encounters in which God and man are both present.

Again, we shall not confound the living God with any ideas we may have of him, nor his grace with the requirements which we think we see in his fatherly goodness, nor his Spirit with our spirituality, nor his essence with our idols. This condemns at once all natural theology, which postulates God on the basis of what we think we know and experience concerning him. It safeguards the revelation of his being in the gesture which he himself makes on his own initiative. Similarly, whatever qualities we think we see in ourselves must now be regarded as fully and exclusively human. There is no need to attribute something more than natural to them to establish their value. It is likely enough that they reflect certain divine perfections. But they are images and not the original. The responsibility of the creature depends on this refusal to mix the two natures, which enjoy their integrity on condition that they are free to be themselves in this association. Is it not a wonderful thing that submission to the Creator does not mean any subjection or any diminution of our powers, but a true realization of our potentialities?

Nevertheless, to attain this balance, it must be remembered that our actual nature, i.e., our nature ruined by the fall, has to be overcome by grace in order that our integrity may be restored from its present corruption. This is a further reason for avoiding confusion. For who is to say that any element which we think worthy of God is truly pleasing to him? Confusion necessarily leads to an arbitrary rehabilitation of certain human values which we declare to be pure even though they are still in the twilight of the fall. True unity is perfectly free, not forced. It comes as the unexpected miracle of grace making alliance with what it saves from disaster and not with what we think is worthy to enter the kingdom. Unity is always an unforeseen fruit. It is often contrary to our own spontaneous ideas. It results from the intervention of the Spirit who destroys the past and seizes on unexpected realities to associate with them. In other words, the truth is always different from what we suppose it to be.

This is why we must not confound our humanity with his, or what he says we are with what we think we are. How can we see what we are to be in the light of what we have become? The true nature of man is the result of a revelation. No intermingling of its demonstration and our intuitions can lead to the truth.

This Chalcedonian term is thus a simple commentary on the freedom of God and a guarantee of the authority of revelation and of the authenticity of the work of the Holy Spirit. In short, it attests the resurrection of the dead, which is not just an amelioration of nature, nor an evolution of our present state to future perfection, but the necessary break between life and death, past and future, falsehood and truth. It respects the authenticity of God and man and protects both against perversion. It is thus the criterion of truth, not merely in the sphere usually reserved for religion, but throughout creation. For if God is transformed into human realities, he disappears; and where are we to find him again? This death of God, which almost always follows his reduction to our stature, destroys our hope and purpose. The result is absurd. It is also true that if certain human values are absolutized and canonized, idolatry becomes rampant and the result is that we trust blindly in things which not only do not deserve it but will deceive us. Either way we are tragically robbed of the one thing that is truly indispensable, namely, the true God in his Word.

Confusion usually takes some very religious forms. Mysticism, pietism and institutionalism all make use of it, and their fervour is impressive. In fact, falsehood and imperialism lurk behind the appearance of consecration, and the truth demands at this point both perspicacity and also profanation. The veil of illusion must be torn off and the honest integrity disclosed which is both sober and luminous.

Thus the rejection of confusion sets aside any human pretension to make a spontaneous pronouncement on truth or to impose it. In theology, it is the criterion of the poverty of spirit which has sufficient respect for the truth of God—and for human virtues—not to try to seize upon the latter and to become subject to them. This attitude is that of the gratitude which joyfully welcomes the gifts of God wherever they come from without trying to turn them to personal advantage.

2. 'Without division' sets aside the contrary error which rather strangely may sometimes merge into that which we have just described. Division annuls the work of reconciliation which is supposed to surmount it. In effect, if full reconciliation does not clearly result from divine intervention, the latter has not succeeded in vanquishing the Prince of darkness whose evil act it is to divide. And if we deny the work of God in this subtle and devious manner, the most elementary faith is rendered futile. The incarnation thus becomes a myth, as do also the resurrection, miracles, and anything covered by the famous term 'supernatural'. In this case we must immediately find another solution to the problem of man, imagine other meetings with God on the basis of human powers, and thus fall back again into the preceding error. Division can never be the last word, for it takes from us all hope. Either God overcomes it, or man is thought to do so, and division leads directly to confusion.

This fault often takes the more attenuated form of separation. Here the work of salvation is recognized. Man is reunited with God through Christ. But there is still a certain distance between the two. The actual chievement of unity is in suspense. Reconciliation is not denied, but for fear of absorption there is separation even within the unity.

It is interesting to examine the hidden motives behind this attitude. It seems that they are found in a concern to maintain to some degree the liberty of man. For fear he might be completely subjected to God, an attempt is made to preserve for him a relative independence in their encounter. Unity is no longer a total engagement in which the creature paradoxically rediscovers his full freedom in submission. It is rather an association in which each preserves his prerogatives in a kind of peaceful coexistence. The presuppositions of this conception of the alliance are as follows. (1) In entering into the association, man has no need to die wholly to himself. He maintains his free will. This term finally denotes all that within him which is still supposed to be worthy of God in spite of the fall. The basis of his being remains, for he is not totally corrupted by the fall. (2) Hence even in his encounter with God this man preserves his measure of dignity. He places himself in some sense alongside God. Thus the unity is regarded as the association of a certain humanism with grace, and this justifies the co-operation of man with God. (3) The creature brings to this meeting a group of natural values which are thought to be worthy of divine approbation and which constitute his participation in the contract.

On this view, proper value is accorded to man, and his unity with God is like the convergence of related elements which come together in a twofold movement from God on the one side and man on the other. Dualisms both Protestant and Roman Catholic, Pelagianism and synergism, all rest on this kind of conception. The covenant is a juxtaposition in the order appropriate to both parties rather than a unity in which freedom results from the victory of God alone, which carries within it the full and complete restitution of man. For fear of total engagement, man as it were hangs back, keeping a number of supports within himself and therefore providing logical justification for apologetics, the philosophy of religion and natural theology.

It will be seen that separation does not denote merely a fault in Christology in the stricter sense. He who cannot accept the mysterious unity of the person of Christ in his two natures gives evidence of a retarding reservation. At bottom he will not admit his own need to die or the contradiction between man as he is and God. He does not apprehend the rigour of judgment which demands our own complete disappearance and the miracle of our resurrection. He thus halts midway, trying to steer a mediating course like the third man in the parable of the talents. He will not let go of self, but wants to enjoy the benefits of the covenant just the same.

This error joins forces with the first because it implies the exaltation of certain faculties in man. If God does not accomplish our full salvation, if the religious man plays his part, it must be admitted that this man is able to do so, though naturally under the influence of prevenient grace. Whether in terms of the Church, consciousness or history, these human factors take on a quasi-divine authority which enables them to join forces with grace. Separation thus presupposes confusion, or else it leads to it. It is for this reason that secularization can take a religious form and sacralization a profane. Secularized Neo-Protestant institutionalism can sometimes agree with sacralized Roman Catholic institutionalism in attributing religious value to its own nature. Natural theology flourishes either way. Whether clericalist or humanist, it springs from the same conception. The Church and believers are no longer thought of as assumed into Christ and restored to themselves by his death and resurrection. A relatively independent existence is conferred upon them. On this is built an ontology which rests on a direct affirmation of the analogy of being.[1]

3. In face of these two perils, which are first manifested in imprecision at the heart of our faith, but which have effects on the whole of our theology and life, unity in difference is able to protect a number of truths on which the correctness of our witness depends.

It first emphasizes the full achievement of our reconciliation in Jesus Christ. Everything is completed here. God and man are reunited. While there is neither transformation nor confusion, they are brought into a communion in which each belongs to the other. What we cannot know of ourselves, and what no phenomenon can demonstrate, is re-established at this one spot. Man has here overcome all hesitation, contradiction and revolt. He is again in God. Nothingness and idolatry are vanquished. The end of history is attained. That which torments man is outmoded. Synthesis is achieved. Who can estimate the importance of this restoration at the heart of our divisions or illusions?

This unity is not an ideal to be attained. It belongs to the Lord. It is his living work, the fruit of his intervention and the effect of his presence. It is a decision on his part, an act of his election, a gift of his grace. It is not a permanent factor nor a pre-established association. It is the event of his coming, the personal and decisive gesture corresponding to his love and freedom. In this sense Jesus Christ

---

[1] Thus, although Roman Catholicism is mainly Eutychian and Neo-Protestantism Nestorian, each implies the other. Deviation is always to be expected where human autonomy is asserted and there is unwillingness to receive our unity by revelation alone.

is not the symbol of our elevation to God, nor the most perfect type of humanity reaching its full flowering. He is the judgment and pardon coming from God to humble us and to transfigure us by divine power. The unity which he gives us is strictly the miracle, the creation, of the new man. His humanity is not ours. It opposes ours with a view to replacing our fallen state. Far from conjoining itself with some of our qualities, it challenges them, overcoming our pretended dignity no less than our distress. How can the flesh be associated with the Spirit? How can there be reconciliation between revolt and sanctity, curse and pardon? Only the cross and resurrection can make this possible.

In Christ the divine and the human do not associate in a kind of compromise. In him our actual humanity is not assumed but condemned. It is rejected in its present orientation and redeemed by being allowed to enter into this new combination. The Holy Spirit applies this judgment to us, and by our participation in the resurrection he clothes us in this newness. Man cannot make good any pretension of his own. He can only receive with astonishment this fulness to which he secretly aspires but which is not to be found elsewhere.

Consideration of the Lord's Supper will perhaps throw some light on the conditions in which this truth is attributed to us. The natural elements which here become the signs of grace have no intrinsic worth. Their value rests on God's decision to select them as instruments of grace. The bread remains bread. There is no transformation. Like the humanity of Jesus, bread is a real element in creation which God uses by association with it. Yet this earthly element is truly united with the reality which it signifies. If we separate it even by a fraction from the mystery of grace, we rob it of its real value. Contrary to what one might suppose, it is the human element rather than the divine which suffers most from separation. The idea is present that we respect it by withdrawing it a little from the divine authority and assuring it of some freedom of action. But by so doing we really make it an illusion, a pure symbol, a meaningless myth. If God alone counts, of what value is this piece of bread? Its function depends on its vocation, i.e., on the divine decision not to ignore or suppress creation, but to re-establish it in its rights. The bread thus takes on significance in the Lord's Supper at the moment when God wills to give it a place and to make use of it just as it is. And it is thus that man rediscovers his role, not against God or alongside him, but in this order in which each element enters into the function which is in keeping with its nature.

This order is necessary. Otherwise the unity would not be complete, as may be seen clearly from the doctrine of *enhypostasis*. The freedom and justification of the creature depend on its incorporation into God. What is at issue is a true and honest meeting of human elements which are purified from their corruption, i.e., which have gone through death to find their integrity in active submission to the true God. This perfection is for the moment realized only in Christ, for our works are not yet free from sin. This is why we receive it from him and await its full manifestation at his return. Actual in him, this unity is for us a promise of which we now have the earnest. There is exchange, however, between what he is and what we are. The dogma of the communication of the attributes has this significance too. A dialogue begins between God and us. His grace is already concretely communicated to us, producing a certain sanctification of our human capacities by association with them. Grace does not elevate the capacities above themselves nor does it confound itself with them. It rather restores to them the orientation in which they prove more true and effective. The conflict at this point between Reformed, Lutherans and Roman Catholics is of great importance. The last two carry the exchange so far that the human elements are already partially divinized in correspondence with their view of the Lord's Supper. But sanctification is not transformation. The term denotes rather restoring to the right place in subjection so that the human may give what is rightly to be expected of it.

The best safeguard of this reciprocal purity is provided by a correct apprehension of the role of the Holy Spirit, who establishes this communication without robbing either God or man of his true nature, but rather by restoring real humanity to man. The Spirit clothes man in powers which are not simply those of nature, but which God wills to confer on him. And it is in this fulness that nature finds again the eminent dignity which God ordained for it that it might reflect his glory. In his true humanity, the Son has received powers which transcend his human resources. Similarly, the witness of Scripture, without ceasing to be human, can tell us more than men alone could do, if God so wills. The Church too, if God so wills, can act in a way which exceeds its own powers. Here again we must be on our guard against any rivalry between the work of God and the forces of the creature. The association brings out the latter, so that one might say that the creature reaches full maturity only when it is stimulated, directed and sustained by the communication of grace, which, while it does not intermingle with it, enfolds it and drives it in the right direction.

Thus the unity is more than the adding together of two units. As in the Trinity, it is the participation of the one in the other in sobriety and in love, with a view to the glorious realization of all the potentialities present.

This leads us to a proper definition of holiness in the scriptural sense. The word is fairly generally used to qualify certain human actualities which are called to act in this unity and service. Thus Scripture is holy, the Church is the communion of saints, the eucharist is holy and the Christian is a saint. In none of these relations does the sanctity crush the human element which it qualifies. Nor does it exalt this element. The terms always denote a unity with distinction in which dependence ensures freedom and the communication of attributes guarantees integrity. The dualities reproduce that which is signified by the name of Jesus Christ, and we may thus apply to them the same order as that which obtains between the two natures of the Mediator.[1]

At all stages, therefore, the word 'holy' denotes that which is of God, that which he creates in us, the use which he himself makes of realities with which he associates himself, not divinizing them but preparing them for his service. The word is synonymous with divine, not in a fixed and static sense, but in accordance with the event of the personal intervention of the living God. Holy means that God acts, promises and accomplishes. It speaks of the choice which God has made of an action commensurate with his being and efficacious for the salvation of humanity. When we come across the term, it puts us on guard. We are perhaps dealing with more than man. There is the possibility of the direct intervention of the living God. We have thus to be attentive and to be ready to go beyond the object in question. This is the direct opposite of a sanctity attributed to the object itself. In this case we find ourselves simply and directly in the presence of a superior, divine, or at least consecrated reality. But 'holy' does not mean this in the Bible. Scripture is holy, not because it is divine in itself, but because it is the place where God

[1] Cf. the relevant article on *hagios* in *TWNT*. In the Old Testament the term applies more strictly to God. For the Rabbis it has cultic significance, e.g., in relation to places, etc. In the New Testament it is proper to God, to Jesus, to the Holy Spirit, then to the Church and to Christians.

might reveal himself. In the last analysis the word 'holy' denotes quite simply the promise and actuality of the intervention of God through a specific object in order that he himself might be the agent of our sanctification.[1]

1. *Holy Scripture*

As we now seek to apply this discipline to problems relating to the Bible—its place in the movement of revelation, its authority and function in the Church, the mode of its interpretation—we shall be struck by the resemblance between these questions and those which encountered us in our study of the person of Jesus Christ. How can this human book become the Word of God? By what miracle is it possible that in listening to the letter of Scripture we may hear God himself? How did this collection come into being through the centuries? Who superintended the formation of the Canon? What is the relationship between the Holy Spirit and this book, not merely at the moment when it was written, but when the various components were brought together and also now that we read it? Why must we study this book to be led to Jesus Christ and fashioned in his name? What is the secret of its power over us in spite of its antiquity?

From an early age attempts have been made to emphasize the concrete authority of the Bible by identifying it almost totally with the Word of God. Although they did not give dogmatic form to their insights, fathers like Clement of Alexandria, Origen and Gregory of Nazianzus espoused literal inspiration. Like the Reformers after them, they did this on the basis of the Bible's own teaching, especially in II Tim. 3.16: 'All scripture is inspired of God' (*theopneustos*), and II Peter 1.20f.: 'No prophecy of the scripture is of any private interpretation. For the prophecy came not in old time by the will of man: but holy men of God spake as they were moved by the Holy Ghost.' To these much-quoted passages we might add II Cor. 3.4–18, where Paul lays down very clearly the main factors in the problem. There is in the Bible, he says, a human element—the letter—and a divine element—the Spirit. The letter kills, the Spirit makes alive. This does not imply a disqualification of the letter. It kills only if not

---

[1] A good example is to be found in the case of Mary, who is holy in virtue of the divine election and ordination. Roman Catholicism, however, ascribes to her an intrinsic sanctity, and thus establishes a mariological norm alongside and finally in place of the christological or Chalcedonian. Neo-Protestantism is mariological rather than christological in principle.

animated by the Spirit. It is useless and even dangerous alone. It receives all its value from the Spirit. The ministry of the letter, the apostle tells us, has its own glory (v. 9). The point is that we must not be imprisoned by it, as were the Jews, for whom a veil rested over the Old Testament. Christ alone can lift this veil. Christ is here almost synonymous with the Spirit, for it is through both that the letter takes on its significance. This is why Paul adds at once that the Lord is the Spirit. The letter of the Bible receives its value from Christ and the Spirit which are its glory, i.e., its true sense. It is also the Spirit who enables us to contemplate this glory of God in the mirror of Holy Scripture, as the Jews could not do until converted. There is now, therefore, no contradiction between the letter and the Spirit if God himself is using Scripture to bear witness to himself by the Holy Spirit. In I Cor. 2.6–16 Paul declares clearly that he is expounding the mysterious and hidden wisdom of God. He is still a man writing his own words. Yet in so doing he confidently claims that he is transmitting the Word of God. If this is so, it is because God has revealed himself to him, giving him access to his own mystery by the Holy Spirit. Only the Spirit can in fact reveal to man the deep things of God and permit man to attest them. Having received God's blessings, Paul is also given the power to declare them. His writings are thus testimonies to the mysterious wisdom of God, thanks to the power which the Spirit confers and which natural wisdom does not have. His human words become spiritual, i.e., meet for the things of God. These autobiographical statements are a commentary on the *theopneustos* of II Tim. 3.16. The Spirit instructs Paul and inspires his words that they may be spiritual. In other words, while Paul's writings are composed by a man, they have more than historical or documentary value. They are included in the event of revelation, since God has inspired them, expressing himself through them. To be properly understood, they should thus be read in the Spirit. Otherwise they cannot give what they promise and what they exist to give. They become a mere letter, are unable to bear witness to the mysterious and hidden wisdom of God and lose their *raison d'être*. One might even say that if we take them merely in their terrestrial historicity we are untrue to the intention behind their composition and we are thus disloyal to history itself, since they were obviously written with this intention. These texts must be received spiritually. As Paul says, 'the natural man receiveth not the things of the Spirit of God' (I Cor. 2.14). Dedicated merely to his own wisdom, he sees in these writings only a letter which kills.

If, however, he judges spiritually, he grasps their true meaning. The hearer, too, must be brought into the miracle of revelation to understand what Paul says, the object which he describes and the true bearing of his testimony. Thus the circle is closed. God acts. Paul can take account of this action only as he is illuminated by the Spirit of God. And his readers can enter this world of revelation, where God and man are associated again in mutual understanding, only when the Spirit apprises them of this mystery. True *theopneustia* is this circuit of the Spirit which allows certain human testimonies to denote the world of God and which allows readers to have access to this world thereby.

From the very first the Church has constantly oscillated between three possible attitudes on these questions.

(i) Fairly quickly this true *theopneustia*, which in the unity of the Spirit neither excludes the part of man nor confounds the divine and the human but rather recreates the human side, was reduced to a kind of neutralization of the human element. Thus for Gregory the authors of these testimonies are no longer true authors. The Spirit has annulled man's part instead of giving man this freedom in the appropriate order. This danger reappears constantly in the doctrine of good works. If all is of grace, man has no more to do. He is, as it were, put between brackets. He becomes an irresponsible and even at times an unconscious instrument in the hands of God. Even in Augustine there are passages where inspiration borders on magic, and this leads to the well-known *opus operatum* of sacramental doctrine. Athenagoras goes so far as to suggest that the Holy Spirit deprives the authors of their own faculties, and according to Hippolytus they are completely passive. We have here a kind of dehumanization. The natural wisdom which is to be effectively set aside is confused with the true humanity which, far from being destroyed by the Spirit, is rather to be rehabilitated and made responsible for cleaving conscientiously to God and bearing voluntary witness to his benefits.

The intention behind these conclusions is less pure than might at first appear. Fundamentally it betrays uncertainty in face of the mystery. God is too distant, the Holy Spirit too vague. Faith wants a more accessible assurance, and it finds this in the Bible. The Bible is itself the Word of God addressing us. In Roman Catholicism we find a comparable movement in respect of the eucharist, where the presence of God is materialized in the host. Here the Spirit is identified with the letter of the Bible. Either way a human element, whether book or bread, is the very expression of God. This identification is no longer the result of the event of a divine intervention. It is a tangible, perceptible fact, a factor in our history.

In itself, however, the Bible is only letter. It is not divine. Yet in its humanity it becomes the Word of God by the Spirit when God expresses himself through it. If we make this a fixed and permanent attribute of the Bible, *theopneustia* is transformed and loses its true value. This deviation was most prominent in the orthodoxy of the seventeenth century. To establish it, recourse was had to Chalcedonian terminology. The divine 'nature' of the Bible was affirmed. No longer, however, did the Bible have two natures; it had only the one, the divine. The term appeared again later, and this shows how convenient it is irrespective of the context in which it is used. Once again the Bible was seen to have only one nature, but this time it was the human nature, now so nearly divine that distinction is difficult. Whether the one nature is that of God attributed either to the Bible or to the eucharistic elements, or whether it is the nature of man, the two deviations merge into one another and show themselves to be simply variations of the one error. In fact, God and man remain distinct. Without confusion or intermingling, and therefore in their distinction, they are united by the Holy Spirit.

The reasoning of Bénédict Pictet[1] is worth noting in this regard. Either the Bible is divine, and thus bears the marks of divinity, so that what it says, the truths which it imparts, can and should be recognized as truths, or it is not divine and no reliance can be placed upon it. The accent has obviously been shifted from the Spirit to the Bible, and the truth depends, not on God's faithfulness to his promises, but on the credibility, i.e., the infallibility of the book. The principle seems to be the same as that of the infallibility of the Church in its head, since the desire is for a more accessible and even perhaps a more certain authority than that of the Holy Ghost alone. It has often been alleged that this attitude attests great faith. But this is an illusion, for it is easier to believe in the Bible, the Church or the real presence, as it is easier to build on the voice of conscience or experience, than to commit oneself to the complete novelty of the mysterious wisdom of God which comes to us by the Spirit. These direct, religious or sacral assurances hide an uncertainty as to the

[1] Bénédict Pictet: theologian at Geneva at the end of the eighteenth century.

object of faith, a search for human security, and a kind of union between nature and grace which authorizes the former not to go through death to resurrection.

However that may be, Pictet is compelled by his presuppositions to adduce lengthy proofs of the divinity of Scripture. He does not begin by confessing God's promise to make use of it. Instead, he tries to show by logical proofs that it has this privilege and that we are thus to put our full trust in it. Here we see the rationalism of this orthodoxy. It tries to prove that of which the Spirit alone can truly convince us. Ultimately the Spirit is hardly necessary in this doctrine, since we have the Bible. Here again there is a parallel to Roman Catholicism, where the Spirit is as it were absorbed in the authority of the Church. What the Church is for the latter, the Bible is for the former. With this kind of *theopneustia*, something very significant happens in relation to the Spirit. His work is strongly emphasized at the moment of writing, and then it fades from the picture. His influence on the authors is decisive, for he dictates the truth to them. But then he is incorporated in Scripture. He thus ceases to be a problem. He is an evident reality, taking concrete form in the Bible and producing by means of it a kind of enthusiasm which may be attributed to him. Once it is possible to prove the divinity of the Bible, the decisions which lead to the formation of the Canon and to our acceptance of it are strikingly simplified. So long as we do not object to the arguments, we accept the truth. There is thus developed in relation to the Bible, or the Church, an apologetic which will be able to overcome all resistance. Certainly the Spirit is still necessary to enflame the heart and to kindle obedience. But he gives only supplementary assurance, since there is certainty already that the Word of God will be found in the whole letter of the Bible.

The well-known work of Gaussen[1] entitled *Theopneustia*, while it moves in the same direction, should not be confused with high orthodoxy. To understand it, we must put it in its historical context, which is very different from that of the seventeenth century. Gaussen is not trying to systematize the results of the Reformation by rationalization. His aim is in fact prophetic and in some sense polemic. He wishes to confess his faith in the Word of God coming through the Bible, and therefore a true *theopneustia*, against the

---

[1] L. Gaussen: theologian of the mid-nineteenth century. He was one of the principal initiators of the Awakening and the chief protagonist of *theopneustia*, and published the book of that name in 1840.

scepticism of rationalistic criticism. But in his warm and in many ways justifiable ardour, he is guilty of incautious expression. He sees quite clearly the humanity of the Bible: 'Scripture is wholly the word of man, and Scripture is wholly the Word of God' (p. 297). Or again, 'All these words are of man, and all these words are of God' (p. 9). He does not deny that God has used this witness as a means of self-expression: 'All the verses, without exception, are of men; and all the verses, without exception, are of God, whether he speaks directly in his own name or whether he uses the whole personality of the sacred author,' so that 'in Scripture God has done nothing except through man, and man has done nothing except through God' (p. 12).

This protestation against a criticism which sets itself up as judge of the Word of God suffers from a threefold inadequacy. In practice, it stresses the action of the Spirit only at the moment of authorship, like all representatives of this movement. Now this moment is important, but why single it out exclusively? When the believer reads the Bible, he knows that it has been inspired, but he waits for it to be inspired afresh for him. And this waiting is necessary, for the Bible does not permanently possess the Spirit. If the second movement is neglected, the final result will inevitably be assertion of the intrinsic divinity of the Bible. This is not very prominent in Gaussen, but it may be seen in the following definition of inspiration: '*Theopneustia* is the mysterious power exerted by the Spirit of God on the authors of Holy Scripture to make them write it, to guide them even in the choice of the words which they use and thus to preserve them from all error' (p. 305). On this view one can hardly avoid clothing the Bible with a certain magical power. If it is the work of the Holy Spirit, it has within it something of the Spirit, and therefore it cannot again become a mere letter, let alone a letter which kills. Like the sacrament of the Church in Roman Catholicism, it thus works by its own power, though in fact, even if inspired in origin, it is nothing unless the Spirit continually animates it. Finally, there is too much concern on this view to show that the Bible cannot contain the least error or contradiction even on the historical, scientific or human level. But this is not really the point. These texts are testimonies to Jesus Christ. Those who produced them did not have infused knowledge or infallibility. They were indebted to the conceptions of their time. What matters is not so much the correctness of their views of the world but the fact that

God gave these relative conceptions the capacity to bear witness to his work. Many of these conceptions have perhaps been corrected. But strictly this has no bearing on the true value of the testimony borne. This has only to be placed in its context to bring out both the intention of the author and the possibly imperfect means which he chose to express himself. Even a historical or technical error might also serve the Word of God if the author had at his disposal no other means of expression. Such human imperfections might ultimately enhance the significance of the spiritual testimony by emphasizing the fact that the truth of God is not necessarily identical with scientific or logical exactness. They might be scandals in the biblical sense, i.e., contradictions of human rationality, to guard us against confusion. Thus, the Word of God does not bind us to the material exactitude of the letter but to the authenticity of this letter as testimony, i.e., to this letter on which reposes the promise to be able to serve the end. This is the meaning of its canonicity, namely, that in its humanity and therefore in its dependence on a given epoch, it may denote, even within a particular history and therefore in all human history, the free and sovereign intervention of the true God. From this angle canonical does not mean perfect or intrinsically infallible or divine, but able by the Holy Spirit to serve the will of God, who purposes to make himself known through these testimonies which are selected and designed to be the instruments of his revelation.

The fact that Gaussen did not go far enough in his pleading explains why his works did not reply as he would have liked either to biblical criticism or to the theological conceptions which accompanied the great advance in historical studies in his day.

(ii) The second attitude taken up by the Church towards inspiration is most clearly illustrated by the movement of historical criticism. When we try to pick out its main features, we note that it regards itself as a reaction against the threat of confusion between the Bible and the Word of God. Its supporters devote their whole energy to destroying this intermingling, which they regard as fatal. Thus Edmond Scherer[1] writes: 'I begin with the fact that the dogma of inspiration has its root in the need for authority, that this need constantly demands a more infallible, more genuine, more absolute

---

[1] Edmond Scherer: Professor of Theology at Geneva from 1838. With Gaussen defended *theopneustia*. Later he abandoned strict biblicism, resigned his chair, and became a literary critic. He ended up a complete agnostic.

authority, and that the instinct of those who surrender to this need is thus to exaggerate as much as possible the nature and degree of inspiration.'[1] To justify its opposition, the movement often caricatures the position which it contests. For inspirationists the Bible is supposed to be a kind of sacred code corresponding to their need for authority, a purely external rule which is divine and therefore infallible, which is equally sovereign in all its parts, and from which are taken ready-made and retrogressive doctrines which cannot be accepted by the liberty-loving conscience of our own age. This idol must be destroyed in order to restore to Jesus Christ his living authority, to put the Bible in its true place, and to free the Church from an authoritarian yoke justified by a text which is received and interpreted with servility. The means to do this is simple enough. It is to rediscover the humanity of the Bible and to free the Word of God from this novel and illegitimate incarnation. 'The Bible is not the Word of God; it contains it. The bond which linked the various parts and the fiction which gave an equal colour of divinity to the whole have now disappeared. Instead of a volume, we now have a number of books, varying in character, contents and importance, which the Christian reads to discover or to rediscover his Saviour, to edify his soul and to receive the life and light which these records impart. And I do not see what harm is done by exchanging the letter of a code for the living products of apostolic individuality, an authority for a history, and, if I may be quite frank, a cabalistic ventriloquism for the noble accent of the human voice' (*ibid.*, pp. 19f.).

Having swung to the one extreme, the pendulum now moves to the other. Stress is now placed on history, textual exactitude, the writers and their writings rather than on the canonical testimony.

For this separation there is, of course, another reason which better explains the movement than either negative reaction or technical development. The eyes of the epoch are now on man, who is to be liberated from tutelage. Almost everywhere there is protest against doctrines which disparage him. The urge is to exalt him. Traditional Christianity is accused of taking malign pleasure in crushing him. Original sin, divine judgment, predestination and the deity of Christ are presented as so many threats to humanity. Conceived at a time when liberty was an empty word, they represent a system of oppression which was in keeping with mediaeval Catholicism and which the

[1] *La critique de la foi*, Paris, 1850, p. 7.

Reformers were unable to shake off completely. 'Protestantism remained a system of authority; the only difference between it and Catholicism in this respect is that it substituted one authority for another, Scripture for the Church' (*ibid.*, p. 6). This oppressive totality must be broken at the root by a new interpretation of the substance of faith which will arise out of a new realization of the true powers of the creature.

Although subjected to all kinds of adverse influences, the creature is always worthy of God and able partially at least to reflect his perfections in spite of its failings. There is a bond between it and the Creator and this permits an exchange which does not have to be subordinated to the miracle of Holy Scripture. Why should God speak to us only through the Bible? Can he not reach us directly in our consciousness? Is it not patent that he also acts in the march of history, in other religions and through the great thinkers of the race? Eugène Ménégoz[1] has given to this insight, which may be novel from the Reformed standpoint but which has a long ecclesiastical tradition, the following unequivocal expression: 'The knowledge of God, perception of his voice and discernment of his revelation depend on subjective dispositions, on an internal criterion which is itself of a spiritual order. There is a mysterious affinity between the spirit of man and the Spirit of God, an active, living and personal reciprocity. And it is thanks to this reciprocity that the Word of God, according to our inner dispositions, affirms itself more or less clearly and energetically in our heart and spirit, and produces a moral impression which creates assurance of faith in those who are of the truth.'[2] The dynamic unity of the Word of God with the Bible is much less necessary and even superfluous once the event of the meeting between God and man can be directly produced elsewhere, in our heart and spirit. If this Word comes to us directly, why should we seek it exclusively in Scripture? This spontaneous affinity between man and God makes revelation less indispensable and less new. The Bible is perhaps the best illustration of this kinship. It is the finest example of man's ability to converse with his God. But once it is no longer received as the unique witness to grace, its authority does not have the same significance. It becomes the precious record of a much more general spirituality in which history, consciousness, life and the Church

---

[1] Eugène Ménégoz: theologian of the so-called Paris school with Auguste Sabatier. He represented the tendency to symbolofideism. His principal works were published between 1900 and 1930.
[2] *Publications diverses sur le Fidéisme*, Vol. I, 1900, p. 67.

all have their say. On the other hand, if it is true that the wisdom of God radically contradicts our own wisdom, and that it bears testimony to this through a death and resurrection, then it will have to be revealed to us somewhere, and the biblical Canon, animated by the Holy Spirit, takes on its full value. If the divine wisdom expresses itself directly, even though only partially, in our own heart and spirit, these texts are no longer the unique instrument of revelation but only an impressive example, among many others, of the affinity between God and man and of the fine spirituality which the human race has always demonstrated. It will be noted here too, in passing, that this conception approximates to the Roman Catholic thesis wherein the Bible is swallowed up in the wisdom of the Church, which is more strictly delimited than in Neo-Protestantism but which is still open to the truths of nature.

The movement of separation which we observe in this period rests fundamentally on another confusion which is no longer that of the Word of God with the Bible but the confusion of revelation with the intuitions of our own hearts. There is thus achieved an intermingling in which the two sources of knowledge are married and give birth to a diffused, general system which combines the message of God and the aspirations of man. This is the meaning of the attempt 'to transport the faith into a new atmosphere and thus to assure it of new conditions of development'.[1]

We may fill out this general description by three observations on the Canon, the part of the Holy Spirit and the use of Scripture in this movement.

(1) The authority of the biblical Canon is not annulled, but it is certainly made conditional and relative. It also depends on a number of verifications which, while they are justified in themselves, considerably modify the classical approach to Scripture in virtue of the importance attached to them.

At first, and without regard to deviations, the Canon was received as a collection of testimonies miraculously given to the Church and gratefully received by it to lead to Jesus Christ under the free control of the Spirit. There was no question of denying the humanity of the texts. But the Church was also conscious of making a discovery in them. God spoke to it effectively through these witnesses, which were thought to be adequate in their actual form and in their totality to serve the Word. Literary, historical and critical study of

---

[1] Scherer, *op. cit.*, p. 28.

the human instrument of revelation was perfectly legitimate so long as there was always a return to the canonical perspective, i.e., to God's promise to speak to us through this collection of prophecies. Whether a text was older or younger, whether it was written by this or that author, whether errors might be discovered in transmission —all these things might have some importance in relation to a correct understanding. But once the work was done it was necessary to return to the body of the received text, not simply to know a historical Jesus, or the facts concerning the foundation of Christianity, or religious doctrine, but to penetrate to the mystery of the personal work which God effected in his Son in human history. Thus, in spite of its humanity, the Bible remained the rule of faith, the authority for knowledge of revelation, the only true norm for the life of the Church. Though fully Scripture, it was also holy, i.e., able to lead us to God by the Holy Spirit.

It is this movement of return to the canonicity or sanctity of Scripture which is now almost completely omitted. The letter is so ardently studied that the promises are neglected. The Bible becomes a source-book of historical science, a religious document, a code of practical morality, but not the unique and normative witness to divine revelation.[1]

(2) Our second observation concerns the part of the Holy Spirit, which seems to be doubly distorted by comparison with classical definitions. The function of the Spirit is both generalized and diminished. It is generalized in the sense that his inspiration is no longer strictly related to Jesus Christ and Scripture, but acts directly and by preference in our consciousness. In opposition to the view which particularly emphasizes the action of the Holy Spirit in the development of the biblical witness, we now have the opposite extreme of emphasis on the actual work of the Holy Spirit in us. Now it is true that the Spirit acts in us. But his office is to declare to us the things of Christ. 'He shall glorify me; for he shall receive of mine, and shall shew it unto you' (John 16.14). Here, however, we do not have the Spirit of Christ commissioned to reveal his work but the assimilation of the Holy Spirit to a much vaguer religious inspiration, to a kind of general fervour which enflames us as we lift up ourselves to God. At work in history, in the consciousness and

---

[1] Cf. Harnack, *What is Christianity?*, p. 6; Ménégoz, *op. cit.*, pp. 64, 71f.; Reuss, *L'Histoire du Canon*, Strasbourg, 1863, pp. 424f.; E. Rochat, *Le développement de la théologie protestante française au XIXe siècle*, 1942, pp. 430f.; A. Malet, *Le Semeur*, December 1958.

in the community, the Spirit is the yearning for God which impels us to seek him and to adore him wherever he manifests himself. To a more general revelation there corresponds a broader inspiration, and the Spirit strictly describes the aspiration of humanity to spiritual heights. This enlargement is particularly palpable in the work of Ménégoz: 'Since the Spirit of God reveals himself in the consciousness of man, the greatest measure of divine revelation is to be found in the collective consciousness of the race, and it is here that we must seek it.'[1] Separated from Scripture, which is simply a striking example, the Spirit operates everywhere. And Ménégoz continues: 'The subjective criterion for this search is the individual consciousness. It is the Spirit of God in personal illumination who serves as a light in the various manifestations of consciousness elsewhere, and we can assimilate of this witness only that which corresponds to our individual consciousness. Hence the final reason for our conviction is always the witness of our own consciousness' (*ibid.*, p. 9). 'We are thus to place ourselves, so far as we are able, under the influence of the witness of the Holy Spirit in humanity, and to do this we must study carefully the contribution of men and books which in our judgment have been and still are organs of the most perfect revelation of the thought of God' (*ibid.*, p. 13).

This enlargement, however, implies a diminution of the true role of the Spirit, for if the consciousness and personal judgment play this role, having the power both to recognize and to apprehend revelation, the miracle of the Spirit is strangely attenuated. For the Reformers, the power of the Holy Spirit must overcome our opposition, as Christ had to do in his death and resurrection. Without the Spirit of the risen Lord, who opens the eyes of the blind, there can be no access to truth. If, however, man has this power, the Spirit does not have to work so complete a miracle. It is enough to direct, stimulate and sustain our own spontaneous search. And the Bible, now brought closer to us, does not have to be opened up by a new intervention on the part of God. This partial confusion between God's Spirit and ours authorizes a new separation between the Spirit and the two other modes of God's being, and therefore between the Spirit and the other elements of revelation, and between the Spirit and the Bible, whose witness is necessarily less supernatural since it is to a mystery less inaccessible and less mysterious.

(3) Finally, there is a marked modification in the use of the Bible.

[1] *Op. cit.*, p. 9.

It is no longer a norm. It is rather a means of knowing and participating in the experiences of its authors. What it expressly declares
is less important than the possibility which it affords us of meeting
either the Christ of history or the Christ of our own experience. The
essential point is the agreement between its witness and history on
the one side and our religious intuitions on the other. In many
passages, however, the Bible expresses conceptions which are no
longer acceptable to modern religious man, i.e., to the man who is in
large measure shaped by nineteenth-century Idealism. It is thus
necessary to select from the whole that which is in keeping with what
we can believe. Selection is of great importance, as Scherer points
out: 'The Christian . . . has within him the principle of spiritual
selection. . . . The reader who is most attached to the dogma of
inspiration can pass by passages which offer him no nourishment
and attach himself, and constantly return to, those in which he finds
edification. There is a kinship, an elective affinity, between the Holy
Spirit in the heart of the believer and the Holy Spirit in the Bible.
Religious truth, which should be the only object of faith, is simply
the spiritual substance of the Bible, the Word of God in Scripture.'[1]
It is common experience, however, that the Bible may contradict the
spontaneous movement of our piety, correcting it, completing it,
even sometimes destroying it in favour of a new growth. But if we
follow only those passages which agree with what we already have,
what progress can we make? This method again resembles that of
Roman Catholicism. The Bible no longer challenges us. It is accepted
to the degree that we can approve it according to our own requirements or Church tradition. This principle leads to a veritable
absorption of the Bible into accepted religion. Biblical criticism has
tried to justify the selection, but it always does so on the basis of a
preconceived position. Once freed from its dogmatisms, criticism
has its value in a restricted sphere. But the well-known slogan of
Harnack that we should distinguish the kernel from the husk[2] has
often been used for good or evil to foist upon the Bible particular
conceptions of the faith. This is a constant temptation for the
Church.

(iii) From confusion and separation we now turn to the unity in
which the authentic elements in the first two positions are reunited
by the miracle of the divine intervention.

---

[1] *Publications diverses sur le Fidéisme*, I, p. 43.
[2] *Op. cit.*, p. 60.

The essential point is undoubtedly that God wills to meet us and to speak to us through these human texts. His Word is Jesus, very God and very man. The person and life of Jesus are for us the message of God. In his humanity and divine sonship, the event of the intervention of the Lord has taken place. This is the history before which we find ourselves placed. It is not simply a terrestrial occurrence but the meeting of God with all men in Jesus.

In these circumstances it was inevitable that the testimonies raised up to record this event should themselves be human, since the divine Word presented itself in this humanity. Yet in accordance with their object they had also to go beyond the visible and to denote the mystery sovereignly present in this man. For if they had restricted themselves to the mere earthly appearance, they would have mutilated that which they purport to describe and set themselves in contradiction with the event which they seek to declare. They would have been highly unhistorical and even misleading if they had been able to record only the external aspect of this reality.

But who was able to lead these witnesses to the core of truth apart from the Spirit in person? 'The things of God knoweth no man, but the Spirit of God' (I Cor. 2.11). His intervention was necessary to allow men to perceive and to penetrate the mystery. Without him, they could not have pierced beyond the external cover. But in this case, how can we for our part dispense with this power if we are to grasp the real content of these writings? Although inspired to correspond with the truth which they sought to denote, they would be closed in their most essential aspect—their aptness to give account of this event—if the Spirit did not enlighten us to see what these witnesses saw and transmitted. The Holy Spirit both makes of these human testimonies an apt description and also causes us to enter into their vision. Thus he himself is the guarantee of the historical integrity of these texts in relation to the event which they indicate. He himself gives us, too, this perspective of truth.

The choice of the Canon is simply this discovery. By the Holy Spirit the Church came to see, and continually does so, that these texts lead it to the incarnate Son of God. It recognizes that this means has been selected by God and brought into his service for this end. It is astonished at the gift which is given to it to assure it of the privilege of coming to the heart of this mighty event, which, although concealed, enables it to live with far greater assurance than its own particular intuitions or ecclesiastical traditions. The authority of the Canon is a promise rather than a dogma. In reading these texts, we, too, may make that breath-taking discovery, and God may thus reveal himself to us as by the Holy Spirit we are permitted to follow these texts to the heart of the mystery which they attest.

The holiness of the Bible denotes quite simply the promise which may well be realized when we read this Scripture which, although inspired in origin, is wholly human. The adjective does not in any sense imply an intrinsic capacity which the Bible has of itself. It recapitulates in a single word the history which we have just recalled. By the Holy Spirit, i.e., according to the wise and merciful will of the Lord himself, men have seen the truth of the central event in human history and have been enabled to speak of it. Similarly, by the Holy Spirit attentive readers of these documents may in their turn penetrate into this vision and encounter the living God. The holiness of the Bible affirms this possibility, which becomes a reality when God fulfils his promise. Hence this term recalls what has taken place and what can take place by the fact that the Bible exists as testimony to the incarnate Word. At the same time it guarantees the historicity of this succession of events from the divine decision, by way of the compilation of the testimonies, to our discovery of their true significance and our reconciliation with God. The Holy Spirit is thus the bond of truth, which is not merely general and abstract, but divine and human in the unity of this totality which centres on the person of Jesus.

In these circumstances the Bible can be revealed to us in its holiness and in its humanity as a full and accurate witness which is sufficient to lead us to the Lord. Although wholly subject to the conditions of its age, it is admirably suited to fulfil this office. It does not tell us everything, but even its silences are eloquent. It is difficult and repelling in places, but its mysteries, and the offence which it gives in some passages, concur in some way or other with the witness which it seeks to give. Every part must be taken in its specific office and in conjunction with the whole if its distinctive teaching is to be fully perceived.

These considerations demand critical study for understanding. But they also demand respect for the whole in keeping with the intention which superintends the establishment of this witness. In other words, even in its humanity the Bible is holy in all its elements in the sense that any part may be the vehicle of grace. The promise applies to every passage. The essentials are not found everywhere,

but every text has its own contribution to make to the true knowledge of the work of God. If we are not to say that every biblical
word *is* the Word of God, we must say that from the very moment
it is canonical, and not merely historical, it participates in the promise of being able to serve this Word as the Spirit declares it to us.
The fact that a text is closed to us does not justify us in ignoring it,
for our lack of understanding cannot destroy the promise. On the
contrary, this text may some day speak to us, and our failure to hear
it at a given time is more of a judgment on us than on it. Our lack of
understanding is a warning. We should impeach, not the Bible, but
our own resistance to grace. Accepted and understood, Scripture
edifies us; rejected, it condemns us. Criticism must not become an
excuse for exempting ourselves from this judgment or an occasion
for substituting our own ideas for its instruction.

The holiness of the Bible encircles its humanity and gives it its
meaning. It lets it keep its distinctive features, but it also bears
witness that in this specific humanity and in all its parts it may
become the instrument of the personal revelation of God. When this
event takes place, this letter, for all its limitations, truly becomes the
Word of God. There is then complete unity between the Spirit and
the letter, the holiness and the humanity. No element is suppressed,
but all are associated without either constraint or faltering.

This holiness is not merely a promise and a guarantee of truth.
It is also a requirement of freedom. The Bible does not compel. It
simply announces that God can and will make use of it. It attests
this possibility. Here, then, 'holy' means that God proposes to act
through this book, and that he does act through it. In this case the
authority of the Bible is simply that of the Lord himself, and our
adherence to his Word is free and joyful faith which does not rest
on a book nor on the authority of the disciples alone but on the
discovery of the living God. There can be no compulsion here by
blind submission to these texts. Either God uses them and himself
reveals their incomparable worth, or he does not speak and our
attachment to these documents has only secondary interest in comparison with what might be. It is thus in full liberty that God gives
us Scripture as the means of his revelation. If he does so, there is no
further problem. If he does not, nothing can prove to us that the
Bible is his Word. This liberty does not imply independence in
respect of the text itself. On the contrary, it binds us more closely
to it, since God gives it as a means whereby we may hear him. It is

in accepting this movement of revelation that we receive the liberating Word. In this free adherence, we see how well adapted the humanity is to its goal. It is fulfilled by the fact that it is put at the disposal of the Spirit, as our humanity is rehabilitated in Jesus Christ by submission to God. It is no longer mutilated by the fall but integrated with grace, which does not crush it but opens it to new possibilities. It has thus to be considered in this fulness, i.e., both in its historical features and also in its aptness to bear witness to God.

This unity is a miraculous and balanced unity. The human receives its integrity and royalty in its own sphere. The divine, denoted in all its interventions by the adjective 'holy', does not compete with this humanity. It restores it to its function, encircles it and gives it its meaning. It limits it too, but in so doing it truly exalts it by giving it its full autonomy within this unity.

The definitions which help us to trace the contours of unity in Jesus Christ also allow us to describe this meeting of the Word of God with a human text. Movement is here again dominant in the sense that it is all true when God sets himself in motion. Grace, the Holy Spirit, the personal intervention of the Lord, all lead to this result. The order which unites the holiness and the humanity of the Bible corresponds to that which obtains between the deity and the humanity of Christ. God is sovereign and the human depends wholly on him. There can be no question of reversing this order or of shifting the accent, for it is thus that the two magnitudes find their truth. The *enhypostasis* tells us clearly that the Bible receives its power only in dependence on the Spirit. Once these documents are separated even in the slightest degree from his active presence, they lose their value and become inauthentic and unhistorical in relation to the event which they are commissioned to proclaim. Their true humanity, that which is capable of God, depends on their submission to the Spirit, who makes them living and efficacious. We also have here the communication of attributes in the sense that in this situation these human words can produce effects beyond their natural strength. All the power of God can take charge of them and enable them to fulfil, by the grace communicated to them, that which the Lord alone can do. These texts thus impart to us more than their human wisdom when they are placed in this unity with the divine Word. Again, there is here a parallel to the *extra calvinisticum*. For God remains God. He remains above the Bible. He will not be enclosed in it. This point is extremely important, for ultimately it is God whom we seek in our investigation of Scripture.

Received in this way, the Bible is an unheard of miracle. That human texts should speak of God, or that God should be pleased to speak effectively through them, in spite of the fall which has made all human speech unsuitable as witness to the true God, is truly astonishing. Of what value are all our traditions, experiences or doctrines compared with this promise? But this miracle may be perceived only when it happens. This book may be mishandled in all kinds of ways until the moment when God, overcoming all our resistance and prejudices, accomplishes that which we have just described. Hence we should not be too greatly concerned. The Lord will always see to it that this event of the Spirit is reproduced. This hope and expectation are not rules. They are the gift of the grace which can be given to us, when the living God decides, through these texts as they are set in their historical context and truly understood according to the sense of their authors. Applied to the Bible, the Chalcedonian 'very God—very man' emphasizes both the truth and the sovereignty of the promise indicated by the adjective 'holy', and also the full humanity of these testimonies, in the miraculous unity which God himself fashions in giving us, when he so wills, his own living Word in this book which he has thus prepared to serve him.[1]

2. *The Church*

Our christological findings also exert a decisive influence on the problem of the Church, determining its setting, orientation and limits. It is in the light of them that we appreciate the dangers of confusion and of separation, as also the true and mysterious unity of Jesus Christ and his people. Thus Calvin says at the commencement of his doctrine of the Church that Christ must be preserved in his entirety,[2] i.e., with his body. In the pages which follow we shall be concerned with this unity of the total Christ, i.e., with his existence as it embraces that of his members gathered to him by the Holy Spirit. This brief description does not pretend to be exhaustive. Its aim is to present the Church as an implication of Christology, and

---

[1] Preaching is to be viewed in the same way. If the Lord is to speak through it, it must be biblical, but not slavishly so. Attesting God's work, our words may become God's Word in a true apostolic succession. There is here a miracle of unity analogous to that of the Jesus Christ and the Bible. The unity which is perfect in Christ and normative in the Bible is more derivative here. Yet the miracle does take place, although, as in the case of Christ and the Bible, the Holy Spirit is again necessary if the truth is to be perceived.　　　　　　　　　　　　　[2] *Inst.* IV, 1, 3.

K*

to show the conditions in which this unity is realized both in fulness and in distinction by the miracle of reconciliation.

(i) *The origin of the Church*

In the first place, the work of the Son urgently invites us, in our ecclesiology, to stress the unique and perfect incarnation of the Son of God and the ineffable perfection to be found in him. Even when we deal with the Church, and especially in face of the many temptations, we must not fail to remember that all fulness dwells in him (Col. 1.19). He bears within himself our righteousness, sanctification, restitution, new life and regenerated humanity. It is thus to him that we must look if we are to describe his body, for this body is his. His person and work are dominant here as elsewhere, and if we can attribute fulness to his Church too, it is precisely because he is the supreme Head, who fills all in all (Eph. 1.23). Thus to speak of the Church is first and always to speak of Jesus Christ who is life, truth and reality in the members which he creates and animates.

It is not that the Church as it is in itself, and as we see it, may be identified with Jesus Christ. Only the converse is true. Christ is the Church, but the Church which we see is not directly the body of Christ. On the contrary, the discipline which compels us not to try to describe the Church directly, but to look to Jesus and to find the Church in him as his possession and the expression of his being, also introduces into the discussion an ultimate judgment on the visible, concrete institution. For there is the strong possibility that the two realities do not coincide, since the one belongs to the Head as his expression and the other to history as in part at least the work of men. Certainly we must be careful not to come to the hasty conclusion either that they always coincide or that they never do so. It is not for us to say. Sane discussion demands, however, that we recognize the possibility of a final contradiction even though we hope that God will himself create identity.

Since it is his body, it is in Christ that we are to seek the Church even though it is necessarily visible, human and historical, and not in the sociological and religious structures which bear this name. The possibility of divergence between the Church which we believe and the Church which we see is implied in the very definition of this organism.[1]

[1] Cf. the encyclical *Mystici Corporis Christi*, 1943. What is here said regarding Christ and the Church is quite correct so long as we are thinking in terms of grace and not of an automatic state. The latter approach, which seems to be that of the encyclical,

The Church, therefore, does not merit direct consideration. Although it is visible and human, it cannot furnish the essentials of its definition by what we see of it. Even in its humanity, it is explained by its mystery. And this mystery does not really belong to it. Hence we cannot treat it directly even if we try to look through its external structures to its soul or spiritual substance. In this sense the common Roman Catholic comparison between the two natures of Christ on the one side and the soul and body of the Church on the other is dangerously equivocal. It is suggested that the Church possesses this twofold reality, both divine and human, within itself, as though the privileges of its Lord had been purely and simply made over to it.[1]

To respect the sovereignty of Jesus Christ over his Church, while emphasizing their unity in distinction, it is as well to call the relation between his two natures and the constitution of his body an analogy rather than a parallel. In his divinity and humanity, as the Lord made flesh, Christ is the Head of the Church. This exists both in him and on earth. Its mystery, soul and very being are Christ Jesus, even though it is fully terrestrial and therefore human. This body is the actual, historical form of the existence of its Head, so that if we are to speak of duality in the Church it must be described as a unity of grace, real but full of tensions, between this divine and human Head who is now at the right hand of the Father and the terrestrial organism. On the one side is Jesus Christ, true God and true man; on the other is Jesus Christ and the Church. The analogy is between the two natures of Christ on the one side and Christ and his Church on the other. There are here two different unities. The second derives from the first. They are not parallel. The Church

leads at once to the erroneous conception of the Church as an extension of the incarnation, to a false view of apostolic succession, to misunderstanding of the sanctity and authority of the Church, etc.; and criticism of the Church becomes a sin against the Holy Ghost.

[1] Cf. the definitions in the encyclical *Satis cognitum*, 1896, and also *Immortale Dei*, 1885, where there is a failure to distinguish properly between the perfect humanity of Christ and the fallen humanity of the Church. To meet the facts of human sin, there is, of course, distinction between the soul of the Church and its body (Journet, *Théologie de l'Eglise*, 1958, pp. 236, 238), and the soul itself is divided into the uncreated (the Holy Spirit) and the created (charity) (*op. cit.*, pp. 193f.). Bartmann draws a similar distinction between the Church as an institution of salvation and the Church as the communion of saints (*Précis*, II, p. 165; cf. also de Lubac, *Méditation sur l'Eglise*, pp. 8of.). Parallels are drawn with the person of Christ on the one side and the constitution of man as soul and body on the other (Journet, *op. cit.*, pp. 265f.). It is forgotten, however, that the divine aspect of the Church can only be Christ himself and not an intrinsic quality. There is also no basis for the distinction between the Church and its members.

does not have two natures. In its humanity it is united to Jesus Christ, and it is he who is its divinity, to use the Roman Catholic term. Moreover, he is directly both its divinity and its humanity, since the natural humanity of the Church must pass through death to find itself again in him. The flesh of the Church is to disappear by participation in his death and to be resurrected in and with him in a newness which is its holiness. This renewal of its humanity will always be partial so long as history lasts. This explains the weakness of the Church, the tensions which exist between it and its Lord and the judgments which overtake it until God is all in all at the coming again of Christ.

The association 'Christ—the Church' is thus in no sense identical with that of the Word made flesh. There are great differences between them. The one association is perfect, the other provisional. The one is the image of perfected reconciliation, the other the sign of a preceding accomplishment, the ambiguous intimation of the final redemption. The one implies the end of time when God and man are together; the other yields the vision of recollection and expectation, but not of full appropriation. In other words, the Church is not the kingdom of God. It is neither the incarnate Christ nor the New Jerusalem which he will cause to descend from heaven at his return.

It is for this reason that the Church must take all necessary precautions to maintain this distinction even within its unity with Christ. In no sense can it pretend to reproduce the truth in itself without deceiving those whom it purports to instruct. It can never present the image of perfection in its own existence, both divine and human. It is there to bear witness to another perfection than its own. Hence it is not divine in itself. It is not without sin. It does not have two natures. In its own misery, it bears signs of the fulness which is in Christ and it waits impatiently for its transfiguration at the end of the age. It is fully human, though its humanity is already sanctified, i.e., it bears a promise, and must therefore continually die to rise again. It does not possess the truth. It does not save. It does not distribute grace. It is only an instrument, bearing witness in its imperfection to the fulness which is in Christ. Hence its witness can participate in the truth and reach its goal only if it renounces any pretension to possession of a divinity of its own and joyfully recognizes that, in its simple humanity, it is the chosen bride of Christ, elected by him, sanctified by the grace of his judgments and promises, and already glorified in part by its Lord. Its existence and mission depend on this direct link with Christ, who himself alone is the first aspect of its constitution. Thus the Church is never more than a human and fraternal community. The other aspect is Christ in it, though this does not prevent it from being our mother to the degree that Christ, present in it, truly makes of it his body. Institution of salvation, sanctifying Church, power of reconciliation, cradle, mother—these things are all the work of the living Christ within it, not a privilege which he has in some sort delegated. The relation between the community and Christ is thus without intermediary, and in this new unity of Christ and the human community, as in that of the Word of God and human words in the Bible, we find an analogy to the relation between the two aspects of the person of the Saviour.[1]

Although it necessarily takes the form of a social body or a society the true Church lives in Jesus Christ. It is set first and always in him. It is he who bears, manifests, fashions and protects it. To define it, therefore, we must begin with its mystery, i.e., with its Head, and then follow the movement from the Head to the body by which it is actualized.[2]

The Church is not a body as a social organism, though it becomes this too. The concept 'body' seems to have given rise to tragic misunderstanding. Applied to the Church, it does not primarily denote its sociological structure but its existence in the person of Christ, whose reality it expresses in the same way as the body translates the impulses of the soul. It is simply an epithet attached to this name, a form of his existence, a part of his own essence. We cannot conclude that it is not visible or human. Quite the contrary! But in its humanity it is the expression of his life, work and presence. The distinction which Roman Catholic theology makes between the social body and the mystical body is inadequate, since it introduces into the Church two aspects which are real only if we keep them strictly together. It is when it is truly in Christ that the Church is a

[1] On the sin of the Church cf. L. Newbigin, *The Household of God*, 1953, and Journet, *Théologie de l'Eglise*, pp. 111f. The Church, like the individual believer, is holy only in virtue of its justification in Christ. Its sinfulness thus gives point to its message of salvation by grace, and its sanctity is its constant recourse to grace, i.e., its constant mortification and renewal. Any thought of intrinsic sanctity, infallibility or authority is itself a form of sin.
[2] A very different course is followed in the encyclical *Mystici Corporis Christi*, in Neo-Protestant definitions, and even in the *Constitution of the Church of Geneva*, which all present the Church primarily as a human society. Calvin in Book IV of the *Institutes* and Barth in *CD* IV take a more scriptural path.

real society. It is in the world as a spiritual body. Otherwise, it may be a social, religious or ecclesiastical body without necessarily being the body of Christ. Its existence in Christ and in the world is thus simultaneous, and it is in this sense that it is visible, but only for faith. It lives both in its Head at the right hand of the Father and on earth as the representation of its Saviour. Its two forms are simply one notwithstanding its imperfections, for it is not its merits which cause it to abide in Christ, but only the grace of God. Although imperfect, the Church is already with Christ in God, and it is as such that it is earthly, to the degree that it exists only by the grace of God, i.e., by his promises, judgment and pardon.[1]

Hence it is not so much a question of seeing Christ in the Church (cf. the encyclical *Mystici Corporis Christi*) as of seeing the Church in Christ. If we take the former course (*op. cit.*, p. 46), it may be logically concluded that there must be unconditional submission to this body, and especially to its more exalted members. This reveals, however, the ambiguous nature of the reasoning. For joyful sub-mission is to Christ alone, who creates the Church as one of the benefits which result from our participation in his life. The Church is not automatically his body. Those within it necessarily become this body which he himself gives and manifests by his creative dynamism in accordance with his promises.

The Church does not have its life in itself. Indeed, it can only lose it if, by pretended confusion between itself and its Lord, it obliter-ates the distance which forces it constantly to turn away from itself and to let itself be judged and saved by the sovereign Christ. This distance, implied even in the presence of its Lord, is absolutely necessary to force it incessantly to repentance and faith, because its Head, i.e., its righteousness, sanctification and life, is not in itself but above itself. It is essential that the Church should always follow the road which leads from itself to Christ by death, resurrection and restitution. Otherwise how can it truly be the expression, the body, of Christ on earth?

Our present task, however, is to see how this Church which is perfect and complete in Christ, and which he already presents to his Father in purity (Eph. 5.26f.), can be manifested and solidly assembled on this earth. It is so by the Holy Spirit, its ministers and

---

[1] The incorporation of the earthly Church in Christ is to be understood along the same lines as that of the individual Christian, cf. Eph. 1.22; I Thess. 2.14; Rom. 12.5; John 17; Phil. 2.2; Gal. 3.28.

the Word and sacraments, i.e., by the will and activity of Jesus Christ.[1]

(ii) *The structure of the Church*

It is thus that the Church is born. It is the product of God's action according to a clearly defined plan and a logic, i.e., a succession of interventions, in keeping with his wisdom. More precisely, the Church is itself one of these interventions. By the very fact that it exists, it attests the efficacy of this action, its ability to reach the envisaged goal, apart from which it would have no more value than a hypothesis or a myth. If we take away this creation, we throw doubt on the whole plan. What is the effect of a promise which is never fulfilled, of a grace which remains as it were suspended in the air, of tongues of fire which do not change those on whom they descend, of an apostolic work which does not cut men to the heart (Acts 2)? As Calvin says, the Church exists necessarily because the death of Christ is fruitful.[2]

Its *raison d'être*, constitution and reality is simply that God acts and that he accomplishes what he has promised. Active in the Holy Spirit, the Word of God in its three forms as the living Word (Jesus Christ), the written word (Holy Scripture) and the oral word (the Church's preaching), brings about this new reality which is its signature, the sign of its victory.

This power reaches sinful men, i.e., lost rebels and slaves. It justifies, sanctifies and already glorifies them. This action gathers and unites them by the deployment of this distinctive dynamism. The principal element in the Church, its primary note, is truly to believe in this action, to receive it and to put all one's confidence in it. Infinitely more important than other preoccupations, this expectation is the condition of its existence, since God is faithful to his promises. No other subjective basis can be found for the Church than this openness—created by the Holy Spirit—to the work of God, for then the Lord can work as he wills and something will appear which will finally be in keeping with its true nature and which may be called the Church.

This first definition is both very precise and yet also very hard to

[1] Thus Pentecost, with all that follows in Acts, reveals God at work. New believers are united to Christ, and as such they are brought together by the Word, that they might continue in it. This assembling is the Church. There is no super-Church above the communities of brethren. There is no intrinsic perfection. Believers are holy because they are objects of God's continuing action.

[2] *Inst.* IV, 1, 2.

grasp, since it depends on an intervention which is external and superior to the reality which we seek to delineate. This definition, however, controls all other descriptions that may be given of its structure, development, organization and mission.

The structure of the Church is supremely defined by the correspondence between its own existence and the conditions in which Jesus himself lived. The truth of the life of the Church may be measured by the authenticity of this parallel. The effect can only represent the cause; the mirror can only reflect the object before which it is placed. The life, death, resurrection and ascension of Jesus should mark the Church to such a degree that it is not their extension, but their image and concrete demonstration. As the body expresses the movements of the soul, so the Church reveals by its form of existence this history which is its *raison d'être* and the effects which it produces. It attests Christ, and it does so as itself the creation of this particular history. It thus represents what he has been and done. All that has taken place in him is manifested in it.

The Church clings, therefore, to the existence of its Lord, who fashions it and makes it his own expression. The moment it no longer portrays his face, in the strict sense it is no longer the true Church. The curve of its life follows exactly that of the life of Christ from its foundation, which is parallel to the birth of Christ, through baptism which is death and resurrection, the Lord's Supper which produces the same alteration, repentance which is its purification, to the resurrection which constitutes its new existence.[1]

The truth of the Church lies in this correspondence. The Church illustrates the comportment of Christ. Receiving its life from the Spirit, who introduces it into the existence of its Lord, it constantly dies to self in him and is raised to a new life. It is thus compelled to put off its body of death (Rom. 7) in order to be born again in the glory with which it is invested by its Lord. It is by experiencing this break and reconstitution that it can witness to the incarnate, suffering and victorious Word. If the Church did not follow this movement, how could it preach the work of Christ? It would then preach itself. But its privilege is to be able to attest, even as it suffers the effects thereof in the flesh, that which Christ has accomplished for all men. The Church itself does not save, or dispense grace; Christ

[1] There is an instructive parallel between Pentecost and the Virgin Birth (cf. Acts 2, Luke 2 and John 1). This is true in respect of the process, the instruments and the result. It implies correspondence, not between the Church and Mary, but between the Church and Christ (cf. the image of the body and the Head).

is salvation and grace. It declares him by letting itself be judged and saved by him; this is the best way to show what he has done.[1]

As Christ is the image of the eternal God, so the Church for its part is the image of Christ as Prophet, Priest and King. The truth of its ministry attests the sovereignty and efficacy of the work of its Lord, who himself actualizes all the perfections of God. It is the image of his body which was broken and miraculously restored for the salvation of men. Though this does not in the least excuse its infidelities, it is in the plan of God and commensurate with the demands of the concrete situation that the Church should proclaim the necessity and fact of the sacrifice of Christ by its failings too, and that it should thereby show also the power of the restoration which he accomplishes. God uses inevitable human betrayals to show how well-founded is his decision to save humanity by his own condescension. Is it not thus that Paul explains the successive revolts of Israel (Rom. 9–11)? Like a concentric circle the destiny of the people of God follows that of its Head. The revolt of Israel bears witness to the death of Christ and the election of Paul attests the victory of the risen Lord. Far from having a good conscience, the Church constantly goes through this break of death and resurrection, and it is thus that it can be of service, actualizing in its own life the decision which God took and executed to remedy the present human situation. In other words, the Church can present itself only as a pardoned Church which has some awareness of what has to be overcome in it if it is to be once again a witness of grace. Only on this condition can its true historical comportment lead to the essential event.[2]

The Church, therefore, conforms to its own definition when, possibly in its humanity and certainly in humility and gratitude, it truly depends only on the election, bearing in its flesh the visible mark of the death and resurrection of Christ and letting itself be fashioned by this event even in its works, which should also correspond to those of Christ. Its true structure is its conformity, as body and witness, to the movements of divine and human truth incarnate, condemned and resurrected in Christ.[3]

[1] The Church cannot possess or dispense grace, for grace is Christ himself in his person and work.

[2] This does not divest the Church of responsibility. It means, however, that God overrules even its failure for his own gracious purposes. It also means that he is faithful to it in virtue of his gifts and calling (cf. Rom. 11).

[3] The witness of the Church depends on this conformity. If it draws attention to itself, it mars the work of Christ. It will certainly do this. But it must be ready to see and confess its failure, not preaching its own perfection, but the judgment of God on itself as on all men, and the victory of his grace in Jesus Christ.

The terms 'growth' and 'development', when used of the life of the Church, denote the progress which it is summoned to make towards an increasingly faithful representation of the destiny of Jesus. This movement is not necessarily in extent or power, but in depth. It is progress in the truth, which is grace, death and resurrection. That is, it is an increasingly strict, lucid and intelligent association with what Jesus lived out in our condition. The image must take on more and more of the object which it reflects. We do not have here a long historical development or a tranquil ascent to plenitude. There is rather an increasingly acute awareness of the break which is necessary for more complete renewal. To bear fruit, the vine must be pruned (John 15.2). The growth of the Church is thus supremely a growth in mortification by trial and chastisement in order that the truth of its burial with Christ may make possible conformity to his resurrection. God chastises us 'for our profit, that we might be partakers of his holiness' (Heb. 12.10). How can it be denied that progress is necessary in this direction, and that this must be our true growth in Christ?

The Church thus makes better progress in the truth the more it participates in the death of its Lord. It dies with him, and is delivered from its sin as it renounces its pretensions, its illusions, indeed, its very self, for 'he that is dead is freed from sin' (Rom. 6.7). Being thus 'planted together in the likeness of his death' (Rom. 6.5), we advance towards the mystery of our own resurrection. How else can it be for the Church which preaches the Crucified, and which receives him by baptism in his death and resurrection and by communion with his broken body? How else can it progress but by taking this death and resurrection seriously, i.e., by living it out in repentance and faith? The Church which pretends that it is exempt from sin has no need of this growth. It can know only a majestic development in extent which will justify its apologetic and imperialism. It will thus preach itself instead of bearing witness to the miraculous superabundance of grace. But does not the exceptional truth of the message which the Church has to deliver lie in the effective pardon of its sin? If this is true, the Church must turn away visibly and concretely from itself in order to attest the reconstructive power of its Lord. Otherwise it will conceal the magnificent possibility which God offers to those who are not perfect and who are not able to become so.

Contrary to the general view, the growth of the Church consists

in an increasingly realistic awareness of its own obduracy and a confession of its rebellion, blindness and evasion, that it may receive
unmerited pardon and newness of life. It is a progress in abasement
parallel to that of its Lord, and a glorious elevation like that of
Easter. This twofold movement takes place simultaneously, since
judgment is already grace and divestiture deliverance. The slightest
confusion between the victorious Christ and the Church destroys for
the latter any possibility of growth in this sense. It carries with it a
good conscience which paradoxically separates it from the Lord and
closes it to his true action.

The organization of this community is directly based on the
succession of events which create and perfect it. This may be seen
very clearly from the well-known passage in Ephesians 4. The first
condition of its edification is the sovereignty of Christ and his abasement and exaltation (Eph. 4.9–10). This event is to be declared and
ministers are given for this purpose. By the apostolate, prophecy and
teaching, they proclaim this act of God. The authority of Holy
Scripture is implicit, since it is the first and determinative testimony
to this event. When God works through them, these three basic
elements lead to 'the perfecting of the saints in view of the work of
the ministry and the edifying of the body of Christ' (v. 12). No other
method can produce this result. Assembled by this divine intervention, the community listens, receives, prays, and gives thanks for
the work which is done in it, which constitutes it and which leads it
into the service of its Master. The more simple the order is—the
work of God in Christ, Scripture, proclamation, hearing and obedience, all quickened by the Spirit—the more chance there is of
efficacy according to the will of God. The life of the Church must
display very clearly this succession of the truth if it is to receive its
growth from Christ alone (v. 16). This is its unique discipline,
commensurate with its nature and full of promises for all its
functions.

The mission of the Church is to be fashioned thus in order that it
may serve this dynamism of the Word and Spirit, which attain
thereby their own objectives. The Lord who moulds it will use it
according to his mysterious wisdom, granting it power and intelligence, charity and humanity, being and action, that it may accomplish his work.

(iii) *The marks of the Church*

There has been much discussion of the marks or notes of the Church. These are to be understood only as a commentary on what we have already said. The Nicaeo-Constantinopolitan Creed gives us the number, viz. unity, sanctity, catholicity and apostolicity. In addition to differences of interpretation, however, other marks have often been distinguished for specific reasons.[1]

It is to be noted that these marks are always interpreted in the sense which best fits the church adducing them. Thus unity for the Roman Catholic Church is primarily ecclesiastical and even sociological. It is the unity of this body. Though deriving from the Head, it is limited to this particular hierarchy and order. Thus Journet links this note with the third: 'The expression "catholic unity", which comprises two correlative properties of the Church, namely, unity in relation to the soul and catholicity in relation to the body, is almost a pleonasm, for all this is contained in catholicity.'[2] Unity in this sense is disciplined rallying around the vicar of Christ in the communion of this faith, of this 'cultic and sacramental' charity, of this organization. There is seen here an argument for the truth and a proof of the superiority of such an organism over the multitude of sects. From this angle schism is a worse evil than heresy. In the necessity of unity of this kind there is also found justification for the powers of the papacy, as stated by Leo XIII in the encyclical *Satis Cognitum*: 'This authority, being a principal element in the constitution and organization of the Church, since it is the principle of unity, the basis of security and perpetuity, cannot possibly disappear with the blessed Peter, but must necessarily pass to his successors and be transmitted from the one to the other' (pp. 39f.). Here the pope rather than Christ is the principle of unity, and a sociological rather than a spiritual flavour is thus given to the concept.

In Neo-Protestantism, probably by way of reaction against this transposition, we find an almost exclusively spiritual understanding of unity. Subjected to docetic spiritualization, real unity evaporates in favour of a federation of churches. Thus Lemaître asks: 'Is the

[1] Thus the *Dictionnaire de Théologie catholique* adds characteristics which seem rather to express the pretensions of the Roman Catholic Church (E. Dublanchy in art. *Eglise*; cf. also Bartmann, *Précis*, II, 200; the encyclical *Mystici Corporis Christi*; de Lubac, *Méditation sur l'Eglise*, p. 96). For Calvin the basic notes are preaching the Word and administration of the sacraments, *Inst.* IV, 1, 9.

[2] *Théologie de l'Eglise*, p. 367.

character of unity essential to the idea of the Church?... Is the multiplicity of Christian confessions and churches intrinsically an evil, a scandal, a disloyalty to the will of Christ? I do not think so. ... For us Protestants, Christian unity can be made concrete only in a federation of churches each having its own independence and distinctive form.'[1] Thus unity is not essential either in doctrine or structure. A similar awareness of Christ, which permits divergent formulations, a similar zeal and a similar prostration before the irrational are enough to define, in tolerance and love—at any rate up to a certain point—this spiritual kinship which constitutes our unity.

The Reformers for their part tried to relate this idea to the person of Jesus himself and therefore neither to a government nor to a common sense of his presence. Unity is the fruit of the victory of Easter over the division of Good Friday both between God and men and among men themselves. It is the work of the reconciliation which was effected by the Mediator and in which the Holy Spirit causes us to participate by our own death and resurrection. Christ himself is this attained and perfect unity. By associating us with him, the Holy Spirit establishes between him and us, and among believers, the bond of peace. Christ being both very God and very man, this unity has both a spiritual and a concrete aspect. In him we find again the human solidarity which is one of the chief signs of our rehabilitation. This notion in all its fulness is both christological and eschatological. We already have the signs, in order that the world may discern in us the first effects of his victory: '. . . that they all may be one; as thou, Father, art in me, and I in thee, that they also may be one in us: that the world may believe that thou hast sent me' (John 17.21). Unity among ourselves thus proceeds necessarily from unity in him. It is the work of grace: 'Fulfil ye my joy, that ye be likeminded, having the same love, being of one accord, of one mind' (Phil. 2.2).

There are similar differences in relation to the sanctity of the Church. In Roman Catholic theology this term denotes both the consecration and the purity of the ecclesiastical edifice, which has an intrinsic perfection even though its members are sinners, and which shines out with majestic splendour. The apologetic bearing of this property is not overlooked, for the perfection of this society reinforces its authority and constitutes a visible proof of its divinity.

[1] *Foi et vérité*, p. 460.

'Real sanctity attaches to holy objects. This sanctity may be passive, conferred by consecration (churches, altars and sacred vessels), or it may be active in the sense of producing personal holiness (sacraments, the doctrine of faith). It is in this twofold sense that we may call the Church holy.'[1] This idea has in Roman Catholicism a religious sense (the perfection of faith), a moral sense (meritorious obedience) and an ecclesiastical sense (service of the Church).

In Neo-Protestantism the term is strongly moralized in spite of the religious framework which always characterizes it. A holy church is a church without spot or wrinkle, which perfects itself in love and which seeks to promote, 'by spiritual life, the progress of moral civilization'.[2] But since no church can present the image of this perfection, sanctity is an ideal rather than a reality. The Church is not holy. It seeks to progress in this direction in order to attain to a certain level of moral purity and of mutual love which will be an example to those who watch it. The most serious thing here is not schism but the scandal of an aggressive spirit or of moral failure.

The Reformers again place our full and total sanctity in Christ, who fulfils the Law and who secures our perfection by his death. This holiness is communicated to us by the Holy Spirit, who clothes us with the new man, received by faith and not obtained by good works. In this setting the sanctity of the Church is simply its openness to grace, its thirst, its waiting for a remedy, which is the more necessary now that it has a keener awareness of its own infidelities. A holy church is not a perfect community. On the contrary, it is a community which counts on the miracle of pardon, which grows in its own justification and which allows the work of sanctification to be done in it. This influence begins by strengthening in it the sense of its own unworthiness that it may die to itself and rise again to a new life. The term denotes the efficacy of the work of God in it, made more real by its own readiness. It recalls specifically the eternal decision of God, the election, the work of Jesus Christ and the reparative work of the Holy Spirit. As with all the concepts which the adjective qualifies—Holy Scripture, Holy Communion, the communion of saints—the word denotes the work of God and its effects in man.

Catholicity is used by Roman Catholics for the universality of their church, and apostolicity for the true succession which guarantees 'the legitimacy, truth and purity' of its essence and especially of its

[1] Bartmann, *Précis*, II, p. 209.   [2] Lemaître, *Foi et vérité*, p. 453.

instruction. Distinction is made between apostolicity of origin, doctrine and succession, but the third is 'already adequate and decisive'. 'In effect, where Peter is and his succession, there is the whole Church, and therefore the infallible teaching office. The infallible teaching office guarantees the purity and truth of apostolic doctrine'.[1] This succession borders on replacement, as may be seen in the encyclical *Mystici Corporis Christi*, which argues that Jesus Christ now rules, not by the voice of the apostles, but by that of bishops (p. 20). The pope, who confers on them their power of jurisdiction (p. 21), fulfils the role of Christ on earth: 'As the divine Redeemer has sent the Spirit of truth, the Paraclete, to assume in his place the invisible government of the Church, so to Peter and his successors he has given the mandate to fulfil his own role on earth in order to ensure also the visible government of the Christian city' (pp. 34f.). Here apostolicity signifies a delegation of power rather than obedience. This is indicated by the fact that the 'locus of true doctrine' is found in the actual hierarchy rather than the apostolic testimony.[2]

In Neo-Protestantism catholicity denotes the universality of the religion of the spirit and apostolicity the rather elastic bond which links the Church of the present with the exemplary experiences of the first witnesses of Christ.

Here again Reformation theology centres on Jesus Christ and aims at the re-establishment of all things. For it, catholicity signifies that the grace which is promised to all men and which encloses the fulness of truth is accorded by the Holy Spirit wherever two or three are gathered. The totality of grace is given wherever it operates, and communion between the various groups results naturally from the fulness which each has received. The true body of Christ is found both here, in a particular place, and everywhere where Jesus Christ manifests himself. Catholicity does not imply sociological unity or universal spirituality, but the truth of the work of God wherever it intervenes, and the real communion which results therefrom. As for apostolicity, Barth is right in treating it apart from the other three marks.[3] It is in effect the guarantee of the sovereignty of Jesus Christ over his Church, by which it is united, sanctified and universally gathered as his body. This property has two senses. The true Church has been founded by the Holy Spirit through the testimony of the

---

[1] Bartmann, *op. cit.*, II, pp. 214f. [2] Journet, *Théologie de l'Eglise*, p. 183.
[3] *Dogmatics in Outline*, ET, 1949, p. 145.

prophets and apostles, and these are always its unique foundation as witnesses of Christ. They remain alive and active in it, for it is through them that God has decided to communicate to us his personal and victorious Word. Secondly, this Church which is apostolic in its origin and by the supremacy of Scripture over it, is also apostolic in its witness to the degree that this conforms to that of the apostles. Hence this mark attests the sovereignty of Christ himself over his body according to the succession of events which he has chosen that he may communicate himself personally to it.

On the basis of these main characteristics we may take up some of the resultant definitions. The Church is certainly visible, as Christ himself was visible. Nevertheless, it is seen in its true structure only by faith. Though one may also see it, one believes the Church, its marks being accessible to faith alone and not to mere observation. If the tendency of Roman Catholicism is to make the mystery of the Church evident by confusing it with its own institution, that of Neo-Protestantism is so to spiritualize it as to separate it from its concrete organization. On the one side we have a materialization of the mystery, on the other an evaporation. Both lead inevitably to the same result. Again, the perpetuity of the Church is true, as is the patient and constantly victorious faithfulness of God, even though the victory is hidden until his glorious return. The Church is not immutable in itself. On the contrary, it varies incessantly, and is always straying in every conceivable way from the grace which calls it. But its Lord is faithful and he will not abandon it.

(iv) *The Christology of the Church*

Throughout this section we have been confronted by three main forms of the Church, and we can again take our bearings from the Chalcedonian adverbs. The divergences are known, but are the explanations advanced for them really relevant? Bartmann deals with them thus: 'From the whole treatise there results the importance of the doctrine of the Church for our age. This may be summed up as follows. For Protestants the Church is a human institution. For Modernists, it is the product of the natural evolution of living immanence and vital permanence. The two conceptions are objectively identical. For Catholic doctrine, the Church is a divine institution. It is Christ, the man-God, who has founded it. On the Day of Pentecost the Holy Spirit united it in permanent fashion to its divine Head and introduced it into the world. From this time, it has fulfilled the mission entrusted to it within humanity.'[1] To what decision does Christology direct us in face of these three interpretations? Let us close by briefly reviewing the main features of these three doctrines.

(1) The conception of a Church allegedly divine inevitably leads to a generalized confusion between what is of God and what of man, and therefore to a partial transformation of human realities, which are as it were absorbed in the divine. These activities are not just holy because of their election and the operation of God in and through them. They have become truly sacred, i.e., penetrated by the divine, by infusion. The mixture produces a kind of sacralization of the whole ecclesiastical sphere. The distinction between the divine and the human is blunted by an association of such a kind that each element has the power to place us directly in the presence of God's own work.[2]

Although this deviation has been victoriously overcome in Christology, there can be no doubt that it has left some traces in Roman Catholic ecclesiology, and that later Catholicism has in some sense returned to it. Certain aspects of the question will be enough to afford brief illustration of this thesis.

(a) The pretension of this Church to divinity is incontestably the first sign. After having underlined the marvellous development of the Roman institution, the continuity and indefectibility manifested in its history, E. Dublanchy concludes thus: 'Such a fact can derive only from a divine action exerted in favour of the Catholic Church and therefore proving its divinity.'[3] Now divinity, as we learn from the person of Christ, never becomes a mark of humanity. It is the personal intervention of God, not a characteristic of the flesh. Nevertheless, Dublanchy goes on: 'Since the Church, considered as a supernatural society, consists essentially in the divine authority established by Jesus Christ to continue his mission until the consummation of the ages, the divine institution of this Church obviously results from the previously quoted texts, which positively confirm the powers conferred by Jesus Christ on his disciples and their successors until the consummation of the ages—absolute

---

[1] *Précis*, II, p. 227.
[2] This might be called a Eutychian tendency, although Eutyches himself, whose teaching is not clear, is part of a whole movement which includes Cyril of Alexandria, Diodore of Tarsus and Theodoret. By it the door is opened to Mariology, the Virgin being the necessary link between Christ's humanity and ours.
[3] *DTC*, art. *Eglise*, col. 2133.

powers equal to those which Jesus received from the Father.'[1] This equation places the Church on completely different ground from that of the truth. It continues the work of Christ, and we may sometimes ask whether it does not replace it. In its twofold nature it is so parallel to the Mediator that it seems to represent him in its own structure. It embraces him, displaying him in its own history, which accomplishes, develops and pursues his work. 'The Church is Jesus continuing in his members a life which he has begun in himself and which will never end. The Church is the continuing Gospel.'[2] We are constantly told that the Church is a perfect society, that it is sinless, that it is true and spiritual, that it is the incarnation of the kingdom of God.[3] It is thus elevated above itself. 'The saying of Joan of Arc to her judges expresses both the mystic depth of faith and the practical good sense of the believer: "I am persuaded that Jesus Christ and the Church are one, and that this should not give rise to any difficulty." This cry of the faithful heart is the sum of the faith of the doctors.'[4]

(b) The holiness with which this Church declares itself to be permeated is equivalent to an inner transformation of which the image of transubstantiation is finally the most eloquent illustration.[5] *Mutatis mutandis* the same conversion takes place in the Christian by sanctification and in the Church. 'Jesus Christ penetrates it by his virtue as the trunk of the vine nourishes and makes fruitful the branches united to it.'[6] The perfection of Christ is communicated to the Church like sap. It is infused into it. Journet speaks of a 'plenary collective inhabitation by the Spirit' (p. 97), which is more than the communication of attributes. De Lubac has no hesitation in affirming that 'the Holy Spirit will never be lacking to the Church' (p. 181). He is within it as a richness integrated with its life.

Thus Christ and his Spirit are in it. This power is dispensed by the sacraments. In the words of *Mystici Corporis Christi*, 'as the human body is supported by means suited to supply its life, so the Saviour . . . has provided for his mystical Body in miraculous ways by enriching it with sacraments . . . By the water of baptism men are invested again with spiritual character . . . By the holy oil of confirmation the faithful are permeated by new power . . .' (pp. 10f.). Nature undergoes a kind of divinization or sacralization.

---

[1] *Ibid.*, cols. 2135f.   [2] Journet, *Théologie de l'Eglise*, p. 257.
[3] *Ibid.*, p. 16.   [4] De Lubac, *Méditation sur l'Église*, pp. 162f.
[5] Cf. the definition of this transformation of the species at Trent, Sess. XIII, c. 4.
[6] *Satis cognitum*, p. 7.

Nevertheless, it remains human. Its humanity, even though secular, is as it were transported into this new sphere of the sacred. This is why it can be at one and the same time both very spiritual and yet also sometimes very earthly and human.

(c) The authority of this Church naturally flows from this twofold pretension. If things are as it claims, then it disposes effectively of all the powers of Christ, whether in teaching, government, or in the last resort redemption. The three offices of Christ are its prerogatives. It teaches the truth infallibly (prophetic); it assures the salvation of humanity (priestly); it governs humanity according to the intention and plan of God himself (kingly). This threefold conviction, which may be variously worked out in detail, explains its infallibility. It is 'preserved from all error by the supernatural assurance which it receives from the Holy Spirit'. And it is part of the logic of the system to confer this authority on the vicar of Christ on earth: 'The Roman pontiff . . . enjoys this infallibility with which the divine Redeemer has willed that his Church should be endowed in decisions of faith and conduct.'[1]

In spite of the reservation of Pius XII—'we must reject any form of mystical union by which the faithful transcend the order of the created and arrogate to themselves the divine to the point at which even one of the attributes of the eternal God can be attributed to them as their own'—there is here an interfusion which is justifiable neither in Christology nor in ecclesiology. Certain forms of Protestantism arrive at much the same result. Pietism in particular represents a very similar religious sacralization by the transformation of certain human realities, e.g., the moral or religious consciousness, experience or feeling, into semi-divine values. The partial identification of the religious consciousness with the voice of God confers on those who have the privilege of possessing it a distinctive and superior nature which is heightened by communal life, so that the Church is a high place of spirituality and sanctity.

(d) It is, however, in the Roman conception of the visibility of the Church that we best see the true nature of this deviation. The Church is, of course, human and therefore visible. But this mark expresses in Roman theology a much more profound and very subtle intention. The Church is not merely visible in the body. It supposedly makes visible the mystery itself, i.e., Christ, who is present not merely in the host but in the organs of the Church. Already the

---

[1] *Vatican Council*, Sess. IV, c. 4.

kingdom of God is manifested in it. The identification goes so far that in it we may see the Saviour directly self-manifested. Now it is true that this privilege of being able to represent the Lord visibly is promised to the true Church. This is the meaning of the term 'body' as applied to it, and it is the result of his faithfulness. But it is never produced by the Church itself and it is always indirect. In other words, there is no confusion. It is a grace and not a certainty, a miracle and not a proof, a correspondence and not an identity, a reflection and not the reality, a hope and not a pretension. It is in dying with Christ that the Church becomes in some measure his witness, not in imagining that it is automatically a demonstration of him.

(2) In face of this premature glorification of the Church, and for ancient theological reasons which have been appropriated and developed, Neo-Protestantism has advanced the opposite extreme, namely, that of more or less pronounced separation between the divine and human elements in the Church.[1]

This is the trend in all the main currents of Neo-Protestantism, first in Christology and then in ecclesiology. Certain general remarks may be made in this connection.

(*a*) The unity of the Father and the Son is attenuated. 'The saying of the Fourth Gospel: "I and the Father are one," surely does not suggest any other unity than that of spirit and of will. The Son of man never dreams of identifying himself with the one of whom he says: "My meat is to do the will of him that sent me".'[2] The starting-point is the humanity of Christ. Full correspondence is seen between the inspiration which animates him, the ends which he pursues and the works which he realizes on the one side, and the merciful wisdom of his Father on the other. But no more than this convergence is taught. The functional divinity of Christ is preferred to his supposedly too metaphysical deity.[3] This implies spiritual and moral union. 'The relation in which he is conscious of being with the Father is this normal relation which all men could retrieve if divested of the abnormality of sin in which he has no part.'[4] Thus the sonship of Jesus is in no sense different from ours once sin is overcome. It is the right relation of creature to Creator rather than a substantial identity, which would radically change the perspective.

---

[1] This is a Nestorian tendency, according to which the union is moral rather than essential, so that an element of dualism remains.

[2] A. Lemaître, *Foi et vérité*, p. 242.

[3] *Ibid.*, p. 310.   [4] *Ibid.*, p. 243.

At this point we are not far from a definition of the divinity of Christ simply in terms of the perfection of his unfallen humanity, i.e., of his holiness. Adoptionism is quite compatible with this conception, and the pre-existence of the Word becomes unnecessary, since Christ may just as well come from below as a perfect creature. The essential truth of Trinitarian doctrine, i.e., that God intervenes personally, is plainly attenuated and even set aside, as is that of the incarnation, which is less the unforeseeable movement of God than an illustration of this encounter. Expiation loses its profound meaning, as does justification, for we are no longer dealing with the suffering and sacrifice of God himself, but in this drama a man is made capable of attaining again to creaturely fulness and of carrying his fellows with him in this victory over corruption. The miraculous birth loses its value, for the accent shifts from the abasement of God to the elevation of man. In reality, this doctrine is basically Ebionite, even though it goes beyond pure humanism in many of its formulations.

(*b*) The unity thus attained is inadequate both in the mystery of the relationship of Father and Son and in that of the person of the Son. It is thus equally inadequate in all the implications of this encounter, i.e., in the relations between the Word of God and the text of Scripture, between faith and works and between dogmatics and ethics, and especially in ecclesiology. We are here in the sphere of religion, which seeks to join two magnitudes originally considered in isolation. Revelation, while it does not involve fusion, yields an infinitely fuller reconciliation. At root there is here simply another form of the *homoousia* dispute of the fourth century, and the iota makes all the difference between similitude and the true assumption of man by God.

But how can we conceive of this unity from within the separation of sin in which we are? The perspective of this trend is too naturalistic. Instead of starting with the mysterious unity which is brought into being by the intervention of God and which is neither juxtaposition, convergence nor even association, but true unification by way of death and resurrection, yet in a true liberty which preserves and even achieves the integrity of the two elements, Neo-Protestantism remains in the sphere of separation and simply draws attention to certain spiritual and moral links between the two partners. In sum, it does not begin with the miracle of the incarnation, but with the actual situation which has to be overcome. This method can never hope to vanquish dualism. As we have seen, this remains the distinguishing feature of the whole movement.

(*c*) In ecclesiology, this attenuated unity, which is more a rapprochement that true reconciliation, is expressed in two complementary forms. The first is Docetic spiritualization, the second an Ebionitism which necessarily leads finally to secularization.

If the essence lies in this spiritual and basically mystical communion, then material organization and human and social forms are of little account. The experience of the love of God can be cultivated outside the rigid framework of the ecclesiastical institution, which is often an obstacle to this elevation. Moreover, the Spirit is by definition a very fluid, elusive and numinous reality, and therefore he cannot be tied either to ritual or to a text. He moves in the vague sphere of the supernatural and cannot be in any way restricted. He blows where he wills, so that he can neither be forced into precise forms nor clearly distinguished from other intellectual, spiritual or religious inspirations which certainly merit our respect and which can also lift us up above our actual condition.

This perspective, which is proper to all the rather evanescent spiritualizing of this whole trend, has several implications for the reality of the Church. (i) The Church is not essential to the development of spiritual life. (ii) Religious individualism is more likely to favour this development than too close connection with a necessarily defective community. (iii) Faith is more a mystical elevation based on the sense of God and contemplation than knowledge of the Word of God, confession and obedience. (iv) Dogmas are an intolerable limitation and a tyrannical materialization of religious intuition. (v) The necessity of the meeting of various converging spiritualities opens Christian doctrine and the faith of the Church to various influences from without. Multiplicity is the result of this prudent syncretism which admits and respects other inspirations and forbids any impoverishment by exclusion. The more the Church is tolerant, i.e., the more it is capable of appropriating other visions of the ineffable, the more universal it is and therefore the richer for the treasures acquired by the race. (vi) As concerns the unity of the Church, it is invisible and spiritual, and as wide as the domain of the spirit. 'If the Johannine Christ prays that one day there may be one flock and one shepherd, we accept the spiritual meaning of these expressions. . . . To believe in this unity is not to reject the idea that in the house of the earthly Church there are several dwellings (i.e., several forms of the Church which need only be federated), as in the invisible house of the Father.'[1] The visible Church, therefore, is of secondary importance. It is a convenient way of assembling believers and co-ordinating their efforts, though with no cramping or diminishing of their religious freedom. It will accept all ideas and impulsions so long as they fit in with the climate of this spiritual association. The body of Christ is evaporated in the spirit. A. Bouvier in his *Dogmatique* does not even speak of it. The sacraments, ministerial organization, finance—these are not worth mentioning. Politics, sexual problems, real life—these have no place in spiritual assemblies in which one seeks refuge from the obsession of everyday life and bathes in the beneficent atmosphere of contemplation of the hereafter. This more or less Platonic idealism provoked the vehement protests of Karl Marx.

But separation may produce a slightly different attitude. Since fusion of the human and the divine is ruled out from the outset, preoccupation with concrete and often very natural realities may go hand in hand with spiritualizing evasion. Not without astonishment one may discover that acute realism can accompany the most advanced spiritualizing. But these two lines are parallel and not subordinate the one to the other. The most extreme mystical penetration can suddenly end and yield to the most interested calculations. In other words, spiritualizing can accommodate itself very well to a secular humanity which is the more demanding because it balances mystical exertion.

This tenuous unity, in which the two elements exist in intentional autonomy, may take a third form. Wearied of ineffective spiritualizing, those who have hitherto sought escape in religion and piety may be suddenly constrained to reverse their outlook and to emphasize the human element in its most earthly form. This return is not so astonishing as it might seem at first sight. For now it is the second pole which is predominant. The humanity of Christ, the letter of the Bible as a historical document, the government and organization of the Church suddenly take the first place. Nothing matters but man and common sense, history, criticism and morality, ecclesiastical administration hardening into a secular institutionalism which is the more intolerant because it is conscious of basic weakness. Docetism thus leads finally to Ebionitism of what is often a very crude type, though the religious superstructure remains, expressing itself in

[1] A. Lemaître, *Foi et vérité*, pp. 461f.

every imaginable form so long as it does not contradict the traditional social and juridical structure. At this higher level toleration has full scope, since everything is permissible, and nothing finally matters, within the limits of the constitutional organism, which is now the only absolute truth and fixed dogma. This is how there can often be within modernism the very rapid or sometimes more gradual transition from apparently the most authentic spiritualizing to the most trivial (religious) materialism.

(3) To avoid oscillation between the two extremes it is necessary to adhere firmly to the decisive elements in the mysterious unity which God himself has actualized in the life and work of Jesus Christ for the whole of creation.[1]

In the light of what we have said already, we need only give some brief indications of the main elements in this unity.

(*a*) In the incarnation as in the life of the Church what dominates the scene is the movement of God towards his creature, i.e., his personal intervention. But God meets a fallen and rebellious humanity with which he cannot unite himself directly without denying himself. Neither in Israel nor the Church is there any ground prepared and disposed to receive him. He thus creates for himself a partner with whom to enter into covenant. This fact is unique. Elsewhere there is only disruption. Here is perfect unity which is inconceivable to those without. In this man God and man relive the drama of history—the fall, the curse and death—in order to overcome the breach. They take it to themselves in order to conquer it. In this way unity is truly restored for us in him.

(*b*) The Church is the consequence of this one history. It is already perfect in him who has obtained the victory for all men. It does not exist prior to the moment when God makes of this movement a living and actual reality for us, i.e., when we discover that he bears us in him, that we are already dead in his death and justified, sanctified and glorified in his resurrection. Then we are raised up with him to the right hand of the Father even though we do not as yet cease to dwell on earth.

(*c*) That this Church which is hidden in him should exist visibly it is enough that he should act and that he should manifest concretely what is already actual in the secret of his own existence. By

[1] An admirable balance is achieved in the *Tome* of Leo and the Chalcedonian definition, though the conception is more static than dynamic (cf. Tixeront, *Histoire des dogmes de l'antiquité chrétienne* III, 1912, pp. 86f.; ET, *History of Dogmas* III, 1916, pp. 81ff.).

his election, Word, appeal and inspiration, he delivers us from bondage and clothes us in his fulness. The Church is the effect of this action on us, the manifestation in us of what he has been for us. Do we cease to be human? On the contrary, his new humanity is attributed to us. Does this action cause sin to disappear? Yes, but only when he intervenes to apply his death and resurrection to our existence. The Church thus exists only as it lets him act, listening, praying and praising God that he creates it in the image of his Son. Knowing that its own truth is outside it, the community recognizes that it is human and sinful, and it receives this grace of its constant transformation. The least confusion between the two contradicts the necessity of the death of Christ, while separation annuls the efficacy of the victory of God for us.

(*d*) This unity is a miracle and a mystery, since it is the presence of Jesus Christ among us, in us and between us. But it is real, full and total, and as certain as the incarnation of God and the resurrection of Christ. It implies a total subordination of man to his Lord, a strict dependence and yet a perfect freedom in this association. The partners are neither diminished nor crushed by this union. They find their integrity and even their autonomy in belonging to one another. To enter this union man undergoes an effective transformation, though not a change of substance. He remains human, passing from a marred to an authentic humanity. He does not acquire divinity, but human fulness in keeping with his destiny. This is what is clearly indicated by the image of the head and the body. There is no rivalry between them. There is rather a harmony which restores the truth of creation.

(*e*) This unity is thus a truth of faith, i.e., a reality which is discerned in Christ but only partially in us until its full manifestation at the *parousia*. There are signs of it in the confession of his grace, in gratitude, in obedience and perhaps in suffering. The main lesson of faith, however, is that this unity is always the gift of God and his personal creation. Hence it can never be integrated into a legal or social structure, even though it does also take this practical aspect when God gives it. Until its final manifestation at the end of the age, we receive and believe it as a reality which is still concealed, and we work and pray that it may be actualized as fully as possible.

(*f*) To define this unity more closely, and in analogy with the incarnation, we may apply to the relations of this body to its Head the terms used to describe the person of Jesus. The *enhypostasis*

L

tells us that the Church is actual in conscious and full submission to its Lord. The *extra calvinisticum* indicates that the fulness of Christ infinitely surpasses that of the Church, and that the latter should constantly turn from itself and glorify him alone to receive from him its reality. The communication of attributes is an unheard of promise. God communicates his own perfections in order that in its being and action, even though it is fully human, it may achieve infinitely more than it might do by its own powers.

Thus the Church is the real, human and historical, though provisional, presence of Jesus Christ in and by his own people to the world. He acts in and by it, pursuing his own work and attesting his victory. In this sense it is true that there is no salvation outside it, so long as it does not pretend to do other than serve and glorify him alone. In all its impotence, like Mary, it is truly his life, his concrete manifestation, if it is zealous to be fashioned by its Lord. And it is this joyful obedience which sets it to work in the liberty and responsibility which it receives the moment it submits to him. It will be understood that its main effort relates to the prayer that God himself will truly act, since it is this action alone which causes it to exist.

3. *Faith in Life*

The Chalcedonian statements finally cast a vivid light on moral problems considered from the standpoint of revelation, i.e., on the relations between being and doing, between faith and works, between dogmatics and ethics, between the Church, the state and the world.

Confusion is most common, if not most dangerous, in this sphere. Separation is practised in some sectarian circles, which claim that they are abandoning the world to Satan in order to withdraw into piety, or which reject all political authority on the ground that they have been freed from all human tutelage by grace. At the beginning of the chapter on civil government Calvin makes it plain that he has this extremist position in view. He treats of the political sphere in terms of the analogy between the two dominions in man, the soul and the body. Having spoken previously of the inward man, he now goes on to deal with outward manners, because the two are conjoined and especially because there are in his day violent people who would overthrow all civil power even though it is established by God.[1]

[1] *Inst.* IV, 20, 1.

Further on, he is even more emphatic: 'Some fanatics, who are pleased with nothing but liberty, or rather licentiousness without any restraint, do indeed boast and vociferate that since we are dead with Christ to the elements of this world, and, being translated into the kingdom of God, sit among the celestials, it is a degradation to us, and far beneath our dignity, to be occupied with those secular and impure cares which relate to things altogether uninteresting to a Christian man.'[1] For the Reformer the two spheres, even though they are distinct, are linked in the same way as the soul and the body, and, if he sometimes leaves the impression that the link is stronger than the distinction, he tries to hold to the middle line in which there is neither confusion nor separation.

Separation is usually present in a more attenuated form both among theologians and among believers who out of an instinct of purity, and a certain lack of concern, hold up holy hands at the idea that the Church should intervene in public life. But confusion is predominant in our so-called Christian civilization, whether in the form of Catholic clericalism or in the rather less blatant form of Protestant secularization.[2]

In the sixteenth century the Reformers had to face the same dangers. Calvin first attacked the mediaeval confusion both in its theological intermingling of the findings of revelation and reason and in its practical synthesis in the form of the *corpus christianum*. This twofold intermingling was the result of the invasion of the faith and life of the Church by natural theology. But later Calvin was also forced to combat the opposite extreme of anarchical separation.

What is the position today? Can it be denied that in spite of the events of the last generation—the theological renewal and the opposition of a great part of the world to established religion—confusion is still the general rule? It is true that this is now beginning to yield, but the fact that most churches are now separated from the state is not a very convincing sign of this progress, since the separation has often been a purely external arrangement with no great effect on the real situation. Little by little the world has invaded the Church, and there will be ambiguity so long as a definite return to the sole lordship of Christ does not affect theology first and then

[1] IV, 20, 2.
[2] For analyses cf. R. de Pury, *Christianisme social*, June–July, 1958, p. 466; Ph. Maury, *Évangélisation et Politique*, 1957, pp. 15, 25ff., 32, 53, 55; K. Barth, *Brief an einen Pfarrer in der Deutschen Demokratischen Republik*, 1958, p. 14; H. Vogel, *Aufgabe und Zeugnis*, Prague, 1958, p. 17.

every sector of practical life. Having appropriated the human values which it adjudges not to be in opposition to its faith, the Church has enveloped them, as it were, in Christianity. It has baptized or Christianized them, not by transforming them, but by covering them with a Christian layer in order to justify their assimilation. There have thus developed within the Church itself doctrines and practices which are purely pagan but which have a religious veneer and which thus give the impression of belonging to the faith. One of the most typical of these appropriations, among many others, is found in the conception of man, where ideas which are originally Greek or which have been borrowed from modern Idealism have been so well integrated into the faith that they have now for a long time seemed to be the official teaching of the Church. The association between humanism and revelation which we have examined both in its Neo-Protestant and its Roman Catholic form can hardly lead to any other result. How can paganism be prevented from penetrating the practical life of the Church once it has invaded its theology? This intermingling is the main feature of the Romanist position, and it has become that of the Protestant also in spite of the Reformation, whose obedience finally consisted quite simply in the rejection of these adjuncts. Christ alone, grace alone and Scripture alone were the themes of the Reformation reaction. Very quickly, however, nature claimed its rights again, and we are now faced once more by a divine-human synthesis in which alien values are fused with the teachings of revelation to constitute Western Christianity. The *corpus christianum* has reappeared in another form.[1]

The most urgent task today is not to remedy individual evils but to summon the Church back to its vocation by return to its only Lord and therefore by a break from the world. Do we have to wait for the world itself to destroy the fiction that Christians may realize again their status as strangers and as ambassadors of a completely different dimension?[2]

By a curious dialectic confusion and division are often associated even in their opposition. Unity with Jesus Christ separates from the

---

[1] Evil results of this development are the secularization of the Church, the replacement of the body of Christ by an ecclesiastical institution, the easy admission of pseudo-Christians, the destruction of the true ministry of the Word and therefore of the authentic pastoral office and the dilution of the witness of the Church in its confession and supremely in its internal life and order.

[2] What the Church has largely forgotten is that it is not of the world. Cf. John 15.19; 18.36; 17.14; I Cor. 2.12; Eph. 2.2f.; Matt. 6.24; Col. 2.20; Rom. 12.2; I John 2.15; James 1.27; 4.4; Luke 14.26f.; Matt. 19.21; 16.25; also Tertullian, *Apol.* 1.

world, and intermingling with the world separates from the truth. When the Church allows itself to be integrated in society, it practices intermingling, but it also separates itself inevitably from its own truth. This is why, in clericalism no less than secularization, there are in the intermingling innumerable traces of inner division. Conversely, when the Church separates itself completely from the world on the pretext of total communion with Christ, we often find that the world comes back into it, producing at the very heart of the separation a subtle and often unconscious confusion. Since the truth is both divine and human, those who take refuge in the divinity alone are constantly overtaken by the most profane humanity which they affect to despise, while those who espouse the humanity alone almost always end up by idolizing what they have chosen as their only truth, since in spite of every effort they are unable to silence the profound yearning for God which is in all of us. Hence the two deviations combine. They are simply two aspects of the same failure to recognize the fact that God has effectively achieved unity in Christ in the freedom of a concluded alliance which allows neither fusion nor independence.[1]

These general remarks apply particularly to ethics, in which some fusions favour the independence of spheres and some divisions entail confusions which are even more harmful to true unity than the apparent synthesis. These phenomena are even clearer in the relations between dogmatics and ethics, but they lead to the same result in relations between the problems of existence and of action, the problems of faith and of works, or the prerogatives of the Church and the state.[2]

Is this really in accordance with the teaching of Scripture? Can it be denied that if we begin, not with a derived synthesis between human precepts and divine, but with the one authentic encounter between God and man enacted in Jesus Christ, we shall have to approach the problem of morality from a completely different angle? On this view two events dominate the scene, objectively the reconciliation effected in the history of the God-man and

[1] Cf. the way in which secular values are appropriated in clericalism, or alien elements are condoned in mysticism, or new and often very elementary mythologies recur where there is complete critical or liberal or even philosophical autonomy.

[2] On the interrelation of dogmatics and ethics, especially in Thomism, cf. T. Deman, *Aux origines de la théologie morale*, 1951; A. D. Sertillanges, *La philosophie morale de Saint Thomas d'Aquin*, 1946; *Le Christianisme et les philosophies*, 2 vols., 1939–41; E. Gilson, *Le Thomisme*, 1942. The work of the Protestant Centre of Studies at Geneva has shed light on an interesting parallel in the Neo-Protestant sphere.

L*

subjectively the complete renewal of man by his participation, under the moving of the Holy Spirit, in the death and resurrection of the Son of God. If Christ had to die, humanity is condemned along with its knowledge of good and evil, and it cannot enter directly into the kingdom of God. The death of man implies that he renounces his natural prerogatives truly to receive everything from his Saviour.[1]

But what is a morality which derives only from the grace of God? What form does it take? The following points are to be noted.

(1) Considered from the standpoint of the work of God, the moral problem is strictly a theological rather than a philosophical problem. For it is God who both poses it and resolves it. The good of human conduct is an object of revelation and not a discovery or effect of creaturely initiative. 'He hath shewed thee, O man, what is good' (Micah 6.8). Man has, of course, his own solution. Having rejected the divine order, he has been pleased to try to regulate his own conduct to prevent disorder. But this new morality is a product of revolt against the divine commandment. It takes the place of the latter. Whatever the value of its intentions, it is a result of defection. Its aim is to try to limit the disastrous consequences of the breach by bringing a little order into human relations. But it can do this only relatively, since the starting-point is vitiated. Thus God decides to intervene to re-establish man in his true condition and to regulate his conduct. In the light of this event, morality finds its only source in the will of God, in his decree of salvation and in the transformation of man. How can the morality which derives from reconciliation be combined with that which derives from sin?

(2) In this form the morality of grace poses first the question of existence rather than of action. Everything depends on the relation of man to God, to himself, and to his neighbour. If he belongs to God, he can only obey him in praise and gratitude, while if he remains in revolt he can only obey his natural impulses even though he attributes their origin to a divine, religious or ecclesiastical law. Thus the moral problem is secondary. It is conditioned by the situation of the subject. Being precedes doing, and decides in a sovereign manner its practical orientation. It is thus erroneous to divide theology into two parts, the one intellectual, theoretical and speculative, the other practical. Grace, revelation and the knowledge of God enable man to act in a completely new way, and are thus as practical as possible. They have an immediate moral bearing.

[1] Cf. Calvin, *Inst.* III, 7, 1; *Heidelberg Catechism, Qu.* 86.

It is morality which becomes theoretical to the degree that it detaches itself from the Word of salvation, for it then shows itself incapable of changing man and impotent to make him obey it. In fact, all authentic moral systems deal with being before acting. A true Marxist, for instance, will act in conformity with his belief once he has adopted it, whereas a half-hearted supporter will act in a hesitant manner. The same is true of a capitalist or existentialist.

(3) God also resolves the moral problem. He does this, not by giving the Law, but by giving the Gospel. Here again there is reorientation. What God expects and requires is not that we obey his precepts. He knows our powerlessness. If he had only to reveal his will for us to conform, the cross of Christ would have been unnecessary. What God wills, however, is that Christ should die in our place and that we should receive from him our justification and sanctification. What he wills is our salvation, not our spontaneous obedience, which is impossible. He wills the obedience of his Son, even to the cross, in place of our deficient service. He wills our deliverance by the accomplishment of this salvation which he ordains, which he ordains for himself as it were. It is only by this detour that he wills our obedience, which is thus made possible again. As may be seen clearly from the parable of the wicked servant (Matt. 18), as from many other passages, God takes to himself our faults and leaves us only his love and holiness, his pardon and our freedom. This is his will, his law. The end of this Law is to show us grace by the life, death and resurrection of Jesus Christ. His commandment is that Jesus Christ should take away our sin and impute to us his holiness, thus enabling us to obey him by his action in us. His will is thus the will of his grace. This is his requirement laid upon us. His Law is contained in his Gospel. If it were not, it could only condemn us. But it now delivers us from our revolt and makes it possible for us to serve him. It is thus his grace which constrains us by giving us the power to meet this demand. This is the great reversal on which our morality rests. The justice of God, his legitimate requirement, effects our justification and pardon. It is not content to summon us to become just; it makes us just.

(4) In face of this sovereign event, our perspective is completely modified. What constrains us to obedience is not the requirement of righteousness, but the gift of God's righteousness, i.e., his pardon. The Law of God is concealed in the Gospel, the Gospel in the Law. Once we separate the commandment of God from his promises and

therefore from the reconciliation accomplished in the death and resurrection of Christ, the Gospel loses its true significance. In other words, the righteousness of God does not expect us to make satisfaction by works. It is no longer fulfilled in punishment. It is satisfied by the death of Jesus Christ, which restores us with a view to the obedience which we can now render in the works that he has 'before ordained that we should walk in them' (Eph. 2.10).

There is no doubt that we see God's requirement in this liberating action which he wills, undertakes and accomplishes. But it has a new meaning. He requires that we receive his grace, and he gives us the power to do so. His Law is an authorization, a gift. Our first obedience, taking precedence in our morality, is thus to receive his grace. We are not first to try to do good works in the attempt to acquire a measure of holiness or perfection by our own means. We are to receive this grace which will transform us into new men and which will thus produce in and by us works corresponding to his. We thus avoid two equally fatal errors. The one is legalism, which by-passes Jesus Christ and commands us to do what we cannot do, namely, to do again what God has done, instead of receiving the remedy which he imparts. The other is antinomianism, which makes the Gospel a facile solution that brings benefits with no corresponding effects on our lives (cf. the 'cheap grace' of Bonhoeffer's *Discipleship*). The Law of God wills the sacrifice of Jesus Christ. It thus becomes grace— the grace which commands a response and obedience even as it gives them.

(5) In effect, Jesus Christ has obeyed the Law of God for us. He has done this in his life. He has not done this for himself alone, for if so he need not have been made sin. It is as our Representative that he meets the requirements of God. He is thus himself obedient man. And he attributes his obedience to us. He is both the Holy God who commands and the holy man who obeys in our place and who imputes to us his docility. As such, he does not merely bring the solution to our moral problem. He is himself the solution. For himself and for us he lives out the response of God to the question of existence in conformity with divine truth. He is perfect man. In him, everything is done. For us, therefore, the moral question is how we can receive this response rather than how we can find a solution. How are we to make our own the solution which he brings by living it out? This is a question of faith alone, in which all morality is contained. Jesus Christ as our righteousness and sanctification is the

good which is commanded and given us. The will of God is that we should be reached by this grace, associated with his death and resurrection and clothed with his righteousness and holiness. We are to be planted together with him (Rom. 6.5). His life becomes ours, his obedience ours. In a sense all morality is to be found in this.

(6) Our works are thus the necessary consequence of our being in Christ. They are our participation in his history, an imitation, a service. Christian ethics is in effect related to a past, present and future history between God and man. God acts, and this action summons man also to do something. It is God's work which provokes ours. Here is the motive, criterion, norm and power of our action. Here is the tree on which the fruit of our works is produced. This history demands and makes possible a corresponding attitude on our part. We have to live our human life on the way opened up to us and in the liberty which we are given to reflect it in our conduct.

The imitation in question is not a simple copy. It consists in a twofold movement: first to let ourselves be associated with God's work and transformed by a new birth, and then to accept the fact that this new thing, which is the Holy Spirit in us, produces in our lives works analogous to those effected by God. The main point of our works is to express this new reality which dwells in us. In this sense we may say that they are prophetic, for they translate the reality by which we live, or tell out our faith. They are the outer witness corresponding to our inner life. They are signs of the resurrection accomplished in us.

(7) This is the morality of the Spirit. These are the fruits of the Spirit. For it is the third person of the Trinity who effects our incorporation into Christ, enabling us by his intervention to believe, to confess and to obey. At this level it is the Spirit who, in his witness to Christ, becomes our Law. The work of God in Jesus and the work of the Spirit in us take the place of pre-established principles, of rules and of casuistry. We are in the freedom of the Spirit and will not be subjected afresh to the Law. J.-P. Sartre has rightly accused all legalistic moralities of destroying the freedom of decision.[1] But he has forgotten the Spirit, as we also do, replacing him by our religious principles. What then is the point of the Ten Commandments, of the Sermon on the Mount, and of the many apostolic exhortations? They indicate the territory on which God

[1] *L'existentialisme est un humanisme*, 1946, pp. 4of.

himself by his Spirit can come to give us his order. For the order of God is always personal, living and concrete. It never becomes a regulation. Open to the action of the Spirit and informed by biblical teaching, the Christian lives by the personal command of the living God as it is given in specific instances. Relying on God, he thus lives in the freedom of his grace. He advances in and by faith, knowing that the Lord who has taken his existence watches over him and guides him. From this standpoint our morality can be summed up in the single Pauline admonition not to grieve the Holy Spirit of God (Eph. 4.30).

(8) Nevertheless, our obedience will never be perfect and our works will always stand in need of forgiveness. This is why the morality of faith can be finally justified only by the eschatological tension which animates it from first to last. We are held between recollection and expectation. This is true of history in general, which is bordered by the incarnation on the one side, and the Lord's return on the other. But concretely it also means that we live daily and from week to week by the recollection of what God has already given us and in expectation of a new intervention on his part. This is the conflict of faith. The horizontal plane of our life is enclosed by the faithfulness of God, who pardons, demands and promises and who patiently begins again to overcome the powers of darkness and to make good our failings. Thus our morality can never be self-sufficient. It brings us back constantly to the work of God which is its origin, centre and end. A horizontal morality alone is naive, since it takes into account neither the attacks of Satan nor our own weakness. We must be protected by more than our own conscience and good will. The work of God thus comes to rehabilitate our works as required, and it constantly substitutes for our approximate conduct the impeccable obedience of Jesus Christ. Christian morality is thus permeated by grace. It is constantly torn away from itself and attached to the Gospel. At the commencement, centre and end of all our thoughts, decisions and actions, whether in the private sphere or the confessional, the political or the economic, there is this grace of the judgment and pardon of God. Grace does not merely lie once and for all at the beginning of our human enterprises, then leaving the responsibility to us under its remote influence. Grace intervenes at the very heart of even our most practical dispositions. This is what confers on our morality its distinctive character, which is to refuse to take itself seriously in itself

as though it were a sphere apart, and to refer itself constantly to the morality of God, which is simply the action of Jesus, the new man who is obedient for us. Eschatology is recourse to this work already accomplished by Christ, to its actual bearing for us and to its approaching manifestation. It is not a flight from immediate reality but our own chance of existing usefully in this intervening time. Expectation of the last judgment confirms this perspective. Our actual conduct is important because he who is coming again will establish its real significance. Thus, in the words of Pierre Maury, 'biblical eschatology is truly our greatest moral obligation'.[1]

Hence the authentic criterion of good and evil is simply the conduct of Jesus Christ. Taking the role of man, God restores man to his true place. This man is the truth of the being and doing of every creature. He restores us in this truth by making us like him through his own power. Thus every human question is resolved by his being and action among us. The response which we are summoned to make to all these problems, if it is to be valid, can only be witness to this solution, confession of his life and his work. We cannot deal with them by the criteria of law, of intuition, of consciousness or of philosophical, historical or political systems. Whether it is a matter of our personal conduct or of collective problems—capital punishment, abortion, prisons, atomic armament or the organization of labour—our concern must always be to attest the ethical bearing of the life, death and resurrection of the man Jesus. This is why all dogmas which serve to describe this history have an indirect and very concrete relevance to morality, i.e., to the personal and public life of all men.

What, then, is our part in this ethics? Are we simply passive and irresponsible intermediaries? We are certainly not. There arises here once again the very complex problem of liberty, which is as it were the hinge between the existence of God and that of his creature, between his work and ours, between dogmatics and ethics, faith and obedience, being and action, the Church and the state. The liberty of man before God is a distinctive feature of the unity in which the two are neither confounded nor separated but associated in the fulness of their communion. With this important aspect we must close.[2]

[1] By way of biblical illustration cf. esp. Rom. 12 and Gal. 5.25. Along the same lines, cf. also Barth, *CD* II, 2.

[2] On this immense subject cf. esp. the two works of Anselm, *De libero arbitrio* and *De concordia*. Cf. also Luther's *Bondage of the Will* and the more popular statement of

The freedom ordained for us in the Gospel has nothing whatever to do with the freedom of self-disposition which from the very first has been the dream of a race eager for autonomy. On the contrary, it is a victory over this autonomy, a liberation, the discovery of a completely new dimension, an illumination which carries with it a discipline, the glory of God himself reflecting itself in our life, a harmony between our existence and the perfection of God which produces a parallel harmony between our conduct and our destiny, between our life, that of our neighbours and the whole of creation. It is the mark of truth and peace, a quality of being, in adherence and not in defence or licence. This right relationship, as we have seen, is the presence of the Holy Spirit, who fulfils this office by applying to us the life, death and resurrection of Christ, so that he is the Spirit of the Lord. This liberty, therefore, follows our own death and characterizes our new existence. It is the fruit of the grace which reaches us through this judgment and transfiguration. Up to this point of restoration we are subject to vanity. 'His servants ye are to whom ye obey; whether of sin unto death, or of obedience unto righteousness. . . . Being then made free from sin, ye became the servants of righteousness' (Rom. 6.16–18). This liberty is thus synonymous with submission, bondage and obedience, not to death, but to Jesus Christ. The dialectic of these ideas coincides exactly, for there is no other liberty for us than that of his victory over us in our justification, sanctification and glorification.

But this is real liberty. For submission to Christ is not resigned and passive subjection. It is an active, resolute and responsible participation. The part of man is here fully restored. More strictly, the whole man is put to work. Co-operation is no longer a vain pretension nor autonomy a revolt. In this harmony the creature expands, for God respects his children. There can be no rivalry in the covenant. Each has his own tasks in mutual confidence and recognition. 'Henceforth I call you not servants; for the servant knoweth not what his lord doeth: but I have called you friends; for all things that I have heard of my Father I have made known unto you' (John 15.15). Friendship now controls the relations of man to God, and this friendship implies difference in unity, mutual participation in privilege and the division of responsibilities in love. It is thus that one may truly speak of collaboration. There is association

Barth in his Address to the Autumn Synod of the Evangelical Reformed Church of the Canton of Berne, Oct. 24, 1956.

of the partners in tasks which derive from their respective vocations, with no suppression, but in accomplishment of their specific potentialities.[1]

The work of God enables us to fulfil our destiny in this royal humanity which he grants us as our participation in his divine sovereignty. To be man is to live and act in this correspondence and to fulfil freely and cheerfully the tasks prescribed by our vocation. Morality at this level is simply the exercise of our royalty as creatures reconciled with their Creator. There is here not the slightest confusion between the free grace of God and the equally free work which man can nevertheless accomplish in virtue of this deliverance and under the friendly authority of his Lord. Nor is there independence, for man is pleased to be able to put all his abilities at the disposal of the one who alone has restored the harmony of creation. Liberty is no longer a pretext for continued rivalry. It is voluntary adherence in the service of truth which is both human and divine. Everywhere free association triumphs over either tyranny or licence.

This royal morality, fully human, active and responsible, is that of which we must now speak. It occurs in the free association which follows our death and resurrection. It is absolutely dependent on grace, and for this very reason it is autonomous. It is a morality of gratitude, and for this very reason vigilant and resolute. It is a morality of reconciliation, and for this very reason it is open and generous. It gives each man his chance.

This morality directs our conduct in three main directions.

(1) All human relations are transformed on this perspective. Gratitude and freedom now characterize not only the relations between man and God but also the life of the married couple, which becomes an open dialogue and a mutual participation in which there is neither encroachment nor alienation, each occupying his own place and facing his own responsibilities in mutual confidence and with mutual assistance. Around this first encounter—with neither confusion nor division—human solidarity finds again its climate of truth in respect, justice and friendship. Indeed, all creation participates in the vocation of man, being associated with his glory and through him with the glory of God.

(2) In the life of every being reconciled with its Lord order is established on an equal basis between truth and love. The soul no

---

[1] Cf. the life of the man Jesus in submission to the Father.

longer despises the body, nor does the body revolt against the soul. Grace does not suppress works, but stimulates the will and the imagination in an engagement conformable to our function as men. Faith does not quench obedience but includes and produces it. Dogmatics does not scorn ethics, but at every point leads to the most concrete action. The Church does not take the place of the state, but, leaving to it responsibility in its own domain, helps it honestly to fulfil its task. There is no question of integration, but rather of a free association which excludes every fusion or imperialism as well as every division. This disposition becomes the truth of all human relations, whether political, economic or social. There is mutual interrelation in the appropriate order, without either absorption or competition. This is the result of the re-establishment of man under the sovereignty of God. The Church and the world are not intermingled but associated under the sole sovereignty of the Lord.

(3) Finally, this rule of grace establishes correct relations between the revelation of God and human disciplines. To man is restored possession of his own instruments and mastery over nature. There is no confusion of spheres, as when faith humanizes itself or culture idealizes itself, psychology becomes religious and history becomes mystical, theology interferes where it has no business to be, science absolutizes itself, technics lead to mythology and medicine, politics, civilization and state try to be Christian. Simple honesty is at a loss in such confusions. In fact, all these disciplines profit by sticking to their own fields. They differ in object and method as well as in specific task. God makes no pretence of interfering directly in sectors which he has left to the intelligence and freedom of man. Again, man gains nothing by trying to attribute to revelation what he thinks he has discovered by specialized research. When we apply to other fields ideas which have been demonstrated in a specific sector, we run every risk of reaching false conclusions through the inevitable confusion of disciplines.

Nevertheless, one cannot separate them entirely, for God is the Master of man in the totality of his life and man is an indivisible whole self-expressed personally in his work. Truth lies on the one hand in respect for revelation as the act of God, on the other in human research, and finally in their meeting, which is still hidden but very real. It is not a systematic synthesis established from below. It is a dialogue which, while it does not exclude tensions, also admits from time to time the unexpected event of a rapprochement in the depths. To the objectivity of grace there corresponds that of human disciplines, and with a similar integrity.[1]

Thus true relations which unite the work of God and the works of creatures—the authentic co-operation of morality under the commandment of grace—are an image of the unity of deity and humanity in Christ. One may apply to them the definitions which have helped us to understand the person of the Mediator. The *enhypostasis* signifies that the decision of God dominates the situation and that our integrity is restored only on the basis of his intervention. In this dependence we are ourselves and we are again able to fulfil our human vocation. The *extra calvinisticum* reminds us that God remains the Lord of our lives and that he always limits our specific dispositions. He is before us, above us and after us, and it is these limits which give validity to our efforts in our own sphere. The work of God commands our works; it is not identical with them. Humility and gratitude are thus our true attitude, whether before God or before the tasks which he entrusts to us that we might therein manifest our royalty. The *communicatio idiomatum* shows us that in this subjection we fully recover our human dignity, this being enhanced by the fact that in this unity God reinforces our capacities by the shining forth of his own perfections in them. But all this is subordinate to the event of his incarnation, i.e., to the movement of his grace, which alone can fully restore us. It is in this miraculous correspondence that we finally become free, rational and active creatures.

Conclusion

Christology, as witness rendered to the work of God in Jesus Christ, is thus a true humanism. It attests the perfect rehabilitation of man in reconciliation with God. What is true in Christ is attributed to us and makes us ourselves. The drama of humanity is fully resolved. History continues under the sign of this definitive accomplishment.

The ancient dogmas can certainly be formulated in other terms, but, when we perceive their original sense, we see that they are

---

[1] It is for this reason that an authentic attitude in human research may contain more truth than a pious totalitarianism. Truth resides, however, in a twofold honesty and a proper relation under the government of the one who was both true God and true man. Cf. 'L'Eglise et l'Université', *Bulletin du Centre protestant d'Etudes*, Sept. 1957, and, by way of illustration, the study of the work of Teilhard de Chardin by E. Fuchs in the same *Bulletin*, Dec. 1958.

perfectly able in their own language to lead us to a true appreciation of the situation. What we have lost to the dualisms analysed in this work is repaid a hundredfold the moment we cease attempting an arbitrary union of nature and grace and cleave firmly to the one reconciliation effected by God, not in us, but in Jesus Christ, the only Mediator, dead and raised again for our transfiguration. By the Holy Spirit all the riches of truth are open to us and the Lord himself is active to give them to us. Here we are in the light of his work, not in the half-light of our own premature fusions. It is in him that we fully possess all things.

Are we then to see in premature attempts to unite what is of man and what is of God signs of this perfect rehabilitation through the victory of the Son of God? They certainly express the yearning for the truth which in spite of everything is still in us. On the other hand, by partial syntheses they may conceal from us the fulness which God truly gives us in his Son. This is why we do best to be on guard against them and to go back to the source of a grace which is demanding but which as such is truly and totally beneficent. To the degree that we attach ourselves exclusively to God we become truly human again. Is it not the message of the Gospel that everything is restored to us the moment that we think we have lost everything?

This fulness is not yet our possession. It is promised to us at the end. Thus far we have only the earnest of our future perfection. Christology thus receives its full meaning only from eschatology, and it is of our waiting under the sovereignty of Christ that we must now speak. Pierre Maury has finely formulated it as follows: 'Without eschatology, faith is a hallucination and even a delusion. . . . What does our completed reconciliation really tell us? I am righteous before God, I am fully justified, I am fully reconciled, I am a saint. Now this is not true if I look at myself, even if I look at my Christian self. I am not a saint, I am not righteous, I am an unrighteous sinner. I am neither the man who prays nor the man who loves nor the man who fully and completely believes without the slightest weakness. I am always the man who does not pray, who does not love, who does not believe. If I look only at myself, if I am not at the eschatological frontier looking in faith and the mystery of faith . . . I can only say that it is fantastic to be a Christian. It is a deception, a Pharisaism, or a great illusion. . . . There is needed something beyond me if I am to be what I am declared to be by the reconciliation effected in Jesus Christ. . . . To men, it is impossible to be a believer. But God can make the most unbelieving believers; he can make the last of men a believer and a Christian. This reality of the incomprehensible contrast between the biblical affirmation regarding us and the reality which we can see is for me one of the greatest evidences of eschatology. God can say Yes even where I see myself saying No. It is because of God, of the *eschaton*, of what is beyond ourselves, of the last things, that, even though we have every reason to say the opposite, we can say: I believe.'

In other words, eschatology is not a separate doctrine. It affects our interpretation of creation as well as Christology. In its total reach, however, it demands a special study on which we cannot now embark. For here again there must be neither confusion nor complete separation. Some day, perhaps, we shall be able to undertake this study in the same constant confrontation and with a view to the unity of truth.

INDEX

INDEX OF AUTHORS CITED